Retailing Management

Retailing Management

RETAILING MANAGEMENT

W. Stewart Howe
Head of the Department of Business Studies
Dundee Institute of Technology

with contributions from

David Couch
Principal Lecturer, Department of Retail Marketing, Manchester Polytechnic

W. C. H. Ervine and Fraser P. Davidson
Senior Lecturers, Department of Law, University of Dundee

David A. Kirby
Booker Professor of Entrepreneurship, Durham University Business School

Leigh Sparks
Senior Lecturer, Institute for Retail Studies, Department of Marketing,
University of Stirling

MACMILLAN

First published 1992

Published by
MACMILLAN EDUCATION LTD
Houndmills, Basingstoke, Hampshire RG21 2XS
and London
Companies and representatives
throughout the world

Typeset and illustrated by TecSet Ltd, Wallington, Surrey

Printed in Hong Kong

British Library Cataloguing in Publication Data
Howe, W. Stewart (William Stewart) *1945–*
Retailing management:
1. Retailing Management
I. Title
658.8700941
ISBN 0–333–48298–0 (hardcover)
ISBN 0–333–48299–9 (paperback)

'Without distribution there would be no civilised life.'

M. D. H. Ross, *Organisation of Retail Distribution*
(London: Macdonald, 1955) p. 18.

Contents

List of Figures   x

List of Tables   xi

Acknowledgements   xiii

Introduction   xiv

Notes on the Other Contributors   xviii

PART ONE: THE RETAILING ENVIRONMENT

1 **The Impure Economics of Retailing**   3
1.1 Introduction   3
1.2 The Functions of Retailing   3
1.3 Conclusion   6
References   7

2 **The Development of Modern Retailing**   8
2.1 Introduction   8
2.2 Elizabethan Origins   8
2.3 The Retailing Revolution   10
2.4 Into the Twentieth Century   13
2.5 Retail Distribution Since 1950   17
2.6 Forms of Retailing   24
2.7 Conclusions   36
References   37
Appendix   41

3 **Retail Competition**   44
3.1 Introduction   44
3.2 The Role of Competition   44
3.3 The Forces of Retail Competition   45
3.4 Directions of Competition   47
3.5 Competitive Responses by Retailers   51
3.6 Combined Dimensions of Response   59

3.7   Conclusions 60
References 65

4   Retail Corporate Strategy 70
4.1   Introduction 70
4.2   Corporate Strategy 71
4.3   Strategic Analysis in Retailing 75
4.4   The Longer Term 85
4.5   Strategic Implementation and Control 94
4.6   Conclusions 98
References 100

5   The Small Firm in Retailing 105
5.1   Introduction 105
5.2   Definitions and Data 105
5.3   The Declining Role of the Small Retailer 109
5.4   The Survival of the Small Retailer 117
5.5   Conclusions 121
References 123
Appendix 125

PART TWO: MANAGING RETAIL
ORGANISATIONS

6   Retail Merchandising and Marketing 131
6.1   Introduction 131
6.2   From Strategy to Merchandise Choice 132
6.3   Supplier Choice 134
6.4   Retail Marketing 136
6.5   Some Operational Issues 144
6.6   Conclusions 150
References 151

7   Physical Distribution Management 154
7.1   Introduction 154
7.2   Retailing Changes and Distribution Challenges 155
7.3   Physical Distribution Management 159
7.4   The Total Costs Concept 162
7.5   Customer Service in Distribution 163
7.6   Inventory, Packaging/Unitisation and Warehousing 165
7.7   Transportation 170
7.8   Information Systems and Communications 173
7.9   Sub-contracting Distribution 177
7.10   Physical Distribution Strategy 180
7.11   Conclusions 183
References 185

8 Retailing Organisation Structure and Personnel Management 187
8.1 Introduction 187
8.2 Retail Employment 189
8.3 Personnel Credibility in Retailing 192
8.4 Creating the Right Climate 194
8.5 Changing Management Types and Practices in Retailing 199
8.6 Retail Skills and Qualities 201
8.7 Personnel Expertise in Retailing 204
8.8 Conclusions 209
References 210

9 Government Control in Retailing 212
9.1 Introduction 212
9.2 The Nature of Policies 213
9.3 Policies to Regulate Competition 214
9.4 Policies to Safeguard Consumer Interests 224
9.5 Regulation of Trading Conditions 227
9.6 Conclusions 229
References 230

10 Legal Issues in Retailing 234
10.1 Introduction 234
10.2 Legal Background 234
10.3 Supply of Goods 236
10.4 Transfer of Property in the Goods 237
10.5 Termination 248
10.6 Advertising and Marketing 248
10.7 Enforcement of Consumer Protection Legislation 250
10.8 The Retailer and his Employees 250
References 268

11 Conclusions 274
11.1 Introduction 274
11.2 The Continued Evolution of Retailing 274
11.3 Retail Competition 277
11.4 Retailing Information Technology 280
11.5 Retailing Corporate Strategy 286
11.6 International Retailing 290
11.7 Conclusions 292
References 293

Index **297**

List of Figures

3.1 Framework of competition in retailing 46
6.1 Merchandising operations flow 132
6.2 Economic order quantity 146
6.3 Supermarket store layout 149
7.1 The elements of the distribution mix 161
7.2 Customer service in physical distribution 164
7.3 The 'new' physical distribution 176
9.1 The consumer policy formulation process 225

List of Tables

2.1   Unit retail traders and total retail trade   16
2.2   Categories of shop by number and turnover   20
2.3   Categories of enterprise by number and turnover   21
2.4   Department stores   26
2.5   UK retail Co-operative Societies   27
2.6   Multiple shop organisation store numbers and size   30
2.7   UK franchising   34
A2.1   The retail sector in the Great Britain economy   41
A2.2   Retail establishments by structure   42
A2.3   Retail sector organisations or enterprises   43
3.1   Distribution of retail turnover between types of outlet   48
3.2   Grocery sales by type of retail outlet   49
3.3   Share of total sector turnover accounted for by out-of-town stores   56
4.1   The strategic decision-making process   73
4.2   The retail task environment   78
4.3   Major retail organisation resource variables   80
4.4   Key strategic variables for retail differentiation   83
4.5   Advantages of vertical integration in retailing   87
4.6   Strategic implementation and control actions   95
5.1   Single outlet retailers in Great Britain   107
A5.1   Single outlet retailers   125
A5.2   Total numbers of retail outlets by sector 1980–87   126
A5.3   Sales per employee   127
A5.4   Stock turnover   128
6.1   Supplier selection and evaluation   136
6.2   Dimensions of the retail marketing mix   139
6.3   Purposes of retail advertising and promotion   143
6.4   Classification and arrangement of merchandise   148
9.1   Christaller's central place system   223
9.2   Typical five-tier hierarchies   223

11.1   Strategic and tactical opportunities for information
        technology   281
11.2   Information technology in retailing   282
11.3   Personal disposable income, expenditure and retail sales
        1980–89   289

Acknowledgements

Even at the end of what has again been largely a solo effort in writing my own chapters in this text it is a pleasant duty to thank those who have provided help and guidance. The chief librarian and his staff at Dundee Institute of Technology have been unfailingly helpful in providing access to a range of material to which reference is made in the text; and my departmental colleague Dr John Fernie has been a valued source of information and discussion on retailing matters in general. I am also grateful to the small number of retailers whom I visited during the course of writing this text for the insight which I gained in discussing matters with them.

I am particularly grateful to the other contributors for the efforts which they have put into their chapters over the fairly lengthy gestation period of the text, for the quality of their work, and for the smooth administrative relations which I have enjoyed with them.

My wife and family too have been aware that I have been involved for some time in producing a book on 'shopping', despite a manifest reluctance to engage in practical aspects of such activity. They wonder what next. I express my sincere thanks to all of the above for their assistance and contributions, but accept the author's usual responsibility for the standard of the work as a whole.

W. S. HOWE
Dundee

September 1990

The individual chapters in the text were contributed as follows: Chapters 1–6 and 11, Dr Howe; Chapter 7, Dr Sparks; Chapter 8, Mr Couch; Chapter 9, Professor Kirby; and Chapter 10, Mr Ervine and Dr Davidson.

Introduction

Retailing, or retail distribution, is an essential and not insignificant part of total economic activity in industrially developed countries. The activities covered in this text, which exclude the retailing of services such as banking and the work of building societies, or the utilities of gas and electricity, contributed total sales of £95 782m (excluding VAT) and net output or value added of £24 472m in the UK economy in 1987. The latter figure comprised 7.5 per cent of the UK total. In the same year the contribution of retailing to employment was 2 319 000 which was about 10 per cent of total employment in the economy.[1] A further indication of the importance of retailing to employment in the UK is the fact that in 1984 the distributive trades provided the first employment destination for 18 per cent of male and 26 per cent of female school-leavers.[2]

In addition to these magnitudes, another significant feature of the retailing sector of the economy is the large number of independent decision-making units which it comprises. Thus although in common with much of manufacturing industry some sectors of retailing are characterised by high levels of market concentration, the retail sector as a whole is still today (1987 data) made up of 240 853 individual business decision-making units. This sector is thus one which deserves particular study in the context of Professor Mathias's view that:

> The dynamics of many key processes which determine change in the 'macrocosm' – such as innovation, capital formation, entrepreneurship, changes in organisation and structure – involve the summation of change within the 'microcosm' of individual units of enterprise and cannot be effectively understood without analysis at the level of the individual firm.[3]

It is, of course, true that as a result of high levels of market concentration in, for example, grocery retailing, many significant decisions for the economy as a whole are made by a relatively small number of multiple supermarket store groups. But, as we shall see in Chapter 5 of the text, the small firm in retailing is still very significant, particularly in certain trades.

One special attraction of retail distribution as an area of study is that it is a part of the workings of the economy which affects almost everyone on a daily basis. In addition to this, the 1970s and 1980s saw significant changes taking place in the way in which retailing is carried out in the UK. A *Financial Times* survey of retailing referred to the industry as 'one of the most dynamic sectors of the UK economy'.[4] Changes have occurred most obviously in the geography of retailing as seen in the growth of edge-of-town and out-of-town shopping facilities as well as in the development of city centre shopping complexes. Equally obvious has been the increase in the scale of individual retail establishments, both in city centres and out-of-town sites. Less obvious but none the less important have been changes in the nature of competition among retailers and in the competitive balance between manufacturers and distributors. As an example of structural changes in retailing, when this Introduction was first drafted one could look back at the year 1985 during which major acquisitions alone in retailing amounted to £3542m: a year which saw the takeover of Debenhams by the Burton Group, the amalgamations of British Home Stores with Habitat–Mothercare and Asda with MFI, and the further expansion of Guinness into retailing through acquisition of the confectioner–tobacconist–newsagent chain R. S. McColl.[5] It is equally a measure of the dynamism of this sector that within less than two years serious questions were being asked in the financial press regarding the strategy and management of Sir Terence Conran's Storehouse (the holding company of BHS, Habitat and Mothercare), Asda had sold off MFI in the largest management buyout to date, and in the wake of wider trouble within the Guinness group McColl and the other components of Guinness's retailing subsidiary Martins had been sold to an Australian consortium.[6]

These and other changes have been responsible for some of the more obvious physical developments in retailing; and the changing nature of competition in retail markets has equally resulted in new strategies being adopted by many retailing firms. In addition to these structural developments, information technology is likely to impose further changes upon the retailing scene for both shops and shoppers as electronic funds transfer at point of sale (EFTPOS) is added to existing EPOS (electronic point of sale) developments in this sphere. Furthermore, although the 1986 Shops Bill providing for a relaxation of the present restrictions on Sunday trading failed in its passage through the House of Commons it is unlikely that the present inconsistent law on this matter will remain long unchanged, with possibly quite significant implications for retailing strategies.

It is in this dynamic and complex environment that, along with the independent shopkeeper, retailing organisations are developing which are not only large but also sophisticated in their strategy and operations: organisations such as W. H. Smith or Storehouse which are collections of distinct product groups or strategic business units, and which in an increasing number of instances are trading multinationally. It is organisations such as these that require to be increasingly professionally managed.

The purpose of this text is to offer the reader an insight into the major dimensions and issues in retailing today, with a strong emphasis upon retailing management. The text is therefore designed to be of value both to undergraduate students and practitioners of retailing: to offer students of economics and marketing an insight into the working of the retail sector of the economy, to provide businessmen (including independent retailers) and students of business with an understanding of the practice of corporate strategy in retailing, and to give all retailers a basis on which to improve the management of their businesses. Part Two of the text in particular is concerned specifically with management issues in retailing, and has been written with both students and practitioners in mind. This latter part of the text thus considers in some detail merchandising and marketing decisions in retailing, physical distribution management in this sector, government policy and requirements in retailing, organisation structure and personnel matters, and specific legal issues which arise for retailers in dealing with their suppliers, employees and customers.

The choice and order of the material in the text reflects this concern to relate to students and practitioners of retailing, and to contribute to management practice in the sector. Part One of the text analyses the retail environment through a consideration of the economics of retailing, the historical development of the retail trade, the nature of competition in this sector, strategic decision making, and the particular role of the small or independent retailer. These are considered to be the major dimensions of the retailing environment which indicate its role in the economy, the impact of recent developments, the factors determining the efficiency with which the sector operates, and policy or strategic decision making within retailing organisations.

Part Two of the text is concerned with administrative or operational issues in retailing organisations which determine the efficiency of individual firms. Five major areas are highlighted: merchandising and retail marketing decisions, distribution management, government control, retail organisation and personnel management matters, and legal issues in retailing. Part Two is directed especially at retailing practitioners and undergraduate students planning to make a career in retailing management.

A text such as this has to be selective. In particular it is concerned exclusively with the retailing of goods and not services. No reference is made to financial institutions such as banks, building societies or insurance companies. Nor is reference made on any scale to non-shop forms of retailing such as garage sales of petrol and other goods, or sales through public houses. It is hoped, none the less, that the text covers the vast proportion of the retail trade as recognised by shoppers, and that it will be of interest and practical

value to all concerned with the operation and management of this sector of
the UK economy.

References

1. Data given in Business Statistics Office, *Retailing* (London: HMSO, Business
   Monitor SDA 25, biennial).
2. S. Segal-Horn, 'The Retail Environment in the U.K.', in G. Johnson (ed.),
   Business Strategy and Retailing (London: Wiley, 1987) p. 13.
3. P. Mathias, *Retailing Revolution* (London: Longmans, 1967) p. ix.
4. *Financial Times*, 30 July 1986.
5. See data in S. Shamoon, 'High Noon on the High Street', *Business*, April 1986, p.
   87.
6. See *Financial Times*, 21 August 1987; 5 October 1987; and 29 September 1987.

Notes on the Other Contributors

David Couch is Principal Lecturer in Personnel Management at Manchester Polytechnic with special responsibility as retail co-ordinator for the BA (Hons) in Retail Marketing. He is author of a number of studies on retailing employment, and has made a special study of graduate recruitment and assessment methods used by retailing companies.

Fraser P. Davidson and **W. C. H. Ervine** are Senior Lecturers in the Department of Law at the University of Dundee.

David A. Kirby is Booker Professor of Entrepreneurship at Durham University Business School and is Director of the School's Centre for Entrepreneurship in the Service Sector. He is author of a large number of publications in the field of retail and distribution management and has held visiting research appointments in the Norwegian Fund for Market and Distribution Research (Oslo), the Swedish School of Economics and the Distribution Economic Institute of Japan, Tokyo. He is a Fellow of the Royal Society of Arts and a member of the Society's Education for Capability Committee.

Leigh Sparks is a Senior Lecturer at the Institute for Retail Studies, Department of Marketing, University of Stirling. Dr Sparks has been researching retail and distribution topics for many years and has published widely on many aspects of retailing and physical distribution. He is the co-editor of the *International Review of Retail, Distribution and Consumer Research* , editor of *Area* and a member of the Scottish regional committee of the Institute of Logistics and Distribution Management.

Part One

The Retailing Environment

The Impure Economics of Retailing 1

'Among those prejudices, inhibitions, and predilections
which compose the English tradition a prominent place is
occupied by the conviction that there is an essential
element of unworthiness about retail trade, a blend of the
sinister and the ridiculous.'

H. Smith, *Retail Distribution* (London: OUP, 2nd edn,
1948) p. 1.

1.1 Introduction

In contrast to the ideal expressed in the title of the opening chapter of Henry
Smith's book (*The Pure Economics of Retailing*) our view is that there is in
fact no pure economic theory of retailing. There is a set of economic functions
which most retailers carry out to a greater or lesser extent; and there are
broad markets in which those retailers compete with one another along
various dimensions. Beyond this, however, there is no pure theory of
retailing. This chapter seeks none the less to clarify those particular functions
of retail distribution as a prelude to the later analysis of competition, strategy
and operations in retailing today.

1.2 The Functions of Retailing

In order to avoid the tautology of simply defining retailing as what 'retailers'
are observed to do, any study of retailing must begin by establishing what
particular functions those enterprises in the retail sector of the economy
perform that may be separately and clearly thought of as retailing. One
starting point is their role of bridging the gap between producers and
consumers: enabling the former to specialise in manufacture and the latter to

3

obtain a range of goods with their money from a limited number of physical sources. As McClelland puts it, 'We must . . . regard the retailer from a logistical point of view as one who receives a variety of articles from different sources and on the basis of inefficiently and irregularly received instructions sorts them to their appropriate destinations.'[1]

Within this focus five unique retailing functions can be identified.

- Physical movement of goods
- Availability of a range of goods
- Change of ownership
- Advice to potential customers
- Other services to customers

Physical Movement

One of the most obvious functions of distribution is the physical movement of goods from the place of production to a point where consumers are willing to buy them. Where a retailer offers a home delivery service this function may involve moving goods from the place of production to that of final consumption. Only from carrying out this distributive function can production on any scale be converted into value; and one writer instances the discovery on many sites throughout England and Wales of axes made of stone in late Stone Age Penmaenmawr in North Wales as an example of the possibility and necessity of the distributive function early in the development of civilisation.[2] In our own time one of the reasons for the increased importance of retailing and rising costs of distribution is that production of goods is increasingly carried out in specialised, large scale, geographically concentrated factories. Such production conditions lead to the achievement of many economies of scale; but they impose a corresponding burden upon the distributive process in terms of the physical movement of goods.

Range of Goods

Although there may be held to be different policies which retailers can adopt with regard to product range, shops do not generally stock only one narrow type of a commodity or the goods of one producer only. Shoppers' time and effort is saved and a service is provided through retailers offering a range of goods within one category (groceries), by providing an opportunity to do a variety of shopping under one roof (in a department store), or offering a wide selection of a narrower class of items (engagement rings in a jewellery shop). In the case of a mail-order catalogue the range of goods is brought by illustration to the shopper's home, and when ordered the chosen items themselves are sent to the customer. These are merely some of the ways in which the retailer serves the consumer, whom two early writers in this field characterised as 'a lazy animal who expects to be able to buy goods as, when, and where he wants and who is willing to pay a price which will cover all the necessary costs of ministering to his convenience'.[3]

In addition to the issue of the range of goods, the distributor, in providing for an uncertain incidence of consumer purchases, has to hold a certain level of stock of items. Too high a stock level relative to his turnover reduces retail productivity and increases costs; while being out of stock of a requested item may result in a lost customer. In trades such as bookselling the retailer may act largely as a taker of orders for items which he in turn orders from a wholesaler or the producer (publisher). In other fields such as newspaper distribution the newsagent buys a particular daily quantity of, for example, the *Financial Times*, and customers cannot necessarily expect to find any copies left for sale after mid-day. In intermediate cases the retailer, while keeping his stockholding to a reasonable minimum, hopes to reorder efficiently so as to meet demands made upon him by his customers.

Change of Ownership at the Discretion of the Customer[4]

Other than in cases of hiring or hire purchase, a fundamental characteristic of retailing is the change of ownership of goods from the distributor to the purchaser and the corresponding exchange of value from the buyer. The need to carry out this function in respect of millions of transactions and with a high degree of accuracy (involving accurate pricing of items, weighing of goods, avoiding pilferage, proper handling of currency for cash transactions, and administration of any consumer credit given) accounts for a significant part of the costs of retailing.

Furthermore, the display of goods by a shopkeeper is merely an 'invitation to treat', and the commercial initiative to the transaction is with the buyer. Without advance notice the purchaser can at any time during shopping hours choose what to buy and in what quantity at any one time. There may be exceptions to this randomness, as when a retailer offers a special incentive by way of a price reduction to buy at one particular season or in larger quantities, or when a customer places a regular order (usually accompanied by home delivery as in the case of newspapers). By and large, however, the retailer is subject to the 'inefficiently and irregularly received instructions' of the shopper in these matters which add further to the costs of retailing.

Retailer Advice

Not all of this advice may be strictly required in a retail transaction, and some is simply part of the salesmanship of the shopkeeper. But when asked which household medicine is best for a child's cough, how to remove a stain from one's tie, whether to use crossply or radial tyres, or how long it will take to defrost a particular size of frozen turkey, the retailer is assisting in the use of the product by the consumer. In the past it has been argued in respect of certain classes of goods that the need to preserve a minimum retail margin for the distributor could be justified in order to ensure that such advice did in fact accompany the sale of the products.

Other Services

This category of distributor functions also embraces a range of services some of which are simply part of the marketing activities of the retailer. Generous lighting, background music or spacious 'gallerias' are optional extras designed to entice customers. Large car-parks on the other hand are a necessity for edge-of-town, bulk shopping grocery stores. Credit, as we shall see in Chapter 2 in examining the historical development of retailing, is a facility which has ebbed and flowed in its importance in retailing. While it was important at all social levels in the latter part of the nineteenth century – 'society ladies seldom pay their dressmakers' bills before two or three years'[5] – the multiple and department stores which grew up in the 1870s and 1880s tried strongly to operate without it. In the last decade, however, there has been a marked increase in credit extended by many individual stores through the introduction of charge cards.[6]

1.3 Conclusion

In this chapter we have outlined the principal functions of retailing. It was through carrying these out on an enlarged and more specialist scale that a separate activity of retailing first emerged in Elizabethan times; and in Chapter 2 we shall trace the evolution of retailing from the seventeenth century to the present time, noting the different ways in which retailing functions have been provided. This separate retailing function has come about as conditions relating to manufacture or importing have altered, and in response to changing demands by shoppers. These demands placed upon retailers by manufacturers and particularly by shoppers create the special management issues of retailing. Physical distribution management for retailers is now a subject in its own right, and is the topic of Chapter 7 in this text.[7] The provision of a range of goods in response to relatively unpredictable demand from shoppers who must be drawn to the retail outlet, and a fairly low value of each sales transaction require management decisions on merchandise range and stockholding levels, employment, store location and financial investment. Equally there are rewards to be gained by the retailer who manages physical distribution efficiently, who makes strategically correct decisions regarding merchandise and store location, and who controls labour, stockholding and other financial costs.[8] It is by providing appropriate distributive services efficiently that one class or type of retailer assumes greater or lesser importance in the sector; and within any one type of retailer (for example, multiple grocery stores) the recognition of the need for a particular service and the ability to provide this efficiently will determine the survival, profitability and growth of individual retailing enterprises. These matters are the subject of analysis in Chapters 3 and 4 of this text. Before this, however, we turn in Chapter 2 to a historical account of the development of retailing.

References

1. W. G. McClelland, *Costs and Competition in Retailing* (London: Macmillan, 1966) p. 6.
2. M. D. H. Ross, *Organisation of Retail Distribution* (London: Macdonald, 1955) p. 12.
3. D. Braithwaite and S. P. Dobbs, *The Distribution of Consumable Goods* (London: Routledge & Sons, 1932) p. 9.
4. See P. McAnally, *The Economics of the Distributive Trades* (London: Allen & Unwin, 1971) pp. 21–4.
5. Quoted in W. H. Fraser, *The Coming of the Mass Market* (London: Macmillan, 1981) p. 92.
6. Associated with the rapid expansion of bank credit cards in the 1980s, and also lending by finance houses and other credit companies, there has been some reduction in consumer credit extended by retailers themselves. There was, none the less, £7.1bn of retailer credit outstanding at the end of 1987. See data in CSO, *Social Trends*, No. 19 (London: HMSO, 1989) pp. 109–110.
7. A very useful specialist text in this area is M. Christopher, *The Strategy of Distribution Management* (London: Heinemann, 1986).
8. See the emphasis upon this in the American text B. Berman and J. R. Evans, *Retail Management* (New York: Macmillan, 2nd edn, 1983) Ch. 1. For a treatment of UK retail location issues see C. M. Guy, *Retail Location and Retail Planning in Britain* (Farnborough: Gower, 1980).

The Development of Modern Retailing 2

'Histories make men wise.'
Francis Bacon, 'Of Studies', *Essays*
(London: John Haviland, 1625)

2.1 Introduction

The purpose of this chapter is to trace the development of retailing from the seventeenth century to the present time. Following this development allows one to see the emergence of a distinct retailing function and to trace the growth of different forms of retailing such as the department store and multiple-shop organisations, the co-operative movement and the variety chain stores. It is on the basis of an understanding of the development of retailing in general and its different forms in particular that one can more fully understand the analysis of competition and strategy in this sector which are dealt with in Chapters 3 and 4 of this text.

2.2 Elizabethan Origins

The functions of retailing discussed in the previous chapter have always had to be carried out in any developed society. That expression 'the carriage trade', for example, referring to various accessories bought by the more wealthy classes, derives from Eliabethan times when, not to dirty their clothes on unpaved streets, such people bought at shops without leaving their carriages. In the London of the late sixteenth century 'The way the coaches were allowed to block the streets was becoming daily more of a scandal. Two or three of them might cumber up the thoroughfare for half an hour, while

8

their fair owners bargained in the shops for earrings for themselves or collars for their pet dogs'.[1]

It is in fact from Elizabethan times that we can trace the emergence of a distinct retail trade – a distinguishing of the retail distribution function from that of production. Prior to this time in the Middle Ages when consumption by a scattered population was largely limited for most to basic necessities, and when self-sufficiency in food and clothing was a major concern, there was no place for a separate retailing function on any scale. Suppliers of food and clothing sold their produce and wares directly to buyers in the local markets or at larger fairs. 'Middlemen might be unavoidable evils if goods had to be carried over a long distance, but otherwise they thrust an unwanted service between producer and consumer.'[2]

By the reign of Elizabeth I (1595–1603) however, a separate retailing function was beginning to develop, at least in London and a few other large centres of population. A more geographically concentrated and wealthier population, combined with a greater range of goods available (including imports), justified a vertical disintegration of retailing from manufacture; and by the early years of the seventeenth century, in Mrs Davis's view, 'there is no doubt that shopkeeping, as distinct from random trading and the keeping of a miscellaneous warehouse, was becoming an important occupation'.[3] This development began in London; but by the end of the eighteenth century it had spread across the country as standards of living generally rose and as newer centres of population emerged. By then the retail shop had become a normal part at least of the urban environment.

The advent of the industrial revolution at the beginning of the nineteenth century was not immediately accompanied by further developments in retailing. Jefferys, for example, writing of the contrast between the old and new production systems at this time, considered that 'The wholesale and retail trades in Britain in the middle of the nineteenth century were examples of those trades that still bore the marks of the old system rather than of the new. . . . The distributive system as a whole still bore the marks of a pre-industrial economy'.[4] It would seem as if, following the rapid changes in distribution which had begun two centuries before, retailing required a period of consolidation. It had certainly emerged as a function separate in many sectors from production; but older forms of distribution none the less remained. In the case of food (poultry, meat, eggs, fruit and vegetables) markets were still of prime importance, and ready-cooked foods such as sausages, pies and gingerbread were still sold in markets by those who made them. In clothing and footwear also there was for most people direct contact between the final consumer and the craftsman tailor and shoemaker. Here too one must bear in mind that much clothing, both underwear and outerwear, was still made at home. Pedlars also continued to form an important part of distribution, both wholesale and retail; and the products of the new textile mills were frequently sold around the countryside by Scotch

Hawkers or Scotch Drapers who acted as middlemen between factory and customer, often extending credit to the latter.[5] The fixed shop was therefore at this time only one of a number of avenues through which final consumers obtained their wants.

The rapid population growth of the nineteenth century, and the accelerated trend to urbanisation were, however, creating the conditions for new forms of retailing. Over the century following the first census in 1801 the population of Great Britain expanded by 12 to 18 per cent each decade. Between 1801 and 1851 the population doubled from ten million to more than twenty million; and by 1911 it exceeded forty million. At the beginning of the nineteenth century only one person in five of the population lived in towns of more than 10 000 inhabitants. By the middle of the century this proportion had risen to more than one in three, and at the time of the 1851 census more than 50 per cent of the population could be described as 'urban'.[6] As the historian of the Allied Suppliers multiple shop grocery group put it in accounting for the development of this new form of distribution, 'They owe their life completely to the new urban society spawned by the process of industrialisation'.[7]

2.3   The Retailing Revolution

The next stage in the development of retailing thus began to take off shortly after the middle of the nineteenth century on the basis of a much enlarged, urbanised and increasingly well-off population; and it is from then that the retail trade as we know it today appears to have started to evolve. Developments in particular began from this time which by the early decades of the present century had produced a pattern of shopping clearly similar to that of today. First, there was a gradual displacement of the hawkers and street sellers by fixed shops. London in 1851 was reported to have more than 43 000 street sellers.[8] These included costermongers selling fruit, vegetables and fish; sellers of foods such as oysters, kidney puddings, mutton pies, plum duff and currant cake, together with drinks such as tea, coffee, ginger-beer and milk; pedlars offering a whole range of manufactured articles of metal, glass, china and cloth; and finally a miscellaneous group of street sellers of caged birds, goldfish, shrubs and combs, along with purveyors of ballads, songs and broadsheets. However, the street sellers, or the market stallholders and the packmen of the rural areas, seem to have declined markedly in importance by the end of the last century. They were replaced by the fixed general store, particularly in poorer areas, and also by specialist shop retailers of soap and candles, of cheeses, and of hardware. One further trend at this time was a degree of disintegration as the retailing of such products as meat and bread became separated from the earlier stages of the making of the product. Butchers, for example, by the end of the nineteenth century were less likely to buy live cattle, but to purchase carcass meat from wholesale meat markets.

This trend accelerated in the 1880s as refrigeration brought carcass meat more economically from the United States, South America, Australia and New Zealand. A similar separation of roles occurred, albeit more slowly, in the case of milling, bread-baking and retailing.

The importance of the individual stores and specialist shops which developed from the middle of the last century was soon, however, to be overtaken by the multiple-shop organisations which became established during the final quarter of the century. The early individual retail outlets appear neither to have been particularly efficient, nor to have offered good value to customers. While retail profit margins on common items such as bread or sugar were 14 per cent, on the range of standard items they averaged 25–30 per cent. Within these margins the quality of service offered appears in many cases to have been extremely poor. According to Fraser:

> The working class, by shopping in the streets or in the corner store, got neither cheapness nor quality. They paid dearly for their small quantities and for any credit obtained. The quality was abysmal, with frequent adulteration of the most common products to squeeze a few pence more profit from the poor. Nor was there much effort to attract customers, and the only sales technique applied in the better-off shops was servility and deference.[9]

A response to this was the growth of multiple-shop organisations, initially in the field of groceries but later in other areas. The strategy of these new retail organisations was to combine relatively low prices with a higher quality of service than traditional shops in terms of cleanliness, provided to a population characterised by a rising level of incomes. This strategy was achieved on the part of the multiple grocery shops by offering customers a relatively limited range of goods (including, however, the greater number of imported foods then becoming available), selling these in clean but standardised shops, with an absence of credit and delivery services given by earlier shop retailers. Maypole, for example sold only four articles in its shops to begin with: margarine, butter, condensed milk and tea.[10] On this basis retail trade margins were reduced to 10–15 per cent compared with the 15–30 per cent in traditional shops. In the grocery trade these developments occurred from 1870 onwards; and the last quarter of the nineteenth century saw the establishment and growth in this field of firms such as Lipton, Massey, Templeton, Galbraith, Maypole, and Home & Colonial Stores. Most of these enterprises gradually expanded their range of goods; and as the number of branches also grew they became business organisations of considerable size and importance, and posed a significant competitive threat to the traditional, single shop retail business. Thomas Lipton, for example, opened his first shop in 1872, and by 1878 turnover was at a level 6000 hams, 16 tons of bacon, 16 000 dozen eggs, ten tons of butter and 200 cheeses per week. In the years immediately preceding the First World War Maypole was responsible for one third of national margarine distribution.[11] A similar development of multiple retailing occurred, a little later, in the meat trade, in bread, and in non-food areas such as books (W. H. Smith and John Menzies), sewing machines, boot and shoe retailing, clothing, and medicines. In a number of instances, both food and non-food, retail operations became vertically integrated with manufacturing or processing, thus providing a further basis for the low-price policy of these organisations. In the case of the multiple grocers Maypole established creameries and packing stations in Denmark, and Lipton acquired tea plantations in Ceylon and hog-packing plants in Canada.[12] A number of retail butchers were meat processors and importers, and other multiple chemist organisations also followed Jesse Boot in integrating backwards (at an early stage) into the manufacture of medicines. There was frequent integration between retailing and manufacturing in clothing, and by 1900 45 per cent of multiple shoe retailing was undertaken by retailing-manufacturing integrated firms.

These multiple outlet developments were accompanied, and in some respect anticipated, by the growth of Co-operative stores. Indeed, it is often forgotten that it is to the Co-operative movement that we owe two major retailing innovations of this time: vertical integration, and ownership by a single organisation of a number of branches (i.e. multiple retailing).[13] The consumers' co-operative movement took off in the middle of the last century, and by 1863 membership totalled around 100 000 with a turnover, mostly in groceries and provisions, of £2.5m. The Co-operative Wholesale Society (CWS), founded that year, gave the Co-operative movement the advantage of vertical integration; and by the end of the century the CWS had one million shareholding societies and provided these shops with a wide range of grocery products, including goods imported in its own fleet of ships and tea grown on its Ceylon plantations. As its range of goods was extended to clothing and other areas the Co-operative movement added a boot firm, a shirt factory, hosiery manufacturing and cabinet making facilities under the control of the CWS or the SCWS. By the end of the nineteenth century the working-class co-operatives and their middle class or civil service equivalents were a major retailing force in the economy.[14] Jefferys estimated that in 1900 the Co-operative Society share of the total retail market was 6–7 per cent, and in food and household items the proportion approached 10 per cent.[15]

If the multiple stores, including the co-operatives, grew up on the basis largely of an expanding trade in foods for working-class shoppers, the development of department stores from around the same time was based upon not dissimilar policies applied to clothing and a wider range of goods and the shopping habits of middle-class consumers. The department stores which grew up from the 1860s provided a range of clothes and material at keen prices; and although they offered services such as delivery and rest rooms, no credit was extended and prices were clearly fixed, in contrast to earlier practice of haggling. Retail margins were low, and aggressive selling and advertising, including bargain sales, were used to attain sales volume.[16] From 1860 onwards these stores were established, many of which names survive today, including Whiteley ('the Universal Provider'), Harvey Nichols, Derry & Toms, Selfridge, and Harrods in London, and Lewis in the provinces. These organisations too operated on a large scale – Selfridge's Oxford Street store expanding to a total frontage of 1400 feet and employing 5000 staff.[17]

2.4   Into the Twentieth Century

The latter half of the nineteenth century witnessed quite revolutionary changes in the pattern of shopping which changed the structure of retail distribution from a pre-industrial form to one which we would recognise today. Both demand and supply factors were at work. On the demand side were features such as the increased urbanisation of the population, and particularly up to 1900 the rise in the level of real incomes. From the supply side also a number of forces operated which encouraged in particular the advance of large-scale retailing. The increase in the scale of manufacturing of a range of goods, the appearance of new items altogether such as factory-made footwear and clothing, margarine and patent medicines, and the large-scale importing of foods (incuding latterly frozen meat), all made demands upon the distributive system which could not be met by the traditional producer/retailer. At the same time the increased standardisation of many goods facilitated mass distribution by a less skilled retail distribution network; and changes in the law relating to limited liability also played a role in facilitating an increase in the size of business units in both manufacturing and distribution.

By the early decades of the present century the pattern of the newer forms of retailing had become established, and indeed in the years leading up to the First World War a further divergence appeared in the policies of the department stores on the one hand and the multiples (including the co-operative stores) on the other. While the department stores moved further in the direction of providing a wide range of goods from which customers could choose, together with increased levels of amenity, comfort and service, the multiple shops continued to appeal predominantly to working-class customers in terms of price. In Jefferys' analysis:

Until well after the turn of the century the multiple shop branch units in most trades made little or no attempt to provide comforts or amenities for their customers. Only the barest essentials by way of shop fittings were installed, but every effort was made to advertise in spectacular and noisy ways the goods for sale and the low prices at which they were being offered.[18]

It was not until the inter-war period that the multiple chains began to increase their range of goods in an effort to reach more customers; and it was only at this stage of their development that they began to expand into fields previously occupied by the department stores. In 1915, for example, food represented 72 per cent of total multiple shop sales, and footwear and clothing (mostly the former) 15 per cent. By 1939, however, food sales had fallen to only 45 per cent, and clothing and footwear had risen to 26 per cent.[19]

By the early decades of this century the multiple chains were able to enjoy economies of scale through their ability to buy in bulk (in addition to being vertically integrated in many cases) as well as standardisation and specialisation of retail functions such as buying, merchandising, administration etc. They became large incorporated, professionally managed organisations. By the turn of the century Home & Colonial Stores had 200 outlets, and by 1910 Lipton had 245 branches throughout the UK;[20] and with the more than doubling of the proportion of total food and household goods retail sales accounted for by multiple shop firms over the period 1900–1920 it must have seemed as if the small independent shopkeeper was about to disappear from the retailing scene.[21] But competition among these stores was increasing during this period. The very success of a small number of multiple grocery stores brought each into competition with the others in a manner aptly described by Mathias in his Introduction to the history of Allied Suppliers. Writing of the separate emergence of those grocery chains which later came to form Allied Suppliers, Mathias points out:

> These separate stories do not converge much until the first decade of the twentieth century for the reason that direct, one-to-one competition (when awareness of the moves of the other party directly induced counter-action) had to await the emergence of the few giants astride the national market. The process of growth up to that point was such that even the fastest-growing companies were not in direct serious conflict with each other. A rapidly growing national market, less efficient independent shops which were continuing victims of the multiples' expansion and natural specialisations blunted the edge of head-on conflicts between the emerging giants. Only after 1900 has the growth of the largest firms mainly occurred by amalgamation and absorption of other companies and not by the simple extension of the numbers of their own branches.[22]

The falling off in the rate of expansion of the population and in spending power led to consolidations among the multiple food retailers accompanied by a hard core of 'the best and most business-like and most wide-awake of the small shopkeepers'.[23] This trend is reflected, for example, in the slowing down in the rate of expansion in the number of branches of multiple shop firms even by the end of the nineteenth century. While in the case of firms having ten or more branches (which continues to be the definition today of multiple shop organisations) the annual rate of store expansion over the period 1876–1900 was 10.8 per cent, the figure for the period 1901–1920 was 3.8.[24] Competition in retailing was also addded to in the pre-1914 period by the emergence of the variety chain stores, although the major development of these occurred in the inter-war period. Although they were a form of multiple shop organisation, the distinguishing features of the variety chain stores were an emphasis upon high-volume trading in a wide range of low-priced goods, with shoppers operating a system of self selection.[25] Although they have now largely left behind the Penny Bazaar or 6*d*. Store image, organisations such as Woolworth (established in the UK in 1909), Marks & Spencer, Littlewoods and British Home Stores offered competition in the inter-war period both to department stores and traditional shops.[26] Selfridge, among the more success-ful of the department stores, found itself in the 1930s having to react to these 'fixed-price chains [which] appeared to be consolidating their position at the expense of the department stores', and was forced to respond by opening a sub-bargain basement on 'sixpenny bazaar' lines.[27]

In the period between the two world wars supply conditions continued to favour large-scale retailing with an increase in the scale of manufacture of standard goods, extended use of branding of both home produced and imported products, and a further taking over by producers of many of the functions such as weighing and bagging of groceries previous carried out by retailers. The new products of this era included domestic electrical app-liances, radios, motor cars, new textiles, and a wide range of chemists' goods and toiletries.[28] On the demand side real incomes were rising more slowly, and there was a reduction in the rate of population increase; but at the same time there was a growing homogeneity of demand for many products as regional and even income group differences in consumption of many goods decreased. These developments favoured national marketing and distribution of many products, and thus the growth of large scale, multiple shop organisations; and estimates for the years 1920 and 1939 indicate a rise in the proportion of total retail sales accounted for by multiple shop retailers from 7–10 per cent in the former year to 18–19.5 per cent in the latter, representing a doubling of their importance in the retail trade.[29] As in the case of the department stores, where this period saw the emergence of large groupings such as Debenhams, United Drapery Stores and the John Lewis Partnership, the interwar period was marked by significant amalgamation among the multiple shop retailers. In the meat trade the formation of the Union Cold Storage group in 1923 brought together more than 2000 branches; Home & Colonial Stores in groceries brought more than 3000 branches within its control through amalgamation by 1931; and a similar pattern of amalgama-tions led to the hegemony of Boots and Timothy Whites and Taylors in chemists' goods, Freeman, Hardy & Willis in footwear, and the United Dairies group.[30] As might be expected, these amalgamations were stimulated partly by a desire to gain further economies of scale and specialisation which accompanied increased size, and partly in order to reduce the level of competition in some overcrowded markets. As we noted before, this period saw a widening of the range of goods of the multiple shops; and at this time there was also a move to a greater emphasis by multiple shops upon service – demonstrated not only in the wider range of goods but also in the provision of more elaborate facilities for shoppers (including in some cases free credit) and the occupation of main street sites. The interwar period thus appears to have been marked by increased competition and a reduction in the earlier differences in the trading policies among the larger-scale retailers who were now appealing to less differentiated groups of customers.

Where did these developments leave the unit or independent shop, whose numbers Braithwaite and Dobbs put at 500 000–600 000 in 1930 – accounting for 'well over 90 per cent of the total, and . . . for something like two-thirds of the entire turnover'?[31] Some indication of their situation can be gained from a comparison with Jefferys' estimates of 1938 and also with the data from the first Census of Distribution for 1950 (Table 2.1).

Although the data for 1930 and 1938 are not strictly comparable, the three observations taken together indicate a decline in the role of the independent shop. This certainly occurred between 1938 and 1950 in terms of numbers, where there was a reduction of almost one third, representing a considerable departure from the picture painted by Henry Smith in 1931 of an average of nearly six shops of one kind or another per street, or one shop for every seventy persons.[32] Comparison of the last two columns of Table 2.1 indicates that even the reduction in numbers underestimates the decline in importance of the unit retailer as his share of the total trade fell away considerably by 1950.

The independent shopkeeper appears in the years before 1939 to have begun to lose his competitive place as a result of the continued urbanisation of the population (and with this the demise of the local village shop) and

Table 2.1
Unit Retail Traders and Total Retail Trade

Year	Establishments	Proportion of total	
		No. %	Trade %
1930	5–700 000	90	67
1938	657 000	88	66
1950	447 426	84	53

SOURCES: D. Braithwaite and S. P. Dobbs, *The Distribution of Consumable Goods* (London: George Routledge, 1932) p. 239; H. Levy, *The Shops of Britain* (London: Routledge & Kegan Paul, 1948) p. 32; M. D. H. Ross, *Organisation of Retail Distribution* (London: Macdonald, 1955) pp. 19 and 21.

increased mobility on the part of consumers, allowing them in particular to travel greater distances to centres of population in order to make comparisons in buying shopping goods. In the case of some trades such as butchery the increased level of fixed costs of retailing in terms of more hygienic and sophisticated shop fittings, and also possibly a delivery van, further militated against the survival of the small retailer. On the other hand trends such as the growth of semi-rural housing estates on the fringes of urban communities, and the requirement for joint retailing and repairing of the new generation of domestic electrical appliances, radios and gramophones favoured the small retailer, who remained also for many a convenient source of short-term credit in shopping.[33] Nevertheless, and even allowing for the impact of the wartime economy, there is some evidence, in comparing the number of independent retailers between 1938 and 1950 and the falling share of the total retail trade accounted for by unit retailers from 1930 to 1950, to suggest that this class of retail distributor was beginning to be reduced in importance except in those fields where a more personal service was offered (and here the retailer was often in fact a producer/retailer as in bespoke tailoring and dressmaking) or where the shopkeeper offered greater locational convenience – often accompanied by long working hours – and thus enjoyed something of a geographical monopoly.

2.5 Retail Distribution Since 1950

The years following the Second World War are an appropriate point in time at which to begin an account of retailing as it is today. By the early 1950s wartime restrictions – including rationing and building controls – were coming to an end, and retailing was ready to resume its peacetime developments. Since 1950, too, we have the advantage of the data in successive Census of Distribution reports on which to base an analysis of trends in the pattern of retailing. Thus although Jefferys' data for earlier years may be quite reliable, they do not have the robustness of properly organised census data.

We noted that in the early decades of the present century and during the inter-war period a number of developments in retailing had occurred, most of which consolidated the trends of the last decades of the nineteenth century. Both supply and demand factors operated in favour of larger retailing groupings. However, new forms of retailing such as the variety chain stores emerged; both the department stores and the non-Co-operative multiples changed part of their trading policy; and the fortunes of different forms of retailing changed. In this section bringing our history of retailing in this chapter up to the present time we shall highlight a number of features of this period. Some of these will be dealt with in more detail in Chapters 3 and 4 in analysing competition and strategy in retailing. In the remainder of this chapter we first provide a picture of the retailing scene from 1950 to the present time through analysing Census of Distribution data. We then examine new trends in retail competition which came about with greater freedom in retail pricing, and phenomena such as trading stamps and private label goods. Finally we return to an earlier theme of examining the proportion of the retail trade accounted for by different forms of retailing and try to account for these changes.

The Data of Retail Distribution

Using the figures in the Census of Distribution is a frustrating exercise. Data which ought to be comparable between one census and another turn out not to be so; definitions of, for example, multiple shop organisations in terms of the number of branches change; and the levels of aggregation of different types of shop also change from one census to another.

None the less an examination of the data in successive census reports provides a reasonably consistent global picture of the development of the retail trades over the past 25 or 30 years. The first data, presented in full in Appendix Table 2.1, indicate the global size of the retail sector of the economy in terms of the number of shops (establishments), its output relative to total economic activity as measured by Gross Domestic Product (GDP), and the number of people employed in this sector. The first data column, relating to the number of establishments or shops, provides a simple indication of the physical presence of retailing in the community. From these data we can see that while the freedom from rationing and building restrictions by the mid 1950s permitted an increase in the number of individual shops, this trend had reached its peak by the time of the 1961 census at which stage there were almost 9 per cent more shops than in the first census year of 1950. This total fell off quite rapidly – by a rather surprising 13 per cent over the five years to 1966,[34] and again between 1971 and 1977 – and has continued to decline more steadily from 1977 to the present time, at which point the number of shops (in 1987) is 40 per cent below the peak total twenty-six years ago. Retailing activity has thus become physically more concentrated in the decades since the Second World War; and that this rather than a significant reduction in the total amount of economic activity is behind the fall in the number of shops may be seen from the last two data columns. The penultimate column in Appendix Table 2.1 relates retailing activity in value added terms to total economic activity as measured by GDP. The pattern of this ratio indicates that, contrary to the assumptions made by some writers concerning the emergence of a service economy, retailing has not (allowing for the difficulties of comparing the 1950–1971 and 1977–1987 periods) become a more dominant part of total economic activity. Nor on the other hand has it become less important, and remains accounting for over 7 per cent of the total. Similarly, although problems abound here in counting and comparing full-time and part-time employees, employment in terms of the total number of persons engaged in the retail sector has remained remarkably stable, although there has been a downward movement observable since 1971.

Appendix Table 2.2 breaks down the total of shopping establishments into those which were independent units (although for statistical purposes this figure also includes shop units which were part of a multiple shop organisation having up to nine units under its control), multiple shop units (i.e. outlets in organisations controlling 10+ units) and Co-operative Society retail establishments. What is immediately apparent is the decline in the number of independent shops relative to the total of establishments. In 1950 there were 448 999 shops classed as independents (376 446 or 84 per cent of which were actually single units); and at that time units classed as independent shops made up 85 per cent of the total number of establishments. Although this total rose along with the general increase in the number of shops up to 1957, the figure fell off after that time and has declined steadily since then. None the less as the data in Table 2.2 show, independent shops have retained their importance in terms of numbers and still account for more than four out of every five establishments. The data relating to sales, however, tell a very different story. Despite a decline in numbers in recent years, those shops classed as multiples have continued to increase their share of retail sales – to a point in 1987 where, together with Co-operative Stores, they accounted for 60 per cent of the total. There has thus been a very significant swing away from the traditional retailer, identified as the independent shop establishment, who was responsible in 1950 for almost two-thirds of retail sales to a situation at the present time (1987) where this form of retailing accounts for only two fifths of the total. Correspondingly non-Co-operative multiple sales, although such outlets represent less than one in five shops, have increased to an extent which has more than doubled their proportion of the total from 25 per cent in 1957 to 56 per cent in 1987. The story of the Co-operative retail movement is one of steady decline from a not insignificant proportion of the retail trade in 1950 to a halving of this in terms of sales by 1987.

The data in Table 2.2 thus indicate clearly the rise in the importance of multiple shop retailing, not predominantly in terms of the number of outlets but with regard to their share of total retail turnover. Correspondingly although shop outlets classed as independents still represent more than four fifths of the total number their share of total retail turnover has declined from almost two thirds in 1950 to 40 per cent in 1987.

The data in Appendix Table 2.2 relate to establishments or individual shop units. Of equal concern is the distribution of economic power among retailers in terms of business decision-making organisations, and data on this are presented in Appendix Table 2.3. Organisations or enterprises are separate legal decision-making units and as such represent the locus of economic power and strategic decision making in the sector. Obviously only in the case of true unit shops are establishments and enterprises the same thing. Table 2.3 shows the proportion of organisations within each category of retailer on the same basis as Table 2.2 from which are also repeated the proportions of retail turnover. What stands out clearly from the data in Table 2.3 and Appendix Table 2.3 is the overwhelming concentration of decision making on the part of multiple shops. Not only has there been a significant increase in

Table 2.2
Categories of Shop by Number and Turnover
(Establishment data in proportions)

	Total No.	Independents No. %	Independents Sales %	Multiples No. %	Multiples Sales %	Co-operatives No. %	Co-operatives Sales %
1950	529 684	85	65	10	23	5	12
1957	574 218	84	63	11	25	5	12
1961	544 873	80	52	15*	36*	5	12
1966	504 046	80	58	14	33	6	9
1971	471 369	83	55	13	37	3	7
1977	387 588	80	48	17	45	3	7
1980	368 253	82	46	16	47	2	7
1982	356 590	82	44	16	50	2	6
1984	349 728	83	43	16	52	2	5
1986	343 386	82	41	16	54	2	5
1987	345 468	82	40	17	55	1	5

* The definition of a multiple shop organisation was changed for this year only to one having 5+ establishments.

SOURCES: *Reports of the Census of Distribution*, and more recently Business Monitor SDA25 *Retailing* (London: HMSO).

the proportion of total retail sales accounted for by multiple shops, but also the power of these organisations is reflected in the fact that in terms of numbers of enterprises these multiple organisations comprise a negligible proportion of the total. In 1957 1151 non-Co-operative multiple organisations (each with an average of 53 shops) accounted for 25 per cent of total retail sales, while by 1971 1031 such organisations (each by then with an average of 61 shops) accounted for 37 per cent of the total. In 1987 the number of these organisations had fallen to 772 (each having an average of 75 branches), and they accounted for over half of the value of retail trade. Even these figures understate the concentration of power among the largest multiple retailing groups. The 1977 census report showed that among the multiples seven organisations, each with more than 1000 branches, controlled a total of 9305 outlets which together accounted for almost 8 per cent of total retail sales. By 1982 the number of organisations in this largest size category had fallen to four; and these businesses (all of which were in the food retailing sector) controlled 5981 outlets which with combined sales slightly in excess of £3bn accounted for 4.4 per cent of total retail sales. (The concentration of sales within the food sector was obviously very much higher, and this issue is dealt

Table 2.3
Categories of Enterprise by Number and Turnover

	Total No.	Independents No. %	Sales %	Multiples No. %	Sales %	Co-operatives No. %	Sales %
1950	404 845	100	65	−*	23	· ·	12
1957	· ·	· ·	63	· ·	25	· ·	12
1961	416 606	99	52	−†	36†	−	12
1966	· ·	· ·	58	· ·	33	· ·	9
1971	352 256	100	55	−	37	−	7
1977	262 443	99	48	−	45	−	7
1980	256 139	100	46	−	47	−	7
1982	248 950	100	44	−	50	−	6
1984	246 931	100	43	−	52	−	5
1986	244 006	100	41	−*	54	−	5
1987	240 853	100	40	−	55	−	5

* No separate organisation data on Co-operative available
† The definition of a multiple shop organisation was changed for this year only to one having 5+ establishments.
· · = not available.

SOURCES: *Reports of the Census of Distribution*, and more recently Business Monitor SDA25 *Retailing* (London: HMSO).

with in more detail in Chapters 3 and 4 in looking at competition and strategy in individual retailing sectors.)

For all their imperfections Census of Distribution data provide us with a reasonably consistent picture of the retail trades since 1950. Four features stand out. First, within the greatly reduced number of shops, whose total has fallen by 40 per cent since its peak in 1957, the non-multiple retail establishment is still today the dominant physical feature of retailing. These establishments represent more than four fifths of shops by number; and in 1987 there were still 213 378 single-shop retailing organisations, accounting for 62 per cent of all outlets. Second, independent shops have, however, suffered a significant loss in their share of retail trade over the years since 1950. This proportion has fallen from 65 per cent in 1950 to 40 per cent in 1987; and the decline indicates both the cost competitiveness of multiple shops and the extent to which they have been able to attract an increasing proportion of shoppers with a wider range of goods. Third, from the enterprise or business decision-making unit data in Table 2.3 it is clear that at the present time there is also a trend towards an increased concentration of economic power in retailing. Thus the picture painted by Jefferys and Knee in 1961 of 'the existence of a vast number of individual entrepreneurs . . . in retailing', and their reference to retailing as 'still a very small scale and human occupation' is increasingly less accurate as a number of very large professionally managed retailing organisations possessing oligopolistic market power emerge in a number of sectors.[35] Fourth, it is evident from the data in Tables 2.2 and 2.3 that the Co-operative movement is no longer the force in retailing which it was at one time. Some of the reasons for this decline are discussed later in this chapter when we look at changing forms of retailing.

Price Competition

A major development in retailing since the 1950s has been the emergence of price competition in many areas where prior to this time it was dormant or proscribed. The newer multiple retailers of the last quarter of the nineteenth century developed and expanded their share of the retail trade on the basis of their lower operating margins from which they were able to undercut the traditional retailers; and the growth in the range of packaged and branded products at this time made such price differences more obvious to shoppers.[36] Not surprisingly, in this environment the practice emerged of manufacturers determining the price at which all retailers could sell a product to shoppers – a policy known as resale price maintenance (r.p.m.). The practice of r.p.m. became established in the last decades of the nineteenth century mainly as a result of pressure upon manufacturers from the traditional retailers of household medicines, groceries and cigarettes and tobacco who were suffering from the cut-price trading methods of the new multiple and Co-operative retailers. In a few fields – books, confectionery, domestic electrical appliances and motor vehicles – some of this initiative appears to have lain with the manufacturers themselves. Estimates of the proportion of consumer expenditure on goods which was affected by r.p.m. have varied. However, from a figure of 3 per cent of total consumer expenditure so affected in 1900, the proportion of goods subject to r.p.m. rose to 30 per cent in 1938 and to 40–50 per cent by the mid-1950s.[37] In a more detailed analysis shortly prior to the 1956 Restrictive Trade Practices Act Yamey listed a range of goods including bread and cereals, cigarettes etc., confectionery, radios and electrical goods across which r.p.m. was applied almost universally, and a further list covering preserves, manufactured foods, clothing and footwear, furniture and floorcoverings within which r.p.m. applied to many brands.[38]

It is unnecessary here to go into the argument and counter-argument relating to the practice of r.p.m. Of more significance in our analysis is the fact that as part of its general move against anti-competitive trade practices embodied in the 1956 Restrictive Trade Practices Act the government outlawed collective enforcement of r.p.m.; and in the 1964 Resale Prices Act it provided that only in clearly defined and defended instances could individual manufacturers continue the practice of r.p.m. in their particular sector. In fact even prior to the 1956 Act the price-cutting policies of the large multiple grocery chains had begun to break down any effective r.p.m. system in the areas of branded foods and other household goods; and by the mid-1960s a similar sequence of events had brought about the demise of r.p.m. in the field of domestic electrical appliances. Indeed in a wide range of products, including cigarettes and tobacco, gramophone records, cosmetics, newspapers, bicycles, razor blades, wallpaper and paint, the system of price maintenance crumbled away between the mid-1950s and mid-1960s partly as a result of the legislation on the practice and partly as a result of the trading policies of the large retailers. Only in the cases of four trades did hearings relating to the practice of r.p.m. occur in the Restrictive Practices Court. In respect of confectionery (1967) and footwear (1968) the arguments put forward by the manufacturers for continuing r.p.m. were turned down by the Court, while with regard to books (1962) and household medicines (1970) manufacturers are still permitted to dictate retail prices, except under special conditions such as second-hand book sales or remaindering in the case of books.[39]

The demise of the practice of r.p.m. brought about a number of changes in retailing. Most significantly it increased the availability of the price dimension of retail competition. The extent of this change for retailing management may be gauged from Pickering's comment that 'After the influence of so many years of rpm retail pricing tended to be a lost art in those trades which relied almost entirely on manufacturer branded goods'.[40] Equally importantly, in terms of the evolution of the structure of retailing the advantages in the use of this 'lost art' of price competition lay with large-scale distributors: those retailers who benefited most in spreading their high incidence of fixed costs over increased volumes of sales, and who enjoyed low variable cost levels through using these high volumes in bargaining with manufacturer suppliers. The main competitive weapon of these retailers tended to be price. This competitive situation was exacerbated for the smaller retailer by the fact that, although the econometric evidence on the matter is not robust, there is some evidence to suggest that at this time of post-r.p.m. price reductions there was in a number of retail trades a reduction in distributors' margins, thus increasing the general extent of competitiveness in this sector.[41] This and other pressures led to the establishment of voluntary groups among independent retailers in order to attempt to trade on the same terms *vis-à-vis* manufacturers as the multiple retail groups. Thus the point about these changes – some of which were indeed brought about essentially by the behaviour of the larger retailers themselves – is that certainly from the mid 1960s onwards those lower-cost retailers were able fully to exploit their economies of scale in competing in terms of price with traditional distributors, and there is no doubt that in many trades – grocery distribution being a prime example – the ending of r.p.m. increased the rate of penetration of those multiple shop organisations able to exploit this advantage.

Trade Stamps

Another dimension of retail competition which developed to significant proportions after 1950 was stamp trading. Although the practice of giving stamps with goods originated in the 1920s in the UK, it was not until the 1950s that the practice developed on a more significant scale. None the less it was estimated that even in 1964 less than 4 per cent of total retail trade was affected.[42] Stamp trading – providing shoppers with stamps in proportion to the value of their purchases where these may be redeemed through a catalogue or other outlet for a choice of goods – provided retailers with an indirect means of price competition. Where the stamps were those of a particular store, as opposed to those of a stamp organisation such as Green Shield, this practice not only afforded a means of indirect price competition but also built store loyalty. This form of indirect price competition was obviously appealing to some retailers while the practice of r.p.m. obtained, but continued to grow even after that policy had been largely discontinued. In fact although stamp trading continued to expand throughout the 1970s the practice remained concentrated in a relatively few trades. It was estimated, for example, that in 1970–71 13 per cent of grocery/supermarket turnover was covered by stamp trading; but the figure was only about 1 per cent in the case of other food and non-food shops. In the case of garages 26 per cent of total outlets gave stamps.[43] The practice of giving trading stamps has now almost entirely ceased and is overwhelmingly restricted to garage sales of petrol.

2.6   Forms of Retailing

As we have gauged already in looking at the Census of Distribution data for the post-1950 period, quite significant changes have been continuing over the past forty years in the pattern of different forms of retailing. Such change was relatively slow to begin with after 1945 as the effects of wartime controls in the forms of food rationing, price and margin control as well as building restrictions continued. Wartime controls did, however, have the effect of generally encouraging greater efficiency in retailing as these tended to depress gross trading margins at the same time as male and juvenile labour was becoming more scarce. On the other hand these controls on supplies and entry into retailing made the sector much less competitive in its structure.[44]

This section looks at the major changes in the forms of retailing over the period since the Second World War and the chapter then concludes with an appraisal of the development of retailing since its early beginnings.

Department Stores

Of those forms of retailing which have been in decline, perhaps the most obvious is the department store. We saw earlier in this chapter how these grew up in the last decades of the nineteenth century on the model of innovative French establishments of the 1860s. Department stores in the UK thrived on rising standards of living among the middle classes and expenditure on clothing, furnishings etc. in particular. In the early decades of the present century, as in the case of multiple grocery stores, the department stores experienced increasing competition with each other, realising that 'giant must compete with giant and that they must watch one another for points'.[45] Up to the interwar period, however, department stores benefited from the increasing proportion of consumer expenditure on non-food items and a greater fashion consciousness among their customers; and over this period the department stores also took steps in terms of price policies and their range of goods to meet competition from other forms of retailing. From this time on, however, the department stores began to encounter problems in terms of a population drift further and further out to the suburbs on the part of their traditional customers, increased physical limitations and rising costs associated with their city-centre locations, and perhaps most of all the incursions into their product ranges of the multiple and chain store organisations. As these shops moved increasingly into clothing the multiple stores demonstrated that they too could offer a range of items; and these could be offered at prices which reflected the much greater purchasing economies of the multiples, each with a more restricted range of merchandise overall than the typical department store. Changes in conditions of manufacture also aided the multiples as large-scale production of clothing, which could incorporate both fashion and variety, became a possibility. Thus, starting at the lower price levels in men's and women's clothing, the multiples began to creep up on the department stores.

In fact Davis points out that the era of department store expansion came to an end between the two world wars, and by the 1950s the multiple and chain stores were beginning to take away from the department stores large quantities of standard popular lines of both men's and women's underwear and outerwear, all offered at prices reflecting not only the scale economies of the more modern forms of retailing but also the absence of rest rooms, doormen or credit.[46] Stacey and Wilson described the department stores of this era as 'surviving mastodons from the pre-history of large scale organisation', and pointed out that although in 1950 they were responsible for 13–15 per cent of all clothing and footwear sales, that position had been static for some twenty-five years, and over the 1950s their share of the total retail trade dropped from approximately 6 per cent to nearer 5 per cent.[47] In fact it was not until 1971 that department stores were omitted from separate analysis in the Census of Distribution reports, and Table 2.4 traces their role in the retail trade.

These and other data show that department stores tended in this period to remain independent (i.e. non-multiple). In 1957, for example, independent shop department stores accounted for 52 per cent of total establishments, and the Co-operative Societies for a further 26 per cent. In 1966 the nineteen

Table 2.4
Department Stores

	Enterprises (No.)	Establishments (No.)	Proportion of retail sales (%)
1950	. .	529	6.3
1957	. .	718	5.8
1961	335	784	5.4
1966	. .	760	5.9
1971	243	818	6.1

SOURCES: *Reports of the Census of Distribution*, (London: HMSO)

multiple-shop department stores still accounted for only 55 per cent of establishments and merely 26 per cent of department store total sales.

Since 1971 the department store sector of retailing has further declined, particularly in respect of independent outlets. Well-known names such as London's Whiteleys, Swan & Edgar, and Bournes closed in the early 1980s,[48] Debenhams was acquired by Burton in 1985,[49] and Sears sold its loss-making Lewis's department store chain to its management in 1988.[50] This leaves the department store sector dominated by the Al Fayed brothers' House of Fraser with about 62 individual stores including Harrods, and the John Lewis Partnership which has 21 department stores in addition to its 84 Waitrose supermarkets.[51] The sector is now estimated to account for 4.5 per cent of total retail sales – a figure which has remained quite constant for most of the 1980s.[52] It would seem unlikely that department stores as a whole can regain much of their previous retail market share as an increasingly car-borne shopping population prefers out-of-town locations for more convenient and price-competitive shopping for consumer durables, and a combination of increasingly 'up-market' chains such as Marks & Spencer together with fashion multiples such as Next and Richards take away clothing customers. It would seem that only the very distinctive traditional department stores such as Harrods, Fortnum & Mason and Harvey Nichols, or the John Lewis Partnership with its particular image, keen pricing policy of being 'never knowingly undersold' and unique form of ownership can survive in this sector.[53]

The Co-operative Retail Societies

During the latter part of the last century the Co-operative movement, whose distinguishing features are that its share capital is provided by a large number

Table 2.5
UK Retail Co-operative Societies

| | *Number of* | | *Market share of total* | |
| | *Organisations* | *Outlets* | *Retail trade* | *Grocery trade* |
			%	%
1950	· ·	26 458	12.0	23
1957	940	30 585	12.2	23
1961	835	29 396	11.8	20
1966	697	28 198	9.3	16
1971	313	16 480	7.5	15[*]
1977	238	10 921	7.0	14[†]
1980	186	8 197	6.4	14
1982	144	6 653	5.7	13
1984	111	5 569	5.2	12
1986	98	4 859	4.6	11

[*] 1970 data.
[†] 1975 data.

SOURCES: *Census of Distribution*; Business Monitor SDA25 *Retailing* (London: HMSO); grocery trade data from A. C. Nielsen.

of individual subscribers and that these investors are rewarded by a dividend related to their level of store purchases, was responsible for major innovations in retailing: the establishment of multiple branches, and backward vertical integration. Again, after the Second World War the Co-operative movement led the way in the development of self-service and the establishment of supermarkets in grocery retailing; and of this era one writer concluded 'co-operative societies displayed in some directions greater enterprise than their private competitors'.[54] With regard to self-service shopping, in 1950 the Co-operative movement operated 90 per cent of such outlets, with some 2000 out of its 16 000 branches being self-service stores; and in 1958 its share of these outlets was still 60 per cent.[55] The year 1957, as one author points out, was the high-water mark for the UK Co-operatives, when their share of total retail trade was 12.3 per cent and their proportion of the food trade was 19.7 per cent. By 1961 even, 42 per cent of all UK self-service outlets and 26 per cent of supermarkets were owned by the Co-operatives.[56]

Yet as we saw in Tables 2.2 and 2.3 above, and as detailed in Table 2.5, the Co-operative share of the total retail trade halved over the period 1950–1982. This has come about essentially because of the Co-operatives' loss of market share in groceries on which they remain dependent for about half of their turnover. The Co-operative movement share of the grocery trade fell from 23 per cent in 1950 to 16 per cent in 1966, and now stands at 11 per cent.[57] Given this lengthy period of steady decline it is not unreasonable to feel that the Co-operative movement has reached a point at which, as the *Financial Times* consumer affairs correspondent concluded, it 'appears to many to be a spent force'.[58]

The UK retail Co-operative movement is an example not of a retailing form or technique, such as the department store, which has been overtaken by changes in retailing economics, consumer shopping habits or location, but of the relative failure of a form of business management. The Co-operative retailing movement has many of the advantages of size – it is still nominally the largest single retailer in the UK and only in 1982 fell behind Sainsbury in terms of its share of the packaged grocery market[59] – but has not been able to capitalise upon this. Indeed, explanations for the reduced state of the Co-operative societies are normally couched in terms of their organisational structure and managerial policies. The Co-operative movement is still a loose federation of some 95 retail societies, many of which are comparatively small, and under management committees dominated by lay members who may have more emotional loyalty to the philosophy of the Rochdale Pioneers than knowledge of modern retail merchandising practice. Indeed, at an overall strategic level it has been argued that the Co-operative movement clung for too long to its 'basic values' of profit sharing, consumer service, fair prices and equity; and that this prevented the organisation from responding to competitive pressures, including changes in consumer demand.[60] Thus the individual Co-operative societies have remained decentralised at a time when economic and other forces have dictated the need for more centralisation in retail management. Despite recommendations for more centralisation and rationalisation within the movement from the time of publication of the Gaitskell Commission report in 1958 onwards, the Co-operative movement has continued to be characterised by significant local management autonomy, which like the payment of the 'divi' is out of step with modern retailing.

Some have argued that the Co-operative movement never recovered from the onslaught upon it by the newer multiple grocery groups in the post-r.p.m. era of the early 1960s. Thus despite a widespread cost- and asset-reduction programme of the late 1960s, when it closed one third of its shops and shed one quarter of its employees in three years, the retail Co-operative movement has been able neither to match competitors much smaller than itself in 'low cost' price competition nor to 'differentiate' itself in terms of the quality of its merchandise and service from other chains.[61] Certainly for all of its apparent size as a retailer, the Co-operative movement and its retailing formula appear, like the department stores discussed above, to be phenomena more of yesterday than tomorrow.

Multiple Shop Groups

In contrast to department stores and the Co-operative society movement whose post-1950 developments were dealt with above, multiple shop retailing (including the variety chains) has advanced steadily over this period. As we saw in Table 2.3 non-Co-operative society multiples increased their share of the total retail market from 23 per cent in 1950 to 55 per cent in 1987, and this advance was especially rapid around the time of the breakdown of r.p.m. in the late 1950s to mid-1960s. In the grocery sector in particular these multiples advanced from a 20 per cent share of this market in 1950 to 40 per cent in 1968. By 1975 their proportion of the trade had reached 49 per cent, and by 1986 it was 71 per cent.[62]

Both cost and demand conditions have continued to favour large-scale retail distributors since the Second World War. First, pre-packaging and branding of foods (in ever more sophisticated forms thanks to Clarence Birdseye and other innovators) created a national product market. These ideas were also applied to many other goods and made possible national retailing. Second, the ending of building restrictions for retail development in 1954 permitted the creation of large-scale retailing units; and both the Co-operative societies and other multiple-shop organisations began to take advantage of this to establish supermarkets.[63] The number of these outlets increased from 175 in 1958 to 1366 by 1963;[64] and although the supermarket movement was contributed to significantly in the early years by the Co-operative societies, today it is dominated by a small number of non-Co-operative organisations including Sainsbury, Tesco, Gateway, Asda and the Argyll Group.

Third, the size of the multiple-shop organisations, both at the business firm and individual outlet level, gave them access to significant economies of scale in their operations, to which may be added the reduction in their direct costs arising from enhanced buying power *vis-à-vis* suppliers. For example, labour costs as a percentage of sales (which account for more than half of retail operating costs) are generally between 10 and 20 per cent lower for supermarkets than smaller grocery shops;[65] and the 1985 Office of Fair Trading study of comparative performance of different categories of food retailers found that the average buying price differential advantage between multiple and independent retailers was 15.5 per cent.[66] Fourth, as already commented upon above, the abolition of r.p.m. allowed large-scale retailers to convert their cost advantages into the weapon of price competition. In the case of groceries this pricing freedom resulted in reported savings for shoppers in multiple stores of 1s.4d. in the £ (6.5 per cent) in 1958; and comparable savings in contrast to independent shop prices were reported in another survey in 1961.[67] Again in 1971 the National Board for Prices and Incomes in its report on food distribution provided similar evidence of savings for shoppers;[68] and a 1977 Ministry of Agriculture, Fisheries and Food survey found that food prices at the largest stores were 6–13 per cent lower than at traditional food shops.[69] The multiple-shop organisations have consolidated many of their cost advantages by continuing to rationalise their operations in terms of individual store numbers and size, as indicated in Table 2.6.

These data indicate the increase in size of the average multiple-shop organisation in terms of outlets, and also the increased size of these outlets in terms of employment. Further indices of the increased scale of operation of multiple-shop operations and of their market power are the previously mentioned data on 'giant' retail organisations having 1000+ branches and their market concentration figures. In 1977 there were seven 'giant' retailers which together had 9305 establishments or shops and accounted for 7.6 per cent of total retail trade. By 1982 the number of such organisations had fallen to four, with a total of 5981 outlets and 4.4 per cent of the market. The 1984 and subsequent *Retailing* Business Monitors unhelpfully fail to separate this category, but show that in 1987 the top 24 retail organisations each having 500+ outlets had a total of 21 573 branches, or an average of 896 each, and a total of 17.6 per cent of the retail market.[70] At present the largest ten UK retailers account for 27 per cent of total retail sales, while in the grocery market the 'big five' supermarket operators alone (Sainsbury, Tesco, the retail co-operatives, Argyll and Gateway) have 64 per cent of that market.[71]

On the demand side retail consumers across the country have in many sectors become more uniform in their tastes, and this more homogeneous market has also been characterised by a steady increase in real incomes. As a result, multiple-shop groups have not only been able to replicate their particular retailing formulae across the economy, but have also moved 'up market' in terms of the quality, style and price of their merchandise. As part of this process multiple shop operation has spread to a number of sectors of

Table 2.6
Multiple Shop Organisation Store Numbers and Size[*]

	Organisations	*Outlets*	*Outlets/ organisation*	*Employment/ outlet*	*Total retail market share (%)*
1980	818	57 933	71	17.0	47.2
1982	843	56 555	67	16.9	50.0
1984	721	55 224	77	18.9	52.3
1986	763	55 497	73	19.4	54.6
1987	772	58 015	75	19.4	55.6

[*] Excludes Co-operative Societies

SOURCE: Business Monitor SDA25, *Retailing* (London: HMSO).

the market where independent retailers once felt protected in providing a high level of personal service or expertise, or in catering for a particular level of consumer tastes. In clothing, for example, Next has not only competed with other multiples but also taken custom away from independent men's and women's clothiers;[72] while Ratner has successfully applied a multiple-shop formula in part at least of the jewellery trade that was previously dominated by independent outlets.[73] The DIY trade too has moved out of the hands of countless independent ironmongers and paint sellers to a situation now where Kingfisher's (formerly Woolworth's) B & Q and the Ladbroke Group's Texas Homecare together account for about 20 per cent of total sales.[74]

The inescapable conclusion is that for a number of reasons relating both to cost and demand factors, the multiple-shop form of organisation has come to dominate UK retailing. These 'retail corporations', as one author has described them, have capitalised upon their scale cost advantages (at both the outlet and organisation level), have used this base to compete successfully against smaller retailers, and have so managed their merchandise policies as to take the multiple shop into almost every area of retailing, while in many sectors the independent shop plays only a very modest role.[75] It is, of course, the additional skills required to manage these retail corporations which provide a major focus for this text.

The Independent Retailer[76]

As we noted from the data in Tables 2.2 and 2.3, there has been a very significant reduction in the role of the independent retail organisation. Those shops classed as independents saw their numbers almost halved and their share of total retail sales fall by twenty percentage points between 1950 and 1982, at the end of which period they accounted for less than half of retail turnover. In 1987 the proportion of retail sales accounted for by independents was 40 per cent.[77] The place of the single unit shop within this group has also been significantly reduced as their numbers fell from 376 446 in 1950 to 231 329 in 1977 and 213 378 in 1987: a decline of 43 per cent over the whole period. Over this period the share of total retail trade accounted for by unit shops fell from 48 per cent in 1950 to 28 per cent in 1987.

In these figures there is, however, perhaps some ground for believing that the rate of decline in the position of the independent shop is slowing down, and that a core of independent shops – larger in some sectors than in others – is likely to remain viable. Three factors may contribute to the survival of the smaller retailer. First, we saw that one response of certain independent retailers as a class to the outcome of price competition following the ending of r.p.m. was to form voluntary buying groups. These comprise organisations trading under such names as Spar, VG, Mace and Wavy Line whose individual retailer members agree to purchase a weekly or monthly minimum of goods from the group in order to qualify for price discounts and other services provided by the group. Discounts are available because of the buying power of the group *vis-à-vis* manufacturers arising from the larger orders that it can place. This practice has most noticeably developed in the food trades where by 1970 44 per cent of a sample of independent grocers were members of a voluntary group, although voluntary group independent grocers accounted at that time for only 21 per cent of total grocery sales.[78]

At one stage in their development it was felt that such groups would play a major role in preserving the existence of independent food retailers. One of the Bolton Commitee research reports considered that:

It is generally agreed that this (formation of buying groups) has been a highly successful defensive strategy for independent retailers. A typical appraisal is that 'there is little argument that the development of voluntary purchasing groups has been the most successful measure the independent firms have adopted to counter the severe inroads made into their trade by the multiple store and large scale organisations'.[79]

Initially in the post-r.p.m. era it looked as if voluntary group independent grocers would come to dominate this sector of the market. A. C. Nielsen data show that while the share of total grocery turnover for indpendents as a whole fell from 53 per cent in 1961 to 42 per cent in 1971 the symbol or voluntary group shops raised their market share from 13 per cent to 22 per cent, resulting in a halving of the non-symbol shops market share from 40 per cent to 20 per cent over this period.[80] However, although the major symbol groups held on to a total grocery trade market share of about 12 per cent until the mid 1970s, this had halved by 1981.[81] The proportion of independent grocery retailers belonging to voluntary groups has remained little changed; and over the period 1975–1984 the packaged grocery market share of symbol group members actually fell rather more steeply than that of other independents: from 13.5 per cent to 5.4 per cent over this period for symbol shops, and from 11.1 per cent to 5.3 per cent for other independents.[82]

Second, as a further development in this area, however, independent retailers may in effect take over some of their own wholesaling functions by purchasing at trade cash-and-carry outlets. The largest firms in this sector are Landmark, Nurdin & Peacock, Linfood and Booker McConnell.[83] The retailer in this case is particularly saving his supplier the labour and transport costs involved in making small deliveries. Cash-and-carry warehouses – a number of which are operated by voluntary groups and may be open to unaffiliated retailers – have expanded in scale and in the range of goods carried as independent retailers have become more affected by competition from multiples. Thus although there was no major volume growth in the cash-and-carry wholesaling business during the 1980s, this remains an important source of supply for independent food retailers. Cash-and-carry accounted for about two thirds of the grocery wholesale trade over the 1980s, the remaining one third comprising the delivered trade. In turn 50 per cent of this grocery cash-and-carry trade is accounted for by grocery retailers, with caterers taking a further 39 per cent.[84] The importance of cash-and-carry wholesaling for independent grocers may be seen in the data from one survey which found that 55 per cent of expenditure of a sample of independent grocers was accounted for by cash-and-carry, compared with 32 per cent by wholesale delivered goods. However, only 7 per cent of these grocers relied entirely upon cash-and-carry.[85]

Thus while there may be some drawbacks for independent retailers in buying through a voluntary group or cash-and-carry outlet – such as a lack of variety of lines or the absence of certain merchandise altogether – these may be worth accepting in return for the increased trading margins available to the independent retailer in obtaining supplies in this way.

Finally, with regard to patterns of demand or custom, two features may promote the continued survival of independent retailers. First, in those areas where the 'corner shop' offers a unique service by virtue of personal attention and hours of opening, shopper demand may be fairly inelastic in response to the higher prices charged to cover greater unit costs. Such retailers may therefore expect to survive on the basis of both service and geographical monopoly. Second, the independent retailer will survive, even in larger centres of population and in open competition with multiple-shop organisations, where a clearly differentiated product-service combination is offered at a price that some proportion of the shopping public is willing and able to pay. This demands from the independent retailer a high level of expertise in merchandise choice and retail buying, personal selling, and retail business management, including finance: all, often, on the part of one or two people in the organisation. This can, however, still be achieved on the part of the independent wine and spirits shop, the jeweller-cum-watch-repairer, the clothing boutique or gentlemen's outfitter, the independent chemist, the fruit and vegetable shop, or even the traditional counter-service grocer/ delicatessen. But as we saw above, even in a number of these trades the onward march of the multiples is steady; and in Chapter 5 the particular issues confronting the single-shop retailer are analysed in more detail.

Franchising

An increasingly popular form of retailing is the business-format franchise. Franchising – deriving from the French verb *'affranchir'*, 'to free' – involves a relationship between a franchisor, who has developed a particular form of product or service, and a number of franchisees, who are independent businesses which pay the franchisor for the right to conduct the franchise operation in a particular locality. Although franchises may take a number of forms, the most relevant to retailing are wholesaler–retailer franchises such as the Spar, Mace, VG etc. 'voluntary groups', and certain business format franchises including Body Shop, Circle 'C' Stores, Clarks Shoes, Knobs & Knockers, Late Late Supershop, Yves Rocher, and Tie Rack.[86]

Franchising first developed at the beginning of this century in the United States; but the more recent major growth in Britain has occurred as a result of the increased popularity of business format franchises, including the retail operations instanced above. Annual turnover of business format franchises rose from some £670m in 1981 to around £2200m in 1986, and was forecast to reach £6bn by the end of the decade.[87] The total number of franchisees in the UK more than doubled from 1984 to reach nearly 20 000 in 1986, while over the same period employment in franchised outlets trebled to almost 150 000; and forecasts for the end of the decade were for 42 000 franchisees with 350 000 employees.[88]

A 1988 survey of all forms of franchising in the UK reported the data shown in Table 2.7.

Table 2.7
UK Franchising

	Annual sales from franchised units	Number of units operated	Jobs attributable to franchising
1984	£1.0bn	8 300	71 000
1986	£2.2bn	12 500	149 000
1987	£3.1bn	15 000	169 000

SOURCE: Power Research Associates report quoted in D. Ayling, 'The Universe of Franchising', *Management Today*, April 1988, p. 117.

The advantages of the franchise format are that the franchisor gains rapid geographical expansion of the business without massive capital investment, and has a highly motivated self-employed 'workforce' of franchisees – often possessing useful local contacts and knowledge of the market. These franchisees, on the other hand, gain the advantages of self-employment and independence while at the same time benefiting from being able to develop an established product or service format, enjoying continued business support from their franchisor, and being protected by having exclusive rights to the franchise within a particular locality.

Some retail organisations – such as Body Shop, with over 300 outlets in 31 countries – have expanded very successfully in niche markets, operating the franchise form with a blend of tight central control over merchandise, display etc. combined with local entrepreneurship.[89] On the other hand the experience of Flash Trash – the niche franchise fashion accessories chain which was established in October 1986 but which went into receivership in March 1988 – shows that success is not guaranteed for this business form when faced with problems of lack of clear market focus, insufficient access to good retail sites and possible overtrading.[90] Franchising – and retail business format franchises in particular – seems likely to increase in popularity in the UK as a desire for self-employment increases and attracts greater 'political' support, as service industries come to predominate in the economy, and as the franchising concept itself becomes more acceptable and attracts support from financial institutions such as banks and other lenders. This form of retailing too is also likely to play a role in maintaining the 'independent' retailer in the face of competition from multiple shops.

Mail Order

Although the proportion of total retail sales accounted for by general mail order has tended to decline in more recent times – from 4.0 per cent in 1976 to 3.3 per cent in 1985 – it continues none the less to occupy a not unimportant role in retailing.[91] Furthermore, developments in retailing technology and marketing may tend to increase the importance of this form of shopping in the next decade.

Although some of the present firms in the mail order sector can look back more than a century to their origins,[92] the roots of the mail-order catalogue business are to be found in the early years of the present century among lower income groups in the north of England who valued the availability of the tallyman or clubman's credit for clothing and household items.[93] At the present time the mail-order sector can be divided into two parts. The traditional agency mail-order system – accounting for 90 per cent of home shopping sales – where the part/spare time agent sells usually to a close circle of friends from a catalogue, and direct mail order where customers order by telephone. Although the latter presently accounts for only 10 per cent of total sales it is by far the faster growing sector, and likely to benefit from changes in marketing and technology.[94]

For post-war generations the attractions of traditional mail-order buying have been the convenience of shopping from home – taking one's time in making a choice at a convenient hour of the day; the wide product range available within a single catalogue; the ability to order goods on approval and then return them if not satisfied; the availability of apparently 'free' credit over an extended payment period; and the convenience of free home delivery of goods. In addition mail order as a form of retailing has benefited from the involvement of the agents who earn a return for their work of encouraging sales in terms of a commission, a discount off the catalogue price of merchandise, and the general social involvement that is part of being a mail-order agent.

The traditional form of mail-order retailing has declined in recent years as some of the loyalty of its lower socioeconomic group customers has waned, as some form of consumer credit has become available in most larger stores, and as mail-order prices are not only perceived to be generally less competitive than those of shops but also cannot quickly respond to store promotions. The mail-order organisations are reacting to this by using new technology (and information technology in particular) to reduce their storage and handling costs, and presenting a more attractive image of mail order or direct selling. Many of the mail-order companies have invested in information technology not only as a means of reducing stockholding levels and improving ware-house, delivery, agency and credit management but also to improve market-ing. Existing customer profiles can be built up; and mail-order firms can use these and other data to produce catalogues – sometimes known as special-ogues – for particular customer segments. Not only have there been ta-keovers in this sector,[95] but the advent, for example, of the Next Directory based upon Next's acquisition of Grattan in 1986 indicates the potential for this form of non-stop retailing.[96] The Next Directory – at a current cost of £3 – offers a very wide merchandise range with 48-hour delivery in response to local-rate telephone orders 8 a.m. to 10 p.m. seven days a week. Further advances in this field in the form of ordering from a video or television channel catalogue, possibly by home computer, may lead to a revival generally of non-shop retailing.[97]

2.7 Conclusions

This chapter has traced the evolution of retailing from its Elizabethan beginnings to the present time. We have seen how over this period the 'fixed shop' gradually took over from self-sufficiency in clothing and in food, and how it took the place of the itinerant packman, the hawker and the travelling fair. We also saw how the nature and size of these shops and retailing organisations changed particularly from the last decades of the nineteenth century onwards. The forces behind these changes have been economic, demographic, social and technical. Thus increased economic standards of living along with the growth of large centres of population contributed to the establishment of fixed shops in the seventeenth and eighteenth century and also to department stores in the nineteenth century. Advancing technology in manufacture, construction and distribution permitted the building of large retail emporia with their plate glass windows and lifts, provided longer shelf life products and frozen/convenience foods, changed the nature of physical distribution for wholesalers and retailers, and more recently through EPOS and EFTPOS has revolutionised retail selling and consumer buying and paved the way for genuine 'home shopping'. Social changes in one form or another led to the establishment of the various retail Co-operative movements, the early multiple-shop grocery retailers and department stores, the movement of the former variety chain stores into clothing, and in the past decade the emergence of the 'lifestyle' retailers.

In the final chapter of this text we shall look at some theories which attempt to explain the past evolution of retailing and thereby predict future develop-ments. Meanwhile, in Chapters 3 and 4 we examine the nature of competition in retailing – both among retailers of a given class and between different categories of retailing – and the use by retail organisations of the concepts and process of corporate strategy in competing in their markets.

References

1. M. St. C. Byrne, *Elizabethan Life in Town and Country* (London: Methuen, 1925) p. 70.
2. D. Davis, *A History of Shopping* (London: Routledge & Kegan Paul, 1966) p. 6.
3. Ibid., p. 60.
4. J. B. Jefferys, *Retail Trading in Britain 1850–1950* (Cambridge: CUP, 1954) pp. 1 and 5.
5. See Davis, *A History of Shopping*, Ch. 11. Alexander has analysed this period of retailing development in some detail, and while recognising the economic and other forces at work changing the system of retail distribution in the first half of the nineteenth century cautioned that in respect of this period 'the extent of change must not be exaggerated. . . . We must . . . give attention to what was static, or changing very slowly, as well as to what was new and dynamic'. See D. Alexander, *Retailing in England during the Industrial Revolution* (London: Athlone Press, 1970) pp. 11–12.
6. See W. H. Fraser, *The Coming of the Mass Market 1850–1914* (London: Macmillan, 1981) Ch. 1.
7. P. Mathias, *Retailing Revolution* (London: Longmans, 1967) pp. 38–9.
8. See Fraser, *The Coming of the Mass Market*, p. 95. Much of the material in this section is based upon Chs 8 and 9 of Fraser's study.
9. Fraser, *The Coming of the Mass Market*, p. 110.
10. Mathias, *Retailing Revolution*, p. 230.
11. Ibid., pp. 97 and 216.
12. Ibid., p. 8.
13. Davis, *A History of Shopping*, p. 280.
14. On the middle-class co-operatives see J. Hood and B. S. Yamey, 'The Middle-class Cooperative Retailing Societies in London, 1864–1900', *Oxford Economic Papers*, 1957, Vol. 9, pp. 309–22.
15. See Jefferys, *Retail Trading in Britain*, p. 58.
16. See N. A. H. Stacey and A. Wilson, *The Changing Pattern of Distribution* (London: Pergamon Press, 2nd edn, 1965) pp. 37–42.
17. R. Pound, *Selfridge* (London: Heinemann, 1960) pp. 1 and 153.
18. Jefferys, *Retail Trading in Britain*, p. 27.
19. See Stacey and Wilson, *The Changing Pattern of Distribution*, p. 44.
20. Davis, *A History of Shopping*, p. 283.
21. Jefferys' estimates indicate that the multiples' share of total food and household stores retail sales increased from 3.5–4.5 per cent in 1900 to 8.5–11.0 per cent in 1920. See Jefferys, *Retail Trading in Britain*, p. 28.
22. Mathias, *Retail Revolution*, p. xix.
23. Davis, *A History of Shopping*, p. 284.
24. Jefferys, *Retail Trading in Britain*, p. 22.
25. Stacey and Wilson, *The Changing Pattern of Distribution*, pp. 45–6.
26. Jefferys, *Retail Trading in Britain*, pp. 69–71.
27. Pound, *Selfridge*, pp. 238 and 243–4.
28. Jefferys, *Retail Trading in Britain*, p. 41.
29. Ibid. p. 73.
30. Ibid., p. 64. Boots increased its number of branches from 200 in 1900 to 1180 in

1938, and Timothy White from 562 in 1933 to 1149 in 1937. See H. Levy, *The Shops of Britain* (London: Routledge & Kegan Paul, 1948) p. 185.

31. D. Braithwaite and S. P. Dobbs, *The Distribution of Consumable Goods* (London: George Routledge, 1932) p. 239. Levy gives an equally authoritative estimate of as high as 750 000. See Levy, *The Shops of Britain*, p. 32.

32. H. Smith, *Retail Distribution* (London: Oxford University Press, 2nd edn, 1948) p. 39. One should, however, allow in making comparisons over the period 1939–50 for the effects of the Second World War in reducing the number of independent shopkeepers in particular as a result of the lack of goods to sell over the period 1939–45 and a lack of staff due to war service. See Ibid., p. 146.

33. See Smith, Ibid., pp. 82–3; and Levy, *The Shops in Britain*, pp. 7–9.

34. Conclusions regarding trends at this time must be stated with some caution as the comparability of successive census data is at its worst in these early years, and significant revisions to figures are habitually reported in successive census reports for this period.

35. J. B. Jefferys and D. Knee, *Retailing in Europe* (London: Macmillan, 1962) p. 24.

36. A measure of the extent to which this price competition could operate may be seen at the time of Lipton's entry into the tea market in 1889. According to Mathias 'He found tea prices at 3s to 4s per lb in family grocers; and retailed his own blends at 1s 2d to 1s 9d.' See Mathias, *Retailing Revolution*, p. 101.

37. See Jefferys, *Retail Trading in Britain*, pp. 53–4; and Stacey and Wilson, *The Changing Pattern of Distribution*, p. 36.

38. See B. S. Yamey, 'Resale Price Maintenance and Shoppers' Choice', in R. Harris (ed.), *Radical Reaction* (London: IEA, 1960) p. 68. Yamey estimated at this time that one quarter of personal consumer expenditure was affected by r.p.m.

39. These details are taken from W. S. Howe, 'The Ending of Resale Price Maintenance: Implementation of Government Policy', *Economics*, Summer 1973, Vol. 10, pp. 5–16.

40. J. F. Pickering, 'The Abolition of Resale Price Maintenance in Great Britain', *Oxford Economic Papers*, March 1974, Vol. 26, p. 137.

41. Ibid., pp. 138–45. The reaction at the time of Jack (later Sir John) Cohen of Tesco to the 1964 Resale Prices Bill was that "The abolition of RPM will be the green light for the most intensive retail development this country has seen. We shall now go ahead with our plans to expand the Tesco supermarket chain into a nationwide enterprise comprising multi-purpose cut-price general self-selection stores". Quoted in M. Corina, *Pile it High, Sell it Cheap* (London: Weidenfeld & Nicolson, 1971) p. 30.

42. Stacey and Wilson, *The Changing Pattern of Distribution*, p. 367.

43. These data relate to the Green Shield Trading Stamp Co., which at this time accounted for 58 per cent by value of stamp trading in the UK. The CWS accounted for 35 per cent and the American Sperry & Hutchinson and others together for 7 per cent. See C. Fulop, *The Role of Trading Stamps in Retail Competition* (London: IEA Eaton Paper No. 3, 2nd edn, 1973) pp. 69 and 72.

44. See Jefferys, *Retail Trading in Britain*, Ch. 3.

45. Davis, *A History of Shopping*, p. 287.

46. Ibid., pp. 293–4.

47. Stacey and Wilson, *The Changing Pattern of Distribution*, pp. 37 and 41.

48. See S. Sharples, 'Is there a Future for the Department Store?', *Retail & Distribution Management*, March–April 1982, p. 19.

49. *Sunday Times*, 26 May 1985. Other 1980s department store acquisitions included UDS (Allders) by Hanson Trust, and Owen Owen by Ward White (now in turn owned by Boots). See Y. Musannif, 'Store Wars – the Background to U.K. Retailing', in A. West (ed.), *Handbook of Retailing* (Aldershot: Gower, 1988) p. 20.

50. Corporate Intelligence Group, *Retailing and 1992 – The Impact and Opportunities* (London: Corporate Intelligence Group, 1989) p. 40.
51. Despite a number of acquisitions, House of Fraser individual department store numbers have fallen from 136 in 1973 to 120 in 1985 and 62 at the present time (1990). See Monopolies and Mergers Commission, *The Boots Co. Ltd. and House of Fraser Ltd.* (London: HMSO, 1974, HCP 174) paras 51 and 54; and *Lonrho PLC and House of Fraser PLC* (London: HMSO, 1985, Cmnd 9458) para. 3.1; and *Financial Times*, 3 and 8 March 1990.
52. See Musannif, 'Store Wars', p. 16.
53. An interesting analysis of the earlier years of department stores is contained in H. Pasdermadjian, *The Department Store – Its Origins, Evolution and Economics* (London: Newman Books, 1954).
54. C. Fulop, 'Revolution in Retailing', in R. Harris (ed.), *Ancient or Modern?* (London: IEA, 2nd edn, 1964) p. 84.
55. Ibid., p. 65; and National Board for Prices and Incomes, *Prices, Profits and Costs in Food Distribution* (London: HMSO, 1971, Cmnd 4645) para. 83.
56. See J. Bamfield, 'Rationalization and the Problems of Repositioning: U.K. Co-operatives Caught in the Middle', in G. Johnson (ed.), *Business Strategy in Retailing* (Chichester: John Wiley, 1987) pp. 157–9.
57. See NBPI, *Prices, Profits and Costs in Food Distribution*, para. 83; W. S. Howe, 'Competition and Performance in Food Manufacturing', in J. Burns *et al.* (eds), *The Food Industry* (London: Heinemann, 1983) p. 111, and subsequent A. C. Nielsen data.
58. See 'The Rochdale pioneering spirit adrift among the high street store groups', *Financial Times*, 24 May 1986.
59. See A.G.B. data in D. McCarthy *et al.*, *U.K. Supermarkets* (Manchester: Manchester Business School Centre for Business Research, 1983) p. 9.
60. See Bamfield 'Rationalization and the Problems of Repositioning', p. 159.
61. For example, during the 1970s the Co-operative movement failed to follow up its earlier rationalisation. Between 1971 and 1981 non-Co-operative grocery super-market operators reduced their store numbers by 49 per cent whereas the figure for the Co-operative movement was 35 per cent. One result of this was that when in 1980 53 per cent of non-Co-operative multiple grocery stores were of less than 4000 sq.ft. in size, 86 per cent of Co-operative stores accounting for 53 per cent of sales fell into this size category. See D. McCarthy *et al.*, *U.K. Supermarkets*, pp. 10 and 13. See also D. Arnott, 'When the Co-operating Faltered', *Management Today*, October 1983, pp. 88ff. More recent data show that while the average sales area for a Sainsbury or Tesco store is 20 000 sq.ft., the 1985 average for non-Co-operative multiple supermarkets was 10 180 sq.ft., and for Co-operatives it was 3617 sq. ft. See J. Bamfield, 'Competition and Change in British Retailing', *National Westminster Bank Quarterly Review*, February 1988, pp. 19 and 21.
62. See data in Howe, 'Competition and Performance in Food Manufacturing', p. 111, and subsequent A. C. Nielsen data.
63. A supermarket was originally defined as a large self-service shop, with size criteria of 2000 sq.ft. of sales area and three or more checkout points, selling a range of food and also basic household requisites such as soaps and cleaning materials. See W. G. McClelland, 'Economics of the Supermarket', *Economic Journal*, March 1962, Vol. 72, p. 154.
64. Ibid.
65. See J. A. N. Bamfield, 'The Changing Face of British Retailing', *National Westminster Bank Quarterly Review*, May 1980, p. 35.
66. Office of Fair Trading, *Competition and Retailing* (London: OFT, 1985) para. 5.15.
67. These examples are given in J. F. Pickering, *Resale Price Maintenance in Practice*

(London: Allen & Unwin, 1966) p. 138.

68. NBPI, *Prices, Profits and Costs in Food Distribution*, para. 110.
69. Quoted in *The High Street of Tomorrow* (Cheshunt, Herts: Tesco PLC) p. 3.
70. These data are taken from Business Monitor SDA25, *Retailing* (London: HMSO).
71. Total retail data quoted in *Financial Times*, 30 March 1989; grocery supermarket figures given in *Sunday Times*, 3 February 1991.
72. See G. Davies, *What Next?* (London: Century, 1989) Chs 5–8.
73. See A. Ferguson, 'The Jewels in Ratners', *Management Today*, April 1987, pp. 66ff. Ratner presently accounts for 31 per cent of the UK market in its sector. See *Financial Times*, 3 July 1990.
74. N. Wrigley, 'Retail Restructuring and Retail Analysis', in N. Wrigley (ed.), *Store Choice, Store Location and Market Analysis* (London: Routledge, 1988) pp. 25–30. Retail market concentration has further increased in this sector with the amalgamation in June 1990 of W. H. Smith's Do-It-All and Boots' Payless which, according to Verdict Research, would produce a market share of 7.8 per cent for the combined venture, putting it in second market place after Kingfisher's B & Q. See *Financial Times*, 5 and 6 June 1990.
75. Wrigley, 'Retail Restructuring and Retail Analysis', p. 5.
76. This analysis of the independent retailer uses as a definition of such businesses those organisations not classified as multiple-shop firms. That is, included here are all retail businesses having nine or fewer branches. In Chapter 5 the problems of the small retailer are examined in the context of the more restrictive definition of the unit or single-outlet retailer.
77. See the latest reported data in Business Monitor SDA25 *Retailing* (London: HMSO).
78. NBPI, *Prices, Profits and Costs in Food Distribution*, paras 91 and 98.
79. A. D. Smith, *Small Retailers: Prospects and Policies*, Committee of Inquiry on Small Firms Research Report No. 15 (London: HMSO, 1971) p. 26.
80. A. C. Nielsen *Annual Review of Grocery Trading* data quoted in W. S. Howe, 'Competition in the United Kingdom Food Manufacturing and Distributive Industries since 1956', paper presented at Economics Association Conference at Loughborough University, 5 July 1972.
81. See *The Nielsen Researcher*, 1977 No. 2, 1980 No. 3, and 1982 No. 3.
82. Data in Monopolies and Mergers Commission, *The Dee Corporation PLC and Booker McConnell PLC* (London: HMSO, 1985, Cmnd 9429) para. 2.33.
83. See Institute of Grocery Distribution Bulletin, *Distribution & Technology* (Watford: IGD, December 1988) p. 3.
84. Ibid., pp. 1–3.
85. Monopolies and Mergers Commission, *The Dee Corporation PLC and Booker McConnell PLC*, para. 2.23.
86. The other forms of franchise are manufacturer–retailer franchises, such as motor car or truck dealerships and petrol service stations, and manufacturer–wholesaler franchises, epitomised by soft drink manufacturers and independent wholesale bottlers. See P. Stern and J. Stanworth, 'The Development of Franchising in Britain', *National Westminster Bank Quarterly Review*, May 1988, p. 40.
87. See R. Hall and R. Dixon, *Franchising* (London: Pitman, 1988) p. 10.
88. Ibid.
89. See D. Oates, 'Keeping Body and Soul Together', *Director*, June 1988, pp. 65–7.
90. See J. Richards and L. Clarke, 'Flash in the Pan', *Management Today*, January 1989, pp. 80–5.
91. Data given in Musannif, 'Store Wars', p. 16. The figure for clothing is somewhat higher at 4–5 per cent.
92. See P. Beaver, *A Pedlar's Legacy: The Origins and History of Empire Stores 1831–1981* (London: Henry Melland, 1981).

93. See B. Sharp, *Entering the Mail Order Market* (London: Brian Sharp Marketing Ltd, 1979) p. 48.
94. *Financial Times,* 19 September 1989.
95. The market remains dominated by GUS/Kay with an estimated 41.3 per cent of total mail order sales, followed by Littlewoods wth 24.5 per cent, Freemans (acquired by Sears in 1988) with 14.0 per cent, and Grattan (owned by Next) with 11.0 per cent. See *Financial Times*, 19 September 1989.
96. See D. Jones, 'Grattan', in R. Nelson and D. Clutterbuck (eds), *Turnaround* (London: W. H. Allen, 1988) pp. 183–8; and *Financial Times*, 28 September 1989.
97. See Davies, *What Next?*, pp. 110–13.

Appendix

Appendix Table 2.1
The Retail Sector in the Great Britain Economy

	Establishments (No.)	Sales (£m)	Value added/ GDP (%)	Employment ('000)
1950	531 143	4 923	7.8	2 265
1957	573 988	7 798	8.3	2 569
1961	577 307	8 919	8.1	2 524
1966	504 412	11 132	8.1	2 556
1971	509 818	16 949	8.4	2 853
1977	387 588	39 056	7.3	2 442
1980	368 253	59 757	7.1	2 408
1982	356 590	70 167	7.1	2 258
1984	349 728	82 794	7.2	2 317
1986	343 387	97 296	7.6	2 334
1987	345 467	104 627	7.5	2 319

SOURCES: Establishments, Sales, Value Added and Employment, *Reports of the Census of Distribution*, and more recently Business Monitor SDA25 *Retailing* (London: HMSO); GDP from CSO *Economic Trends* (London: HMSO).

Note The third data column in the table relates value added in retailing (less taxes) to expenditure-based Gross Domestic Product at factor cost, which is also, of course, a value-added measure of economic activity. Measuring retail output in terms of value added gives a true reflection of the amount of economic activity in the sector, and also allows for changes in the degree of vertical integration on the part of retailers. *Caveat*: for the years 1950–1971 the ratio of retail value added to GDP has been calculated before deduction of taxes – both in the numerator and in the denominator. The transition from this series to a net of taxes basis following the introduction of Value Added Tax (VAT) has resulted in a set of data for the period 1971 onwards which is not strictly comparable with the earlier figures.

Appendix Table 2.2
Retail Establishments by Structure

	Total (No.)	Independents (No.)	Multiples* (No.)	Co-operatives (No.)
1950	529 684	448 999	54 227	26 458
1957	574 218	482 606	61 027	30 585
1961	544 873	434 063	81 618†	29 396
1966	504 046	404 312	71 536	28 198
1971	471 369	392 354	62 535	16 480
1977	387 588	309 770	66 897	10 921
1980	368 253	302 123	57 933	8 197
1982	356 590	293 382	56 555	6 653
1984	349 728	288 935	55 224	5 569
1986	343 386	283 030	55 497	4 859
1987	345 468	282 762	58 015	4 691

* Within organisations having 10+ establishments.
† Within organisations having 5+ establishments.

SOURCES: *Reports of the Census of Distribution*, and more recently Business Monitor SDA25 *Retailing* (London: HMSO).

Appendix Table 2.3
Retail Sector Organisations or Enterprises

	Total (No.)	Independents (No.)	Multiples* (No.)	Co-operatives (No.)
1950	404 845	403 076	1 769	
1957	· ·	· ·	1 151	940
1961	416 606	414 471	1 300	835
1966	· ·	· ·	1 281	697
1971	352 356	351 012	1 031	313
1977	262 443	261 069	1 136	238
1980	256 139	255 135	818	186
1982	248 950	247 963	843	144
1984	246 931	246 099	721	111
1986	244 006	243 145	763	98
1987	240 853	239 991	772	90

* Organisations having 10+ establishments.
· · = not available.

SOURCE: As in Appendix Table 2.2

Retail Competition 3

'To found a great empire for the sole purpose of raising up
a people of customers, may at first sight appear a project
fit only for a nation of shopkeepers.'

Adam Smith, *An Inquiry into the Nature and Causes of the
Wealth of Nations* (1776), Vol. II, Book IV, Ch. VII.

3.1 Introduction

The purpose of this chapter is to provide an economic analysis of the
competitive environment of retailing and of the major dimensions of retailer
response to this. These are important aspects of retailing insofar as an analysis
of the competitive environment and the behaviour of firms within it allows us
to assess whether or not the community as a whole benefits from the system of
retailing which we have at the present time. This analysis also sets the scene
for the topic of corporate strategy in retailing which is dealt with fully in the
following chapter.

3.2 The Role of Competition

Competition or competitiveness is a central theme in that area of microeconomics known as welfare economics. It is through the competitive operation of
the market forces of supply and demand that consumers are satisfied in the
most 'efficient' manner – that is, at the lowest resource cost. Thus the
question we want to be able to ask of any economic system or part of a system
such as retailing, is 'are goods being supplied to consumers in the economy at
the lowest possible resource cost consistent with the quality of service that
shoppers want?' The matter of 'what consumers want' is, however, an unclear
one in a number of respects. Not least are the issues which it raises for the

measurement of retail productivity, where a small number of retail transactions per employee may reflect shoppers' desire for a high level of customer service rather than the inefficient use of labour in retailing. As Fulop points out, for example, wartime reductions in retailing employment and supplies give rise merely to a specious improvement in labour and other productivity as consumers are obliged to shop around for supplies and queue for a limited selection of goods.[1]

The earlier almost exclusive interest of microeconomics in price competition and the structural conditions of 'perfect competition' (basically a large number of sellers and buyers in the market and freedom of entry and exist with respect to the market) has given way over past decades to a recognition of a broader range of issues. These include the importance of having regard to the longer term, the concept of efficiencies other than allocative (for example, X-efficiency and organisational slack), the role of competition in technology (as in the writings of Schumpeter and Downie), and an acceptance that imperfectly competitive market structures are inevitable and need not of themselves be bad for consumers (as exemplified in the general theory of the second best, the writings of the 'workable competition' school, and Galbraith's claim for the beneficial effect of countervailing power).[2]

It is not the purpose of this chapter to adopt a highly theoretical approach to the analysis of retail competition, but to rely upon the basic microeconomic framework as a means of identifying the major determinants of competitiveness in retail markets and the criteria for judging the outcome.

3.3 The Forces of Retail Competition

One way in which to identify the 'actors' or participants in retail markets is to adapt Porter's 'five-forces framework' as set out in Figure 3.1.

The centre box in Figure 3.1 relates to the traditional locus of market competition: competition among existing producers or retailers of the same product, offering consumers broadly the same product or service. Each of these market participants seeks to make a profit between its relationship with suppliers and customers or shoppers by convincing customers that it offers the best value for money in shopping, and maximising the gap between the income obtained from shoppers and the costs of supplies and value added inputs involved.

The forces in the boxes in Figure 3.1 above and below Existing Retail Competitors comprise two additional dimensions of retail competition. New Entrant competition is a frequent possibility in retailing where for many forms of retail distribution market entry costs are low and diversification from one branch of retailing to another is readily possible. This will be distinguished in our analysis below from competition arising from New Forms of Retailing, as when multiple shop or supermarket organisations move into product areas previously dominated by independent retailers.

FIGURE 3.1
Framework of Competition in Retailing .

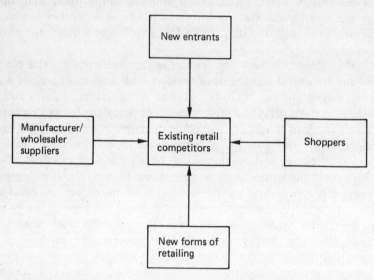

SOURCE: Adapted from M. E. Porter, *Competitive Advantage* (New York: Free Press, 1985) p. 6.

The structural forces to the left and right of Existing Retail Competitors in Figure 3.2 also influence retailer profitability and strategy. Retailer–supplier relations are dealt with in detail below under the heading of vertical competition. In very few instances are individual retailers confronted by a limited number of customers possessing oligopsonistic buying power. Retailers' relations with shoppers in general do, however, enter into their strategic decision making; and not only is the law increasing the power of consumers as a whole *vis-à-vis* retailers (as discussed at length in Chapter 10) but consumer organisations such as the Consumers' Association allow at least more affluent and articulate shoppers to make more detailed comparisons between distributors' offerings, and facilitate through their advice the application of the law in exercising consumer sovereignty.[3]

It is within this framework that retail competition takes place. According to the prevailing direction and intensity of these forces retailers will choose to emphasise particular forms of competition (price, service, location etc.); and as we argued above, these forces and the resulting distributor behaviour will determine retailer profitability and the efficiency with which retail markets operate.

3.4 Directions of Competition

As was shown in Figure 3.1, competitive forces impinge upon retailers from a number of directions. The purpose of this section is to examine these forces and their operation in more detail using a distinguishing terminology to identify three principal directions.

Horizontal Competition

Horizontal competition in retailing is the competition which takes place between retailers of the same broad class. This also embraces the possibility of entry into a retail market by further retailers of that class. It is this type of competition, as Palamountain stresses, with which traditional economics is most at home.[4] Within the scope of horizontal competition one can analyse the struggle for customers between competing independent grocers, rival department stores, or neighbouring jewellers. Such competitors having broadly similar cost structures, competition tends to take the form of marginal price differences, competition in service (customer attention, credit, delivery etc.), the range or choice of merchandise, and, particularly in respect of the 'corner shop', location.

Intertype Competition

In contrast to horizontal competition, intertype conflict has traditionally been less specifically stressed in economic analysis. This latter type of retail market competition in Palamountain's analysis is 'competition between different methods of distribution'.[5] It is competition between the independent and the multiple grocer; between, say, the specialist record store and Boots; the children's clothing and toys multiple and Marks & Spencer; or between the traditional furniture store and Texas Homecare.

Heightened competition in this dimension, and in particular its impact upon the smaller independent shop, has been the outcome of three factors: first, the growth in the scale of retail outlets, in terms of both shop and firm size; second, freedom since the early 1960s for retail outlets to compete along the dimension of price as resale price maintenance (r.p.m.) was prohibited or withered away; third, the increased diversification of merchandise among large-scale retailers which has resulted in groups such as Marks & Spencer and Boots becoming, in effect, department stores without the burden of overhead cost which traditional outlets of this type have had to bear.

The growth of large-scale retailing was a post Second World War phenomenon which emerged as wartime building restrictions were lifted and materials became available. It was encouraged in the grocery trade by food technology and marketing supply conditions relating to nationally branded and longer-shelf-life packaged goods, by scale economies available to large, self-service outlets, and by an economic and demographic environment of higher standards of living on the part of a geographically more concentrated population. The demise of r.p.m., which actually occurred in the grocery trade from the late 1950s onwards, enabled large-scale, price-cutting multiple grocers to emphasise the advantages of self-service supermarket shopping to cumstomers in terms of lower prices.[6] The essence of this competition in the food trades was thus the reduction in costs of new forms of food retailing *and* their ability to use this to compete on price with traditional grocery outlets. The results of this intertype competition may be seen in the data in Table 3.1 which relate to the period during which the practice of r.p.m. was under institutional and legislative attack.

The data in Table 3.1 show clearly how for the retail trade as a whole the share of the market taken by multiple shops grew from 1957 to 1961, and particularly between 1961 and 1966. In the food trade, where r.p.m. began to crumble from the late 1950s onwards, the advance of the multiple shops was even more rapid, again particularly after 1961. Over the period 1957–66 the multiple shops' share of the food trade increased from one fifth to more than a third. Analysing the trend in grocery sales (a broader definition than Food) A. C. Nielsen data reveal the trend shown in Table 3.2, indicating clearly the continued progress of multiple retailers in this sector.

Intertype competition has taken place most noticeably in the UK between traditional independent shops and larger-scale multiple shop organisations, with the latter coming to dominate retail distribution in many markets. This competition has not only been based upon the price advantage of the newer forms of distribution arising from their higher levels of productivity and lower supply costs, but has also taken the form of the appeal to a more mobile

Table 3.1
Distribution of Retail Turnover Between Types of Outlet (%)

	Total retail trade			Food shops			Non-food		
	1957	1961	1966	1957	1961	1966	1957	1961	1966
Independents	63.2	60.3	55.5	59.9	57.4	51.3	66.2	62.8	59.0
Multiples	24.8	28.9	35.2	20.4	25.0	33.5	28.8	32.4	36.7
Co-operative Societies	11.9	10.8	9.2	19.7	17.6	15.2	4.9	4.8	4.4
	99.9*	100.0	99.9*	100.0	100.0	100.0	99.9*	100.0	100.1*

* Errors due to rounding.

Sources: Census of Distribution data tabulated in K. D. George, *Productivity and Capital Expenditure in Retailing* (Cambridge: CUP, 1968) p. 20.

Table 3.2
Grocery Sales by Type of Retail Outlet (%)

	1950	1957	1961	1966	1970	1975	1980	1982	1984	1986
Independents	57	55	53	48	43	37	25	22	19	18
Multiples (10+ branches)	20	22	27	36	42	49	61	65	69	71
Co-operative Societies	23	23	20	16	15	14	14	13	12	11
	100	100	100	100	100	100	100	100	100	100

SOURCES: 1950–1980 data tabulated in W. S. Howe, 'Competition and Performance in Food Manufacturing', in J. Burns *et al.* (eds), *The Food Industry*, p. 111; 1982 data from A. C. Nielsen, *Grocery Industry – Trade Statistics*.

population of a larger selection of merchandise available under one roof with easy, free car-parking provided.[7] At the same time some more specialist retail outlets have also had to face competition from large-scale diversifying retailers who have moved into their segment of the market.

Vertical Competition

As was emphasised in Figure 3.1, retailers not only have to contend with competition from distributors of the same type and from new forms of retailing, but also have to recognise and react to the 'vertical' market relationship with their suppliers. The outcome of this vertical relationship, as Palamountain points out, is dependent upon the relative bargaining strengths of the participants.[8]

Historically in the UK, as the National Board for Prices and Incomes (NBPI) pointed out in its 1971 report on food distribution, the balance of market power had lain with manufacturers.[9] Production economies of scale in food processing had encouraged horizontal mergers which had led to much higher levels of firm size and market concentration in manufacture than in distribution. Along with high fixed manufacturing costs went large advertising expenditures designed to persuade food shoppers to buy particular brands, and the phenomena of high fixed overhead production costs, widespread advertising and horizontal amalgamations intensified as sophisticated convenience foods became an increasingly important part of the food market.[10]

However, also as a result partly of technical factors such as food processing methods, and arising too from the abolition of retail outlet building controls and food rationing, amalgamations began to take place in the 1960s among food distributors. Their market power *vis-à-vis* manufacturers or processors thereby increased significantly. As we noted above in the context of intertype competition, the growing power of the large-scale distributors was also assisted in a range of markets by the early 1960s by their freedom to compete on price. A situation was reached early in the 1970s where large food manufacturers such as Cadbury-Schweppes, Brooke Bond and United Biscuits, as well as Unilever subsidiaries Birds Eye and Van Den Berghs and Jurgens found that their largest twenty customers accounted for 30–65 per cent of total sales.[11] Alarmist headlines appeared in the business press on this issue as firms even of the size of Unilever's Birds Eye, with a frozen food market share of 47 per cent, admitted that its discounts to retailers 'were not created at the initiative of the manufacturer but were an unavoidable response to the power of the retailer'. According to Birds Eye, 'the discounts earned by these ("top 20") retailers exceeded the cost savings in supplying them as compared with supplying the generality of customers'.[12]

As a result of these factors the Monopolies and Mergers Commission was asked in 1977 to look into the general issue of manufacturers' discounts to retailers and published its findings and conclusions in its 1981 report *Discounts to Retailers*.[13] The major findings of the report relating to vertical competition were that along with the increased dominance of the grocery distribution market by a small number of multiple retailers, the practice had grown up of manufacturers according to retailers discounts which were not related to manufacturer cost savings. The 1981 Report (para. 4.29) calculated that the special discounts awarded by a sample of twelve manufacturers to their top ten retail customers amounted to 6.6 per cent of these manufacturers' total sales, and that the value of these special terms for their top ten retail customers was 3.1 percentage points above that for all other customers. In arriving at its conclusions and recommendations, however, the Commission was influenced by the impact upon manufacturers and distributors of the static level of demand for grocery products, and the high degree of competition among large multiple grocery distributors. The Commission noted in particular (Appendix 6) that the larger retailers appeared to reflect closely in their prices the advantages gained by them in buying at lower costs. Indeed the gross profit margins of the sample of four major multiples were in the case of all products covered by the inquiry lower than those of other multiples whose margins were, a little surprisingly, not significantly different from those of the sample of independent distributors. The Report did not, therefore, recommend any specific action on the part of the government in this area. An updating of the 1981 Report data carried out by the Office of Fair Trading (OFT) and published in 1985 noted that the overall cost of manufacturers' special terms to retailers relative to their total turnover had risen from 6.6 per cent in the 1981 Report to 8.6 per cent, although the advantage in their terms to the top ten retail customers compared with all other customers had fallen from 3.1 percentage points reported in 1981 to 2.7 percentage points reported in 1985.[14] These findings in particular suggest that while manufacturers have come under increased pressure from their grocery retailer customers as evidenced by the overall scale of special discounts, there has perhaps been a spreading of these discounts among a wider group of retailers which leaves the remainder marginally less disadvantaged compared with the very largest.

These findings connect Palamountain's intertype and vertical dimensions of competition in retailing. It is clear, at least so far as the documented case of the food/grocery market is concerned, that an initial round of successful intertype competition from the late 1950s onwards which substantially advanced the position of multiple distributors (see data in Table 3.1) had a significant subsequent effect upon vertical relationships in these markets within some fifteen years as this 'balance of power' swung from manufacturers to retailers. Equally, the enhanced trading power of a small dominant group of grocery retailers – whose four largest constituents accounted for 41 per cent of the total Great Britain market in 1984[15] – has enabled them further to advance against independent distributors in this sector.

This trend has come to affect the operation of intertype and horizontal competition as what the Monopolies Commission in its 1981 Report referred to as a 'dual market' in the grocery trade has emerged.[16] Despite the importance of intertype competition, retail markets, it is argued, are increasingly characterised by separate competitive environments of multiple shop and traditional retailing. Whatever their power over smaller outlets may be, multiple grocery stores face considerable competition from each other. The finance director of Tesco once commented that 'Tesco stores opposed by Asda are not making any money';[17] and the consistent striving for market share among the largest food multiples contains all of the elements of competition.[18] On the other hand smaller retailers are beginning to follow strategies which in some measure allow them to avoid competition with the multiples. The geographical monopoly of the former type of outlet is an obvious source of protection, as is the quality of service given, including longer opening hours. Other avenues of differentiation may include the stocking of special items such as health foods, fresh locally produced bread, or the requirements of ethnic minorities. Before arriving at any final conclusions relating to competition or consumer welfare we shall now, in the context of this analysis of the retail environment, consider the competitive responses of retailers.

3.5 Competitive Responses by Retailers

The first major part of this chapter dealt with the competitive environment of retailing, and was largely concerned with how the forces of competition in retailing served the needs of consumers. In this section, looking at matters more exclusively from the point of view of the retailer, we examine how retail organisations can respond to their competitive environment. This section is therefore linked to the preceding one in terms of possible responses by retailers to their environment. It also serves as an introduction to Chapter 4 on strategy in retailing; for although strategy is concerned with the organisation's total response to its environment, including longer-term developments, it embraces the use of the various competitive responses covered in this section.

McClelland identifies three major dimensions of competitive response available to retail organisations: price, location and service.[19] Although, as we shall see in this section and again in Chapter 4 on retail corporate strategy, both retailers and their customers see the variables or characteristics of price, location etc. as part of a package to be offered or sought in the retail market place, we shall initially look at these phenomena separately below.

Price

Although price is not necessarily the sole, or even the major, variable upon which shoppers base their choice of retail outlet, it is the variable which is given most emphasis in formal analysis of consumer behaviour, and is the one most susceptible to rigorous examination.[20]

As we saw in Chapter 2 on the history of retailing, it is only within the past fifty or sixty years that the practice by retailers of clearly pricing goods has become almost universally established. Practically all items in shops are therefore now clearly priced, and this price may under certain circumstances be accompanied by reference to a price at which the same goods were previously sold (see further on this in Chapter 10 below). This is not to say that in buying high unit value goods such as domestic appliances shoppers may not be able to negotiate a discount from the showroom price, especially if payment is being made in cash. Moreover, when a retail sale involves a trade-in, discounts may effectively be given by means of enhanced trade-in allowances. Thus goods are not universally sold at the advertised price. The practice of unit pricing – indicating clearly the price per unit of weight, for example, and thus allowing consumers to make accurate price comparisons between packages of a product of different weight – is not far advanced in the UK as yet.

The other more recent major development in retail pricing which one must bear in mind is, of course, that retailers now in all cases except those of books and household or proprietary medicines, where r.p.m. still applies, have the power to establish their own selling prices. This is not, however, entirely without restriction. Section 2(1) of the 1964 Resale Prices Act prohibits manufacturers from refusing to supply a retailer because the distributor is not adhering to any minimum published or recommended price. However, manufacturers may, under Section 3 of the same Act, refuse to supply a retailer when the distributor has been using the goods as 'loss leaders', where these are defined as goods sold 'not for the purpose of making a profit on the sale of those goods, but for the purpose of attracting to the establishment at which the goods are sold customers likely to purchase other goods or otherwise for the purpose of advertising the business of the dealer'.[21]

Retail pricing is a complex and under-researched area of considerable significance for management. The starting point must be a rejection of traditional, mechanical and uniform mark-ups across the range of products, and a recognition of the importance of the price image of a store or chain's merchandise assortment. This is particularly important for variety chain or grocery stores stocking a wide range of goods, and may involve the adoption of leader line pricing, i.e. the identification of products that consumers accept as key indicators of the store or chain's total assortment price level. Within this overall context of pricing, retail managers must make decisions on short-term price promotions (the timing, extent and choice of products for such price reductions), and comparative price levels of national brands and own label products, if the latter are stocked. For multiple-shop organisations, decisions have also to be made regarding relative price levels for the same products in different geographical locations. Departures from uniform national price levels should be based not only upon cost factors but also with regard to regional differences in 'macroeconomic' features such as income levels, as well as the incidence and strategies of local retail competitors. In all of these pricing decisions retailers must recognise the importance of consumer buying behaviour in factors such as the relationship between the price of goods and their perceived quality, and cross elasticities of demand where price reductions on some items result in changes in quantities bought of other goods.[22]

In practical terms, the context of retail pricing behaviour is that of organisations with both variable and fixed costs (the latter becoming increasingly significant), which are in most cases selling a variety of goods to shoppers who themselves may be making a number of purchases on each shopping visit, and the possibility of whose repeat visits the retailer must bear in mind. Furthermore, although there may be alternative retail outlets available to them, shoppers are characterised by limited price consciousness and price sensitivity, and even a tendency in the case of some goods to judge the quality of the product by its price.[23] These last characteristics reflect a point already made, that price is not the sole variable influencing shopping decisions, and that this influence may not be straightforward.

On the demand side, therefore, the retailer in his pricing decisions must be concerned not only with the pricing of individual lines but also with the price of the assortment or range of goods which he is offering to representative customers. The retailer has to manage price changes over a period of time, and has to maintain the price image which buyers have of a store or chain, as well as reacting to changes in these variables on the part of competitors.[24] It is the existence of these aspects of retail consumer demand, as well as the cost structure of retailing, which gives rise to some of the more sophisticated approaches to retail pricing outlined below.

The conventional approach to retail pricing and the determination by retailers of sales margins or mark-ups on individual lines is to set the retail selling price at the cost to the distributor plus a margin which reflects the level of service provided with the product, the rate of stockturn (and thus the financial cost and shelf space involved in holding the product), and the unit value of the goods.[25] Now, however, with fixed overhead costs (including an increasing proportion of labour costs) making up the largest part of total retail organisation expenses, the emphasis in retail pricing is much more upon maximising the total contribution of a line of goods towards these costs.[26] This has created an emphasis upon increasing the volume of sales per store or throughout the organisation; and a further attraction of this is that as the volume of sales increases the organisation may be able to buy its supplies at lower unit prices. Retail organisations may thus be expected to conform to sales revenue maximising behaviour with opportunities for price distribution.

Price discrimination in retailing arises as retailers reflect in their margins or mark-ups the different price elasticities of demand for each line of goods. The profit maximising position under these conditions is where the marginal returns (marginal revenue minus marginal cost) of all product lines are equal, which with different elasticities of demand will result in a variety of profit percentages being earned across the merchandise range. Higher percentage profit margins are enjoyed on lines with lower demand elasticities, while where price elasticities between stores are high, low margins must be accepted.[27] Within this type of policy retailers may attempt to present a low-price image to shoppers. In the early period of distributor freedom to set prices this image was created through retailers cutting prices deeply on a restricted number of lines rather than implementing more limited price reductions across their product range. This policy was doubtless considered more appropriate when manufacturer recommended prices were prevalent and consumer price consciousness, at least over a limited range of goods, quite high. The trend now is for low-price retailers to offer price reductions off a wider range of goods in order to create a consistent price image for their stores, and there is some evidence that this policy is actually preferred by shoppers.[28]

However, stores may choose none the less to offer quite significant price reductions on a limited number of products where these will stand out in customers' perception, where competitor retailers will not necessarily respond, and where these price reductions will increase overall purchases within the store. These chosen products must enjoy high levels of consumer price consciousness, which implies fairly frequent purchase. At the same time widespread staple products should not be used in this context as price reductions on these invite competitor retaliation. McClelland adopted the term 'suggestion articles' to refer to these traffic builders: something a little special to which the housewife is none the less receptive.[29] Livesey emphasises the criteria for such offers established by the American retailing researcher Holdren. These include articles characterised by high levels of consumer price consciousness, having a sufficiently high unit price to allow significant absolute price reductions, and which are important to shoppers in their total budget.[30] A final characteristic of such limited number price cut goods is that this strategy should lead consumers to increase their purchases of other goods in the same store. That is, there should be a high price cross elasticity of demand between the price of those price-reduced goods and the quantities purchased of other goods in the store sold at normal mark-ups and prices. In these cases the profit-reducing impact of the price reductions is anticipated to be more than offset by the beneficial effect of additional purchases of items whose margins have not been reduced.

Turning again to the concept of the consumer price image of a store, it should be emphasised that these price cross elasticities referred to above will not operate psychologically entirely within the store. Rather the price reductions will have to feature in the price advertising of the retailer and influence the total price image of the store. Consumers will then generalise from such limited advertised price reductions to assume that the store offers low assortment prices (that is, across the range of goods), although as we saw above the store may in fact compensate for its limited price reductions by charging normal or even higher margins on the remainder of its lines.[31]

Finding these relationships is likely to be a matter of experimentation for the retailer rather than an exact science; and it is quite likely that consumer behaviour in this respect will change over time.

Location

It is recognised that location – involving both the siting of new stores and the closure of existing ones – is an important and also difficult managerial issue in an increasingly competitive retail environment. Retailing is on the move: from city centre to edge of town, to retail park, and most recently to giant retail complexes. An Oxford Institute of Retail Management report, for example, argued that 'it is the massive decentralisation of retailing in the 1980s which is the most marked aspect of change in the retail environment', and instanced the proliferation in that decade of out-of-centre retail ware- houses for DIY, domestic appliances and household furnishings, the 800 shopping centres which had developed by the late 1980s, and the advent of large-scale regional shopping complexes in the form of the Metro Centre at Gateshead with 1.6m square feet of gross retail space, 10 000 car-parking spaces and associated leisure activities.[32] The data in Table 3.3 show just how rapidly such change took place in a number of retail sectors in the 1980s. The filling up of the best available retail sites, the fact that in a socially and demographically changing world past experience is not necessarily an ade- quate guide in present decision making, increasingly oligopolistic locational competition among retailers, and the high cost of locational mistakes all combine to highlight the importance of retail location decisions.

Before looking at specific techniques that may be applied in this area, three general issues should be mentioned. First, there is the question of the population size which will support particular retail establishments. This is determined broadly by the size of the population catchment area and the amount of retail expenditure per head. A store will only be located in a particular place if, allowing for the reaction of competitors, the expenditure

Table 3.3
Share of Total Retail Sector Turnover Accounted for by Out-of-Town Stores

	Grocers	DIY	Furniture and carpets	Electrical
1980	13%	17%	4%	6%
1985	22%	50%	17%	11%
1990*	38%	60%	26%	18%

* Estimate

SOURCES: Verdict Research Ltd. data quoted in Monopolies and Mergers Commission, *Kingfisher plc and Dixons Group plc* (London: HMSO, 1990, Cmd 1079) para. 3.4.

of the existing population of the centre and that of 'migrant' shoppers from surrounding areas provides a sufficient sales turnover. More sophisticated analyses of this distinguish between three sources of custom for individual retail outlets: generative business created by the store itself as a result of its advertising and the appeal arising from its merchandise; shared trade which comes from the total business generated by a group of shops, who may be competitors or retailers of other goods as in a shopping centre; and suscipient custom which arises from a retail outlet's proximity to a particular non-retail activity such as a railway station, cinema complex or tourist attraction.[33] Use may be made in planning store location of quite sophisticated models encompassing the gravitational pull to larger shopping centres from surrounding areas and comparative *per caput* expenditures of the local and migrant populations of shoppers.

The second dimension of retail location concerns the distinction between convenience and shopping goods. The former category, as the name implies, comprises goods where convenience of location is an important part of shoppers' requirements. Groceries, confectionery, cigarettes, tobacco, newspapers and inexpensive household requirements may be regarded as convenience goods. Shopping goods are those with a higher unit price, bought less frequently, and where consumers wish to make comparisons of prices etc. between competing products before final purchase. This means that shoppers will be prepared to invest time and money in making such comparisons. However, it also produces a situation where competing retailers of shopping goods – jewellery, domestic appliances, furniture – will tend to congregate together. This is not only more convenient for potential buyers in reducing their expenses of 'shopping around', but an existing centre for a particular shopping good will also exert considerable locational pull upon any new retailer entrant to this market. This tendency at the same time increases the degree of competitiveness in such markets as comparisons between retailer offerings are easier for shoppers to make.[34]

Third, there is the aspect of geographical or locational monopoly enjoyed most frequently by the small 'corner shop'. In offering convenience of location, and often extended hours of opening, such a retailer is in a position to earn a substantial margin on each unit of sale of convenience goods; and because there is within any one of such areas only a limited amount of retail custom available, these enhanced mark-ups do not necessarily entice competitive entry. This absence of new competition may also be explained by the patronage or loyalty which the existing small shop enjoys despite its higher prices. Thus the growth of large scale, lower cost retail outlets has by no means eliminated the corner shop which, despite increased mobility on the part of consumers, still provides a convenient service for smaller unit value items and is able to survive largely on the basis of its locational characteristics.

A range of techniques is available to retail managers in making store location decisions. These may be broadly divided into *search* techniques designed to determine particular geographical areas which are appropriate to individual categories of retailer, *store viability* techniques which involve forecasting sales turnover for individual stores in a particular location, and assessment of *micro* factors at a particular store location which will influence sales levels.[35] The appropriateness of each technique will depend upon the level at which the location decision is being made; and it is possible also to take account of outlet-dominated and product-dominated retailing situations, and to distinguish between convenience-good and shopping-good stores.

At the broadest level of location analysis – search for suitable geographical areas – the most appropriate techniques are those of spatial marketing. These involve the identification of quite detailed geographical areas (such as population census enumeration districts) by socioeconomic category, which may in turn be regarded as representing certain retail spending levels and patterns. The aim is to identify spending catchment areas which will justify establishing certain types of shopping facilities in the area; and detailed databanks and processing techniques designed for spatial marketing are provided by commercial organisations such as CACI (ACORN) and Pinpoint.

The spatial marketing approach to retail location decisions is really appropriate only at the general search level, and is more suited to product-dominated, larger-scale specialist outlets. Assessment of individual shop viability, on the other hand, depends more upon store turnover forecasting techniques. These recognise the importance of the volume of potential customers, the costs to shoppers of travelling to stores, and the influence of competitor shops. The original 'gravitation' models in this field concentrated upon the relative pull of population areas of different size and the cost for shoppers of movement between these.[36] More sophisticated store turnover models, however, refined to include a number of explanatory variables and built up on the basis of multiple regression techniques, can now be used to assist in location decisions for new outlets. A regression model is drawn up on the basis of the statistical determinants of sales levels in 'analogue' stores, i.e.

outlets having similar merchandise to the one planned. These independent variables are then measured in possible new store locations in order to determine the viability of the proposals. Store turnover models thus assist in location decisions at the level of the individual outlet, and are especially useful where location itself is a major determinant of sales levels. This is particularly the case with convenience goods, where there are large numbers of smaller outlets, many of which may be operated by multiple shop organisations.

The most detailed level of location analysis is referred to as micro assessment. This takes account of the influence upon store turnover and profitability of pedestrian flows, neighbouring shops, car parking and even architectural ambiance. Naturally, a distinction is made between the influence of these factors on convenience and specialist stores. The task of this analysis is to identify the relevant micro-level factors and to assess the impact of each of these in any particular case. Surveys and analysis of micro-level characteristics are held to be more important in making location decisions concerning product dominated, specialist shops for which simple store traffic forecasting models may be less appropriate, if only because of a relative lack of 'analogue' outlets.

Guy's survey of retail location decision making by multiple shop organisations in the mid-1970s revealed considerable reliance on 'rules of thumb': 'a combination of hunch, experience and a few rudimentary calculations'.[37] Certainly there was no evidence of firms distinguishing between the various levels in the 'geographical search, store viability and micro factors' hierarchy outlined above. More recent research, however, indicates increasing use by retailers of more sophisticated store location techniques – although complicated mathematical methods were eschewed, and there was, surprisingly, an inverse relationship between the number of stores operated by retail organisations and the quality of store location techniques used. Disappointingly, one of the overall findings of this study was that 'Probably as a function of the financial and manpower demands, research is generally simplistic and hurried',[38] although it is unlikely that large multiple superstore operators such as Tesco or Sainsbury who are currently spending more than £20m on each new store (including site acquisition costs) would agree that this view fairly reflects their approach.

Service

Service in retailing relates to many of those principal functions of this sector which were outlined in Chapter 1 of this text. These features include explicit services such as the provision of credit and delivery, facilities such as accommodation for trying on clothing or looking after shoppers' children, and extend to the range of stock, the standard of personal service given to customers, and the quality of the fittings and surroundings in a retail establishment. The hours of opening are also, of course, part of the service offered by retailers.

Although it is possible to charge consumers directly for some individual additional retail services given (such as credit or delivery) it is more usual for retailers to differentiate themselves by the standard of service provided and to reflect this in their general level of prices. Furthermore, although retailers therefore broadly compete by offering some combination of 'more service and higher prices' and 'lower prices with less service', service competition may be attractive not only as a means of differentiating a store or chain from others but also as a subtler, more oblique form of competition. Such competition less aggressively invites retaliation; and unlike price competition cannot be responded to so rapidly or accurately. However, some fairly obvious forms of non-price competition – such as offering charge credit cards – once adopted by one chain tend to have to be operated by all competitors.

With the rise in the cost of labour in retailing not being matched by increased labour productivity in the provision of many of these services, there has been a general tendency to reduce the level of retail services provided. The alternative is to provide such services, but at what may be perceived by shoppers to be vastly increased prices. Even so, however, there is some evidence of a 'counter' revolution occurring as some grocery chains, for example, have experimented in offering a delivery service at a nominal charge. As we shall see in more detail in Chapter 4 on retailing strategy the task of each retailer is, in responding to the market, to offer most efficiently that appropriate differentiated combination of goods and services at a price level which affords an adequate return on investment.

3.6 Combined Dimensions of Response

As emphasised at the beginning of the second major part of this chapter, the dimensions of retailer response to competition (price, location and service) cannot be considered separately. Nor is this list of headings exhaustive.

Store loyalty may be increased, for example, by the use of private label products. These are defined as products identified as unique to a particular retailer through bearing his brand name. Examples include St Michael (Marks & Spencer), Kingsmere and Winfield (Woolworth), Keynote (Littlewoods), Prova (British Home Stores), and Delamare (Tesco). Other store groups such as Safeway less adventurously use their store name on own-label goods. The proportion of a store's total turnover accounted for by own-label sales may range from 100 per cent in the unique case of Marks & Spencer's St Michael brand through about 60 per cent in respect of Sainsbury to around 40 per cent at Tesco.[39] The proportion of merchandise sold under retailers' own labels also varies from one sector to another. It is highest in packaged groceries (at around 35 per cent), footwear, men's and women's wear and chemist's goods, lower in radio/electrical goods, furniture and DIY, and largely absent in confectioner–tobacconist–newsagent (CTN) lines, jewellery and toys etc.[40]

Although own label products were adopted under conditions of r.p.m. as a means of permitting retailer pricing flexibility, their greater incidence may now be more largely attributed to the increased vertical market power of retailers *vis-à-vis* manufacturers which has built up since the ending of r.p.m. At the present time the advantages for retailers of own-label goods are twofold. First, they heighten store identity and so assist a retailer in creating an image which is unique to his store, and hopefully increased store loyalty. Second, they provide retailers with an opportunity at one and the same time both to offer lines at reduced prices (by 5–10 per cent in comparison with national brands) and also to enjoy higher gross margins (possibly by 5 per cent). Thus, providing a retailer can obtain quality own-label goods from manufacturers at attractive prices through ordering in quantity, offer a sufficiently wide range of own brands to create store identity and loyalty, and still also in many trades stock leading national brands to satisfy some customers and provide a comparison with lower own-label prices, then retailers' own-brand products may constitute an important competitive weapon.

Internal consistency of policy is obviously necessary in the price and service dimensions of retail competition, and this also applies to the choice of merchandise. In addition each retailer must adopt the correct overall emphasis in dimensions of competition, relative both to trends in retailing and the behaviour of competitors. As the economy develops there is a general trend away from an emphasis in retailing competition purely upon low prices to a more sophisticated combination of the competitive variables dealt with in this section.[41] There is evidence, for example, in the highly competitive grocery distribution sector that firms which built up their reputation and market share on the basis almost entirely of low prices are moving 'up market' through emphasising convenience, variety, and quality and freshness of merchandise. Increased amounts of retailer advertising (£13.5m in the case of Asda in 1987) are being spent in conveying a quality store image to create store loyalty;[42] and part of the rationale for the acquisition by Argyll Foods (the Presto superstore and Templeton, Hinton and Lipton supermarkets group) of the 132 UK Safeway stores in February 1987 was the desire to move Argyll up market through association with the more attractive and successful Safeway image.[43] In Chapter 4 we shall examine in more detail the longer-term strategic decision making of retail organisations.

3.7 Conclusions

This chapter has been concerned with competition in retailing: with the directions in which retailers encounter competition, and with the ways in which they compete. A major concern in this context is the resultant efficiency of the system of retailing in the UK in serving the needs of consumers.

As in many economic studies, however, reservations have been expressed regarding the possibility of drawing any strong conclusions concerning the resource allocative outcome of competitive forces in the retail sector. Nyström, for example, expressed the view that:

> The question of what market form or form of competition is most applicable in various retail situations usually leads to strong disagreement among economic writers. On the whole, the lasting impression one receives from such discussions is that there is no acceptable general retail market theory and that traditional microeconomic theory is not very useful for the study of retail competition.[44]

In fact retailing appears generally to have presented economists with some difficulty in arriving at firm conclusions on the welfare aspects of competition. Early concern was expressed regarding a tendency to an 'excessive' number of shops in the retail sector, and the propensity of the system of r.p.m. to divert retail competition wastefully into the provision of 'excessive' levels of service, which might be accompanied by additional pressure upon manufacturers further to increase their maintained prices in order, supposedly, to protect retailers' profit margins. These earlier studies seemed, however, quite unsure as to whether retail markets should be analysed in terms of (local) monopoly, oligopoly, monopolistic competition, or something approaching 'perfect' competition.[45]

In terms of its immediate effect upon consumers there seems to be no doubt that the initial restructuring of many retail markets and the emergence of price competition by the early 1960s operated to the advantage of shoppers. The development of food multiples, self-service and supermarket operations at this time, for example, introduced consumers to a variety of goods and provided a new form of shopping which many found more convenient than traditional counter service. The price-cutting policies of the multiple grocers also offered considerable savings to shoppers. A survey in the early 1960s revealed savings on branded grocery products from manufacturer recommended prices of 4.7 per cent; and a similar inquiry in 1964 revealed savings of 7.7 per cent, with by far the largest savings to be gained by shopping at large self-service supermarkets. In particular, regional analysis of the 1964 data revealed a close link between the extent of price reductions and the penetration of self-service stores.[46] In the case of domestic electrical appliances price cutting was such that following the general breakdown of r.p.m. in this sector in January 1967, a survey in March 1968 found that only 47 per cent of refrigerators and space heaters, 43 per cent of kettles, and 36 per cent of washing machines and vacuum cleaners were being sold at or above the manufacturers' recommended prices, and that in each of these categories around 10 per cent of sales were taking place at discounts of more than 10 per cent off recommended prices.[47]

Additional evidence of the beneficial impact of pro-competitive forces on retailing arises, paradoxically, from the differential impact of the ending of r.p.m. in a number of retail sectors. This is brought out in Ward's study.[48] We have already seen above (pp. 61–2) some examples of the extent of price cutting following the ending of r.p.m. Ward's evidence on the changing structure of retailing in the years after 1965 – the growth in the importance of multiple grocers, the emergence of discount stores selling domestic appliances, and DIY supermarkets in the hardware sector – along with changing distributor margins and a reduced role for wholesalers, suggests that no Procrustean, manufacturer-dominated system of distribution is likely to remain ideal for consumers over time. In some of the trades examined by Ward – in confectionery and cigarettes, for example – there were relatively few changes in the structure of distribution or wholesale/retail margins. There was, on the other hand, some tendency for large carpet and hardware retailers to enjoy improved margins over this period, and in both of these cases the wholesaler began to play a much less important part in the distributive system. The contrast between these situations and the outcomes in the grocery and domestic appliances sectors indicates the way in which a release of competitive forces moves a distributive system towards a structure which is in some sense optimal for each individual sector.

Some doubts have been expressed, however, whether the emergence of a dominant group of grocery multiples in the 1970s has operated to the benefit of consumers. Such doubts are based upon the implications of the sheer increase in size and market power of such outlets, a fear that as they enjoy oligopsony power in their buying they may behave as uncompetitive oligopolists in their selling, and a limited amount of evidence that not all of the buying advantages of such retail organisations are passed on to consumers.[49] On the other hand the Monopolies and Mergers Commission and OFT surveys found not only that larger multiples had lower gross margins than other retailers but that they tended more than other outlets to translate lower buying prices into reduced selling prices.[50] Thus the benefits of the buying power of large-scale retailers over traditional independent outlets – estimated at 10 per cent in 1981 and 15.5 per cent in 1985[51] – do appear to be passed on to shoppers; and there is no conclusive evidence to suggest that manufacturers recoup their lower prices to large buyers through a general increase in prices or specifically inflated charges to smaller distributors. Rather, given the low rates of market growth in many retail sectors, surplus manufacturer capacity and import competition, together with a desire on the part of manufacturers to ensure the survival of more efficient smaller retailers, manufacturers themselves have been forced to bear part of the cost of enhanced trade discounts for larger retailers by a reduction in their own profitability.[52]

At a further practical level international comparisons of retail labour productivity indicate at least considerable scope for improvement in retailing efficiency in the UK. Data relating to 1981 show that US retailing labour productivity was 32 per cent above the level in West Germany, which in turn was 18 per cent higher than in the UK.[53] These data suggest that the British shopper is not well served in this respect. Nor, despite our earlier reservations concerning the interpretation of retail labour productivity figures, can we simply assume that UK shoppers are expressing a desire for a higher level of personal service etc. in accepting these lower labour productivity levels. Indeed writing in the context of the then more recent abolition of r.p.m. Ward emphasised that retail services in a protected environment tended to rise to fill the available gross margin. Any restrictions upon competition in retailing, such as the limitation on price competition under a system of r.p.m., will, Ward argued, tend to lead to a wasteful use of resources in distribution and a higher than desired level of retail services as 'the [competitive retail] margin available determines the total costs of distribution rather than the reverse'.[54] Thus competition and competitiveness in this sector, as in others, plays a major role not only in ensuring improved levels of technical performance (as measured in this case by labour productivity) but also in leading to the standard of service desired by consumers.

One general finding in the first major section of this chapter is of an improvement in manufacturer's trading terms for larger distributors since the mid 1960s. To some extent we may again see this as a beneficial reaction by manufacturers in recognising the economies of greater turnover or larger single orders given to them by large scale, multiple retailers. Furthermore, we noted above that such manufacturer reaction did not result in a higher level of gross margins for multiple grocers – the sector most affected by this development. These advantageous trading terms do, however, permit large scale retailers to undercut traditional shops in prices; and this opens up a threat of 'excessive' intertype competition which some claim may eventually lead to an undesirable dominance of a number of retail trades by multiple supermarket operators, and which it may already be said operates against those consumers who cannot travel longer distances to shop at lower prices or who want to buy particular goods in smaller units than are stocked by many large retailers. There is, however, no evidence of this threat materialising in substantial form as small-scale entry into retailing remains very largely unrestricted, and such small shops can enjoy an adequate margin between their higher cost of supplies (and possibly also higher unit overheads) and the enhanced prices which they can charge for shopper convenience as a result of their relative geographical monopoly position. Nor should we forget that the large scale, multiple retailers do pass on to final consumers the price advantage gained through their purchasing power. (Indeed, as we have seen, there is some statistical evidence to suggest that they pass on these advantages of lower buying prices more readily than independent shops.)[55]

One further effect of retailer buying power has been an associated decline in manufacturer profitability; and it has been suggested that increasing grocery retailer buying power from the 1970s onwards has been largely responsible for the deterioration in food manufacturer profitability in particular.[56] It should, however, be noted, within the limitations of such comparative data, that food manufacturer profitability has consistently remained above that of Total Manufacturing Industry over the period 1960–1983 when such comparisons on the basis of published data are possible.[57] There has, none the less, been a closing of the gap between these series over time; and food manufacturer profitability (return on capital employed) 'normalised' by reference to Total Manufacturing Industry profitability over the period 1960–1977 shows a significant decline.[58]

Data validity and reliability issues apart, however, there are problems in analysing such results; and one interpretation entirely consistent with the data is that the existence of discriminatory retail discounts arising from the purchasing behaviour of large-scale distributors is explained by the market power of *manufacturers*.[59] Retailer buying power is here seen as a constructive 'countervailing power' to the market dominance of manufacturers; and as long as such a buying advantage is passed on to the final consumer – as it appears to be at the moment – then retailer oligopsony power is not detrimental to the buying public.[60] The present situation is that while the availability of discounts related to the scale of orders may perhaps be the most important stimulant to retailing expansion and acquisitions, there is no evidence of collusion among the largest retailers in any field; and that we may at the present time become too obsessed with one phase of the gradual oscillation of power between manufacturers and distributors in the market. A return to the situation in the 1960s where the balance of power resided with manufacturers could well be the outcome of increases in manufacturer concentration and rationalisation of product lines.[61]

The second major part of this chapter dealt with the competitive response of retailers to their environment. Retailers have a variety of competitive responses open to them, and the balance in the adoption of these will depend upon their market environment, including the anticipated reaction of customers and competitors to the use of any particular competitive weapon.

It has been argued that despite the increase in market concentration among grocery retailers, price has remained the most important competitive weapon in this sector. Evidence for this is found in the increasing centralisation of pricing decisions at the headquarters of large multiple grocery organisations, the abandonment by Tesco of trading stamps in 1977, and the increase in retailer advertising – much of which inevitably concentrates upon prices.[62]

On the other hand it is possible to see these moves in the later 1970s as the product of a particular economic environment. This was a period of high rates of price inflation (25 per cent for 'All Foods' in 1975) and thus increased price consciousness on the part of consumers, combined with static real consumption in this area. It was also a time when the large grocery groups – less oligopolistically structured than they now are – were under attack from discount food shops such as Asda, Kwik Save and Fine Fare's 'Shoppers

Paradise'.[63] Tesco's response in particular – dropping Green Shield stamps as part of its 'Operation Checkout', followed by 'Discount '78' which resulted in Tesco's share of the packaged groceries market rising from 8 to 12 per cent – exerted considerable pressure upon food retailers across the market, and net profit margins fell consistently up to the early 1980s.[64] By this time, however, there was a realisation not only that the public were taking low prices in the supermarket for granted and were looking also for quality and convenience in shopping, but also that in a more tight-knit oligopoly situation of food retailing price was a 'dangerous' competitive weapon too easily responded to by competitors.[65] Thus Tesco abandoned its earlier 'pile it high, sell it cheap' approach as the present chief executive began the strategy of taking the chain up market.[66] This, as we saw earlier in the chapter, is a policy now broadly adopted by most firms in this sector.[67]

Generally, there is no evidence to suggest, within the present law, that the use of various competitive responses as practised by retailers is detrimental to customers or competition. Even in a post-r.p.m. context, legal restrictions on loss-leader selling and price marking ensure that retailer pricing freedom is not abused or the public misled. What is clear from the latter part of our analysis of retailer competitive response is that stores now have the freedom to compete along a number of dimensions, and that price alone is not necessarily the preferred one. Retailers are free to compete on a price basis; but they will respond to competition in ways that reflect changing consumer tastes and lifestyles, the particular strengths of the organisation, and a policy of differentiating oneself from one's competitors. It is this, in part, which has produced the 'dual market' in the grocery sector referred to in the first major section of this chapter, and which has maintained the variety of shopping outlets available to consumers, including the not insignificant contribution still made to retailing by the small-firm sector. (A full discussion of retail strategy making is contained in Chapter 4 below, while the specific issues of small-scale retailing are addressed in Chapter 5.)

Once more, therefore, we would argue that freedom for retailers to compete has produced the variety of shopping service which customers demand, and ensures that pressure is maintained to provide these services efficiently.

References

1. See K. D. George, *Productivity in Distribution* (Cambridge: CUP, 1966) p. 17; and C. Fulop, *Competition for Consumers* (London: Allen & Unwin, 1966) pp. 5–8.
2. A very elegant and comprehensive review of the theory of competition is contained in D. Swann *et al.*, *Competition in British Industry* (London: Allen & Unwin, 1974) Ch. 3. The author of this chapter in the text has used a practical

framework derived from the industrial economics concept of competition in W. S. Howe, 'Competition and Performance in Food Manufacturing', in J. Burns *et al.* (eds) *The Food Industry* (London: Heinemann, 1983) Ch. 6.

3. See C. Fulop, *Consumers in the Market* (London: IEA Research Monograph No. 13, 1967).
4. See J. C. Palamountain, *The Politics of Distribution* (Cambridge, Mass.: Harvard University Press, 1955) Ch. 2.
5. Ibid., p. 38.
6. The author has analysed these phenomena previously in 'Bilateral Oligopoly and Competition in the U.K. Food Trades', *The Business Economist*, Summer 1973, pp. 77–87.
7. The productivity differences, for example, are very much a source of intertype competitive advantage between retail outlets of different scale. In the case of labour productivity the advantages are predominantly at the individual store level. Labour productivity in UK retailing on the basis of 1977 data does not rise significantly over *firm* sizes £100 000 to £100m in terms of annual sales: but labour productivity for firms in this size category is considerably above that for firms having annual sales less than £100 000. See A. D. Smith and D. M. W. N. Hitchins, *Productivity in the Distributive Trades* (Cambridge: CUP, 1985) pp. 41 and 45.
8. See Palamountain, *The Politics of Distribution*, pp. 51–2.
9. NBPI, *Prices, Profits and Costs in Food Distribution* (London: HMSO, 1971, Report No. 165, Cmnd 4645) especially Ch. 2.
10. See K. van Musschenbroek, 'Developments in the Food Manufacturing and Distributive Industries', *Journal of Agricultural Economics*, September 1970, pp. 435–6.
11. See Howe, 'The Ending of Resale Price Maintenance', p. 82 for detailed figures.
12. See Monopolies and Mergers Commission, *Frozen Foodstuffs* (London: HMSO, 1976, HCP 674) paras 125–6. It should be noted, however, that at this time a number of food manufacturers were also recognising the increased costs of servicing smaller retailers by raising their minimum order or drop size or by imposing prohibitive surcharges on small orders. See A. C. McKinnon, 'The Historical Development of Food Manufacturers' Distribution Systems', Occasional Paper 7, Leicester University Geography Department, 1981, p. 16.
13. See Monopolies and Mergers Commission, *Discounts to Retailers* (London: HMSO, 1981, HC 311). The subtitle of the report is 'A report on the general effect on the public interest of the practice of charging some retailers lower prices than others or providing special benefits to some retailers where the difference cannot be attributed to savings in the supplier's costs'.
14. See Office of Fair Trading, *Competition and Retailing* (London: OFT, 1985) Ch. 4.
15. Ibid., Table 10, p. 26.
16. Monopolies and Mergers Commission, *Discounts to Retailers* (1981), para. 7.20.
17. Quoted in Howe 'The Ending of Resale Price Maintenance', p. 83.
18. The product, and to some extent geographical, diversification strategies of the large multiple retailers may also be seen as an index of the competitiveness of the traditional grocery markets in which advances in market share are increasingly more difficult to achieve. See D. F. Channon, *The Service Industries* (London: Macmillan, 1978) p. 29.
19. See W. G. McClelland, *Costs and Competition in Retailing* (London: Macmillan, 1966) Part II.
20. McClelland, for example, quotes a survey of 1957 which found that of shoppers who patronised more than one grocer 44 per cent were influenced by proximity,

13 per cent by price and goods each, 9 per cent by service, and 21 per cent vague or unspecified. Ibid., p. 187.

21. See V. Korah, *Monopolies and Restrictive Practices* (Harmondsworth: Penguin, 1968) Ch. 6, esp. pp. 195–209

22. See P. J. McGoldrick, 'A Multi-dimensional Framework for Retail Pricing', *International Journal of Retailing*, 1987, Vol. 2, No. 2, pp. 3–24.

23. Price consciousness measures simply the extent to which consumers are aware of the price of particular goods through asking them to recall the price at which they were bought. Price sensitivity is a measure of consumers' reaction to price changes and is akin to the economist's concept of price elasticity of demand. See the articles by A. Gabor and C. W. J. Granger, 'On the Price Consciousness of Consumers', *Applied Statistics*, 1961, pp. 170–88; 'Price Sensitivity of the Consumer', *Journal of Advertising Research*, December 1964, pp. 40–4; and 'Price as an Indicator of Quality: Report of an Enquiry', *Economica*, February 1966, pp. 43–70. More recent research in this area indicates that price awareness has declined a great deal over the past few decades, and that this varies considerably both between grocery items (including own labels) and across socioeconomic/age groups. See P. J. McGoldrick and H. J. Marks, 'Shoppers' Awareness of Retail Grocery Prices', *European Journal of Marketing*, 1987, Vol. 21 No. 3, pp. 63–76.

24. The price image of a store reflects shoppers' qualitative or psychological image of a shop or chain and gives rise to their overall evaluation of a shop as, for example, 'pricey', 'value for money', or 'cheap and cheerful'. For further analysis along these lines see H. Nyström, *Retail Pricing* (Stockholm: Economic Research Institute of the Stockholm School of Economics, 1970).

25. See A. Gabor, *Pricing: Principles and Practices* (London: Heinemann, 1977) pp. 137–43.

26. The total contribution of a line of goods is thus the product of the unit margin between selling price and variable cost and the number of units sold.

27. See R. H. Holton, 'Price Discrimination at Retail: The Supermarket Case', *Journal of Industrial Economics*, October 1957, esp. pp. 16–23.

28. See F. Livesey, *Pricing* (London: Macmillan, 1976) p. 122.

29. W. G. McClelland, *Studies in Retailing* (Oxford: Blackwell, 1964) pp. 96–7.

30. Livesey, *Pricing*, p. 120. The impressionistic dimension of retail pricing is emphasised in the following comment on price levels at Kwik Save grocery supermarkets. 'Kwik Save's offer, therefore, depends on a rather subjective view of price. [The chairman and chief executive, Ian] Howe's claim that customers can save 10 per cent to 15 per cent on their grocery bills seems ambitious, if not actually misleading, particularly in the light of the grocery trade's gross margin of around 18 per cent. But in retailing, perceptions rather than cold statistics are what matter, and the perception of Kwik Save appears to be of stores where the temptation to over-spend is not strong.' T. Lester, 'Kwik Save's Chain Reaction', *Management Today*, March 1989, p. 100.

31. See H. Nyström, *Retail Pricing*, Chs 6 and 7, esp. pp. 104–5 and 120–1.

32. See E. B. Howard and R. L. Davies, *Change in the Retail Environment* (Harlow: Longman/Oxford Institute of Retail Management, 1988).

33. See C. M. Guy, *Retail Location and Retail Planning in Britain* (Farnborough: Gower, 1980) p. 49.

34. See P. Zusman, 'The Role of the Retail Trade in the Competitive System', in D. G. Hague (ed.), *Price Formation in Various Economies* (London: Macmillan, 1967) pp. 63–4.

35. See S. Bowlby *et al.*, 'Store Location: Problems and Methods', *Retail & Distribution Management*, September–October 1984, pp. 31–3; November–December 1984, pp. 41–6; January–February 1985, pp. 44–8; and March–April 1985,

pp. 40–4. For a more detailed analysis of this topic see N. Wrigley, *Store Choice, Store Location and Market Analysis* (London: Routledge, 1988).

36. A good survey of this is contained in B. Berman and J. R. Evans, *Retail Management: A Strategic Approach* (New York: Macmillan Publishing Co., 2nd edn, 1983) pp. 185–92; and some interesting examples are given in M. Dickson, 'Forecasting Retail Turnover', in A. West (ed.), *Handbook of Retailing* (Aldershot: Gower, 1988) pp. 178–85.

37. Guy, *Retail Location and Retail Planning*, pp. 54–6.

38. See L. P. Simkin *et al.*, 'How retailers put site location techniques into operation', *Retail & Distribution Management*, May–June 1985, pp. 21–6.

39. See G. J. Davies and J. M. Brooks, *Positioning Strategy in Retailing* (London: Paul Chapman, 1989) p. 41 and data in P. J. McGoldrick, *Retail Marketing* (London: McGraw Hill, 1990) p. 342.

40. In the case of footwear the prominence of retailer brands stems from vertical integration between shoe manufacture and retailing. See Chapter 6. See data in McGoldrick, *Retail Marketing*, p. 241; and the useful review of policy in K. Davies *et al.*, 'The Development of Own Label Product Strategies in Grocery and DIY Retailing in the United Kingdom', *International Journal of Retailing*, Vol. 1, No. 1, 1986, pp. 6–19.

41. On this see also the concept of the 'wheel of retailing' dealt with in Chapters 4 and 12.

42. See 'Price gives way to image', *Financial Times*, 21 October 1986.

43. See *Financial Times*, 24 January 1987.

44. H. Nyström, *Retail Pricing*, p. 70.

45. See, for example, W. A. Lewis, 'Competition in Retail Trade', *Economica*, November 1945, pp. 202–34; J. Hood and B. S. Yamey, 'Imperfect Competition in the Retail Trades', *Economica*, May 1951, pp. 119–37; M. Hall and H. Smith, 'Further Reflections on Retail Pricing', *Economica*, February 1952, pp. 19–30.

46. See J. F. Pickering, *Resale Price Maintenance in Practice* (London: Allen & Unwin, 1966) Ch. 10. The 1971 NBPI Report on food distribution also noted that where retail outlets faced supermarket competition their net sales margins were significantly lower. See NBPI, *Prices, Profits and Costs in Food Distribution*, Appendix E, Tables 2, 3 and 5. The relevant data are tabulated in Howe, 'The Ending in Resale Price Maintenance', Appendix, p. 87.

47. See NBPI, *Distributors' Costs and Margins on Furniture, Domestic Electrical Appliances and Footwear* (London: HMSO, 1968, Report No. 97, Cmnd 3858) Appendix 10.

48. T. S. Ward, *The Distribution of Consumer Goods* (Cambridge: CUP, 1973) Chs 15, 16.

49. See R. B. Heflebower, 'Mass Distribution: A Phase of Bilateral Oligopoly or of Competition?', *American Economic Review*, December 1956, pp. 274–85; observations in NBPI, *Bread Prices and Pay in the Baking Industry* (London: HMSO, 1970, Report No. 151, Cmnd 4428) para. 67; and Musschenbroek, 'Developments in the Food Manufacturing and Distributive Industries', p. 436. A study of the US food retailing industry over the period 1970–74 found that the enhanced sales margins associated with increased retailer market shares were explained entirely by increased prices, as operating expenses as a proportion of sales actually rose with increased market share. See B. W. Marion *et al.*, *The Food Retailing Industry: Market Structure, Profits, and Prices* (New York: Praeger, 1979) pp. 132–3.

50. See Monopolies and Mergers Commission, *Discounts to Retailers,* Appendix 6 paras 9–13; and OFT, *Competition and Retailing*, Ch. 5. In the OFT survey the gross margins of the multiples were found to be not significantly different from those of independent retailers, and the conclusion from the data was that 'These

results are not inconsistent with the proposition that the benefits of lower buying prices are in general passed on in lower selling prices.' (para. 5.19).

51. See Monopolies and Mergers Commission, *Discounts to Retailers*, Appendix 6, para. 8; and OFT, *Competition and Retailing*, para. 5.15.
52. See Monopolies and Mergers Commission, *Discounts to Retailers* (1981), para. 6.19; and also evidence in respect of trends in food manufacturer and distributor profitability in Howe, 'Competition and Performance in Food Manufacturing, pp. 115–19, and OFT, *Competition and Retailing*, Ch. 3.
53. See Smith and Hitchens, *Productivity in the Distributive Trades*, p. 120.
54. See Ward, *The Distribution of Consumer Goods*, p. 176.
55. See Monopolies and Mergers Commission, *Discounts to Retailers* (1981), Appendix 6, para. 13.
56. See C. W. F. Baden Fuller, 'Rising Concentration: The U.K. Grocery Trade 1970–1980', in K. Tucker and C. Baden Fuller (eds), *Firms and Markets* (London: Croom Helm, 1986) pp. 70–2.
57. See. W. S. Howe, 'Competition and Performance in Food Manufacturing' (1983), pp. 115–19; and OFT, *Competition and Retailing*, pp. 31 and 34.
58. Ibid., p. 119.
59. See R. M. Grant, 'Manufacturer–Retailer Relations: the Shifting Balance of Power', in G. Johnson (ed.), *Business Strategy and Retailing* (Chichester: Wiley, 1987) pp. 43–58.
60. For some reservations on the application of this see A. Hunter, 'Notes on Countervailing Power', *Economic Journal*, March 1958, pp. 89–103.
61. See K. Davies *et al.*, 'Structural Changes in Grocery Retailing: The Implications for Competition', *International Journal of Physical Distribution and Materials Management*, 1985, No. 2, pp. 13–14.
62. See Baden Fuller' 'Rising Concentration', pp. 73–4.
63. Although multiple grocers had increased their share of the trade from 20 per cent in 1950 to 56 per cent in 1976, this was to rise to 59 per cent in 1980 and 69 per cent in 1986. In particular the market share of the largest four distributors rose from 26 per cent in 1976 to 34 per cent in 1980 and 45 per cent in 1986. See I. Hunt, 'Developments in Food Distribution', in J. Burns *et al.*, *The Food Industry*, p. 139; and A. Burdus, 'Competition in the Food Distribution Sector', paper presented at conference on *Competition Policy in the Food Industries* (Reading University, Department of Agricultural Economics and Management, 10 September 1987) p. 4. The author is grateful to Miss Burdus for a copy of her paper.
64. See Davies *et al.*, 'Structural Changes in Grocery Retailing', pp. 16–18.
65. See G. Akehurst, '"Checkout": The Analysis of Oligopolistic Behaviour in the U.K. Grocery Retail Market', *The Service Industries Journal*, 1984, Vol. 4, Part 2, pp. 189–242.
66. W. Kay, *Battle for the High Street* (London: Piatkus, 1987) pp. 86–7.
67. Interestingly, however, the depressed sales levels in the clothing sector in the autumn of 1989 saw Littlewoods, the seventh largest clothing retailer in the UK, launch its 'Moneysworth' sales promotion which involved price cuts of about 10 per cent on its 104 top-selling, price sensitive clothing lines which accounted for 40 per cent of its clothing sales. This move may be seen as a reaction to generally depressed trading conditions brought about by a consumer credit squeeze, and also Littlewoods' desire to maintain its reputation for keen prices among its traditional customers in the lower socioeconomic groups. See *Financial Times*, 26 October 1989.

Retail Corporate Strategy 4

'An important consideration in understanding
the retail structure or corporate performance
in any sector or country is . . . the competitive
strategy and decision-making adopted by companies
and individuals.'

D. Lord *et al.*, 'Retailing on Three Continents:
The Discount Food Store Operations of Albert
Gubay', *International Journal of Retailing*, 1988,
Vol. 3 No. 3, p. 3.

4.1   Introduction

In Chapter 1 and Chapter 2 of this text we described the functions of retailing
and the way in which the retail sector of the economy developed particularly
since the middle of the nineteenth century. This description included some
reference to the emergence and relative success of different forms of retailing
such as department stores and multiple-shop organisations. Having analysed
retailing competition in Chapter 3 the function of this present chapter is to
look at how retail organisations respond to competitive and other pressures in
terms of their business strategies. This chapter therefore continues with an
outline of the topic of business strategy. This is followed by more specific
analysis of strategic decision making in the retail sector, including longer term
decision areas such as vertical integration and the role of acquisitions. The
chapter concludes with a consideration of the issues involved in strategy
implementation in retailing.

4.2 Corporate Strategy[1]

Definitions and Comparisons

Strategic management and the strategic management process are concerned with arriving at decisions on what an organisation ought to be doing and where it should be going. Ansoff, one of the most influential writers in the field, defines strategic decisions as those pertaining to the relationship between the firm and its environment, and involving 'decisions on what kind of business the firm should seek to be in'.[2] The business historian Chandler refers to strategy as involving 'the determination of the basic long-term goals and objectives of an enterprise, and the adoption of courses of action and the allocation of resources necessary for carrying out these goals'.[3] In the context of the modern business organisation the editor of the *Harvard Business Review* described strategic decision making as follows:

> agreements reached by top management about how the company should position itself to take advantage of future market opportunity and to outdo its competitors . . . (as a result of having) investigated market opportunity, appraised and invested in the distinctive competence and total resources of the company, and combined opportunity and resources, consistent with the economic goals, personal values, and ethical aspirations that define the character of the company.[4]

These definitions of strategy and strategic management emphasise the central nature of strategic decision making within organisations, and also the need for a logical sequence of decision making in this area.

One way in which to gain further insight into strategic decisions is to contrast these with other management decision areas. Ansoff distinguishes three such areas: strategic, administrative and operating.[5] Operating decisions in any organisation are concerned with the management of the resource conversion process itself, and involve, for example, allocating operating resources, setting price and output levels, and making decisions about necessary marketing and research and development expenditures. Decisions at this level are being made all the time in an organisation, and a stream of such decisions constantly presents itself to be made by managers. Actual decision making in this area thus tends to be relatively decentralised within the organisation. Many of such decisions are repetitive, and while they involve risk and uncertainty they are also characterised by a relatively short time period between recognising the need to make such decisions and the completion of all of the effects following from them.

Administrative decisions within an organisation are essentially facilitative. They establish procedures for acquiring resources, for ensuring an appropriate internal structure of authority and responsibility among those working within the organisation, and for managing the flow of information within the business.

Strategic decisions, in contrast to the first two areas above, concern the interface between the business and its external environment. Such decision making is inevitably centralised at the top of the organisation as the decisions are concerned with the general disposition of the total resources of the business. Strategic decisions, in contrast to operating ones, are made relatively infrequently, and their effects will normally be felt by the business over a considerable period of time. Perhaps the most challenging of all of the characteristics of strategic decisions is that top management does not receive forewarning that such decisions require to be made. Ansoff refers to them as 'non self-generative'. This means that although strategic decisions are relatively few in number, the organisation must be constantly aware of the need to consider making such decisions, and must ensure that a mechanism exists for drawing the need for making such decisions to the attention of senior management. This is particularly true in an environment where lead times relating to such decisions – involving, for example, capital building programmes – are increasingly long.

The Strategic Management Process

It was emphasised at the beginning of this section that there is a logical process by which strategic decisions should be arrived at. The strategic decision-making process comprises six distinct, interrelated steps, as shown in Table 4.1.[6] A strategic decision should only be made and implemented after the senior management of the organisation has gone through the decision-making process outlined in the table.

At *Stage 1*, mission and objective identification, management must answer for itself questions about the nature of the business in terms of its basic mission or purpose. It must also decide in broad terms its corporate financial objectives over the next five or ten years. The basic mission or purpose of the organisation should be expressed in terms of the market in which the business sees itself operating: industrial textiles, financial services, information processing, travel/tourism, etc. Business goals should be considered at this stage in broad terms along dimensions of profitability, growth, stability of earnings etc.

Stage 2 of the strategic decision-making process, analysis of the environment, involves the business in an appraisal of its current and likely future external environment: its market opportunities and threats. Opportunities for the business may include new market areas into which to sell existing products, or the appearance of new market demands which match the company's unique strengths. Threats may be posed by the decline of markets upon which the business has been dependent in the past, upward movements in raw material costs, or demographic changes likely to have an adverse impact upon the organisation.

Table 4.1
The Strategic Decision-making Process

Stage	Steps	Process
1	Mission and objective identification	Establishment of basic mission or purpose of the organisation, and determination of broad performance goals
2	Analysis of the business environment	Appraisal of the opportunities and threats relating to the business arising from its external environment
3	The internal business audit	Review and assessment of strengths and weaknesses of the organisation
4	Review of strategic opportunities	Identification of all possible strategies open to the business
5	Comparison of strategic options	Evaluation of all possible options, and making of the final strategic decision
6	Implementation, evaluation and control of strategy	The translation of strategic into administrative and operating decisions, and ongoing monitoring of strategy.

By contrast *Stage 3* of the strategic decision-making process involves the organisation in analysing its own internal capabilities: its unique strengths and weaknesses. Such an analysis will enable the business to identify the key resources upon which its success in exploiting markets and surviving against its competitors depends, and also the weaknesses that should be remedied if the business is to continue to operate in such markets and survive. For example, a firm may have particular strengths arising from the possession of a nationally recognised name, or considerable financial resources accumulated as a result of past profitability. Such a business may correspondingly have recognised weaknesses in the areas of production efficiency or its physical distribution network. In choosing its strategy any organisation will wish to capitalise upon its strengths while at the same time remedying, or in the short term minimising the exposure of, its competitive weaknesses.

At *Stage 4* of the strategic planning sequence the business should identify and consider as wide a range of strategic options open to it as possible. These may be thought of in very broad terms such as expansion or consolidation of existing activities, innovation, diversification, or divestment and restructuring. This range of options will need to be narrowed down at a later stage to more specific strategies. Indeed *Stage 5* of the strategic decision-making process is the point at which the business evolves a particular strategy. At this stage the organisation seeks to match the goals which it has set for itself at Stage 1 with the results of the external review and internal audit (Stages 2 and

3), and chooses which of the possible avenues identified at Stage 4 should be followed in the light of all of the circumstances. This is arguably the most difficult part of the whole strategic decision-making process, and although there are a number of techniques available which may improve business decision-making in this area, there is undoubtedly a great deal about such decisions which must depend upon the judgement of the business strategist. At the end of this stage the organisation will have decided upon one particular strategy for itself.

Stage 6 of the sequence set out in Table 4.1 involves a process of putting the chosen strategy into effect and of monitoring its implementation in order to ensure the achievement of the business goals identified at Stage 1. This process involves the continuous monitoring of the chosen strategy and its implementation in order, if necessary, to adjust the strategy to the changing circumstances of the business. It is hoped to show in the remainder of this chapter that by following the sequence of steps in the strategic decision-making process senior managers in retailing can improve the quality of the difficult long-term decisions that they have to make.

The Importance of Strategy

Making correct strategic decisions matters for businesses; and corporate strategists would argue that it is probably more important for the long-term survival of the organisation for management to be efficient in terms of its strategy than in respect of its operating efficiency. There are indeed grounds for suggesting on the basis of both American and British research that there is a link between strategic planning and profit performance in business. In the case of the British evidence the study by Grinyer and Norburn, although it was not able to establish a relationship between company financial performance and the formality of business planning, nor between financial performance and agreement upon objectives within the organisation, did find a positive statistical relationship between business performance and the detail of objective setting and the fixing of responsibility for long-term decisions.[7]

Leontiades, in his study of diversification, provides through three short case studies very telling evidence from the American business scene of the importance of making correct strategic decisions.[8] Taking examples from the areas of computers and two retailing sectors, the author shows how in each case over a ten or twenty year period one of two organisations which were equally placed in the market at the beginning of the period had succeeded while the other had failed as a result of superior strategic decision making on the part of the former business. The successful organisations are those which, as events have turned out, had the correct vision of how things were to be in the future and deployed their resources accordingly. The businesses which by comparison failed did so not because of any obvious inherent disadvantage in terms of size or financial resources, but because of poor strategic decision making on their part.

A business is not a prisoner of its past history or present environment; and to emphasise the role of successful businessmen in building up their organisations is not simply to glamorize the task of the chief executive but to recognise the scope on the part of an individual or group of individuals for choosing between possible strategies for their organisations. The roles of Sir John Cohen of Tesco Stores or Michael Marks and his successors at Marks & Spencer in building up in competitive conditions organisations which were to play a dominant role in their sectors of the retail market are merely two illustrations of the choice and implementation of successful business strategies in the face of severe competition.[9]

The function of corporate strategy is to facilitate the achievement by the business of its objectives. This is brought about by the organisation determining for itself a clear idea of its mission or business area objective, and also establishing ultimate performance objectives in terms of return on investment, growth etc. Once these have been established – and at this stage they may have to be tentative or preliminary – the firm must analyse its environment and resources. This external and internal audit of the organisation will not only lead to possible refinement or modification of the business area and performance objectives but will also be fundamental to determining the strategy of the firm; for on the basis of the environmental analysis, for example, will depend the precise geographical or socio-economic markets to be concentrated upon, a recognition of the strength of rivals in the market and the major competitive weapons to use. Thereafter the firm should formulate a number of possible strategies, and on the basis of its earlier analysis choose and implement that one which is most appropriate to its objectives, environment and resources.

4.3 Strategic Analysis in Retailing

In this central section of Chapter 4 we shall examine how strategic analysis should be carried out in the retail sector, using as a framework the sequence of strategic analysis in Table 4.1.

Mission and Objectives

Although in the context of this book it is assumed that the firm is concerned with retailing as a broad business area, an analysis of retailing mission and objectives is obviously necessary for three categories of organisation. First, for smaller businesses starting up in the retail environment; second, for retailers expanding from one sector of the retail market to another, such as the entry by the Asda–MFI superstores group into car sales;[10] third, for manufacturers contemplating forward vertical integration into retailing, as Terence Conran did in the 1960s in moving from furniture design and manufacture into retailing.[11] At this stage the organisation should identify the broad area of retailing in which it is to operate. Also at this stage it will have in mind the form or scale of its activities, dictated perhaps largely by its financial resources. A more detailed view of store location, position in the market and merchandise policy will have to wait until the business has further analysed its environment and resources.

None the less, before any further such analysis is undertaken the firm must have a set of performance goals, however tentative these may be at this stage. The overall performance goal of return on investment (ROI) is usually dictated by shareholders, who have an opportunity cost of their present rewards in terms of returns elsewhere in the market at comparable risk. Obviously the precise makeup of shareholders – whether they are a large number of dispersed small shareholders, a small family group participating in the management of the firm, or a range of financial institutions – will determine the alternative investments available, attitudes to risk and the time horizon adopted in decision making. Whatever the pattern of ownership and control of the business, however, some minimum profit performance, some time horizon for the achievement of this, and some attitude to risk will dictate a set of financial goals for the firm. Failure to satisfy these will ultimately jeopardise the survival of the organisation as an independent entity.

A firm may also have aspirations in terms of the rate of expansion, particularly as this may satisfy management pride or be associated with a greater likelihood of survival in the market. Below this in a hierarchy of goals may come market share, cost control etc. which may be regarded as essentially facilitative to the survival of the firm or the achievement of its financial goals.

The purpose of this combination of business area and performance goals is, first, to allow the organisation to focus on that part of its environment which is strategically relevant; second, thereby to highlight the appropriate dimensions of resources necessary for competitive advantage; and third, to establish for strategists a cut-off level of return and risk in putting forward possible strategies. Indeed, as was pointed out earlier in this chapter the whole purpose of business strategy is to permit the organisation to achieve its goals through interacting effectively (competitively) with its environment.

Analysis of the Business Environment

The environment of a business comprises all of those organisations, circumstances and other parameters within which the firm has to achieve its objectives but which are largely beyond its immediate control. Analysis of the environment for a retailing organisation is particularly important as retailers are at the leading edge of the relationship between the production–distribution chain and the ultimate consumer. This importance is magnified when markets are dynamic, that is when the nature of the environmental variables is changing rapidly.

The general environment comprises broad economic, social (including demographic), technical and governmental features which have an impact upon retail organisations. The level of activity in the economy and its rate of growth ultimately determine spending power and the size of individual markets. So also do the distribution of incomes and spending decisions between the well off and the less well off, between men and women within the family, and between those of different ages. Events during 1989 particularly highlighted the need for retailers not only to be able to anticipate macroeconomic changes but also to react to the impact of these. As the Chancellor of the Exchequer's monetarist approach to controlling inflation through higher interest rates took effect, retailers experienced a reduction in the level of consumer shopping expenditure which had a particular impact in such areas as clothing and television and audio equipment where consumers could easily put off buying, especially where purchases might have been made on the basis of increasingly expensive consumer credit.[12] Economic and social aspects of the general environment merge when we consider, for example, the changing role of women in society. Increased 'activity rates' on the part of married women and a rising proportion of married women in the labour force have not only provided such working women with more money to spend on items such as fashion clothing, but have also increased demand for convenience foods and ready-prepared meals. Demographic trends have produced baby booms and a subsequent ageing population, having strategic implications for retailers such as Mothercare and Pronuptia.

We mentioned in the Introduction to this text the march of microprocessor technology as an example of rapid change in retailing. Certainly the advent of EPOS is having a significant impact upon the way in which shopping is done, the level of necessary capital investment in retailing, the scale of retail organisations and also the locus of management decision making in retailing. Finally, the government plays a role in retailing and retail strategy by setting many of the rules of competition etc. In Chapter 2 we saw how the legislative attack on r.p.m. increased the importance of price competition and further advanced large-scale retailing in the 1960s. Similarly, legislation on hours of shop opening and on employment embodied in the Shops Acts, and weights and measures regulations along with other consumer protection measures circumscribe the ways in which retailers may compete.[13]

In addition to the general environment, each individual retail organisation is faced with a particular task environment. The task environment comprises factors which impinge directly upon an individual organisation. The major dimensions of this are set out in Table 4.2

On the basis of the factors set out in Table 4.2 a retail organisation must analyse its own existing market, or particular retail sectors which it is considering entering. Government publications, specialist journals such as the Economist Intelligence Unit's *Retail Business*, and trade sources should provide factual answers or estimates to questions of size and rate of growth of particular markets. The 'existence of segments within these markets is,

Table 4.2
The Retail Task Environment

Markets	Size and rate of growth
	Existence of segments or niches
	Other market features, e.g. seasonality
	Bases of competition – key factors for success
Participants	Number and size distribution of other sellers
	Supply conditions
	Barriers to entry and exit
Other Factors	Particular impact of technology
	Legislative or other controls specific to chosen retail market

however, much more a matter of marketing judgement. Recognition of these requires not only a possible further breakdown of aggregated market statistics but also the ability to recognise patterns of customer behaviour within broader sectors such as books (student purchases) or food (health foods). Likewise the recognition of the basis of competition, based upon why customers buy a particular product, is a matter partly of market analysis and partly of judgement. Features such as price, service, merchandise range, location and promotional activity all enter into the retail marketing mix.

The choice of avenue of competition in a particular retail sector will also depend in part upon the structure of the market in terms of the number of competitors and their relative sizes, together with their existing strategies. Most retail markets are oligopolistic, both at a national and local level, so that competitive interdependence is strongly recognised, and competitor analysis is an important component of retail strategy. Supplies or supply conditions to the retail trade also form an important part of the task environment of individual sectors, and relationships with suppliers are an important part of retail strategy. This is not simply a question of the balance of market power discussed in the previous chapter, but of both the economics (cost savings) and strategy of the variety of possible supplier–retailer relationships from a purely arm's length linkage to full vertical integration.

As in manufacturing industry so in retail distribution there will exist cost conditions and other institutional circumstances which make it more or less difficult to enter particular sectors. Barriers to entry or barriers to new competition may arise as existing retailers control sources of supply, enjoy cost economies arising from access to particular factors or from the present scale of their operations, or benefit from the loyalty of customers in the market – a loyalty possibly quite consciously built up through advertising or the private brands of a store. In an increasing number of retail markets too now the requirement for large amounts of initial capital constitutes a significant barrier to entry by smaller organisations.

Finally there may be a particular legislative or other aspects of individual retail markets which constitute an important part of their environment. The more obvious examples of this – such as restrictions upon outlets for retailing petrol or alcohol, or the legislation covering the operations of banks and building societies – are not covered in any detail in this text.

The conditions relating to the general and task environments of retailing organisations have a major influence in determining their strategy. It is these conditions which together present the opportunities and threats facing the business, which must guide the firm in choosing its individual strategy, and which provide the context within which the organisation must assess its resources. It is to this internal resource audit that we now turn.

Business Resource Analysis

No strategy can be formulated by reference to the analysis of the business environment alone. Before arriving at its strategy an organisation must have regard to its present and likely future resource position. This involves an internal audit of the firm's resources, and leads to the identification of the strengths and weaknesses of the firm in the context of possible environments. Thus the internal resource audit is always conducted in the light of the principal features of the environment of the business. The major dimensions of the resources of the firm are set out in Table 4.3.

For a retail organisation the principal market resource variables are its present share of the market, the number and location of its existing stores, its current merchandise policy in terms of the products and product range, the share of the firm's sales, profits etc. derived from each major product area, and its general marketing or market research competence.

The firm's present market share tells the organisation something about its current success in the market. It also indicates its competitive position *vis-à-vis* other sellers in the market and its suppliers; and if there are significant economies of scale or learning effects, then market share information may imply something about the relative cost position of the firm in the market. The number and location of the organisation's stores reveals in more detail how the firm operates, as also does information on its products and product range. Within this a firm should know the relative contributions to sales, profits and cash flow of its separate product areas. Finally, and again reflecting the importance of an understanding of the market by retailers, the firm must constantly assess its competence in the marketing and market research area.

Whether or not a retail group competes predominantly on the basis of price, efficiency in store operations is an important consideration. In this

Table 4.3
Major Retail Organisation Resource Variables

Markets	Market share
	Number and location of stores
	Product range
	Dependence upon key products
	Marketing/market research competence
Cost competence	Size of store relative to market average
and supply	Performance data – sales per square foot etc.
	Supply costs, control etc.
Finance	Capital structure – gearing ratio etc.
	Access to additional equity and debt finance
	Pattern of cash flow
	Procedures for financial management, stock control etc.
Organisation and	Organisation structure – form and appropriateness
human resources	Management succession
	Staff quality and development
	Wage and salary levels
	Management–trade union relations

context size of store may be a relevant variable where there are economies of scale at the level of individual establishments. Certainly all of the evidence concerning the increase in average store size suggests that retail groups consider there are such economies, and that increased size of store unit as much as an increase in the number of branches is the preferred means of increasing market penetration. Performance in store operations will be measured by indicators such as sales per square foot or sales per employee, reflecting the importance of these cost categories,[14] and this again is likely to encourage retailers to grow by expanding store size rather than the number of outlets.

Concern over the cost and control of supply reflects the other major cost variable for retailers. For many retailers supply is a question of obtaining at the lowest cost the goods they believe they can sell. In the case of Marks & Spencer, however, the relationship between manufacturer and retailer has been taken to the point where the retailer is seen as determining in large part what, how and under what conditions goods sold in the shop should be produced in what is essentially a vertically integrated manufacturer–distributor system.[15]

Such are the costs of store expansion that finance is a major resource variable in retail strategy, with the largest retailers talking in terms of annual store development expenditures of more than £200m.[16] Cash flow too is an important variable, with grocery retailers, for example, depending upon generating significant liquid resources as a result of paying for their supplies some time after they have received cash from their customers.[17]

Finally, but by no means least, there are the issues of organisation structure and reporting relationships, top management succession, quality and development of staff, and matters relating to wage and salary levels and management–trade union relations. The organisational relationship between the centre and individual stores is a significant determinant of the efficiency with which a retail chain is operated. It will influence the speed and accuracy with which information is passed up and strategy is passed down within the group, and will also affect human relations in the organisation. In addition to providing for senior management succession, the firm must ensure an appropriate quality of staffing throughout the organisation. Management may be able to economise in the latter respect if customer or product conditions do not make staff an important retailing variable; but where either the product requires some expertise on the part of sales staff (as in photographic goods or hi-fi equipment) or a particular standard of staff is considered necessary (as in the case of traditional department stores) economising on staffing costs will be an inappropriate strategy.[18] Wage and salary levels, as we noted above, are a significant cost factor in retailing, while at the same time they will influence the quality of staff; and although the Union of Shop, Distributive and Allied Workers is not normally regarded as a particularly powerful or militant union, good management–union relations are an integral part of retail strategy.

Combined Environment and Resource Analysis

The combined analysis of the environment and resources (sometimes referred to as SWOT analysis: strengths and weaknesses, opportunities and threats) is the basis of all strategic decision making. Thus, for example, the decisions by Marks & Spencer to enter the UK baby products market, by British Home Stores to withdraw from food retailing, and by ASDA to sell motor cars each reflect an alignment of the firm's resources and its environment in an attempt to achieve its profit, growth and other goals. In the case of Marks & Spencer's product extension, the decision was based upon favourable general environment and resource features such as a rising birth rate, and a capitalising upon the firm's experience with children's clothes and the quality and value for money image which should attract existing Marks & Spencer customers. These opportunities and strengths, it is argued, should give the firm a competitive advantage over its rivals in this field, who include traditional children's retailers as well as Mothercare and Boots. Such a development will have the advantage of allowing Marks & Spencer to reduce its dependence upon the slower-growing food markets and more volatile fashion clothing.[19]

By contrast, shortly after its acquisition by Storehouse early in 1986 British Home Stores (BHS) pulled out of food retailing in which it had been making losses, and transferred the 7 per cent of its store space released to other product areas. Storehouse saw BHS operating in an environment of low growth in food sales together with severe competition from the large multiple grocery groups as well as Marks & Spencer. Clearly it was envisaged that the space involved could be put to better use by BHS for selling other goods and its profitable restaurant division.[20] An example of a radical change in retailing was the entry (later reversed) of Asda into the motor vehicle selling, service, repair and trade-in field. 'Hatchbacks, madame? . . . down past the toiletries, and left by the baked beans' quipped the *Financial Times* in April 1986.[21] Here again this strategic departure appears to have been clearly thought out over a considerable period. Despite an environment of low sales growth, significant manufacturer over-capacity and very severe distributor competition Asda perceived that its car-borne customers provided a rich source of potential car purchasers, and that the firm could apply its low margin–high volume trading policy to cars in such a way as further to diversify from its food and existing related sales.

Strategic Choice in Retailing

Having analysed its environment and resource position a retail organisation must make a refined choice of the market or markets in which to operate. The choice of market position and the particular strategy adopted will be determined by the need to attain the maximum competitive advantage. Knee and Walters suggest a sequence through which a retailer first identifies an advantageous broad market *position* on the basis of SWOT analysis. This is followed by market *segmentation*, which involves identifying particular customer groups on the basis of demographic, socio-economic, lifestyle and other variables. Finally the firm responds to these variables through *differentiation*, by which it moves to a unique product-market location in which it considers it has particular advantages, and seeks to defend this position against competitors by developing resources accordingly.[22] The result of this action is a particular image which the retailer has of what the firm is offering customers; and it is of course imperative that this image is shared between the retailer and its customers, is adopted in respect of all of the retailer's strategic variables, and is consistently applied over a period of time. To take an example of a failure in this respect, many people would accept that the relative lack of success of Woolworth's UK subsidiary over the last ten years of its existence before being acquired in 1985 by a British consortium was a lack of clear strategic position in the eyes of potential customers.

At a broad level strategic *positioning* requires retailers to recognise sectors of the market which are viable for them. As the chairman of one of the smaller department store groups put it, 'If you can't beat the chains, don't try to. Do something they cannot do; be different'.[23] At the more detailed level of *segmentation* the Littlewoods chain store has obviously rethought its position in the market in recent years. An earlier attempt by the store to move 'up market' into women's fashion clothes has been reversed in the light of a better identification of its market, which is now perceived as 'quite clearly the mother, particularly the one with a mature family . . . The group is stream-lining its range to go for that market'.[24]

Having chosen a broad position in the market and identified a particular market segment, the retailing organisation will *differentiate* itself in terms of the following key variables, set out in Table 4.4. It is particularly important that in respect of these dimensions and their components the retailer develops resources so as to offer a consistently differentiated combination of attributes to the chosen customers. Consistency here is something which is applied over time (unless it becomes appropriate to revise the strategic approach) and among the competitive dimensions. Thus the approach of the department store is that of offering a wide range of quality products available in a single city-centre shop with an ambience of comfort (possibly even affluence), and which, while it must remain reasonably price competitive with other forms of retailing, emphasises the provision of services (credit, delivery etc.) including a high level of personal attention to customers. By contrast even a high quality chain store such as Marks & Spencer does not claim to offer the same width or depth in its product range, provides a more restricted shopping environment (in terms, for example, of the absence of opportunities for trying

Table 4.4
Key Strategic Variables for Retail Differentiation[25]

Product range	Specialisation
	Width
	Depth
	Availability
	Quality
Location	Local/national coverage
	City centre/edge of town
	Store size
	Ambience
Pricing	National/local policy
	Importance of price variable
Customer service	Standard of service
	Range of services (priced or free): credit etc.
	Quality of staff

on garments), recognises the greater importance of price in its competitive strategy, and in terms of staffing provides only assisted self-selection of merchandise.[26]

An important part of the strategy of any retailer is relative differentiation of his strategy from those of competitors. This differentiation is designed to produce the combination of attributes (price, product range, service etc.) which is closest to the ideal preferred by the chosen market segment. It is also designed to develop particular chain or store loyalty on the part of those customers. It is, amongst other objectives, in order to achieve this loyalty that retailers have developed own-label goods (including the St Michael label under which all Marks & Spencer products are sold), adopted a chosen image applied across the whole store group in the case of 'Boots the Chemist', and placed increased emphasis upon design in shop layout.[27] In the case of some multiple shop groups there is also national uniformity of prices for the same goods.

As with all strategies an important consideration is that of resources. The firm must have a basis for cost efficiency for a low-price strategy, the financial resources with which to extend credit, the quality of staff through which to provide the chosen level of attention to customers, and sources of supply from which to provide products of particular price and quality. As we shall see below in considering vertical integration and similar policies, one of the reasons for a close retailer–supplier relationship is to ensure the availability of appropriate merchandise: goods which are of the right quality and design for the store in terms of its chosen image or differentiation.

The history of Marks & Spencer provides a good example of a retailer deciding to occupy a particular segment of the market, and accompanying this by appropriate merchandising decisions. Following its registration as a limited company in 1903 Marks & Spencer expanded rapidly as a variety chain store selling a very wide range of goods originally at its 'one penny' price point which was replaced in 1927 by 'five shillings'. At the time when the firm became a public company in 1926 its product range comprised 'haberdashery, hosiery and drapery, toilet requisites, glass, china and earthenware, stationery, toys, confectionery and sports goods, fancy goods, jewellery, gramophone records and music, cutlery, household goods, hardware, tin and enamel ware, books and novels'.[28] By this time, however, other chain stores were expanding in the UK. The American Woolworth had been established in the UK since 1909, and British Home Stores began trading in 1928. The threat from Woolworth was particularly felt. 'They [Woolworth] enjoyed the advantage of large financial resources, American experience and American methods of large-scale retailing. Indeed, the threat presented by Woolworth's was one of the factors which forced Marks and Spencer to find ways and means by which it could create for itself a specialised position in the field of chain store retailing'.[29] The response to this situation by Marks & Spencer was to reduce dramatically its product range and to develop particularly in the clothing field. By 1932 over 70 per cent of the items listed in the company's

1926 prospectus had been dropped, and between 1928 and 1932 seventeen departments in the stores had disappeared.[30] The result of this deliberate strategy was that by 1936 two-thirds of the group's sales were accounted for by textiles, and in 1950 the then Board of Trade classified Marks & Spencer not as a variety chain store but as a clothing multiple.[31] Nor was it a matter of accident that Marks & Spencer moved into clothing – particularly lighter women's wear – at this stage. The First World War and the economic and other conditions following it had quite radically changed the nature of demand especially by working-class women for outerwear and underwear; and having been attracted to the market Marks & Spencer assisted supply conditions by transmitting large orders to clothing manufacturers who were encouraged to apply to this market for the first time factory production methods, including the use of new, artificial fibres.

This example illustrates the way in which Marks & Spencer, one of the original variety chain stores, moved away from this form of retailing in response to the emergence of a powerful competitor, and sought to differentiate itself by capitalising on an emerging market for women's clothing which it in turn helped to develop. As a refinement of this strategy Marks & Spencer's progressive movement into higher quality clothing not only removed it from competition from Woolworth but also differentiated it from British Home Stores and from Littlewoods (established in 1937), both of whom entered the clothing market at a slower rate and in a lower price range.[32]

A further contrast may be drawn between the development of Marks & Spencer in clothing and Tesco in groceries at important periods of their development. Whereas Marks & Spencer after the Second World War deliberately moved up market in terms of the range and quality of its merchandise and pricing strategy, Tesco retained its allegiance to its working class, market stall origins. To say that its policy could be adequately summarised in terms of one original slogan of 'No divi, no bonus, no bunk – just plain rock-bottom prices' would be to over-simplify. Throughout its major period of expansion after 1945 the firm did, however, remain close to its working-class customer roots with a vigorously operated cut-price policy associated with Tesco's clear opposition to r.p.m.[33]

4.4 The Longer Term

Retail organisations, as much as others, require to make adjustments to existing strategies and also to make longer-term strategic decisions. The need for these will arise, first, if the present strategy of the organisation is not achieving its performance goals (return on investment etc.); second, if there is a significant change in the environment of the business, requiring the retail organisation to reposition itself; third, the firm may wish to expand, and this will require strategic decisions regarding the increased size of the organisation, the rate of growth, the appropriate direction of expansion and the means (for example, acquisitions) of achieving this goal.

In any of these three situations the firm will have to reassess itself in terms of the environmental and resource variables set out in Tables 4.2 and 4.3 above and adopt an appropriate new strategy. The extent of change from the existing strategy required will depend upon the size of the performance gap or the change in environmental variables. It is also worthwhile bearing in mind that the extent of change which an organisation is capable of undertaking may be constrained by some of its resource variables, and not least the present management.

The first two situations outlined at the beginning of this section (performance gap and changed environment) should not, if diagnosed sufficiently early, require dramatic strategic change on the part of the firm. Such change is likely to fall into the category of repositioning within the firm's existing market area; and this will be carried out after an assessment of the relevant environmental and resource variables.

Very few organisations, and in particular retailers who are in direct contact with the consuming public, are faced with a static environment. Movements in economic and social variables will have an immediate impact upon retail demand; and very seldom is an increase in national income equally distributed among all age, social class or sex groups. Women, for example, play a much more important part in family income and in expenditure decisions now than in the past. This has resulted from increased activity rates on the part of married women in the labour force as well as the generally changed role of women in society. Similarly, increases in earnings and disposable income in any period may vary considerably among social groups, with such differences possibly being reversed in a subsequent period as a result of economic conditions or government policy. Finally, the birth rate, and consequently the age structure of the population, can behave in a quite marked cyclical manner, producing significant changes in the basis of demand for children's clothing, house furnishings, and in the 'Methuselah market' catering for spending by retired people.[34] Furthermore, retailers must respond to changes in the strategies of competitors and also to general trends in retailing, including that phenomenon referred to as the wheel of retailing.[35] This evolution, it is argued, creates a broad upward movement in the standard of retail services provided, caused both by a general increase in the standards of living in the economy and also a tendency for each new form of retailing (department stores, chain stores, discount centres) to compete over time by gradually increasing the level of retail services provided and thus the costs of distribution.

Beyond these changes requiring ongoing adjustments to their strategy by retailers there are three further areas in particular which deserve attention. These are vertical integration, diversification, and the role of acquisitions in retail strategy. Thes are dealt with in three subsections below.

Vertical Integration

Operating at previous stages in the production–distribution chain is a strategic option open to most retailers and may be adopted for a number of reasons. We shall look at this strategic option almost entirely from the point of view of the retailing organisation which has integrated backward, although some mention wil be made of decisions by manufacturers to integrate forward into retailing.

Michael Porter provides a very lucid analysis of the strategic case for vertical integration.[36] From the point of view of the retailer the principal advantages of backward vertical integration may be stated as shown in Table 4.5.

This taxonomy of the gains from vertical integration distinguishes between economies of integration, which are the more immediate and accessible gains from a vertical integration strategy, and the longer term, broader advantages of the policy. Thus where it is possible, combined manufacturing and retailing of the product may allow the retailer to enjoy higher profit margins or charge a lower price because certain costs have been eliminated in combining the two processes in close proximity. Other than instances such as 'the factory shop', however, this is not likely to be a source of major economies as retailing occurs on a widely dispersed scale and is unlikely to be efficiently physically combined with manufacture. A more fruitful source of economies of integration is that of internal control and co-ordination of manufacturing and distribution and the avoidance of certain information gathering and market transactions costs where a retailer possesses manufacturing capacity. Here, ideally, the retailer's shops and associated market research provide the retailer-manufacturer with clearer information on which to make production decisions. There can thus be a stable co-ordinated flow of goods from factory to shops with lower stockholding levels, a reduction in certain transaction

---

Table 4.5
Advantages of Vertical Integration in Retailing

Economies of integration:
    cost economies in combined manufacture/retailing
    economies of internal control and co-ordination
    avoidance of market-related costs
    stable manufacturer/retailer relationships
Knowledge of manufacturing technology
Assurance of supply
Offsetting bargaining power of suppliers

costs, and a more rapid response at the production stage to a requirement for change in quality or style of output. In particular where there is a stable manufacturing–retailing relationship within a single organisation then special and possibly experimental requirements in terms of product or packaging quality or design may be undertaken by the manufacturing unit which it would not be possible to obtain at a similar cost from an independent organisation.

The remainder of the advantages of vertical integration as set out by Porter relate to broader gains which a retailer may achieve through some degree of integration. Thus an integrated retailer will obtain some useful knowledge of the manufacturing process involved in the goods distributed, and this may lead to a clearer understanding of manufacturing costs (with the opportunity of reducing these) and possibilities for using manufacturing techniques to create advantage at the retail stage through product improvements.

One of the most discussed advantages of backward vertical integration is the assurance of supply to which this should give rise, and we shall see below the various ways in which retailers can obtain this advantage of integration. The final strategic gain from vertical integration is concerned with the structuring of the seller–buyer relationship between retailers and their suppliers. As we saw in the previous chapter the balance of power in many consumer markets already lies very much with the distributors. There is thus very little incentive in the UK at the present time for retailers to integrate backwards into manufacture in order to eliminate excess profits being made by their suppliers. The very possibility of this integration, or its existence on a small scale, is sufficient along with other market structure characteristics to maintain the dominance of retailers in many markets.

To set against these possible advantages for retailers in backward integration there are also actual or potential costs. The major one is the capital investment required for full vertical integration, combined with the issue of how cost-efficient such an investment is likely to be. This cost efficiency will be governed by the scale of the investment, the capacity to which it is regularly operated, and the competence of retailing management in controlling the facility. Where such manufacturing plant is established at well below the level at which economies of scale are to be gained, where the plant frequently operates at below capacity (leaving the organisation to carry a high level of unit fixed costs), and if retail management is not attuned to controlling manufacturing operations then whatever the advantages of such an integration strategy in terms of assurance of supply, the cost is obviously going to be high.[37] Again relating to upstream output levels, any significant mismatch between the capacity of the manufacturing unit and the requirements of the retailing organisation is likely to reduce the effectiveness of an integration strategy as either the excess output of the manufacturing facility has to be sold in the market, or occasional requirements of the retailing division not met by in-house capacity have to be obtained from outside suppliers who are aware that they are very much a back-up facility to the integrated organisation's own manufacturing capacity.

Thus in addition to the question of possible shorter term gains or strategic benefits from a policy of integration, as well as the issue of transferability of retail management skills to manufacture, distributors must bear in mind the reaction of their suppliers to the adoption of this policy. The history of W. H. Smith highlights the firm's sensitivities on this issue. Not only was the firm quite cautious at an earlier stage in its history in taking on printing or publishing work on a large scale which would conflict with its distributor relationship with other publishers, but the firm has also had to accommodate to the sensitivities of its retailer customers who may feel that Smith's own retail outlets benefit unduly from the firm's wholesaling activities. Thus

the modest rate of expansion of [Smith's] modern shops in the 1950s may be partly explained by the fear that existed throughout the wholesale division that the independent retailers whom they supplied would be upset by the appearance in their trading area of a Smith retail branch. . . . retailers could be disadvantaged by their wholesaler if he was also a retailer.[38]

In practice the degree of vertical integration among retailers and the reasons for adopting the policy vary considerably. At one extreme, forward vertical integration at an early stage in the development of the industry by footwear manufacturers has produced a present situation where 60 per cent of footwear sales to consumers is accounted for by integrated organisations. J. Sears, for example, unashamedly acquired retail outlets in order to help sell the output of its shoe factories. Originally 'the shops simply serviced the factory'. Now, however, with Sears' 3500 retail outlets accounting for one quarter of the UK market only 18 per cent of the firm's shoe sales come from its own factories, and the footwear strategy of the group is very much retail market dominated.[39] A more recent case of a manufacturing organisation integrating forward to obtain satisfactory distribution arrangements is that of Sir Terence Conran who established the chain of Habitat stores in the mid 1960s as a response to his dissatisfaction with existing furniture retailers.[40] Montague Burton, on the other hand, began as a clothing retailer in 1901, but by 1910 found that it had to acquire its own manufacturing capacity in order to pursue its novel retailing strategy of supplying low-price made-to-measure suits.[41] Boots the Chemist also integrated backwards from its retail origins at a very early stage in its development in order to ensure supplies of its own particular medicines, and especially as a means of achieving the firm's low-price policy which was the key to its early rapid expansion.[42] More recently, however, Burton has shed its suit manufacturing capacity in order to concentrate its managerial efforts and skills upon retailing, conscious of the fact that possession of manufacturing capacity by retailers can lead to shops being treated as captive outlets for integrated upstream (manufacturing) facilities.

The larger food distributors do not normally follow a policy of vertical integration in the sense of possessing food processing facilities. Sainsbury, however, has integrated backward into the production of a number of its own label foods in order to control quality and to give it an insight into manufacturing or processing activities so that it can discuss these matters on a more informed basis with its outside suppliers. The firm even has a prize-winning herd of Aberdeen Angus cattle.[43]

In order to achieve the advantages of a policy of vertical integration retailers need not necessarily make a fixed capital investment in manufacturing plant. Vertical quasi integration, as one economist has called it, is a situation in which, by virtue of his importance to his suppliers as a 'large customer', a retailer is able to enjoy many of the benefits of vertical integration without the costs of having to invest in a fixed supply of his requirements.[44] Retailer 'large customers', who account for a significant proportion of their suppliers' sales, and the withdrawal of whose custom may cause short-term losses for manufacturers, may obtain the advantages of very competitive prices, flexible takeup quantities and satisfaction of special requirements in the manufacture of the product while having no capital invested in production capacity. Thus the previously rapidly growing discount furniture chain Harris Queensway, for example, was able to obtain many of the advantages of being a large customer relative to some household furniture manufacturers. Christie-Tyler committed 20 per cent of its total output to Harris, with some items being manufactured exclusively for that chain. On the basis of this relationship, according to *Management Today*, 'Harris will not only get bespoke sofas, but also power to control output in the Lebus (Christie-Tyler) factory, switching production lines as necessary to meet the stores' changing stock requirements'.[45] Perhaps the best known exponent of this strategy is Marks & Spencer. A crucial part of Marks' retailing strategy has been to develop a very close relationship with its suppliers, the firm seeing itself from its earliest days as an 'interpreter to industry' through its stores of the needs and tastes of the public.[46] As a result of its specification buying from suppliers and the very close control operated by Marks, the firm has been variously dubbed a manufacturer without factories or a manufacturer in disguise, or in the company's own words operating in 'partnership with its suppliers'. From some of its suppliers Marks & Spencer takes around 90 per cent of their output, although the proportion is more normally 30–50 per cent.[47] It is by all accounts a situation which provides this retailer with very tight control over merchandise quality, extremely competitive prices, and flexibility of supply – all without any of the capital investment and the inflexibilities associated with traditional backward vertical integration.

Diversification

The policy of a firm expanding simultaneously into a number of different markets is a common feature of business strategy. The advantages normally sought are an increase in the rate of growth through breaking out from dependence upon expansion within a single market area, and a reduction in business risk resulting from spreading one's activities over a number of distinct market areas. In addition, retailers may become more diversified as a result of adding new product lines to their range which are a natural expansion of their existing activities. W. H. Smith, for example, expanded its product range into gramophone records in the 1960s, video cassettes and cassette players in the 1970s, and satellite broadcasting and cable television in the 1980s as an extension of its commitment to reading and leisure activities.[48]

In strategic terms the contrast of specialisation and diversification in retailing is not necessarily straightforward. Knee and Walters, for example, outline a number of 'specialisation' strategies which may none the less in some cases give the appearance of diversification. These specialisations comprise a particular market direction (Mothercare), product specialisation (MFI), service specialisation (Harrods), and (low) price specialisation (Kwik Save).[49] These are in fact examples of a particular *strategic focus* by the firms involved; and the adoption of such a focus does not necessarily preclude product or geographical diversification, always provided that the particular focus can be translated to other product or geographical areas.

Once a retailer has established a particular strategic focus, and provided the conditions obtain which allow that focus to be transferred, increased rates of growth and a wider spread of risk may be achieved by diversification. The most obvious form of this is to add to one's existing product range. This may be undertaken, for example, through adding womenswear to menswear lines as Burton did quite early in its history, or through expansion by food retailers into non-food areas. Part of the very rapid growth achieved by Tesco in the 1960s was the result of a planned extension from groceries into clothing and household products through its Home 'n' Wear departments. Within five years non-food sales accounted for almost 10 per cent of Tesco's supermarket turnover, and the group now (1989) devotes more than 30 per cent of its total sales area to non-grocery products.[50] Boots the Chemist, which commenced retail business with a fairly narrow range of pharmacy products, gradually moved up market with an increased range of merchandise. The firm not only added baby foods, cosmetics and toiletries, but also now has a department-store range of goods including luggage, jewellery, electrical, photographic, stationery and audio equipment (records, cassettes, stereo equipment). This product range extension and the standard of customer service offered in Boots' larger stores has moved Boots away from its position as a chemist multiple into the department store category.[51]

The development of Tesco also exemplifies an element of geographical diversification as the firm began too in the 1960s to move out from its established base in London and the Home Counties to the Midlands, the North and into Scotland, seeking out larger conurbations and centres of population where shoppers would respond to large-scale self-service distribution.[52] A natural extension to this policy is overseas expansion of retailing operations. A number of UK-based retailers, including C & A, Mothercare, Dixons, Burton and W. H. Smith, have expanded overseas. These efforts have not been uniformly successful as even proven retailing formulae in the

UK have been found difficult to transplant to other economic and social environments. W. H. Smith followed its newspaper, periodical and book reading public overseas in the early years of this century: France and Belgium before 1914, Canada after the Second World War, and more recently the United States.[53] Even in this case, however, despite Smith's successful retailing approach in the UK the path of overseas ventures has not been smooth. An early Canadian executive reported that 'exporting *retailing* was a terribly difficult thing to do', and the recently acquired US interests continue to make losses.[54] Again even Marks & Spencer, with a successful track record in the UK, has experienced a relatively slow build-up of its overseas interests. Marks' multinational operations began in 1972 with a local joint venture in Canada. Subsequent overseas expansion encountered a situation where, according to a senior manager, 'Each foreign store has been plagued with problems', largely created by national differences in taste and style, lack of existing local familiarity with Marks & Spencer retailing formula, and general problems of managing overseas operations.[55]

Diversification in retailing, which normally involves the extension of a chosen retailing strategy to new product or geographical areas, is an appropriate policy for increasing growth, reducing risk or adding new related products. The adoption of additional retailing forms for existing products – such as mail order – may also be classed as diversification. As with diversification in the remainder of the economy, however, it is easy for retailing management to underestimate the transition involved in moving into new market areas; and certainly the time period over which this can be successfully achieved may be protracted. Successful retailers, on the other hand, often possess a unique focus or differentiation which may well be capable of being profitably transplanted into neighbouring product fields or over a wider geographic area.

Mergers and Acquisitions

Leaving aside those situations where a retail organisation is acquired by a non-retailing enterprise (such as the series of retailing acquisitions by Guinness in the early 1980s), merger or acquisition is an important dimension of longer-term strategy for retailers. Certainly the retail sector was a full participant in the upsurge of merger/acquisition activity in the UK during the 1980s; and those fundamental forces at work in this sector to encourage acquisitions – such as computerisation of retailing operations and scarcity of good retail sites – are considered likely to continue to prevail for some time.[56]

As in the case of business in general, there are three principal attractions to retailers of mergers or acquisitions. First, the acquisition or external route to business growth is far speedier than that of internal or organic development; and the external route is particularly attractive where there are physical or legislative constraints upon the speed of business growth as in the case of retail sites. Thus, for example, at the time of the Burton bid for Debenhams in August 1985 it was accepted that this £567m expansion by Burton would have taken the firm perhaps a decade to achieve without resort to acquisition.[57] The importance of acquisitions in longer-term growth also comes through strongly in the case of Dollond & Aitchison, the retail ophthalmic opticians. At the time of the merger of the two original businesses in 1927 there were fewer than thirty branches; but as a result almost entirely of acquisitions of other chains or independent opticians the Dollond & Aitchison group expanded to 268 branches in 1969 and to 452 by 1985. The pace of growth may be judged by the fact that at an early stage in this rapid growth the firms acquired some 28 individual practices in not much more than one year, that in 1968 the group multiplied the number of branches by three within six weeks, and that in the early 1980s a rapid series of four acquisitions enlarged the group from 300 to 450 branches 'at a stroke'.[58] Clearly this growth was achieved at a speed which could not have been accomplished by internal expansion.

The second attraction of acquisition in business strategy is the immediate access which takeover gives both to resources – supplies, premises etc. – and to market share. In the case of Dollond & Aitchison expansion by acquisition provided a supply of trained opticians. In a highly competitive market such as food retailing there are very limited prospects for rapid internal growth, which would inevitably have to be achieved by price or other forms of competition with existing sellers and which would upset the balance of competition in the market. The acquisition route, on the other hand, allowed Dee Corporation to expand rapidly in this virtually static market, increasing its estimated food and drink market share from 5.4 per cent to 8.5 per cent with the acquisition of the Fine Fare and Shoppers Paradise chains in June 1986.[59] The merger of Asda and MFI early in 1985 may likewise be seen as an example of two businesses each seeking to pool their resources and expertise in developing large out-of-town shopping sites, and also to respond to the existence of very powerful competitors both in grocery and furniture retailing.[60]

The third attraction of acquisitions in retail business development is the access which these give to existing management insight and experience in a market area. One is, so to speak, buying a corporate vehicle which has been run in. Thus acquisitions are likely to be particularly a feature of diversifying retail expansion such as that of Dee Corporation into sports goods, and the rapid diversification of Ward White (originally a shoe manufacturer and retailer) into motoring accessories (Halfords), department stores (Owen Owen), DIY (Payless) and confectionery and toys (Maynards).[61] While some retail groups such as Marks & Spencer appear to be content to diversify and expand more tentatively by internal development – introducing classical music records and tapes into some of its stores and experimenting with mail order in 1986 – acquisition is frequently regarded as being required for any more rapid growth or for developments taking retailers outwith their existing range of merchandise.

As with all takeover strategies, however, retail management must consider whether it has the resources to manage an acquisition or merger. Much depends upon the competence of the existing management of the acquired firm (and whether this will remain effectively within the enlarged business) together with the relatedness of the acquisition to the acquiring firm. Retailers wishing to diversify rapidly in response to market changes will be particularly attracted to the acquisition route. Marks & Spencer, on the other hand, has been very conscious of the difficulties involved in controlling a large number of stores, and has placed its greatest emphasis upon internal development and enlargement of its existing outlets rather than acquisitions. Between 1927 and 1939 the company increased the number of its stores from 126 to 234.[62] The number in the UK stood at 289 in 1990; but between 1939 and 1990 UK turnover, net of VAT, rose from £23 448 000 to more than £3bn. Marks' unique style of trading, including its special relationship with suppliers and a desire for a fairly high degree of centralisation, have largely dictated an internal growth path. This has not, however, prevented fairly rapid expansion of the firm to high levels of market share in some clothing sectors. Sainsbury too has concentrated upon expanding output per store as a major means of growth. The number of food stores at the present time (around 250) has not changed much from 1950, and the present chairman has expressed the view 'Do not be misled by the number of stores. It is turnover per store that counts'.[63]

The problems associated with the development of acquisition strategies, choice of partner and implementation have, in retailing as in the remainder of the economy, given rise on occasions to divestment of previous acquisitions and even the break-up of large-scale mergers. The coming together of Asda and MFI in 1985 to enable the former to diversify in order to escape the market saturation and competition of the food retailing sector and to allow both firms to pool their out-of-town retailing expertise, was broken up in 1987. Changes in the combined market environment and a better prospect of each company developing separately led to the break-up, following which both organisations have successfully pursued individual strategies.[64]

4.5 Strategic Implementation and Control

Implementation and control of strategy is now increasingly recognised as one of the most important dimensions of strategic management.[65] Strategic implementation in detail involves the following steps set out in Table 4.6.

The starting point for any strategic implementation and control system is a clearly formulated set of strategic objectives. These objectives should be expressed in clear, verifiable form, agreed with senior management, and communicated across the organisation. It is on the basis of these objectives that the key strategic tasks are identified and allocated, with provision being made for co-ordination of delegated actions. A management information system is necessary to provide for implementation of strategy and as a basis for collecting information on performance, control and appraisal. The last two steps in the sequence in Table 4.6 involve an element of judgement in relating divisional or departmental management performance to rewards, and in interpreting any underperformance as arising from poor strategy, inadequate administration or faulty operations. That is, the system of strategic control should motivate managers efficiently, and help to distinguish the level (strategy/operations) at which corrective action is required.

The early stages in the sequence in Table 4.6 relate very much to internal organisation structure. Research since the 1960s has identified organisation structure as an important determinant of strategic success, and there is more recent empirical evidence which suggests a causal relationship in manufacturing industry between profit performance and the choice of the appropriate organisation structure.[66] The task in designing the organisation structure of a retail business is to achieve that blend of centralisation and decentralisation which will provide scope for initiative and response to local circumstances at the individual store or departmental level yet allow tight strategic control at the centre to ensure the presentation of a common differentiated image throughout the group and to take advantage of centralised buying and other economies.

The trend towards the adoption of an organisation-wide national image for individual store groups, the availability of operational and administrative economies of scale from centralising particular functions, and the benefits of presenting a united purchasing front to suppliers have all tended to keep retail organisations relatively centralised in their management structures. More recently, however, a trend towards some form of decentralisation within retail organisations has occurred. This, it is argued, is a function of the increased size and complexity of these businesses, together with particular

---

Table 4.6
Strategic Implementation and Control Actions

- Identification of objectives and key tasks to be performed
- Allocation of each task to individuals (delegation)
- Provision for co-ordination of separated tasks
- Design and installation of appropriate management information system
- Drawing up of specific programmes of action, including time schedules and operating budgets/standards
- Design of a system for comparison of actual and budgeted performance
- Design of a system of incentives/penalties for individuals or departments relating to actual/budget performance
- Any resulting review of strategy, administration or operations

---

strategies adopted in response to changes in the nature of competition in retail markets. A number of multiple-shop retail organisations initially developed and expanded on the basis of a 'low-cost leadership' strategy appropriate to trading in relatively undifferentiated markets with an emphasis on price competition.[67] At this stage of development their low-cost strategy – dependent upon maximising purchasing and operating economies – dictated a centralised, functional organisation structure which a number of retail organisations have retained. However, as multiple-shop retail organisations have greatly increased in size and merchandise range, both by internal growth and through acquisition, and as maturing retail markets have dictated a movement away from entirely price-based competitive strategies to differentiation, some form of organisational decentralisation through multidivisionalisation has proved necessary. Many of these large retail organisations now see themselves as operating a portfolio of related but differentiated business units.[68] An example is Sears' British Shoe Corporation which has 24 per cent of the UK retail footwear market. While BSC came to dominate the High Street footwear market largely on the basis of low-cost leadership, its strategic emphasis is now upon differentiation and a recognition that the firm is competing in a portfolio of market segments. Accordingly BSC now operates through four market-directed divisions: 'quality' (Saxone and Manfield), 'family' (Freeman, Hardy & Willis, and Trueform), 'fashion' (Dolcis), and 'volume' (Curtess and Shoe City). Each of these separate divisions is responsible for the creation of its own strategic image in the market, and as a reflection of this has its own merchandise buying team.[69]

In other retail markets there may have to be a different balance between centralisation and decentralisation depending upon market conditions and business strategy. The need for a blend of profit-based divisionalisation and functional centralisation in retailing led Channon in his study of structure and performance in the service industries to identify the 'critical function structure' as an appropriate organisation form in this sector. Thus in a multiple retailing firm individual stores or regional groups may be profit centres with considerable autonomy. Central headquarters, however, will be responsible for merchandise and pricing policies; and in Channon's view the lack of success of certain non-food store groups such as House of Fraser and Debenhams in the 1960s and 1970s was due to the failure adequately to centralise and control the critical function of merchandising.[70]

The size and strategy of many large retailers today means that they do not see themselves as passive distributors of what manufacturers feel customers want or can be persuaded to buy. The initiative in much consumer goods marketing has passed to retailers – as exemplified by the dominance in many areas of own label products – who now see themselves as interpreting and responding positively to consumer tastes. The difficult task, as we said above, is to reconcile the role of the branch manager in a centralised retail organisation – described with reference to Sainsbury as 'controlling a prescribed set of tasks'[71] – with the exercise of skills and initiative at this level which can considerably influence store or department performance.

Assuming that a retail organisation can achieve the initial steps in the sequence in Table 4.6, two particular issues arise in performance reporting in this sector. The first is the level at which performance is measured within the organisation, the second is the choice of performance measure. Normally a retailing organisation will be able to identify operating divisions within itself which will constitute 'strategic business units'. These may be branches in a multiple shop organisation or product areas within a department store.[72] In the case of the former (branch shops) where a range of different goods are sold – groceries, newspapers, cigarettes and tobacco – it may be desirable to measure performance at the product level, and information technology is making this increasingly possible at relatively low cost.

The issues of *where* to measure business performance and *what* to measure overlap as it becomes necessary to distinguish between those strategic costs from which a divisional manager benefits but which are not controlled by him, and those costs which he can directly influence.[73] Performance should be assessed at the strategic business unit level where a particular product or product group environment is encountered, and where a unique group of resources is based which is controlled by the divisional manager. At this level a single individual should be identified with the management of the unit.

Turning to the matter of what should be measured, the crucial issue is to link divisional, unit or departmental performance measures or objectives to the corporate goals. This involves the choice both of the measurement variable and the time horizon. If the ultimate goal of the organisation is expressed as a target return on investment then this has to be translated into a business unit goal, often in a situation where not all of the operating costs of the whole organisation can be attributed to, say, each department in a department store, and where in particular there may be no possibility of identifying 'capital employed' in a department. One approximation at the unit level is the sales margin: (sales revenue less all identifiable costs)/revenue. Bearing in mind that at the corporate level return on investment is equal to the sales margin times capital turnover (i.e. sales/capital employed), the sales margin, along with data on sales per square foot etc. is a very good approximation to return on investment at the departmental level. The result of this may be the establishment of an *average* target sales margin for each department; and subsidiary ratios contributing to this especially in retailing, such as sales per square foot of selling space and sales per employee, will also be controlled by comparison of targets and actual performance.[74] The divisional manager will obviously attempt to achieve his average sales margin by optimising the combination of sales margins on his range of goods, thus producing different mark-ups on individual product lines reflecting the particular burden of these lines upon departmental costs, and also market factors such as different price elasticities of demand for individual items. It would, of course, be similarly open to a department store to set different sales margin targets for individual departments if it considered that there were inherent differences in their profitability, or arising from a different burden upon selling space, or different consumer reaction to higher prices.

Some further flexibility in the area of sales margin targets is required in response to particular situations such as local competition; and in addition to this senior management should adopt a longer-term view in relation to new developments such as the introduction of a new line of merchandise, which may require lower sales margin targets in the shorter term.

4.6 Conclusions

In a review of Knee and Walters's text in the inaugural issue of the *International Journal of Retailing* the view was expressed that there were considerable barriers to management acceptance and implementation of strategic planning in retailing. These barriers, it was considered, emanated from the values, ideologies and historical development of retailing companies.[75] A comprehensive article on grocery retailing at about the same time concluded,

> Retailers in general appear to have a negative attitude to strategic planning and so far they have been slow to adopt planning processes as integral parts of managerial activity. . . . our experience of grocery retailing in the United Kingdom suggests that only the top three or four firms can be said to be using any recognisable and consistent form of strategic planning.[76]

Whatever the historical or intellectual inertia may be in this respect, conditions in retail markets at the present time make it essential that managements take a strategic view of their organisations. 'Retail is detail' doubtless still applies to many aspects of this sector of distribution. Wider developments in retailing, however, dictate the adoption of a strategic approach. Foremost among these is the increased competitiveness in retail markets experienced by all sizes of firms as many of these markets reach maturity characterised by low sales growth rates. This makes analysis of the business environment, identification of attractive market areas, and the adoption of appropriate differentiation strategies essential for retailing success. Furthermore, the abandonment by most retailers of low-price, cost-led competition in favour of differentiation strategies demands a clear understanding by managers of the nature of retail markets in terms of the bases of consumer preferences and buying behaviour, the strengths and strategies of competitors, and the consequent relative strategic 'positioning' by retail organisations.[77]

A second feature of retail markets requiring a strategic approach is the increased scope for product diversification and the breakdown of traditional market boundaries in retailing. One can now buy a cuddly teddy bear at the local garage, choose from a range of shoes in Marks & Spencer which now has more than 5 per cent of the market, purchase a car at the grocery superstore, buy and sell shares in a department store, or buy gramophone records at

'Boots the Chemist'. With regard to the retailing of a range of financial services the distinction between banks and building societies is rapidly disappearing. The implications of this collapse of traditional product boundaries in retailing are not only that competition for more specialist shops now comes from a variety of sources but also that while it is possible for retailers to seek growth in a much wider range of markets than previously, there is a corresponding need for accurate assessment of the opportunities and threats over a greater area together with the strengths and weaknesses of the organisation itself.

A third development of strategic significance is the greater capital intensiveness and extended time horizon now characteristic of retailing developments. The increased fixed costs of retailing (site costs, other capital expenditures and management overheads) make profits much more sensitive to sales volumes and exact heavy penalties for poor choice and implementation of strategies. Similarly, increased lead times in acquiring retail sites and building larger stores make it particularly important that careful strategic analysis is carried out in the first instance.

The complexity of retail organisations is further emphasised not only by the size of their sales turnover and capital investment programmes but also by the fact that the largest retailers are operating a number of chains of stores which must each be viewed as strategic business units. Thus Harris Queensway not only diversified into toys in building up a chain of Hamleys shops but also operated Times Furnishing, Harris Carpets, Mad Max, Queensway and General George, among others, as separate chains. W. H. Smith adopts the same approach in operating Our Price, Paper Chase, and Sheratt & Hughes as well as the Do It All out-of-town DIY stores separately from the more traditional W. H. Smith shops.[78]

A frequently heard argument from retail managers (and those in other market areas also) is that in retailing in particular the rate of change in the market is so rapid that long-term strategic planning is not worthwhile. Successful retailing, it is claimed, is about efficient response to changing consumer wants. Such rapid rates of change do not, however, in any way undermine the case for strategic retail planning. Rather, despite the uncertainty of the future retailing environment it is even more important to think about the broad nature of possible market developments and the appropriate strategic response to these: very much along the lines of the Futures Committee at Burton whose job is to advise the board on the impact of trends in society on the pattern of retailing.[79]

Strategy is also of course about the detail of planning and implementing a chosen policy; and in regard to retailing as in other markets, the literature emphasises a distinction between the more formal, normative approach to strategy making largely adopted in this chapter and the everyday reality of strategic planning. Consideration of this 'reality' leads us to accept that few strategic decisions in business come about in the form of a radical 'big bang', but that progress in strategic change is incremental, with the history of the business, its past strategies and present resources having a considerable influence on both strategic choice and implementation.[80] In addition to these aspects of realism in business strategy there are the elements of the unique perception of individual managers, power within the organisation, and interactive decision making which influence which strategy is adopted. From such a perspective strategy change is seen 'as the product of managerial style, sense-making, and interaction as distinct from "technical" competence and experience *per se*'.[81] We would not, however, see this perspective as detracting in any way from the value of the prescriptive strategic analysis of retail business offered in this chapter. The approach and techniques put forward above – involving the establishment of retailing organisation objectives, the analysis of the relevant environment and resources, the subsequent choice of optimal strategy through market segmentation and differentiation, followed by strategic implementation action – clearly need to be recognised by middle and senior retailing management. So also do wider and longer-term strategic issues and behaviour such as vertical integration and even internationalisation, along with acquisitions or joint ventures. The evidence, as we have seen, is quite strong that choosing and implementing appropriate strategies improves business performance; and retail organisations are now too large, complex and sophisticated to be guided solely on the basis of entrepreneurial flair and attention to operational detail.

References

1. This section draws heavily upon the author's text *Corporate Strategy* (London: Macmillan, 1986) Ch. 1.
2. H. I. Ansoff, *Corporate Strategy* (Harmondsworth: Penguin, 1968) p. 9.
3. A. Chandler, *Strategy and Structure: Chapters in the History of the Industrial Enterprise* (Cambridge, Mass.: MIT Press, 1962) p. 13.
4. K. R. Andrews, 'Corporate Strategy as a Vital Function of the Board', *Harvard Business Review*, November–December 1981, p. 180.
5. Ansoff, *Corporate Strategy*, pp. 17–22.
6. This sequence is based upon a more extended one in D. F. Harvey, *Business Policy and Strategic Management* (Columbus, Ohio: Charles E. Merrill Publishing, 1982) Ch. 1.
7. See P. H. Grinyer and D. Norburn, 'Strategic Planning in 21 U.K. Companies', *Long Range Planning*, August 1974, pp. 80–8.
8. See M. Leontiades, *Strategies for Diversification and Change* (Boston: Little, Brown & Co., 1980) p. 63–4.
9. See M. Corina, *Pile it High, Sell it Cheap* (London: Weidenfeld & Nicolson, 1971); and K. K. Tse, *Marks & Spencer* (Oxford: Pergamon Press, 1985).
10. See *Financial Times*, 6 June 1986.
11. See the chapter on (Sir) Terence Conran in W. Kay, *Tycoons* (London: Piatkus, 1985) pp. 38–9.
12. See 'Paying the price of dear money', *Financial Times*, 27 May 1989; and 'A ghastly shopping season in store', *Sunday Times*, 15 October 1989.
13. For a retailer's broad view on this see I. MacLaurin, 'Food Retailing in the Eighties – Technological Opportunities and Social Constraints', *Long Range*

Planning, February 1982, pp. 40–6. Mr (now Sir) MacLaurin is managing director of Tesco Stores (Holdings) Ltd.

14. Labour costs account for about half of retail operating expenses, and as a percentage of sales these are generally between 10 per cent and 20 per cent lower in supermarkets than in smaller grocery shops. See J. A. N. Bamfield, 'The Changing Face of British Retailing', *National Westminster Bank Quarterly Review*, May 1980, p. 35.

15. See, for example, in G. Rees, *St. Michael: A History of Marks & Spencer* (London: Weidenfeld & Nicolson, 1969) p. 112.

16. This figure was given as the capital spending budget of Tesco for 1986, involving the opening of eleven new superstores. See *Financial Times*, 6 May 1986. More recent data suggest that Sainsbury may spend about £500 million in new stores in 1991. See *Sunday Times*, 3 February 1991.

17. It was the retail sector in the 1950s that pioneered the sale-and-leaseback arrangement whereby, following a takeover, shop properties were sold to financial institutions which leased them on a long-term basis to their previous owners. Early exponents of this technique were Charles Clore of J. Sears & Co. and the first Lord Fraser of Allander. See W. Davis, *Merger Mania* (London: Constable, 1970) Ch. 2.

18. Henry Smith referred in this contex to 'the case of Woolworth's . . . where the salesman is a nonentity behind the counter, neither informing nor influencing the consumer, but merely engaged in collecting money and preventing petty larceny'. While the terminology is perhaps a little extreme it does suggest a contrast in staffing policy between different retailing organisations. See H. Smith, *Retail Distribution* (London: CUP, 2nd edn, 1948) p. 26.

19. See *Financial Times*, 6 May 1986.

20. Ibid., 6 June 1986.

21. Ibid., 26 April 1986.

22. See D. Knee and D. Walters, *Strategy in Retailing* (Oxford: Philip Allan, 1985) Ch. 2.

23. Quoted in G. Havenhand, *Nation of Shopkeepers* (London: Eyre & Spottiswoode, 1970) p. 103.

24. 'Littlewoods looks to the mums', *Sunday Times*, 20 April 1986.

25. This table is based upon factors listed in Knee and Walters, *Strategy in Retailing*, p. 25.

26. In common with a number of store groups, however, Marks & Spencer now offers credit facilities through its chargecard, and in 1986 these accounted for 8 per cent of UK turnover. See *Financial Times*, 9 August 1986.

27. For a short account of the importance of this see 'Mothercare: How Conran gave birth to a new image', *Marketing Week*, 22 July 1983, pp. 40–1.

28. Rees, *St. Michael*, p. 66.

29. Ibid., p. 58.

30. Tse, *Marks & Spencer*, p. 25.

31. See Rees, *St. Michael*, p. 58. Subsequent expansion of its food departments from the late 1950s has reduced the proportion of turnover accounted for by clothing to around one half, with food sales making up slightly less than 40 per cent of the total. See Marks & Spencer Annual Reports.

32. See M. Wray, *The Women's Outerwear Industry* (London: Duckworth, 1957) pp. 152–3.

33. See Corina, *Pile it High, Sell it Cheap*, pp. 95, 118 and 192.

34. See A. C. Tynan and J. Drayton, 'The Methuselah Market Part II: Decision Making and the Older Consumer', *Journal of Marketing Management*, Winter 1985, pp. 213–21.

35. See M. P. McNair and E. G. May, 'The Next Revolution of the Retailing Wheel', *Harvard Business Review*, September–October 1978, pp. 81–91.

36. See M. E. Porter, *Competitive Strategy* (New York: Free Press, 1980) Ch. 14.
37. Although it is less susceptible to precise analysis than some of the other variables involved in the vertical integration decision, the issue of the transferabilty of management skills between retailing and manufacturing is an important one. Instancing the withdrawal of department stores from manufacturing one author commented that 'such extensions to the manufacturing sector usually spread the energies and the mental resources of the (retail) management over too wide a field.' H. Pasdermadjian, The *Department Store* (London: Newman Books, 1954) p. 112.
38. C. Wilson, *First with the News: The History of W. H. Smith 1792–1972* (London: Jonathan Cape, 1985) pp. 267–8, 302, 399 and 403.
39. Sears' principal footwear retail outlets are Freeman Hardy & Willis, Dolcis, Lilley & Skinner, Saxone, Manfield and Trueform. See 'The Sears Group of Companies', *Euromoney*, July 1985 (Supplement).
40. See Kay, *Tycoons*.
41. For further details see Burton Group Ltd case in J. M. Stopford *et al.*, *British Business Policy* (London: Macmillan, 1975) pp. 152–71.
42. The firm's founder Sir Jesse Boot 'insisted that he could make most chemist's goods more cheaply than he could buy them, . . . constantly substituting products of their own make for those bought from other manufacturers'. See S. Chapman, *Jesse Boot of Boots the Chemist* (London: Hodder & Stoughton, 1974) p. 91.
43. See *J S 100: The Story of Sainsbury's* (London: J. Sainsbury, 1969) p. 86. One direction in which retailers may choose to integrate vertically is physical distribution from warehouses or regional distribution centres to individual stores. It is generally held that the internalisation of physical distribution which multiple retailers have achieved through vertical integration of this function has conferred upon them a number of operational and other benefits, including greater bargaining power in negotiating with their suppliers. However, although multiple grocery retailers have continued to exert direct control over physical distribution, around 70 per cent of this is now carried out by third party operators such as Exel Logistics, Christian Salvesen and Tibbett & Britten who are employed by the large-scale retailers. See A. C. McKinnon, *Physical Distribution Systems* (London: Routledge, 1989) pp. 65–72; and *Financial Times*, 15 May 1990.
44. See K. J. Blois, 'Vertical Quasi-Integration', *Journal of Industrial Economics*, July 1972, pp. 253–72.
45. See D. Isaac, 'Harris Queensway's Flying Carpet', *Management Today*, January 1984, p. 56.
46. Tse, *Marks & Spencer*, p. 21.
47. See *The Economist*, 4 September 1982, p. 26; and Tse, *Marks & Spencer*, p. 80.
48. Wilson, *First with the News*, pp. 400 and 422.
49. Knee and Walters, *Strategy in Retailing*, pp. 137–8.
50. See Corina, *Pile it High, Sell it Cheap*, pp. 138, 153 and 165.
51. See *100 Years of Shopping at Boots* (Nottingham: Boots plc, 1977).
52. Corina, *Pile it High, Sell it Cheap*, pp. 149–50.
53. Wilson, *First with the News*, pp. 428–33.
54. Ibid., p. 432.
55. See S. Salmans, 'Mixed Fortunes at Marks & Spencer', *Management Today*, November 1980, pp. 67–73.
56. See 'U.K. retailing: new steps in takeover tango', *Financial Times*, 5 July 1986; and S. Shamoon, 'High Noon on the High Street', *Business*, April 1986, pp. 87–96.
57. See 'Designs on Debenhams', *Sunday Times*, 26 May 1985. Interestingly, the same figure of compressing ten years of internal growth into a single takeover was

also quoted in the context of the Argyll Group's 1987 acquisition of 132 UK Safeway stores. See *Financial Times*, 24 January 1987.

58. See H. Barty-King, *Eyes Right: The Story of Dollond & Aitchison 1750–1985* (London: Quiller Press, 1986) p. 213.
59. See *Financial Times*, 5 June 1986.
60. See K. Davies and L. Sparks, 'ASDA–MFI: the Superstore and the Flat Pack', *International Journal of Retailing*, Vol. 1, No. 1, 1986, pp. 55–78.
61. See *Financial Times*, 5 July 1986.
62. Rees, *St. Michael*, p. 125.
63. Quoted in G. Havenhand, *Nation of Shopkeepers*, p. 5. See also C. Kennedy, 'Keeping up with the consumer', *The Illustrated London News*, January 1985, pp. 27–30.
64. See T. Nash, 'MFI's new life after Asda', *Director*, November 1988, pp. 112–16; and A. van de Vliet, 'Can Asda deliver the goods?', *Management Today*, April 1988, pp. 58–63.
65. See, for example, Howe, *Corporate Strategy*, pp. 95–103.
66. See Chandler, *Strategy and Structure*; and P. Steer and J. Cable, 'Internal Organization and Profit: An Empirical Analysis of Large UK Companies', *Journal of Industrial Economics*, September 1978, pp. 13–30.
67. See Porter, *Competitive Strategy*, Ch. 2.
68. See S. Segal-Horn, 'The Retail Environment in the U.K.', in G. Johnson (ed.), *Business Strategy and Retailing* (Chichester: Wiley, 1987) p. 25.
69. See *Financial Times*, 13 August 1987.
70. See D. F. Channon, *The Service Industries* (London: Macmillan, 1978) pp. 19, 184–5.
71. See Knee and Walters, *Strategy in Retailing*, p. 131.
72. In respect of large superstore groups performance may be broken down by store and product area.
73. These strategic costs would not necessarily include activities such as head office accounting expenses. On the other hand central personnel costs which relate to a particular desired quality of recruitment and selection appropriate to strategy should be allocated to business units or divisions.
74. In addition to the fixed asset base of the department not being identified, problems also arise as working capital tied up in stock or in the form of debtors (resulting from extended credit) may not be taken into account, when the latter two variables, stock and debtors, may well enter into the strategy of the department.
75. See *International Journal of Retailing*, 1986, Vol. 1, No. 1, p. 85.
76. K. Davies *et al.*, 'Structural Changes in Grocery Retailing: The Implications for Competition', *International Journal of Physical Distribution and Materials Management*, 1985, No. 2, pp. 38, 39.
77. See G. Davies and J. Brooks, *Positioning Strategy in Retailing* (London: Paul Chapman, 1989).
78. See W. Kay, *Battle for the High Street* (London: Piatkus, 1987) pp. 99–103, 114, 120.
79. See C. Moir, *The Acquisitive Streak* (London: Hutchinson, 1986) p. 51.
80. A current example at the time of writing of the problems of implementing incremental strategic change is the boardroom upheaval at Harris Queensway as the group attempted to broaden its range of furniture, increasing the element of design in merchandising and moving into higher price/quality fields at Queensways itself. The failure rapidly to achieve this change in strategy resulted in the departure of the group's joint chief executive, some City disenchantment with Queensway, and even the suggestion that Sir Philip Harris would have to resign, or that the group would be taken over. See *Financial Times*, 9 June 1987, and

Sunday Times, 23 August 1987. In fact by August 1988 Harris Queensway had been acquired by Mr James Gulliver's Lowndes group, although by early 1990 there were signs that this had not resulted in a total recovery of Queensway's fortunes (see *Financial Times*, 16 December 1989, 21 January 1990 and 15 August 1990) and in August 1990 Lowndes Queensway went into receivership.

81. M. Pitt and G. Johnson, 'Managing Strategic Change: A Chief Executive's Perspective', in Johnson (ed.), *Business Strategy and Retailing*, p. 195.

The Small Firm in Retailing 5

5.1 Introduction

The popular image of the retailer embraces both the large modern super-market and the 'corner shop'. Most of us are as familiar with numerous unplanned visits to the latter as with the weekly trip to the former; and for those who live in smaller towns or rural communities shopping is predominantly carried out in small retail outlets.

This chapter is concerned with small retail businesses, their place in UK retailing, the present problems of small retailers and their future prospects.

5.2 Definitions and Data

The Bolton Committee, which reported in 1971, was responsible for the first major research into the role of the small firm in the UK economy.[1] Its report, in addition to its broad statistical definition of the small firm as one which employed fewer than 200 people, identified three qualitative characteristics of the small business. First, it had a relatively small market share; second, an 'essential characteristic' was that the small firm was managed by its owners in a personalised way; and third, the firm was independent in so far as it did not form part of a larger organisation such that its managers were under the control of other executives or shareholders in decision making.[2]

Leaving aside the issue of market share, which with local geographical monopolies makes this criterion extremely difficult to apply in retailing, produces a working definition of the small retailer as the owner or partner in an individual retailing enterprise where these persons exercise total managerial control over the operations of the organisation. The Bolton Report, adopting a separate statistical criterion of an annual turnover of £50 000 or less for small retailing firms, identified small retailers as responsible in 1963 for 96 per cent of the firms in the sector and 49 per cent of employment.[3]

Other approaches to the definition of a small business are derived from the UK 1986 Companies Act which lays down employment ($<$ 50), sales turnover ($<$ £2m) and balance sheet asset value ($<$ £175 000) criteria; and employment law criteria of four or fewer employees for health and safety legislation, and 20 or fewer in respect of unfair dismissal. Apart from the difficulties of using sales turnover or asset values in making intertemporal comparisons, and the fact that the 1986 Companies Act employment definition is set at a very high level for retail organisations, a better approach would seem to be that derived from the UK Retail Inquiry statistics based upon the number of outlets. Thus in this chapter the definition adopted of the small firm is that of the single-outlet (or establishment) retailer: that is, retail organisations or businesses comprising only one shop. This, in contrast to studies based upon other establishment or outlet data, or financial or employment criteria, is considered to be an appropriate definition for analysis of business decision making and the present position and future prospects of small retail outlets. It is also consistent with the 'economic' definition of small firms adopted by the Bolton Committee discussed above. This definition is not, of course, without its problems. It includes as a 'small retailer' the single unit, large department store while excluding the possibly quite small retail business with two branches. These relatively minor inconsistencies are the price paid for an otherwise clear identification of the small retail outlet.

For a picture of the evolving contribution of small firms to retailing in Great Britain we can turn to the various Census of Distribution or Retail Inquiry reports. Data strictly comparable to those in Table 5.1 are not available for years prior to 1971. From the date of the first Census of Distribution in 1950, however, a broad picture can be drawn of the place of the single-unit retailer. According to the 1950 Great Britain Census of Distribution report there were then 404 845 retail organisations of which 376 446 had only one establishment. The single-unit retailer thus accounted for 93 per cent of business units in retailing; and in terms of the number of shops or establishments 376 446 out of 529 684 or 71 per cent were accounted for by those single-unit retailers. The proportion of total retail sales through single-unit retailers was, however, only 48 per cent. Thus although the independently-owned shop appeared as the archetypal retailer, even in the immediate post Second World War era these businesses accounted for less than half of total retail sales.

The 1957 Census of Distribution report did not, unfortunately, identify single-unit retailers, and thus it is not until the 1961 Census report that we can compare the role of the single-unit retailer with the first published data relating to 1950. By 1961 the total number of unit retailers had fallen to 316 440 – although this apparent reduction of 16 per cent since 1950 may be partly accounted for by a lower rate of response to the 1961 enquiry than in 1950. Single-unit retailers in 1961 accounted for 90 per cent of organisations (93 per cent in 1950), 62 per cent of establishments or shops (71 per cent in 1950) and 41 per cent of total retail sales (48 per cent in 1950). Over the

Table 5.1
Single Outlet Retailers in Great Britain

	Number	Average employment (persons)	Proportion of total retail trade:		
			Number (businesses) %	Sales turnover* %	Employment %
1971	326 735	4.0	92.7	42.9	47.4
1977	231 329	4.0	88.1	32.6	38.1
1978	208 022	4.3	88.6	31.8	37.3
1979	207 530	4.3	88.2	31.7	36.6
1980	225 907	4.1	88.2	32.2	38.1
1982	220 219	3.9	88.5	30.9	37.6
1984	218 700	3.8	88.6	30.1	36.3
1986	217 247	3.8	89.0	28.6	35.6
1987	213 378	3.7	88.6	28.3	33.9

* Excluding VAT.

SOURCE: Business Statistics Office, Business Monitor SDA 25 *Retailing* (London: HMSO, Government Statistical Service, biennial). The 1980–1987 data above are taken from the 1987 inquiry and are not, unfortunately, totally comparable with the 1971–1979 data.

decade of the 1950s, therefore, while the single-unit retailer retained its predominance in terms of the business unit, the independent shop began to become a less typical part of retailing, and its proportion of total retail sales fell by 15 per cent.

As the 1966 Census of Distribution report did not identify single-unit retailers we have to wait a further decade to compare the 1961 and 1971 Census data. These last data are included in Table 5.1. Comparison of the 1961 and 1971 Census data suggests a rather static picture of the position of the single-unit retailer during this intercensal period, although this may be contributed to by the estimated nature of some of the 1961 data. The number of single-unit retail organisations in 1971 – 326 735 – appears to have increased since 1961 when it was 316 440; and as a proportion of organisations the single-unit retailer increased to 93 per cent. The proportion of shops or establishments accounted for by single-unit retailers, which was 62 per cent in 1961, rose to 69 per cent in 1971, while the proportion of total retail trade in 1971 at 43 per cent also showed a slight increase from the corresponding figure of 41 per cent in 1961.

Table 5.1 provides broadly comparable data from more recent Census of Distribution or Retail Inquiry reports outlining the place of the small firm in UK retailing.

From the data in Table 5.1 it can be seen that the single-outlet retailer is still the dominant form of retail organisation in Great Britain, accounting for almost nine out of ten businesses. In terms of outlets too, the single-unit retail business still dominates the shopping scene, accounting for 62 per cent of outlets or establishments in 1987. However, with an average employment of under four persons per business, and very much lower sales per person than larger retail organisations, the small-firm retail sector now accounts for less than one third of total retail sales.

The data in Table 5.1 also indicate the downward trend in the relative importance of the small retailer over the 1971–1987 period, despite some apparent recovery in the number of outlets and proportion of businesses in the 1980s. Overall, the number of such businesses has declined by more than one third over these sixteen years; and while business rationalisation within the remainder of the retail sector has resulted in the proportion of small retail businesses declining only slightly over the period as a whole, the falling proportion of total retail sales accounted for by single-unit retailers – from 42.9 per cent to 28.3 per cent over the period – emphasises the diminishing role of this group.

As the data in Appendix Table 5.1 indicate, the relative importance of the small retailer varies between the seven sectors identified in the Census reports. Single-unit retailers are represented much more in some sectors than in others, most notably Drink, Confectionery and Tobacco. According to the 1987 Census data, unit retailers accounted for 96 per cent of businesses and over half of turnover in this category, and for a slightly smaller proportion of turnover in the Other Non-Food sector which is largely made up of chemists, toys, hobbies and sports goods, and booksellers, stationers and newsagents. The other field in which the small retailer is represented more strongly than average by turnover is the Household Goods sector whose largest components are hardware, china and fancy goods, furniture, and electrical and musical goods.

Appendix Table 5.1 also reveals that the net 5.5 per cent decrease in the total number of unit retailers between 1980 and 1987 is made up of both increases and decreases at the individual product sector level. In line with the overall trend there were decreases in the number of unit retailers in the Clothing, Footwear etc., Household Goods, and Hire and Repair Business sectors. In particular there was a 19 per cent reduction in the number of single-unit Food retailers, which is the product category accounting for the largest number of unit retailers (31 per cent in 1987). There was, however, a marked rise in the number of unit Drink, Confectionery and Tobacco retailers where the total rose by 13 per cent over this period.

The picture that emerges from a statistical analysis of the position of the single-unit retailer in Great Britain is thus a mixed one. It is undoubtedly a picture of decline. But the rate of decline would appear overall to be slowing down; and the unit retail business continues to play a significant, and in some respects dominant, role in retailing in this country. Between product sectors, too, the role of the unit retailer varies; and while in the important Food category there was a significant fall in the number of unit retailers over the period 1980–1987, there was an appreciable rise in the number of Drink etc. unit retailers. It is within this variegated statistical context that we can turn now to examine the changing environment and resource situation of the single-unit retailer.

5.3   The Declining Role of the Small Retailer

Having traced the diminishing overall position of the small retailer in statistical terms we next seek to explain this situation. This will be done by analysing the changing environment and resource position of the single-unit retailer, as in terms of strategic analysis our hypothesis must be that the decline of the small retailer is the result of an adverse movement in the environment-resource situation of this particular group.

Changing Environment

A number of features of the retail environment have changed over the past thirty years in ways that adversely affect the position of the small retailer.

First, an urbanised and mobile population has less need of the single-unit retailer and is less dependent upon the local shop. The UK is now one of the most densely populated countries in the developed world, and this has only been accommodated as a result of an unusually high degree of urbanisation. This trend began in late Victorian times and accelerated immediately after the Second World War. A comparison of the 1951, 1971 and 1981 population census data, however, indicates a much reduced trend in this respect, and more recently there is evidence of a population drift from the larger conurbations to suburban areas, accompanied by some increase in the rural population.[5] In part, however, this more recent reaction to high city-centre population densities has also operated against the small shop as inner city housing clearance policies result in a much greater loss of independent shop outlets than are created in suburban housing developments with their much lower densities of shopping provision.[6] It has also been pointed out that even where provision has been made in housing development schemes for shopping facilities, the retail units available are often much larger than those required by small shopkeepers, and the level of rents or purchase prices are such that these units can only be afforded by much larger or multiple shop organisations.[7]

The small shop, so characteristic of modest centres of population, is thus faced in many instances with a reduced local population, and one which at the same time is more mobile. In this latter context even the remaining 'local' population is now more likely to be enticed away to larger shopping centres whose constituents may together offer more choice of shopping goods and lower prices for convenience items: so much lower in the case of the latter that the opportunity to purchase at a cheaper price overcomes the 'convenience' factor, thus severely reducing the element of geographical monopoly formerly enjoyed by the small, local shop.[8]

The second environmental change affecting the position of the small shopkeeper has been the result of advances in the technology of retailing. The increased levels of prepackaging and branding of goods by the end of the 1950s led to a 'deskilling' of the tasks of the shopkeeper and helped to usher in self-service. This form of retailing is, of course, much more capital intensive than counter service. It has led to increased shop and organisation size in order to achieve the full benefits of labour productivity and economies of scale realisable from the adoption of self-service, and has imposed a higher minimum level of capital investment in retailing. These factors have certainly operated against the small, single-unit shop; and more recent advances in retailing technology – most notably EPOS – although they may not hasten the demise of the very smallest convenience retailer, will undoubtedly increase the trend to larger scale in retailing by further adding to the capital intensiveness of retail distribution and increasing the operating efficiency of retailers who can also benefit from the faster flow of trading information which should arise from the introduction of EPOS systems.

Third, the increased march of the multiple-shop organisation has, almost by definition, led to a reduction in the place of the small unit retailer. The relative success of these multiple-shop organisations has been based upon purchasing advantages, scale economies in operation and a high standard of professional management. We shall return to some aspects of this issue below in looking at supply conditions faced by unit retailers, i.e. the sources from which they obtain their merchandise and the price and delivery conditions etc. which apply to small retailers.

Some writers, such as Dawson and Kirby, have suggested that too much emphasis may be placed upon competition from larger organisations as a cause of the decline in the number of small retailers. This argument is based upon a spatial or geographical analysis of retailing, and in particular upon studies of the impact of supermarket openings upon adjacent small shops. These studies indicate that new superstores or hypermarkets have in fact little impact upon the trade of small local shops. We cannot, however, ignore the broader competitive effect of large scale, low cost retailers upon the survival of the independent shop, particularly in the context of the increased consumer mobility referred to above.[9]

One further direction in which one might look for an explanation of the decline in the role of the unit retailer is the shifting pattern of retail trade. Data from the recent Retailing Census reports do show some differences between sectors of distribution in terms of change in the number of shops, and Appendix Table 5.2 sets out the changes in the total number of retail outlets between 1980 and 1987 broken down into the principal retailing groups. Although there was an overall reduction of 6.2 per cent in the number of shops between 1980 and 1987, this figure was much higher in two particular areas: Food, and Hire and Repair. However, reference to the data in Appendix Table 5.1 shows that in neither of these areas was the unit retailer particularly 'over represented' in terms of the proportion of unit retail businesses to the total. Indeed in the category of Drink, Confectionery and Tobacco, where unit retail businesses are even more strongly represented, there was a 6 per cent increase in the total number of retail outlets over the period 1980–1987. The other side of the coin, however, is that it is in the Food category – where the total number of outlets fell by almost 20 per cent over the period 1980–1987 – that unit retailers themselves are most strongly concentrated. In 1980 36 per cent of unit retailers were in this product category, with the next highest proportion being 18 per cent in the Drink etc. area.

Further statistical analysis looks to their very size as an explanation for the reduction in numbers of small retailers. To demonstrate this Dawson and Kirby measured changes in retail sales 1961–1971 relative to the opening size class of shop by sales, distinguishing six commodity groups.[10] Although there were found to be some differences in the opening size class-change in retail sales relationship between product groups these occurred at higher size classes. For shop size classes up to £20 000 annual turnover in 1961 the relationship was quite clear: the smaller the initial size class the greater the loss of sales over the period. These two authors also adopted a more sophisticated approach – shift-share analysis – to isolate three components of the total decline in shop numbers within any size category. The three contributory components are the national component or the underlying trend in shop numbers in the economy, the business type or structural component which reflects the influence upon the change in shop numbers of a business being in any particular product area, and the size component which indicates the fall in shop numbers in each size class of business which is accounted for by factors unique to that size class. This approach is similar to that of statistical multiple regression where the change in shop numbers within any size class group is the dependent variable being explained by reference to the underlying trend, the retail sector involved, and the opening size class of the business. Dawson and Kirby's analysis of the 1961–1966 and 1966–1971 intercensal changes brings out very obviously the 'penalty' suffered by the lowest size categories of retailers arising from their smallness; and it is clearly this variable rather than the product group characteristic that has been responsible for the observed reduction in the number of small retailers.

This subsection has considered the range of environmental variables operating against the small, independent retailer in Great Britain. These include demographic and regional planning factors, the increased capital intensiveness, technical sophistication and scope for economies of scale in retailing, the resultant benefits enjoyed by multiple shop organisations in comparison with smaller retailers, and the success of these larger organisations in the food trades in particular in which the unit retailer is still strongly concentrated. The result of these developments, as Dawson and Kirby's statistical analysis confirms, is that small size has continued to be a handicap in the retail trades, which has made it increasingly difficult for many independent retailers to survive. We continue now to examine the resource base of these retailers in order to further our understanding of their market position.

Resources

Continuing with our hypothesis that the difficulties confronting small retailers arise from adverse environment-resource factors we now turn to the resource position of single-unit retailers. Four major resource difficulties confront these retailers: supplies, finance, operating efficiency and management.

Supply Problems

One immediate disadvantage suffered by the small retailer is the cost of supplies. Supply sources vary considerably between retail sectors. While in the grocery field voluntary group membership is quite high, and while small confectioner–tobacconist–newsagent (CTN) outlets may make considerable use of wholesale cash-and-carry outlets for purchases of confectionery and cigarettes, traditional independent wholesalers remain very important in household goods and in clothing and footwear. In the last sector a number of retailers still obtain supplies from manufacturers. Even within the category of smaller retailers the larger organisations are more likely to order from manufacturers or wholesalers, while retailers in the smallest category may purchase from a cash-and-carry wholesale outlet.

Although retailers are naturally concerned about the range of stock available from their suppliers, the delivery frequency and 'minimum drop', or the retailers' own time and travel costs in the case of cash-and-carry wholesalers, cost of supplies is not surprisingly a major source of concern and a reason for smaller retailers changing supply source.[11] The Office of Fair Trading (OFT) study of manufacturers' trade terms found that in 1984 the average buying price differential for national brands of a range of grocery products between multiple and independent retailers was 15.5 per cent, and Dawson and Kirby quote one smaller grocer as being able to buy more cheaply from a local supermarket than through a wholesaler.[12] Clearly this dimension of the supply issue puts small retailers at a considerable trading disadvantage in the markets in which they operate.

Finance

Financial problems are highlighted in a number of studies of the small retailer.[13] However, it is not always clear whether these difficulties arise from 'finance' in the narrow sense or merely reflect the harshly competitive environment of the independent retailer outlined above. In terms of finance and ownership structures small retailers are simple organisations even when compared with other small businesses. As part of its enquiry into the financing of small firms the Wilson Committee was able to draw upon commissioned research into the financing of small firms in the services sector.[14] Of 299 small, service sector firms the 48 retailers (16 per cent) formed the largest single group. They were also amongst the smallest organisations, with 77 per cent of the retailers having five or fewer employees. With regard to corporate form, again the retail businesses were the simplest. Of these, 51 per cent were sole proprietorships and a further 21 per cent were partnerships – proportions far above those of other small, service sector firms.

Correspondingly, small retailers were found to be very dependent upon proprietors'/partners' or family funds for business expansion. Of those small retailers which had expanded over the last three years up to the time of this research late in 1978, 75 per cent were dependent upon retained profits and additional capital invested by the proprietor/partners or family; and a further 33 per cent obtained additional funds by way of a bank loan or overdraft.[15]

Despite comment by a number of small firms regarding some inflexibility on the part of bank lenders, small retailers along with other similar service sector organisations appeared relatively untroubled by financial problems relating to access to funds, although lack of internal finance was seen as a significant barrier to expansion. Rather it would seem, as the Research Report expressed it, that in retailing as in other sectors 'finance is far less of a problem for small firms than the overall economic environment in which they have to operate'.[16]

Although Dawson and Kirby's finding of a statistically significant difference in the incidence of 'financial strain' between sectors of retailing would suggest a differential impact of the environment upon small retailers, these two authors also found significant differences between size of business and financial strain, with larger businesses experiencing significantly less financial strain.[17] This would appear to suggest again that the smallest retailers are disadvantaged in terms of financial resources. Unfortunately the responses given in the Dawson and Kirby survey relating to the reasons for financial strain are not very illuminating. Slightly more than half of the respondents (54.1 per cent) gave as the primary reason for financial strain 'National economic situation'; although the fact that none of the respondents placed 'Supermarket competition' in this category again suggests that it is their small size itself rather than that particular competitive aspect of their environment which operates against independent retailers.[18]

Operating Efficiency

In addition to experiencing difficulties or disadvantages associated with supply, small retailers may also be characterised by less efficient operations than larger organisations. Two indices of operating efficiency which can be calculated from data published in the Retailing census are labour productivity as measured by sales per employee, and stock turnover, i.e. the ratio of sales net of VAT to closing stock. Data on these from the Retailing census for the years 1982 and 1987 are presented in Appendix Tables 5.3 and 5.4 respectively. The data in Appendix Table 5.3 for 1982 and 1987 indicate a range of ratios in comparing single-outlet retailer sales per employee with that of multiple shop organisations. With the exception of the category of Mixed Retail Businesses, which include general mail-order houses, independent retailers are disadvantaged in terms of their use of labour according to this measure. The extent of this disadvantage, however, varies markedly from a very significant level in relation to large multiples in the area of Food, in Drink, Confectionery and Tobacco, and in Household Goods, to more modest differentials in Clothing, Footwear etc. and Other Non-Food.

The differential *vis-à-vis* small multiples (organisations with 2–9 outlets) is in all cases less than that in comparison with large multiples, although the extent of this relative differential also varies between trades. In the case of Food there is a relatively modest gap between the labour productivity of unit and small multiple organisations, while large multiples enjoy considerable advantages. In Clothing, Footwear etc. and in Other Non-Food by contrast, the performance gap between all three forms of retailing is much less.

Comparing the 1982 and 1987 ratio data there is some evidence of a reduction in the advantage of multiple shop organisations *vis-à-vis* unit retailers, although by contrast there was a marked increase in the differential between the multiple and unit retailers over this period in the category of Hire and Repair.

In summary these data indicate generally that within their gross margins unit retailers perform less efficiently (and in a number of trade categories much less efficiently) than their competitors in their utilisation of labour. We must also bear in mind that wages and salaries account for the largest part of gross margins. This situation undoubtedly reduces the ability of unit retailers to respond to price competition from larger distributors, and equally puts pressure upon net profit margins among small shopkeepers.

The second available index of retailer operating efficiency is the rate of stock turnover, that is the ratio of sales turnover (exclusive of VAT) to stock held measured by end-year stocks in the Retailing census reports. Data on this for 1980, 1982, 1984 and 1987 are given in Appendix Table 5.4. Here, and on the basis of rather more reliable data than employment figures used in measuring retail labour productivity, a more complex picture emerges, with independent retailers frequently performing better than multiple organisations. This is so, quite surprisingly, in the case of Food; and in Drink,

Confectionery and Tobacco stock turnover rates for both classes of multiple retailer are consistently well below those of single-unit retailers. In 1987, for example, unit retailer stock turnover in this trade was 13.8 times compared with 11.9 for small multiples and 8.5 for large multiples. On the other hand in the cases of Clothing, Footwear etc. and Household Goods single-unit retailers performed significantly less well than large multiples in terms of this measure of stock utilisation.

Comparing the actual stock turnover ratios of unit retailers over the period 1980–1987 there were improvements in all trade categories except Mixed Retail Businesses where the ratio remained virtually constant. If we then compare the indices of multiple to unit retailer stock turnover data for this period the small multiple retailers generally showed a tendency nevertheless to catch up with or draw further ahead of unit retailers, whereas in the case of large multiples with the exception of the Food sector their position relative to unit retailers remained much the same or in some cases worsened comparatively.

Thus in contrast to the relative labour productivity indices, unit retailers do not generally perform worse than their multiple organisation competitors in terms of stock turnover. Indeed in those trade categories where unit retailers are most represented – in Food and in Drink, Confectionery and Tobacco – they particularly out-perform the multiples. Moreover, unit retailers have improved this dimension of their performance quite consistently since 1980, and in this respect have maintained or improved their performance against almost all of the large multiples.

The competitive environment within which they operate, combined with supply disadvantages faced by independent retailers, make it important that they operate as efficiently as possible. As a result of these pressures small retail businesses generally have lower net-of-VAT gross sales margins than their competitors. Taking the comparable data for 1980, 1982, 1984 and 1987 from the 1987 Retailing census, only in one product category out of seven (Mixed Retail Businesses) did single-outlet-retailers consistently enjoy higher gross margins than small multiple retailers. This finding applied to each of these four census years. (The single year exceptions to this were Other Non-Food and Hire and Repair Businesses in 1987.) In comparison with large multiple retailers the data show that in each of the four years, and with the exception of Household Goods Retailers in 1987, unit retailers enjoyed higher gross margins only in Mixed Retail Businesses and in Food. In the latter case the difference was quite slight: 22.9 per cent for unit retailers in comparison with 21.2 per cent for large multiples in 1987.

Within these gross margins unit retailers are characterised by generally much lower levels of labour productivity, associated not only with counter service but also lower turnover per shop and lower average 'till' or individual transaction. In Food retailing, for example, the sales turnover (net of VAT) per shop in 1987 for unit retailers was £104 234 while the figures for small multiples and large multiples were £144 352 and £1 997 534 respectively.

These performance characteristics, despite higher rates of stock turn by unit retailers in a number of important product areas, contribute to the precarious financial existence of many small retailers.

Management

In all organisations successful business performance is likely to be strongly influenced by the quality of the management of the enterprise. In the case of the small retailer he or she, along with any fellow proprietors, is not only involved in the very obvious retailing functions of serving customers but is also responsible for routine purchasing decisions, the employment of others, and business record keeping (including the dreaded VAT!). On top of all of these the proprietor is responsible for the overall and longer-term strategic management of the business as a whole.

The managerial dimension of small-scale retailing has not always been given particular emphasis, and standards of management have been criticised. From a behavioural science point of view the picture of this sector of the economy is that of 'the miseries and deprivations of the under-capitalised retailer eking out a living by dragooning his family into the business, working all hours of the day and night and treating his customers with simpering deference in a vain attempt to retain his clientele'.[19] Concentrating upon the management dimension, Kirby is quite damning about the competence of the small retailer.[20] The situation arises, as he sees it, from the very low financial barriers to entry into the trade and the absence of any requirement for a formal training qualification. As Kirby points out, half of the new entrants to retailing in his survey had come from jobs which had no relevance at all to small-scale retailing. The situation is thus one of many entrants into this trade having little or no idea of the workings of or the problems involved in owning a small retail business, but being drawn into the sector either as a result of unemployment in the wage economy or a slightly naive attraction of being one's own boss. The result, in Kirby's words, is 'the low levels of managerial competence in this sector of the distributive system'.[21] These issues are not, of course, likely to be emphasised by small retailers themselves in analysing their market position; and in all fairness the same remarks concerning the effects of combining management and operations and also the general level of managerial competence might also be made of many other trades such as plumbers and electricians or small bakers or foundry operators. The point is that small independent retailers are to a considerable degree faced by competition from very professionally organised and managed businesses. Some part of the relative failure of small retailers must, therefore, be ascribed to the lack in many cases of distinct managerial competence.

In the light of the particular environmental and resource situation of the small retailer we now turn to consider the future of this sector of retail distribution.

5.4   The Survival of the Small Retailer

Following the line of our analysis, any consideration of the survival of the small retailer must be based upon some amelioration of his trading environment and/or an improvement in the resource position of these businesses. Three broad issues are identified here: the spatial impact of demographic changes, the competitive position of independent retailers *vis-à-vis* multiple shop organisations, and the standard of management of small retail businesses.

Demographics

The population drift away from certain rural areas, together with the increased shopping mobility of those still living in the countryside, are features about which retailers can do very little, although both result in lost incomes for small rural shops. However, in addition to planning bodies permitting rural retailing development where this is requested, joint action by small shopkeepers and various authorities could assist rural shops. Such action could include awareness campaigns along the lines of the National Bus Consortium's 'We'd all miss the bus' publicity. In the case of small rural shops a 'Use it or lose it' awareness campaign could alert local residents to the marginal financial position of these retail outlets, the particular services which they presently offer, and the impact of the loss of such shops. Policy developments could include a linking of tourist facilities and expenditures to rural shops through these acting as centres for tourist information and providing refreshments and possibly also picnic areas, toilets and telephone facilities. The availability and location of these would be advertised in local tourist guides.

Equally, independent shops in inner city areas have been affected by redevelopment schemes. Shops in these areas have either been forced to close as a result of development plans or by the same process have seen their customers disappear; and the provision made for independent shop units in suburban housing schemes has not necessarily been appropriate for small retailers. Here, too, there is a role for the authorities in planning for the development of shopping facilities in new suburban areas where these may often be best provided by independent retail outlets.

The Competitive Environment

A further major disadvantage for the small retailer arises from the trading terms upon which he obtains his supplies relative to larger multiple retailers. The Bolton Committee in 1971 considered that these differential trading terms were 'one of the main reasons for the success of the chains', and that such terms reflected 'their great buying power' rather than true cost savings to manufacturers.[22]

One rather Draconian solution to this problem would be to proscribe such differential trading terms on the part of manufacturers. The model for this is the 1936 Robinson–Patman Act of the United States. This Act makes it unlawful for sellers to discriminate in price between different purchasers where the effect of this 'may be substantially to lessen competition . . . or to injure, destroy or prevent competition'. The only price differentials on the part of sellers between customers accepted under this legislation are those that reflect 'due allowance for differences in the cost of manufacture, sale, or delivery . . . ' including selling in greater quantities.[23] It is not possible to say whether this legislation itself has had any discernible effect upon the pattern of retailing in the United States, and in particular upon the survival of the independent retailer. It is clear, however, that such legislation is very time consuming, expensive and cumbersome to implement, that it blunts the use of the price weapon in manufacturer competition, and also that it introduces considerable uncertainty and caution in the whole area of competitive behaviour. Despite such misgivings there is no present intention of changing the legislation in the United States. It is doubtful, however, whether there would be adequate support for the introduction of comparable legislation in Great Britain given the likely opposition to such law from the larger retailers and from most manufacturers. Smaller retailers also may feel that since differential pricing by suppliers is not necessarily the sole reason for their difficult trading position *vis-à-vis* larger distributor groups, the introduction of apparently anti-competitive legislation would not command popular support.

As set out in Chapter 2, a second approach to reducing the cost disadvantage of independent retailers in obtaining supplies lies in the formation of buying groups, membership of voluntary groups, or the use by small retailers of wholesale cash-and-carry facilities. The purpose of these initiatives is for smaller retailers to gain the trading advantages of large-scale purchasing and to increase their operating efficiency by taking over some part of the wholesaling function. Voluntary groups comprise a wholesaler or group of wholesalers together with associated retailers who may agree to purchase a proportion of their supplies from the group. Examples include the VG and Spar chains of grocery wholesalers each with its group of retailers, and Numark servicing independent chemist outlets. Wholesaling group organisations may also provide promotional and training services for their independent retailer members. Indeed in the case of wholesale grocery groups a large amount of effort is put by the wholesalers into increasing the efficiency of 'their' retailers. Such efforts include advice on in-shop display material, provision for the adoption of computer-based stock ordering systems, and assistance in training in merchandising and general retail management. In the case of cash-and-carry wholesaling the individual retailer travels to a large wholesale warehouse, selects his supplies, pays for these immediately and is responsible for their transport to his shop.[24]

An appraisal supported in one of the Bolton Committee research reports in 1971 was that 'there is little argument that the development of voluntary purchasing groups has been the most successful measure the independent firms have adopted to counter the severe inroads made into their trade by the multiple store and large scale organisations', while Dawson and Kirby's more cautious assesment at the end of the 1970s was that 'there is little doubt that cash-and-carry and group wholesaling have done much to retard the rate of decline of the small shop, particularly in the food trades'.[25] Given the advantages available through these systems it is surprising that they have not developed further. Ten years or more after their foundation voluntary group membership had still not expanded to cover a large proportion of independent retailers. Data in the 1966 Census of Distribution report, for example, show that only in the case of Grocers and Provision Dealers was there a significant proportion of independent retailers in membership of a voluntary group. The proportion so involved was 26.9 per cent; but in no other sector of the retail trade did the figure exceed 10 per cent, and a more representative proportion would be 5 per cent.[26] A decade later A. C. Nielsen was able to report in its *Annual Review of Grocery Trading* that the major symbol or voluntary groups accounted in 1976 for 12 per cent of total grocery trading. However, this same source reported that by 1978 this proportion had fallen to 7.5 per cent and by 1981 to 6.6 per cent.[27] Thus despite some evidence of the trading performance and financial advantages to be gained for small retailer membership of voluntary groups,[28] the low proportion of independent retailers who seek or are able to benefit from such membership means, as Dawson and Kirby put it, that 'To suppose that voluntary group membership is a panacea for the small retailer is quite wrong'.[29] As a number of writers have pointed out, membership by independent retailers of a voluntary group is not without its limitations in terms of the range of stock available, or because of the restrictions upon one's personal or trading independence which such membership gives rise to – a point which is regarded as being of some significance by behavioural scientist researchers in this field.[30]

As a further development in this area, however, independent retailers may in effect take over some of their own wholesaling and distribution functions by purchasing at trade cash-and-carry outlets. The largest firms in Great Britain in this sector are Landmark, Nurdin & Peacock, Linfood and Booker McConnell.[31] The retailer in this case is particularly saving his supplier the labour and transport costs involved in making small deliveries. Cash-and-carry warehouses – a number of which are operated by voluntary groups and may be open to unaffiliated retailers – have expanded in scale and in the range of goods carried as independent retailers have become more affected by competition from multiples. Thus although there was no major volume growth in the cash-and-carry wholesaling business during the 1980s, this remains an important source of supply for independent food retailers. Cash and carry accounted for about two thirds of the grocery wholesale trade over the 1980s, the remaining one third comprising the delivered trade. In turn 50 per cent of this wholesale grocery cash-and-carry trade is accounted for by grocery retailers, with caterers taking a further 39 per cent.[32] The importance of cash-and-carry wholesaling for independent grocers may be seen in the data from one survey which found that 55 per cent of expenditure of a sample of independent grocers was accounted for by cash-and-carry, compared with 32 per cent by wholesale delivered goods. However, only 7 per cent of these grocers relied entirely upon cash-and-carry.[33] Thus while there may be some drawbacks for independent retailers in buying through a voluntary group or cash-and-carry outlet – such as a lack of variety of lines or the absence of certain merchandise altogether – these may be worth accepting in return for the increased trading margins available to the independent retailer in obtaining supplies in this way.

As mentioned above, management is an important dimension of small-scale retailing, and there is no reason to suppose that improvements could not be made in the present level of management competence. The problem, as was also emphasised above, is not only that 'management' in the narrower sense is only a part of the work of the independent retailer but also that barriers to entry into this trade are extremely low and there is of course no formal requirement for any level of qualification.

Independent retail business owners overwhelmingly arrive in their present position either as a result of family succession or entry into small-scale retailing from previous unrelated employment. Only very rarely has the independent retailer had previous experience of being an employee in a larger retail business. In the case of the independent retail manager who has succeeded to the family business the managerial horizon may be very limited and the level of education (business or otherwise) determined by what the young person is capable of or the parent considers necessary for 'running the shop'. Those entering small-scale retailing without a family connection come from a very wide range of backgrounds, the vast majority having no experience (first or second hand) of what to expect in operating a retailing business.

It is these backgrounds that produce the situation depicted in Dawson and Kirby's survey results of a relatively inexperienced, poorly educated and ill-prepared group of small retailer managers. Some 45 per cent of the respondents had owned their business for five years or less, 69 per cent had left school before the age of 15, and 89 per cent had received no training in retailing.[34]

It would seem, however, that there is little that government or other bodies can do with regard to this situation. Licensing of entrants would be out of the question. On the other hand one would certainly not want to see unwary potential entrants over-encouraged by government finance to enter this sector; although there may be a case for financial assistance to particular types of unit retail outlet in certain geographical areas on the ground of maintaining the local economy.

Kirby has described his own attempt to increase the level of small-retailer management expertise by means of a combination of a formal training programme, the creation of a forum for discussion and group action, and the provision of an advisory service. Kirby's assessment of the programme suggests that it was successful. However, he points out that there is little demand within the trade for such courses, and that small retailers are rarely prepared to pay the full commercial costs for such services.[35] In this respect again independent retailers are little different from many groups of small businessmen.

5.5 Conclusions

As indicated in the opening section of this chapter, the small firm – defined as an independent or unit retailer – plays an important role in retail distribution in Great Britain. For a large proportion of the population it satisfies a not unimportant part of their needs, while for a small group – the less mobile and those in rural areas – the local shop is a vital part of their living. The data in Table 5.1 outlined the numerical position of the independent retailer. These showed that while the number of such retailers was in decline and the proportion of total retail turnover accounted for by unit retailers is now less than 30 per cent, the number of these relative both to total retail business organisations and to outlets is such that the independent retailer must continue to be considered an important component of the retail sector of the economy.

A number of forces are currently operating against the independent retailer. These clearly include in some areas the changing pattern of population, town planning and other similar developments, and the increased scale and professional management of multiple-shop organisations. Equally, independent retailers encounter problems over supply and (to a lesser extent) finance. Not surprisingly this sector has taken some steps to try to combat some of these difficulties – including the formation of voluntary groups and the adoption of cash-and-carry buying.

The net result of these forces is that the small-firm component of the retail sector remains in a quite delicate state of continued existence – although the degree of delicacy obviously varies between retail trades. The major key to the survival of the small retailer must be differentiation from the multiple shop. Some of this differentiation will arise simply as a matter of geography or location. In relatively sparsely populated areas, in respect of less mobile shoppers, or for 'emergency' purchases the 'local' shop will always enjoy something of a geographical monopoly. This form of diffentiation has given rise to the phenomenon of 'retail polarisation' as small convenience stores have sought a complementary rather than competitive relationship with multiple-shop organisations. The major convenience stores in the UK have grown up within the grocery voluntary groups referred to above. But in addition to the Spar Eight Till Late and the VG Late Shop outlets are Misselbrook & Weston, the 7-Eleven stores and the CWS Late Late Supershop franchises. These are self-service stores of 1–3000 square feet in size close to housing, selling a wide range of goods (with food normally accounting for up to half of sales) and, as their titles imply, remaining open for long hours. The development of these convenience stores, which appears to characterise many developed economies, represents an important opportunity for the survival of the independent retailer, particularly in the very competitive food/CTN area which in 1987 accounted for 52 per cent of unit retailers.[36]

The other basis of differentiation adopted by independent retailers is that of range of merchandise, personal attention, expertise, service etc. Thus in Furniture, floorcoverings etc., Jewellery, silverware, watches and clocks, and Toys, games, cycles etc., independent retailers still account for about 40 per cent of total sales despite the incursion of multiple shops into these areas. However, in other sectors where one might have expected the need for specialist retailing expertise and the availability of a range of merchandise to permit the survival of the independent retailer – such as Photographic and optical goods, and Audio-visual equipment, home computers and musical instruments – the market share of independent retailers is less than 30 per cent. In the cases of Men's and boys' wear, and Women's and girls' etc. wear the large multiple retailers (those with 100 or more outlets) now account for around 40 per cent of total retail sales, and the proportion in each of these two product areas accounted for by independent retailers is now around 25 per cent.[37]

Increasingly, multiple shop organisations such as Boots and W. H. Smith, as well as more specialist groups such as Dixons, are moving into the audio-hi-fi/home computer fields. For example, when Sinclair decided in the early 1980s to widen the market for its home computers through conventional retail sales rather than mail order, the ZX81 was sold through W. H. Smith – a strategy which turned out to be highly successful for both organisations.[38] In the clothing field independent shops face competition not only from established chains including Marks & Spencer and Littlewoods but also from newer fashion multiples such as Next, Sears' Miss Selfridge, Storehouse's Richards shops, and outlets such as Tammy Girl and Snob within the Etam Group. In jewellery retailing one chain alone, Ratners, accounts for 31 per cent of the UK market in a sector until quite recently highly fragmented and dominated by unit retailers.[39]

The independent or unit retailer thus faces an uncertain and competitive environment and an increasingly disadvantageous resource position. It must sometimes seem that entry into this sector is another example of the triumph of hope over (informed) expectation. There is none the less a role left in the economy for the independent retailer where the geographical or service-intensive environment can be matched by managerial and other required resources; and given that these businesses are yet responsible for more than one quarter of total retail sales and comprise at 20 per cent the largest single group of smaller firms in the economy,[40] the current position and prospects of the single-unit retailer must remain an important part of any study of UK retailing.

References

1. See *Report of the Committee of Inquiry on Small Firms* (London: HMSO, 1971, Cmnd 4811).
2. Ibid., paras 1.4–1.7.
3. Ibid., Table 1.1 (p.3). According to the Bolton Committee's definition of small firms, retailers accounted for almost one half of the total small firm population by enterprises. The proportion of employment, however, was only one third. *Report of the Committee of Inquiry on Small Firms*, paras 5.15 and 5.19.
4. See G. Davies and K. Harris, *Small Business: The Independent Retailer* (London: Macmillan, 1990) pp. 4–5.
5. See J. W. House (ed.), *The U.K. Space* (London: Weidenfeld & Nicolson, 3rd edn, 1983) Chs 2 and 6.
6. J. A. Dawson and D. A. Kirby, *Small Scale Retailing in the U.K.* (Farnborough: Saxon House, 1979) p.78.
7. See D. A. Kirby, 'The Small Retailer', in J. Curran *et al.* (eds), *The Survival of the Small Firm* (London: Gower, 1986) Vol. I, p. 166; and F. Bechhofer *et al.*, 'The Market Situation of Small Shopkeepers', *Scottish Journal of Political Economy*, June 1971, p. 168.
8. One study of rural grocers and general stores found that although at the time of the study U.K. *per caput* expenditure on food was more than £13 per week, *per caput* spending on convenience goods in local shops was £3–4 per week, indicating a 'leakage' of some 70 per cent in this respect. See *Survey of Grocers and General Stores in Rural Tayside* (Dundee: Tayside Regional Council Planning Department, 1986) para 3.4. A more recent published study of this leakage or 'outshopping' includes an analysis of the reasons for outshopping, and contains an estimate of 33 per cent for the extent of outshopping from a small town in rural Wales. See C. M. Guy, 'Outshopping from Small Towns: A British Case Study', *International Journal of Retail & Distribution Management*, May/June 1990, pp. 3–14.
9. Dawson and Kirby, *Small Scale Retailing in the U.K.*, p. 72.
10. Ibid., pp. 24–32.
11. Ibid., Ch. 4.
12. Office of Fair Trading, *Competition in Retailing* (London: OFT, 1985) para. 5.15; and Dawson and Kirby, *Small Scale Retailing in the U.K.*, p. 61.
13. See Dawson and Kirby, *Small Scale Retailing in the U.K.*, Ch. 5.
14. See *The Financing of Small Firms*, Interim Report of the Committee to Review the Functioning of Financial Institutions (London: HMSO, 1979, Cmnd 7503).
15. Interestingly only 12 out of 48 or 25 per cent of the sample of small retailers regarded themselves as having expanded significantly over this period. See Commitee to Review the Functioning of Financial Institutions, Research Report No. 3, *Studies of Small Firms' Financing* (London: HMSO, 1979) Ch. V.
16. Ibid., p. 69.
17. Dawson and Kirby, *Small Scale Retailing in the U.K.*, p. 64.
18. Ibid., p. 68.
19. Bechhofer *et al.*, 'The Market Situation of Small Shopkeepers', p. 161.

20. See D. A. Kirby, 'The Small Retailer', in J. Curran *et al.*, *The Survival of the Small Firm*, pp. 163–4.
21. Ibid., p. 163.
22. *Report of the Committee on Small Firms*, para. 16.22.
23. These passages from the 1936 Act are quoted in Monopolies and Mergers Commission, *Discounts to Retailers* (London: HMSO, 1981, HC 311) Appendix 2, pp. 93–7. A more detailed consideration of the legal and commercial issues relating to retailer buying power – and generally supportive of the case for more control in this area – is to be found in A. R. Everton, *The Legal Control of Buying Power* (London: National Federation of Retail Newsagents *et al.*, 1986).
24. On the origins of these organisations see N. A. H. Stacey and A. Wilson, *The Changing Pattern of Distribution* (Oxford: Pergamon Press, rev.edn, 1965) Ch. 8.
25. See A. D. Smith, *Small Retailers: Prospects and Policies*, Committee of Inquiry on Small Firms Research Report No. 15 (London: HMSO, 1971) p. 26; and Dawson and Kirby, *Small Scale Retailing in the U.K.*, p. 119.
26. Data given in 'The Market Situation of Small Shopkeepers', p. 176.
27. See A. C. Nielsen, *Annual Review of Grocery Grading* (Oxford: A. C. Nielsen Co. Ltd).
28. See Dawson and Kirby, *Small Scale Retailing in the U.K.*, p. 99.
29. Ibid.
30. See, for example, F. Bechhofer *et al.*, 'Small Shopkeepers: Matters of Money and Meaning', *Sociological Review*, November 1974, esp. pp. 477–9.
31. See Institute of Grocery Distribution Bulletin, *Distribution & Technology* (Watford: IGD, December 1988) p. 3.
32. Ibid., pp. 1–3.
33. Monopolies and Mergers Commission, *The Dee Corporation PLC and Booker McConnell PLC* (London: HMSO, 1985, Cmnd 9429) para. 2.23.
34. Dawson and Kirby, *Small Scale Retailing in the U.K.*, p. 156.
35. Kirby, in J. Curran *et al.*, *The Survival of the Small Firms*, pp. 172–4.
36. See D. A. Kirby, 'Convenience Stores: the polarisation of British retailing', *Retail & Distribution Management*, March–April 1986, pp. 7–12.
37. These proportions are from the 1987 *Retailing* Business Monitor.
38. See I. Adamson and R. Kennedy, *Sinclair and the 'Sunrise' Technology* (Harmondsworth: Penguin, 1986) pp. 108–12.
39. Quoted in *Financial Times*, 3 July 1990.
40. See 1988 data in D. G. Mayes and C. B. Moir, 'Small firms in the U.K. Economy', *The Royal Bank of Scotland Review*, December 1989, p. 17.

Appendix Table 5.1
Single Outlet Retailers

Sector	Number		Proportion of total retail trade:					
			Number*		Sales turnover†		Employment‡	
	1980	1987	1980	1987	1980	1987	1980	1987
Food	81 835	66 504	90%	90%	27%	20%	37%	28%
Drink, confectionery and tobacco	39 989	45 241	94%	96%	53%	58%	62%	65%
Clothing, footwear and leather goods	29 069	24 959	82%	80%	28%	24%	33%	27%
Household goods	38 782	37 253	86%	87%	40%	33%	48%	41%
Other non-food	30 759	33 333	86%	86%	53%	53%	55%	55%
Mixed retail businesses	2 887	4 225	77%	86%	23%	17%	18%	13%
Hire and repair businesses	2 586	1 863	89%	91%	15%	10%	22%	16%
Total/Average	225 907	213 378	88%	89%	32%	28%	38%	34%

* Businesses.
† Net of VAT.
‡ Defined as 'persons engaged'

SOURCE: As in Table 5.1

Appendix Table 5.2
Total Numbers of Retail Outlets by Sector 1980–87

Sector	1980	1982	1984	1987	1980–82	1982–84	1984–87	1980–87
Food	121 600	114 481	105 953	98 016	−5.9%	−7.4%	−7.5%	−19.4%
Drink, confectionery and tobacco	56 375	56 462	56 499	59 810	+0.2%	+0.1%	+5.9%	+6.1%
Clothing, footwear and leather goods	61 489	58 044	58 552	58 380	−5.6%	+0.9%	0	−5.1%
Household goods	64 697	62 050	60 104	60 406	−4.1%	−3.1%	+1.0%	−6.6%
Other non-food retailers	48 224	48 160	50 858	52 473	−0.1%	+5.6%	+3.2%	+8.8%
Mixed retail businesses	10 006	11 292	11 231	11 363	+12.9%	−0.5%	+1.2%	+13.6%
Hire and repair businesses	5 862	6 101	6 531	5 020	+4.1%	+7.0%	−23.1%	−14.4%
Total	368 253	356 590	349 728	345 467	−3.2%	−1.9%	−1.2%	−6.2%

SOURCE: As in Appendix Table 5.1

Appendix Table 5.3
Sales Per Employee *

Sector	Unit retailers (£)		Small multiples/unit retailers (Index: Unit retailers = 100)		Large multiples/unit retailers (Index: Unit retailers = 100)	
	1982	1987	1982	1987	1982	1987
Food	22 556	30 946	119.3	104.2	182.6	167.8
Drink, confectionery and tobacco	21 975	31 266	134.5	117.9	153.0	137.0
Clothing, footwear and leather goods	16 925	27 200	118.8	116.6	120.3	118.2
Other non-food	25 030	39 357	115.4	120.5	172.3	155.3
Household goods	23 345	34 575	107.6	102.7	110.3	105.2
Mixed retail businesses	35 746	63 064	58.5	54.4	82.5	69.7
Hire and repair businesses	19 333	22 600	117.2	108.4	120.9	172.0

* Net of VAT.

SOURCE: As in Appendix Table 5.1

Appendix Table 5.4
Stock Turnover

Sector	Unit retailers				Small multiples/unit retailers (Index: Unit retailers = 100)				Large multiples/unit retailers (Index: Unit retailers = 100)			
	1980	1982	1984	1987	1980	1982	1984	1987	1980	1982	1984	1987
Food	23.4	23.0	25.9	26.5	86.3	91.7	90.0	103.0	54.7	64.8	79.8	65.3
Drink, confectionery and tobacco	11.1	11.7	12.4	13.8	73.9	70.9	78.2	86.2	81.1	77.7	79.8	61.6
Clothing, footwear and leather goods	3.6	3.6	3.7	3.7	108.3	108.3	121.6	118.9	158.3	158.3	154.1	156.8
Household goods	4.1	4.0	4.6	4.6	97.6	110.0	104.3	113.0	146.3	147.5	130.4	130.4
Other non-food	4.4	4.6	4.8	5.3	95.5	97.8	104.2	92.5	77.3	87.0	83.3	77.4
Mixed retail businesses	7.4	7.3	7.3	7.3	85.1	84.9	91.8	83.6	123.0	124.7	126.0	126.0
Hire and repair	4.7	6.8	8.0	5.9	127.7	111.8	93.8	132.2	953.2	733.8	862.5	535.6

SOURCE: As in Appendix Table 5.1

Part Two

Managing Retail Organisations

Retail Merchandising and Marketing 6

'In an increasingly competitive trading environment, the
best rewards go to retailers who can profitably assemble a
product and service mix that is carefully attuned to the
requirements of clearly defined consumer segments.'

P. J. McGoldrick, *Retail Marketing* (London: McGraw-Hill, 1990)
p. 68.

6.1 Introduction

Part One of this text was very largely concerned with the analysis of retailing
in terms of retail markets and the strategic analysis by retailers of their
environment. Part Two is concerned more exclusively with retailing management, and as such deals largely with the internal management of retailing
organisations. It is about the conversion of retailing strategies into administrative and operational management. Although 'Retail is detail' is an
expression which we have suggested is an over-simplification so far as total
retail management is concerned, no retailing strategy can work unless it is
effectively implemented.

The first area of implementation to be examined – arguably the most
important in any retailing operation[1] – is merchandising. This is the choice,
within the strategy of the retailing organisation, of the goods to be sold. For
our purposes merchandising management involves decisions on goods to be
stocked, the choice of suppliers, purchasing procedures, in-store merchandise
handling including stock control, display and pricing of goods, and store
security. Figure 6.1 below shows the links between these functions and also
the role of retail marketing.

It is around this sequence of decision making outlined in Figure 6.1 that the
material in the remainder of this chapter is organised. It must be emphasised
here that the concept of retail marketing adopted in this text is narrower than

131

FIGURE 6.1
Merchandising Operations Flow

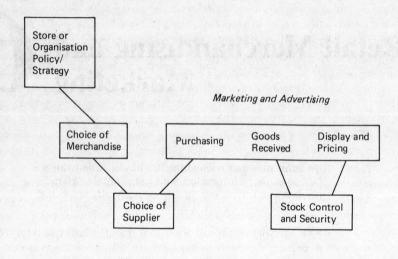

in some specialist books on that subject. For example, Walters and White appear to include within retail marketing the development of:

> A long-term plan based upon a view of the opportunities anticipated from environmental change. The plan will contain an explicit view of the growth rates and relationships between profits, sales and assets and will achieve these by establishing a market positioning in consumer markets strong enough that competitors can retaliate only over an extended period of time and at prohibitive cost.[2]

These are, in fact, issues which have been dealt with under the heading of retailing strategy in Chapter 4 of this text above. Here it is intended to restrict the scope of retail marketing to three important areas: the detailed analysis of retail markets which is necessary to determine the market segment(s) in which to compete, the management of the retail marketing mix, and retail advertising and promotion. These are considered in the second main section of this chapter.

6.2   From Strategy to Merchandise Choice

The strategy adopted by a retail organisation will embrace the clear choice of market or markets in which the store(s) is to operate, including the socioeconomic and other characteristics of the customers to be served, and also the broad sales policy in terms of range of goods, quality of service and approach to pricing. It is the role of merchandise policy to convert this strategy into the choice of appropriate goods to be sold. In any area of retailing – jewellery, men's clothing, books – a choice has to be made within the strategy of the organisation as to the goods to be stocked. Most shops, as a result of their chosen strategy, will operate within a particular price range and thus distinguish themselves as selling at the 'popular' or 'exclusive' end of the market. Thus Ratner's jewellery shops are not operating in the same segment of the market as Garrard (part of Sears Holdings); and Burton's menswear stores are not appealing to those who shop at Gieves & Hawkes.

Less immediately obvious are differences in the range of goods stocked, although there is normally some relationship on the one hand between stores which sell more expensive goods and offer as part of their service a wider range, and on the other, say, discount food stores part of whose image is a restricted range of grocery items. A distinction can also be made between the *width* and *depth* of a range of goods. In men's clothing, for example, the product range refers to the breadth of coverage. Does the shop stock both outerwear and underwear? Within the former does it include shirts, ties, trousers, jackets, suits and coats? Within, say, shirts the *width* of the range refers to coverage of sports shirts, casual shirts and 'office' shirts, while the *depth* relates to choice of collar sizes, normal or 'tapered' fit, and of course choice of colours and patterns within any category of shirt.

Two further characteristics of goods stocked by a retailer are availability and compatibility. The former relates to how far a shop can guarantee to have all of its chosen range of goods in stock, or how rapidly it is willing or able to obtain items normally within the range but not actually in stock at the present time. (These may be obtained from other branches of a multiple store group, or from a wholesaler or the manufacturer.) Compatibility in merchandise relates to the extent to which items in, for example, a clothing range are compatible with each other in wearing. In many chain stores such as Littlewoods the customer is left free to combine items within the clothing range, and no particular emphasis is placed upon this characteristic by the store. By contrast, the essence of 'edited retailing' as practised by Next is the provision of carefully selected ranges of clothes with a high degree of intended compatibility between items in the ranges of skirts, blouses, shoes, gloves etc.

Another dimension of the retail merchandising and marketing decision is that of the choice of own label *vis-à-vis* national brands. We have already discussed some of the rationale for own brands in Chapter 3 above in considering the dimensions of competition in retailing. The attractions of own-label merchandise for the retailer are not only the shorter-term advantage of combined lower consumer price and higher retail margin in comparison with national brands, but also the opportunity which his own label gives a retailer to create a brand of his own outlets. In marketing terms retailers are increasingly wanting to make brand statements about their outlets: to convey to actual and potential customers a statement and a reassurance about the total, unique offering of the retailer in terms of merchandise, quality, service etc. What better way to contribute to this than to be selling one's own unique brand of goods. This, in fact, is now seen as the more important function of the own-label product, rather than its use as a vehicle for price competition (originally as a means of circumventing the practice of r.p.m.). Those retailers most heavily committed to own-label products – most obviously Marks & Spencer with its St Michael label, Boots, and Sainsbury with 60 per cent of total sales under its own label – and also those such as Asda now moving in this direction, are using this approach not to compete on price but to make a unique 'value for money' offer to the consumer that identifies one particular retailer and indicates clearly the segment of the market at which he is aiming.[3] The result of this is that an estimated 22 per cent of total retail sales are made under the retailer brand. In the grocery trade the figure for 1986 was 28 per cent; and in the supermarket sector of retailing it was 33 per cent.[4]

The result of decisions in all of these dimensions is the adoption by a shop or store group of a policy with regard to the goods to be stocked; and one trend embodied in this is for retailers today to have a much clearer idea of what it is *they* want to sell and then approach potential suppliers, rather than the manufacturer seeing the retailer as being there to distribute what, in *his* (the manufacturer's) view, customers want. This trend has of course been carried to its extreme in those cases (described in Chapter 3 above in considering the policy of vertical integration) where, while falling short of distributor ownership of manufacturing capacity, the retailer dictates in detail the characteristics of the merchandise, and the supplier sometimes acts almost as a subcontractor to the retailer in fulfilling product orders. In the case of private-label goods too the retailer is quite largely prescribing the form and content of the product. Small and medium-sized retailers, on the other hand, having adopted a merchandising policy, will buy from warehouse displays, catalogues or sales representatives of manufacturers. Smaller bookshops also selling greeting cards and stationery will choose the range of these that is appropriate to their strategy as a reflection of their market environment and the policy of competitors.

6.3   Supplier Choice

Although the route by which goods arrive at the premises of the retailer will vary from one organisation or trade to another, all retailers face the issue of managing supply; and particularly where the retailer takes a positive role in deciding upon the merchandise to be stocked, the choice of goods leads on to the choice of supplier. This is today a reflection of the dominant relationship of retailer over manufacturer in so many trades; although Lord Sieff revels in recollecting earlier times in which Marks & Spencer actually had to persuade some manufacturers to supply it.[5]

The organisation of the buying department and its location within the firm's total organisation structure will vary between retailers. In particular a balance will have to be struck between the purchasing economies and chain-wide control over merchandise arising from a centralised buying department and the scope for more local initiative and response to competition at the store level which is permissible within a decentralised system. Senior retail management must also decide whether within a multiproduct store all goods should be bought by the same buying team, and also the relationship between the buying function and others in the retail organisation such as marketing. Some part of the organisation of the buying function will also depend upon the relationship between the retailer and its manufacturer suppliers – as in the case of own label requirements or the highly controlled specification buying adopted by Marks & Spencer.

Walters and White suggest a number of criteria to be applied by retailers in choosing their suppliers; and although the fullest rein is given to these factors when the distributor is choosing suppliers to provide specific merchandise, these variables should also be taken into account when a retailer is buying standard goods offered by a manufacturer or wholesaler.

Although some exclusive goods may be available from only a limited number of suppliers, many retailers choose to buy a given range of goods from a number of suppliers, both in order not to over-commit themselves to one source of supply and to maintain contact with a number of possible sources of new merchandise. This may be considered to be an appropriate policy despite the increase in administrative or transactions costs and stockholding to which it will give rise. Retailers will then choose their supplier(s) and the balance of purchases on the basis of the remainder of the criteria set out in Table 6.1.

The identification of retail distribution service requirements in terms of changing seasonal patterns of trade, stockholding locations, frequency of replenishment etc. leads to the formulation of supplier performance requirements. The immediate supplier performance requirements are for the availability of the right merchandise (as determined by the retailer policy decisions set out in the first major section of this chapter), the frequency with which orders may be made, and the reliability of supplier deliveries. Some of these variables, however, are often related to the fourth of the dimensions of supplier selection and evaluation set out above: terms of trade. These will include not only the crucial variable of cost to the retailer but also the relationship between unit cost and size of order, including the imposition of any minimum size of each delivery or 'drop'. The extent of quantity discounts

Table 6.1
Supplier Selection and Evaluation

Number of suppliers and balance of purchases
Distribution service requirements
Supplier performance requirements
Terms of trade, discounts etc.
Financial support
Market congruence
Marketing support

SOURCE: D. Walters and D. White, *Retail Marketing Management* (London: Macmillan, 1987) p. 221.

available from a supplier will obviously, other things being equal, also be a major determinant of the number of suppliers among whom the retailer spreads his custom. Cash flow, and thus retailer working capital requirements, is significantly influenced by the length of credit extended by suppliers to distributors. In fact in many retail trades the expectation is that goods will be sold to final consumers before the retailer is required to pay his supplier; and while this gives rise to the need for additional working capital on the part of the supplier, for retailers it creates an interesting situation of negative working capital, or cash funds available between the date on which the goods are sold to final consumers and the end of the credit period extended by the retail supplier.

Closely related to the issue of terms of trade is the question of wider financial support for retailers provided by suppliers. This may be related to 'finance' in the more restricted sense of providing loans to cover retailer credit sales of major items such as cars or consumer durables; or suppliers may fund advertising or other promotional activities for retailers. Finally, from a marketing point of view the retailer must look for a 'congruence' between supplier and distributor in terms of the market image which each is trying to create; and this may be supported by joint marketing activities either in the form of press publicity or supplier marketing promotions in the retailer's outlets.

Having looked at the decisions involved in merchandise and supplier selection, we now turn to consider the particular role of marketing in retailing management.

6.4 Retail Marketing

Marketing as an activity in retailing management has three important roles to play. First, in the identification and specification of particular market areas for individual retail organisations; second, in the management of the 'marketing mix'; and third, the design and implementation of promotional and similar activities both within the store and in the various media.

Retail Market Analysis

The first, and arguably the most important, function of marketing in this context is to provide for the basis upon which retail organisations can identify particular customer groups and differentiate themselves to serve these. We saw in Chapter 4 above on retailing strategy that this was, in fact, one of the bases of the whole of retailing strategy. Once a retail organisation has decided to operate in a particular product market area – which itself implies a broad strategic choice – it becomes necessary to understand the patterns of demand and bases of consumer behaviour in the chosen field. The essence of retail marketing management at this stage is to identify in numerical terms a worthwhile target market which is not being adequately served at present, and to which the retailer can respond with existing or potentially available resources. Traditionally this task of identification has been thought of in terms of clear attributes or variables such as sex, age and socioeconomic-group. Thus a traditional bespoke tailor may have in mind a segment of the universe of consumers characterised as male, aged 30–55, in the upper income bracket. Responding to this type of self-image, such a unit retailer in the author's home city simply advertises itself as 'Tailors to Gentlemen – Established in 1874'. In this case the market analysis role of the retail marketing manager is simply to identify the existence of such markets by reference to economic and demographic data which will reveal the size of the customer segment and possibly indicate the spending patterns of these relatively well-off males, aged 30–55 in our example.

In order to arrive at decisions in this area the retail marketing manager has to be aware of those types of environmental features and their trends that were outlined in Chapter 4 above. Average levels and growth of income, and the distribution of this in society by socioeconomic group, sex and age are important, as are demographic trends including the regional and urban/rural balance of the population and of course the age profile of consumers. Data on 'geodemographics' are particularly important for the newer style of up-market mail-order retailing where Next, for example, is offering a 48-hour delivery system rather than the traditional 28-day delivery. Increased accuracy in respect of customer profiles allows greater fit between catalogue merchandise and potential customers, economises in the sending out of catalogues, should lead to a lower level of returns (presently 46 per cent in clothing for the market leader GUS), and, as mentioned above, should provide for much speedier delivery.[6]

Because of its particular effect on some areas of retail expenditure such as food or DIY, retail marketing managers may also be concerned with the make-up of the average household. Such groups can range from the traditional extended family of, perhaps, three generations living in the one home to single persons living alone: either as a result of the elderly living on their own or young people living independently away from the family home.[7] More recently arrived phenomena are the mononuclear or single parent family and the dual person household comprising two wage earners in co-habitation. The latter is a particuarly powerful economic unit, with two incomes and no dependants.

These are undoubtedly important characteristics and variables that can be used in retail marketing to identify potential consumer groups and their spending patterns. However, successful retail marketing involves more than demographic or socioeconomic statistics. Walters and White quote the managing director of Harvey Nichol's as saying 'All this AB/C1/C2 stuff is meaningless. What matters is the style and attitude of a person, regardless of age. We are aiming at United Kingdom residents of whatever nationality who appreciate fine quality and fine design',[8] and take this as an illustration of a broader, 'lifestyle' approach to retail marketing. This approach to identifying consumer groups concentrates not so much upon the age or socioeconomic class of a group of consumers but upon a particular cluster of wants. Broader variables include consumers' concept of value for money (what customers are prepared to pay more for in a store in terms of service as they move away from purchasing on a price basis alone), the type of merchandise in which they are interested in terms of 'trendy'/'classic' styles and the degree of exclusivity, the kind of shopping experience which they want in terms of level of services and store design or ambience, and broader attitudes to shopping such as an enjoyment of choosing individual items in specialist outlets such as Sock Shop, Tie Rack and Knickerbox, or some variant of 'one stop shopping' in the form of a large Asda superstore, combined food and clothing purchases at Marks & Spencer, or the 'edited retailing' of Next where the customer is offered a carefully co-ordinated range of clothing. The result of such analysis is the identification of consumer market segments within the total universe of consumers; where a segment may be defined as a set of consumers with common expectations and perceptions regarding particular combinations of merchandise and retailing styles based broadly upon possession of certain income levels and attitudes. It should again be stressed that while some of these features may be susceptible to measurement, others can only be identified as a result of what may be described as retailing flair. Moreover, retailers can of course themselves take the initiative in influencing certain consumer attitudes. Much of the success of Ratners in the jewellery trade, for example, is ascribed to the way in which a particular group of consumers has been encouraged to see jewellery not as individual, expensive items to be worn only on special occasions throughout a lifetime, but to regard jewellery as fashion items, many of which will be bought and worn regularly, then discarded and replaced as fashion changes.[9]

Consumer market segments must possess three characteristics. First, it must be possible to describe or identify them uniquely in terms of the parameters outlined above, and it must also be possible to measure the size of the segment in terms of the number of customers and the volume of expenditure. Second, while a segment of consumers may be unique, it has to be economically viable in terms of being of a size which makes it worthwhile catering for. This is really only to recognise that specialisation on the part of the retailer will be limited by the extent of the consumer market segment. Third, from a practical point of view, it must be possible for the retailer to communicate clearly with the chosen consumer segment. This will influence the media of promotion and advertising adopted by the retailer; and the more clearly a consumer segment has been identified and the clearer the channel of communication then the more specific and possibly more economical will be communication between retailer and potential customer. (Compare, for example, press advertising in a whole city for DIY supplies, and dropping a leaflet on double glazing services through the letter-box of every home in a particular chosen socioeconomic area of the city which by inspection does not presently have double glazing.)

The next step for the retailer, on the basis of the above, is to direct his resources to the chosen consumer segment and differentiate his total offering from that of his competitors. This involves the co-ordination of all of the variables in the retail marketing mix, and it is to this that we now turn.

The Retail Marketing Mix

The marketing mix is traditionally identified as the major components of what a producer is offering. It is often summed up as the four P's: product, price, promotion and place. The dimensions of the marketing mix as applied to retailing are set out in Table 6.2.

Table 6.2
Dimensions of the Retail Marketing Mix

Product	Merchandise defined in terms of quality, range, width and depth, exclusiveness and compatibility
Price	Price level, range and lines
Services	Counter/self-service, credit, delivery, advice, alterations and repair, exchange of goods
Facilities	Car parking, changing rooms, toilet facilities (disabled?), restaurant, store ambience.

The distinction between Services and Facilities above is perhaps a little artificial. Services are rather more specific and are usually provided directly to customers by store staff, whereas Facilities, while none the less important, are part of the general background provision for store customers.

The major points about the retail marketing mix are that it must be appropriate to the chosen customer segment and consistently revised in the light of market research, and that it must be co-ordinated and consistent within itself. The product range in all of its dimensions is obviously funda-mental to the success of the retail organisation, combined with appropriate pricing policies. Most retail strategists would now agree that the emphasis in retailing in many sectors where price was once a dominant consideration has more recently moved to 'value for money', with more consumers now concerned with the range of goods, freshness etc. For example, a survey in 1984 found that at that time two thirds of shoppers felt that convenience was the most important factor in determining their choice of shop, and only 30 per cent were similarly influenced by price. Only three years earlier the proportions had been the reverse, with two thirds of shoppers declaring that price was the most important variable.[10] This presents greater opportunities for retailers, in Porter's terminology, to adopt 'differentiation' strategies rather than 'low cost leadership'.[11] Under the latter, a business emphasises price almost exclusively in its competitive strategy, and correspondingly devotes considerable efforts to minimising its costs; while differentiation, on the other hand, involves retailers in identifying a market to which they can respond in terms of competitive variables other than price alone, and adapting appropriately within the marketing mix.

None the less, although price may now be of less importance in the retail marketing mix, it is a very obvious variable in the 'image' of the retailer, and conveys a very direct message to consumers. Thus, even although value for money may now be regarded as more important in winning customers than price, the latter variable is not only a vital component in the 'value for money' equation but also indicates the target consumer market. Hence retail analysts' critical comments regarding Marks & Spencer's recent apparent departure from its 'natural cultural area of providing B, C1 and C2 people with value for money merchandise', contending that 'people spending £75-plus on clothing are looking for exclusivity'.[12] The criticism being made here is that of inconsistency between one area of merchandise and the image of the remainder of Marks' approach to its target audience defined in socioeconomic terms.

In addition to market or demand influences on retail pricing, regard must also be had to costs. In the last analysis a retailer can only survive profitably if the costs of the goods and services/facilities provided are covered by prices. The retailer must therefore recover all of his costs of differentiation by his prices; and on the cost side, economies of scale and the advantages of moving down the learning curve are as important in retailing as in many other sectors.

More sophisticated retail pricing will take account of consumer price awareness, price sensitivity, and the phenomenon of price as an indicator of quality. Retailers may also adopt pricing strategies such as either 'market skimming' or 'penetration pricing' which refer to longer-term dimensions of pricing; while short-term policies include product range pricing which involves establishing clearly marked single prices for a whole product range, and particular 'breaks' in the range of prices such as £9.99.

Decisions on what we have referred to above as Services and Facilities in the retail marketing mix will quite largely follow from the choice of merchandise (in all of its dimensions) and price. These services and facilities will require to be appropriate to the segment of retail consumers at which the shop is aiming, in the light of which merchandise and pricing decisions will also have been made. Facilities such as car parking will be largely dictated by the nature of the goods – bulk purchases of groceries, DIY supplies – but will also reflect changes in the environment such as increased car ownership. The provision of retail credit through chargecards has now become largely standard in most non-food multiples. Other aspects of facilities such as in-store ambience are much more difficult to quantify in their impact upon customers; although the very large amounts of effort and money now spent on store design indicate how important retailers generally regard this as being within the marketing mix.

As emphasised above, the management of the retail marketing mix is a response to the analysis of the retail environment, and the segmentation and differentiation strategies. This marketing mix requires to be appropriate to the chosen consumer segment, consistent within itself, and regularly monitored to ensure its continuing appropriateness and consistency.

Retail Promotion and Advertising

The third aspect of retail marketing highlighted here is the promotion and advertising role. This relates both to in-store activities and media expenditure. Increasingly, store groups are seeing themselves as brands quite apart from the separate goods which they stock, and this is certainly one factor behind the rapid increase in retailer advertising: to a point where in fields such as groceries retailers are more significant advertisers than manufacturers. An analysis of the top 100 spending brands in 1987, for example, revealed that ten out of the top twenty were retailers; and of the ten non-retailers in this group five (BP shares/prospectus, McDonalds, Electricity Council, BL/Rover Montego and BL/Rover Metro) were either in the cases of McDonald and the Electricity Council providing a 'retailed' service, or were selling goods not normally distributed through retail outlets as defined in this text. This left only national brands such as Nescafé, Whiskas Supermeat, Ariel Automatic and one brand of cigarettes being advertised on a financial scale comparable to the largest ten retailers.[13]

This greater level of retailer advertising is explained by the 'differentiation' strategies which retailers are increasingly adopting, and by the fact that the retailer now sees himself as a brand – or in the case of larger retailers, a number of associated brands. The present levels of retailer advertising are thus taken up not with putting across the message to the consumer of 'low prices' but with promoting the retailer as a differentiated product. Retailing

in total remains a very competitive market. As we saw in Chapter 2
(Appendix Table 2.1) the proportion of retail trade to total GDP has
remained almost constant over the past thirty years; and, more significantly,
retail spending as a proportion of consumer disposable income has fallen in
recent years as consumers have devoted an increased proportion of their
discretionary expenditure to housing, holidays, motoring, and private health
and education etc. New retailing formulae such as Hepworth's Next, Burton's
Principles, or Storehouse's Richards Shops succeed only by taking retail
custom away from established clothing retailers such as C & A, Littlewoods,
Marks & Spencer and traditional department stores. In this context advertising is therefore essential, particularly for those retailers such as The Body
Shop, Tie Rack and Sock Shop trying to create specialist niches in the retail
trade. A common feature of these newer retailers is an appeal to consumers in
terms of quality, distinctness and convenience: characteristics which require
more, and more careful, advertising than purely price-dominated retail
competition.

The purpose of retail advertising is to convey a consistent message to the
chosen customer groups regarding the combination of goods and services
summarised in Table 6.2 above. The relative emphasis within this is,
however, changing. Less weight is now being given to price, and more to
product range, convenient opening hours, quality of own-label products, and
services. DIY, as B & Q advertising reminds us, no longer stands for 'deliver
it yourself'. Advertising and promotion is thus a major way in which the
retailer communicates to potential customers the existence, image and
particular merchandise of a store. More specific purposes of advertising are
set out in Table 6.3.[14]

In addition to these it is hoped that promotions will also lead purchasers to
return to the store and recommend the shop to their acquaintance. In the light
of their overall strategy and these advertising objectives, retailers will make
decisions regarding to whom they will direct their advertising, the media and
content of the advertisements, their timing, and the total level of advertising
expenditure.

Fulop points out, for example, that press and radio are much more
frequently used by retailers than television, and explains this by the fact that
press and radio advertising can be used flexibly to convey relatively inexpens-
ively information on prices and merchandise. Television has, however, been
used increasingly by large store groups to create new, chain-wide images.[15]
Smaller retailers spend almost exclusively on press and radio advertising,
concentrating upon conveying specific merchandise and price information.
For such outlets, 'the public assess the image of the store by the quality of the
merchandise and the manner in which it is presented in the advertisements'.[16]
This attitude is not, however, entirely restricted to smaller retailers, but
explains the policy of some of the larger retailers who engage in almost no
advertising. Thus at Marks & Spencer 'The company's promotion policy is

Table 6.3
Purposes of Retail Advertising and Promotion

Purpose	Applications
1. To inform potential customers of a store's existence	New unit retail outlet, or new branch of a chain
2. To establish or change the image of a chain or store	Increasingly important as store chains become 'brands' in their own right
3. To advertise publicly specific merchandise or price reductions	Designed to attract potential customers to the store
4. Instore advertising and promotion to ensure that customers attracted by 1–3 above do not become 'walkouts', and to increase the level of expenditure by customers through 'impulse' purchases	This includes instore signing, displays etc.

largely based on the thought that good merchandise sells itself . . . Marks and Spencer have 13 million customers per week, most of whom are telling other people about Marks and Spencer's values'.[17]

Fulop also emphasises in her analysis of retailer advertising a distinction between food and non-food retailer behaviour in this area. Somewhat surprisingly in the light of their newsworthiness, food retailers have not significantly increased their share of total retail advertising expenditure, despite several factors that might have led them to do so. These include principally the relatively static level of consumer demand, increased retailer competitiveness, and the greater emphasis by food retailers upon merchandise (including own label products) and store image rather than price competition.[18] The increased proportional incidence of non-food retailer advertising, Fulop argues, has arisen from the impact of the abolition of r.p.m. through the 1970s and the growth of discount furniture, domestic appliances and DIY traders; the increased stocking of non-food items by supermarkets and the variety chain stores (compound trading); and the growth of non-food direct marketing (predominantly catalogue mail order).[19]

Regarding retailer advertising effectiveness, some available evidence suggests that although individual retailers may spend large sums on advertising, it is neither a necessary nor sufficient condition for financial success. One may, for example, contrast the success of the launch in 1984 of Next on the basis of £140 000 of advertising with the failure of much higher advertising spending levels to improve significantly the profit performance of Woolworth at the same time. Marks & Spencer and John Lewis have until quite recently succeeded in their respective fields almost without any advertising.[20] Davies and Brooks suggest on the basis of their own research and that of others that retail advertising is at its most effective when it is informative rather than persuasive: when it is designed to communicate facts such as the existence of a store, the range of merchandise and price levels, rather than attempting itself to create a store image. This may again account for the dominance of radio and the press in retailer advertising in contrast to television; and writing of the important contemporary strategy of store image creation these two authors conclude, 'Without much doubt store design is the most successful method of image formation. Advertising, on the other hand, is unlikely to do more than inform the public about an image. Its ability to create one is, at best, unproven'.[21]

Despite some of these reservations, however, advertising across the range of media is likely to continue to be an important dimension of retailing management, both in attracting new customers through specific offerings or retail image, and in retaining and increasing the expenditure of existing customers. The latter source of consumer spending is obviously an important one – particularly in respect of food and other frequently bought goods.

Because of the importance of certain operational matters in retailing to maintain this custom, a separate section is now devoted below to some of these matters.

6.5 Some Operational Issues

Along with broader, strategic issues regarding retail merchandise and marketing decisions go important managerial matters of merchandise ordering, reception of goods, and storage and display. The last item embraces the whole issue of the design and internal layout of the sales area of the store; and as with all of the matters dealt with in this section, derives its importance from the necessity and cost of stockholding and display in retailing.

Ordering[22]

Having made its strategic merchandise decisions and selected its suppliers, a retailer must place orders such that an adequate instore stock level is efficiently maintained. This will ensure that shelves in the store are not generally uninvitingly empty, and also that specific 'stockouts' do not occur.

At an aggregate level, planned merchandise purchases over a period will be set to equal sales plus the desired level of closing stock minus the actual opening stock; and the size of individual orders will be based upon the economic order quantity (EOQ) calculation discussed below. Thus at its broadest level 'open-to-buy' or OTB reflects the anticipated level of sales of the store, and is a vital component of financial budgeting or cash flow forecasting.[23] However, in addition to total longer-term planned purchases, retailers may use OTB as a means of ensuring that an appropriate stock level is regularly maintained; and with the advent of EPOS databases and other computer applications it is increasingly feasible to apply this to individual lines of merchandise.

'Open-to-buy' fixes a merchandise reorder point on the basis of: the minimum desired stock level, the estimated rate of consumption of the line of goods, and the order lead time with a supplier. Reorder is triggered on the basis of an estimate of when the minimum stock level (units) will be reached at present consumption levels (units per day), allowing for the lead time (days) involved in processing the merchandise order through to the arrival of the goods. Thus in terms of the actual stock level at which reorder occurs, the reorder point is: (merchandise usage rate × lead time) + minimum stock. If the desired or safety stock level of an item of clothing is 40 units, average sales are 10 units per day, and reorder lead time is eight days, then the reorder point is (8 × 10) + 40, or 120 units. This formula can, of course, be used in conjunction with previously planned orders, in which case allowance has to be made for the arrival of these.[24]

In addition to decisions on when to order, retailers must decide how much to order at any one time. This may be based upon the familiar economic order quantity (EOQ) calculation, which is designed to reflect a balance between the *reduction* in unit buying cost as the size of the individual order increases (arising from more attractive trade terms for large orders and some economies in the retailer's own procedures) and the *increase* in physical and financial stockholding costs to the retailer arising from the greater average level of stockholding that comes from buying in greater bulk. The tradeoff between these two forces, illustrated in Figure 6.2, will give the retailer the most economical quantity in which he should buy any line of merchandise.[25]

Goods Received and Stockholding

The next stage is for the retailer to arrange to have inward goods efficiently received. Much sound, if now slightly old-fashioned, advice exists in this area.

> The first stage in reception occurs when the delivery van arrives at the store's unloading bay which should be undercover and well away from the general public. This avoids damage from the rain (and also keeps the warehouseman dry!) and helps reduce losses through pilferage. If a delivery of small transistor radios is made to the front entrance of a shop and left on the pavement for several minutes, no one can be surprised if some of them grow legs and walk![26]

FIGURE 6.2
Economic Order Quantity
Total purchasing costs represented as the sum of ordering costs and carrying costs

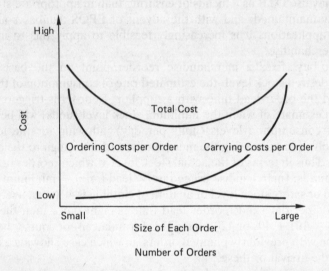

SOURCE: B. Berman and J. R. Evans, *Retail Management: A Strategic Approach* (New York: Macmillan, 2nd edn, 1983) p. 211.

The most important points here are the need for an economical and accurate system for the physical checking of goods received (for quantity, condition etc.) against purchase orders and invoices, security of merchandise held in stock (both against theft or deterioration), and accessibility to stock rooms for goods received and transfer to selling areas. Certain operations such as price marking may be carried out at this stage; although with groceries, prices are often put on items by assistants at the time when goods are placed on the store shelves.

Stockholding involves not just physical control of goods or minimising financial costs, but also comparison of actual and intended stock levels in the light of sales. The rate at which stock is being run down is, for smaller retailers, the clearest indication of the current level of sales; and unpopular lines in particular can be easily identified by slow-moving stock.

Store Layout and Security

The increased incidence of self-service or assisted self-selection in retailing, together with the demise in many cases of a 'planned' shopping list on the part of the consumer and its replacement by in-store decisions regarding both the product to be bought and the particular brand chosen, have combined to heighten the importance of store layout and space allocation decisions.[27] In addition to this, retailers are now spending increased sums of money on the design of the interior of stores in keeping with the various differentiation strategies being adopted and the particular 'image' that they wish to present to potential customers. Store redesign and refurbishment was, for example, a major part of Asda's strategic market changes in the mid 1980s; and the move from traditional 'brown' stores to new 'green' ones increased sales by more than 50 per cent in one instance.[28] More recently Boots has launched a programme designed to make its stores more attractive and inviting to customers, and within three years has redesigned and refurbished two thirds of its 1056 stores.[29] These are not, of course, entirely operational issues, and are being given considerably increased attention by senior retailing management.[30]

In common with the remainder of the issues dealt with in this section, appropriate store design and layout – reflecting the strategic image of the store chain or individual shop – must be translated effectively on to the sales floor. The general principles of store layout, which apply regardless of the particular class of merchandise stocked, are summed up in the following factors.[31]

- Customer convenience.
- Shopper traffic flow through the store.
- Instore location requirements of particular merchandise.
- Purchasing relationships between classes of goods.
- Stock replenishment.

These factors simply serve to emphasise that there is a logic to the internal layout of a store, which can be made more attractive to shoppers – and therefore increase the number of satisfied customers, sales, and profit levels – by the application of certain basic principles. Shoppers expect to find what they want easily, which implies that merchandise should be well signposted and clearly displayed in logical groupings. Traffic flow through the store should be eased; with regard being had to the particular location requirements of certain merchandise (changing rooms for certain clothing) and the effect upon customer traffic flow of popular items such as very regular purchases (bread, fruit, milk) or special offers. Small articles may be displayed adjacent to the store checkout in order both to minimise the incidence of shoplifting and also to appeal to the 'impulse purchase' habit. Articles consumed or stored together at home should be displayed close to one another: or stores which infuriatingly do not adhere to this principle run the risk of being accused of deliberately extending customers' shopping time in the hope of increasing sales! Finally, retailers may also design the store layout with regard to convenience of stock replenishment: restocking some items such as milk from behind wall-based displays, and avoiding frequently having to move pallets of large volume/high turnover items through the middle of the store.

An example of the application of these principles to classes of supermarket merchandise and the resulting instore layout is given in Table 6.4 and Figure 6.3 below. The application of retail space allocation principles – from decisions on overall store design and layout to choice of fixtures and point-of-sale promotional material – plays a very significant role in translating the total strategy of the store chain or individual shop into the achievement of target financial performance. It is therefore necessary that retail managers have an understanding of some of the detail of this.[32]

Table 6.4
Classification and Arrangement of Merchandise

---

1. **Impulse goods**
    Bought:
    As a result of attractive 'visual merchandising' displays
    Should be placed:
    Near entrance in small store – on main aisle in larger stores
2. **Convenience goods**
    Bought:
    With frequency and in small quantities
    Should be placed:
    In easily accessible feature locations along main aisle
3. **Necessities or staple goods**
    Bought:
    Because of an actual need
    Should usually be placed:
    To the rear of one-level stores – on upper floor of multilevel stores (not an infallible rule)
4. **Utility goods**
    Bought:
    For home use – brooms, dust-pans, etc.
    Should be placed:
    As impulse items up front or along main aisle
5. **Luxury and major expense items**
    Bought:
    After careful planning and considerable 'shopping around'
    Should be placed:
    At some distance from entrance

SOURCE: A. E. Spitz and A. B. Flaschner, *Retailing* (Cambridge, Mass.: Winthrop Publishers, 1982) p. 164.

149

FIGURE 6.3
Supermarket Store Layout

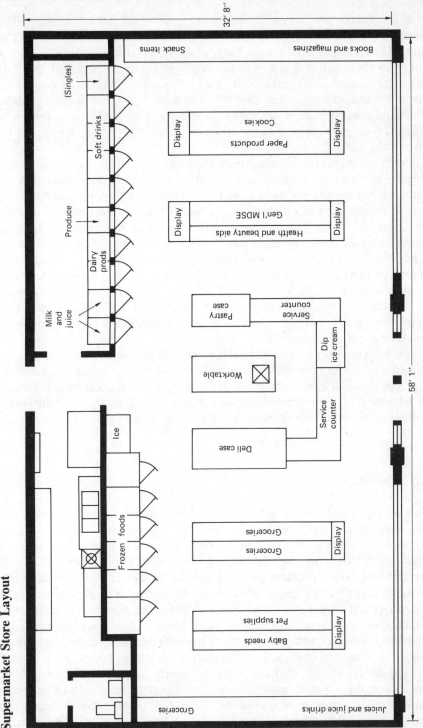

SOURCE: As in Table 6.4 above, p. 165.

A regrettable dimension of store management is that of security. This involves in particular the protection of merchandise from external or internal theft. The former refers to shoplifting, while the latter involves the stealing of goods by shop staff and is sometimes euphemistically termed 'leakage'.[33] In shopping centres additional security may be necessary in order to protect the amenities and, in some cases, shoppers and staff. In a wider security context, retail organisations must also seek to protect themselves from forged or 'bounced' cheques, improper use of credit cards, and, where trade credit is given, bad debts.[34]

Stores can protect themselves from shoplifting – both amateur and professional – by ensuring that they have a clear view of merchandise on display (by using convex mirrors and even closed circuit television), by placing electronic tags or similar devices on merchandise which can only be removed by sales assistants, or by employing store detectives. The possibility of theft of merchandise or money by store employees must also be recognised. This can range from grocery store employees eating off the shelves to large-scale employee theft of garments from clothing stores. Cash may be stolen on a small scale by more junior sales staff, or such theft may occur on the much larger scale of embezzlement by senior managers. Checkout staff may pass items through at reduced prices to family or friends: a process known as 'sweethearting'.

The responsibility of retail management is to use all available techniques and control devices (including financial control) to eliminate these potential losses in the most efficient manner. It is also incumbent upon store managers to be aware of their legal rights and duties as well as those of suspected customers or employees in apprehending and prosecuting persons involved.[35]

6.6 Conclusions

The importance of retail marketing and associated operational issues is becoming increasingly recognised as large, multiproduct (and in many instances multinational) retail organisations compete in oligopolistic markets characterised in a number of cases by relatively low growth. The need certainly for larger retailers to recognise the importance of the marketing function, and to reflect this in their organisation structures, also derives from the movement of the marketing function down the distribution channel as retailers exert increased power in such matters over manufacturers (as analysed in Chapter 3 above).[36] Also of considerable importance, and closely related to structural changes in retail markets as well as social and economic developments, is the changed basis of much retail competition. 'Mass marketing' on a price basis, and a corresponding emphasis on low-cost leadership strategies, gave way in the 1980s to differentiation strategies and recognition of the individual retail outlet or store group as a brand to be marketed. Sir Terence Conran of Storehouse reflected on a number of these factors:

> The great change that has occurred is that retailers no longer go out into the market place and buy what is offered to them by manufacturers. They go now with a much greater knowledge of their customers to manufacturers and say: 'We want our products to be made like this for us and we want them to be our products.'[37]

This more complex approach to retail marketing is also exemplified by statements from chairmen in retailer company annual reports. Thus Burton's 1985 statement that 'Market stratification, not by socio-economic class alone, but by consumer preferences and lifestyles, is fundamental to the Group's approach to the market place', and Dixons' policy that 'Competitive advantage is gained by establishing and maintaining superior ranges of products'.[38] The evidence available suggests that these factors have led to a greater recognition of the importance of the marketing function in retailing as a vital adjunct to longer-term strategic decision making. Indeed, it is impossible in the context of retailing in particular to separate clearly these two dimensions of management. Hence the close link between the material in Chapter 4 and the present one.

References

1. See, for example, G. Pintel and J. Diamond, *Retailing* (New Jersey: Prentice-Hall, 4th edn, 1987) p. 116.
2. D. Walters and D. White, *Retail Marketing Management* (London: Macmillan, 1987) p. 23.
3. See S. Caulkin, 'The Fall and Rise of Brands', *Management Today*, July 1987, pp. 45ff.
4. See S. Caulkin, 'Brand Wars', *Marketing*, 7 May 1987, p. 37.
5. See Lord Sieff, *Don't Ask the Price* (London: Weidenfeld & Nicolson, 1987) pp. 38–9.
6. See G. Nuttall, 'Post Haste', *Marketing*, 5 March 1988, pp. 15–18.
7. It is reported, for example, that in the UK the number of single-person households doubled over the twenty years 1961–1982. See Walters and White, *Retail Marketing Management*, p. 17.
8. Ibid., p. 9.
9. See 'Putting a jewel in everyone's crown', *Financial Times*, 28 January 1988.
10. See J. Harris, 'What Makes People Buy', *Management Today*, November 1984, pp. 68ff.
11. See M. E. Porter, *Competitive Strategy* (New York: Free Press, 1980) Ch. 2.
12. N. Britton and L. Warner, 'Has M & S Lost its Touch?', *Marketing*, 4 February 1988, p. 21.
13. Data given in 'Top 500 Brands', *Marketing*, 25 February 1988.
14. Adapted from a schema in R. W. Hasty, *Retailing* (New York: Harper & Row, 3rd edn, 1983) pp. 299–300.

15. In 1985, for example, retail advertising accounted for 21 per cent and 20 per cent of press and radio advertising respectively, but for only 6 per cent of television advertising. See C. Fulop, *Retailing Advertising and Retail Competition in the U.K.* (London: The Advertising Association, 1986) pp. 32–5.
16. E. Lowe, *Successful Retailing through Advertising* (London: McGraw-Hill, 1983) p. 4.
17. E. J. Ornstien, *The Retailers: A study in successful marketing and promotion* (London: Associated Business Programmes, 1976) p. 143.
18. See Fulop, *Retail Advertising and Retail Competition in the U.K.*, pp. 39–62.
19. Ibid., pp. 63–86.
20. See G. Davies and J. Brooks, *Positioning Strategy in Retailing* (London: Paul Chapman, 1989) pp. 59–60 and 195–6.
21. Ibid., p. 202.
22. See generally P. J. Amer, *Retail Management* (London: Intertext, 1970) pp. 123–6.
23. See Hasty, *Retailing*, Ch. 9.
24. See B. Berman and J. R. Evans, *Retail Management: A Strategic Approach* (New York: Macmillan, 2nd edn, 1983) pp. 343–6.
25. See A. E. Spitz and A. B. Flaschner, *Retailing* (Cambridge, Mass.: 1982) pp. 210–12.
26. A. R. Leal, *Retailing* (London: Edward Arnold, 1974) p. 68.
27. United States data, for example, indicate that almost 40 per cent of department store purchases and nearly two thirds of supermarket purchases are unplanned in so far as the buying intention was not formed prior to entering the store. See F. Buttle, 'Retail Space Allocation', *International Journal of Physical Distribution and Materials Management*, 1984, Vol. 14, No. 4, p. 5.
28. See *Financial Times*, 17 August 1989.
29. The Boots Company PLC, *1989 Annual Report*, p. 8.
30. See, for example, R. Fitch and J. Woudhuysen, 'The Strategic Significance of Design', in E. McFadyen (ed.), *The Changing Face of British Retailing* (London: Newman Books, 1987) pp. 14–21.
31. See Amer, *Retail Management*, p. 77.
32. A very good review of this is contained in Buttle, 'Retail Space Allocation', pp. 3–23.
33. The currently quoted figure for total UK annual shop theft losses is about £2bn – representing up to 2.8 per cent of total retail turnover. Employee theft (1984 data) was twice as great as customer theft; and rather alarmingly one survey based upon responses from retailers showed that 19 per cent of shop staff apprehended for theft were managers or supervisors. See Home Office Standing Conference on Crime Prevention, *Report of the Working Group on Shop Theft* (1986) paras 3–4 and Appendix B, Table 3. Reference to this report and to other literature in the field was kindly provided by a senior crime prevention officer of Tayside Police, Scotland.
34. See D. M. Lewison and M. W. DeLozier, *Retailing* (Columbus, Ohio: Merrill Publishing Co., 2nd edn, 1986) Ch. 11. A very comprehensive treatment of this matter is given in P. H. Jones, *Retail Loss Control* (London: Butterworths, 1990).
35. Any member of the shop staff may arrest someone who is shoplifting or whom they suspect with reasonable cause to be in the act of shoplifting. It is usual to make the arrest after the person has left the shop in order to minimise as far as possible the possibility of arresting someone who is not shoplifting. Such force as is reasonable in the circumstances may be used to effect the arrest. This means that if the shoplifter, or suspected shoplifter, puts up a struggle sufficient force to subdue him may be used. However, if excessive force is used then those responsible will be guilty of assault and, perhaps, more serious offences, depending upon the

nature of the force used and the gravity of any injuries inflicted. In such circumstances the shop staff and the retailer would also be liable to the shoplifter for damages in a civil action. Should a suspected shoplifter prove to be innocent then the question will arise whether those who apprehended him actually had reasonable cause to suspect him or her of shoplifting. If not, then they commit the offence of false imprisonment. More importantly, they and their employer will be liable for the torts of trespass to the person and, if the individual has been detained, false imprisonment, which may result in the award of damages. It should be noted that differences exist between Scots and English law in the procedures that should be followed in these matters as the standard of evidence required in Scotland is greater than that necessary in England and Wales. In Scotland such cases will be heard in the first instance in the Sheriff Court, and in England and Wales in the County Court.

36. See N. Piercy, 'The Role of the Marketing Department in U.K. Retailing Organisations', *International Journal of Retailing*, 1989, Vol. 4, No. 2, pp. 46–65.
37. Quoted in D. Ezra and D. Oates, *Advice from the Top* (London: David & Charles, 1989) p. 32.
38. Quoted in A. D. Morgan, *British Imports of Consumer Goods: A Study of Import Penetration 1974–85* (Cambridge: CUP, 1989) p. 26.

Physical Distribution Management 7

7.1 Introduction

The statement in the Storehouse Annual Report of 1987 that 'Getting the right merchandise to the right place at the right time is still the essence of good retailing' now has an ironic ring given the tremendous difficulties Mothercare experienced in the following year of doing just that. The basic message of the quotation is however still correct. Retailing is only as good as the distribution system supplying the retail outlets. Without product to sell and provide to consumers, most retail operations are in difficulty. This is not to argue that physical distribution supersedes all other management tasks in retailing, but rather to view physical distribution in retailing as an activity that is central with other management areas. A quotation from the Burton Annual Report for 1987 makes the point: 'Any marketing strategy is impotent without the ability to analyse and react to sales patterns and to deliver the right merchandise to the right place at the right time'.

One of the problems for physical distribution in retailing is that it has in the past been neglected. There is now as a consequence only limited awareness of how difficult and complicated it can be to achieve efficient and effective physical distribution.

As the earlier chapters of this book have demonstrated, retailing is a highly dynamic industry.[1] This retail dynamism is occurring at the same time as wider societal and industrial change. The trends in retailing appear numerous, complex and, in some cases, controversial. Whilst change is highly visible at the retail end of the distribution channel, change has also been occurring in physical distribution. As retailing changes so distribution challenges have to be met. The ways in which retailers manage these distribution challenges are the theme of this chapter.

This chapter is structured into ten sections. In order to set the scene, the key changes in retailing bringing forth distribution challenges are analysed in the next section. This builds also on the earlier chapters of this book. Having set the scene, the topic of physical distribution management is then assessed directly by examining what is meant by physical distribution management and why it is important. The remainder of the chapter comprises sections on elements of physical distribution management in retailing. These begin with the key concepts of total cost and customer service before analysing the main functional areas in physical distribution: inventory, packaging, unitisation and warehousing, transportation, and information systems and communications. The analysis of physical distribution management is then concluded by examining the role of sub-contracting in physical distribution and the adoption of physical distribution strategies. This latter section includes some illustrative examples of retailer distribution that aim to show the need for an integrated approach to physical distribution strategy. A summary and conclusions section rounds off the chapter.

7.2 Retailing Changes and Distribution Challenges

The trends and changes in retailing can be divided broadly into changes in business organisation and changes in the operations of retailing.[2] It has to be recognised, however, that both these sets of changes are themselves responses to, or attempts to change, trends in the wider environment of retailing, including, for example, consumer behaviour and social change.

There are under way in Great Britain changes in consumer behaviour and consumption that are influencing retailers and to which retailers respond. First, there are economic changes associated with spending power, disposable income, credit and home ownership. Secondly, there are attitudinal changes through altered perceptions and consciousness (e.g. healthy eating) perhaps reaching an extreme in 'lifestyle'. Thirdly, there are behavioural changes in the use of time and perceived and actual mobility (retail as leisure). Finally, there are locational changes in terms of places of residence and work. All these changes are interlinked and constitute major factors underpinning retail change. Retailers are aware of these changes and respond to them in terms of the quality and format of their retail offering and services. These responses in turn require changes to the physical distribution strategy and operations of both retailers and manufacturers.

Changes in Business Organisation

Within all sectors of retailing there has been a growth of large companies and an expansion of multiple retailers. The largest firms in retailing are amongst the largest companies in Britain. Many retail sectors have become dominated by large firms and have high concentration ratios. Typically the grocery sector is highly concentrated, but other historically less concentrated sectors such as jewellery, toys and chemists have seen the emergence of multiple retailers such as Ratners, Toys 'Я' Us and Superdrug respectively. These large companies depend on the City for finance, and good share price performance therefore becomes a fundamental aim, generally achieved by ensuring profit growth and expansion. As the retail companies become larger so the distribution challenges posed change and the complexities of distribution increase.

The structure of retailing in terms of organisational types is also changing with independents and co-operatives losing market share to corporate chains (multiples) and contractual chains (Body Shop, Spar etc). It is the *chains* of stores that are expanding, based particularly on economies of scale and economies of replication. As these companies have grown larger they have been able to benefit from their size in terms of, for example, buying power from suppliers, administrative centralisation, specialist developments and wider market power. Benefits have also arisen through economies of replication in which a standard or relatively standard retail outlet or procedures can be duplicated over a large number of sites. Such procedures will include stock replenishment ordering by the outlet and delivery of these products. This replication brings cost and operational savings through centralisation of management, speed of store opening and conformity of operation. When companies multiply their retail outlets it becomes imperative to manage distribution correctly not only in the vertical channel dimension but also in the horizontal outlet dimension. Excess stockholding at one outlet may be acceptable, but its cost if replicated over hundreds of outlets is immense. For independent retailers, the performance of the wholesaler and the delivered goods sector has also had to change to reflect the new competitive realities. Wholesalers have had to improve their distribution efficiency and support to independent retailers.

The move to centralised management and control is associated with the emergence of strategic planning and the adoption of a systems approach to retail operations.[3] Small units as part of a larger chain have become profitable again under tight, central control, as for example in Spar, Tie Rack, Knickerbox etc. although the importance of maintaining tight central control on all aspects of the business can be underestimated (e.g. Sock Shop). Arising from these new management methods as well is the emergence of clear corporate strategies adopted by the leading retailers. Leading retailers are much clearer about their strategy and the tactics and operational management that are required to deliver that strategy. Currently favoured strategies are segmentation, often associated with multi-format development (e.g. Burton) and diversification perhaps involving other service sector activities (e.g. Marks & Spencer) or across retail trades (e.g. Kingfisher). As these strategies imply a better focus on the consumer, so distribution operations and strategy underpinning the corporate strategies have had to change to reflect this focus. Distribution strategy has become an important element of corporate strategy.

Changes in Retail Operations

The changes in retail operations are dramatic and widespread. A shop of the 1950s bears little or no resemblance to the shops of the present day. The most basic change in retail operations is that the number of retail units has declined enormously. As a generalisation, there has been an increase in large units and a decrease in traditional small units. New forms of small units are emerging however, mainly as part of a multiple chain with centralised control, producing therefore a polarisation of format size in retail operations. Associated with these developments are fundamental changes in the location of retailing. Larger units, through their size and commitment to economies of scale, spearheaded a move out-of-town or to decentralised locations. The growth of food and non-food superstores, retail parks and regional shopping centres demonstrates the decentralisation of much modern retailing. Even many of the smaller stores are now moving away from former high streets. The change in number of retail units, their polarisation in size and their changing locations all pose new problems and issues for physical distribution management.

Many stores are now located in purpose-built shopping centres where the environment is managed. This reflects an increasing concern to improve the retail environment both in and out of stores and to emphasise customer care and service. There is a recognition in retailing that existing facilities often do not meet consumer needs. This has found expression in greater emphasis on design and service. 'Customer care' is now a by-word in retailing, whether considered as new products, better products, greater range, more financial facilities, accessible location, more consumer information, or better environment and so on. Customer care extends into better pedestrianisation, the increasing use of food courts and the current high level of refurbishment of older shopping centre schemes. At the store level design consultancies are being used widely to help multiple retailers project an image and to improve performance. The whole ethos of better service and customer care however means little if physical distribution is unable to get the goods to the store in the right conditions, sizes etc and at the right time. Managing the retail environment and the consumer also implies better management of the distribution process and channel.

The locational changes in retailing and the re-emergence of the small unit are associated with new technology introduction in retailing. New technology is enabling management control to remain effective in large stores and in chains of small stores. Laser scanning at the checkout, whilst the most visible sign of technology use, is merely one manifestation of technology introduction throughout retailing. For example EPOS tills are now common in many retailers, with the data polled overnight by head office for up-to-date sales information. Laser scanning and computer control are becoming standard in warehouses and distribution centres with replenishment orders from stores transmitted electronically. Communications and payment between retailers and suppliers are increasingly via electronic data interchanges such as TRADANET. At store and head offices increasing use is being made of decision support systems on microcomputers including Direct Product Profitability (DPP) models. The important point to note in all this is the increase in control of all aspects of operation that is offered by technological data collection, transmission and interpretation. Technology is being applied throughout the distribution channel to facilitate rapid and accurate information flows and thus timely and appropriate product distribution. As an illustration Walters shows how technology is helping Argyll manage better its supply chain,[4] whilst Belussi provides detail on the importance of technology for Benetton in linking retail sales, distribution and production.[5]

At the product level in the stores other changes are also under way. Following on from technology introduction at the point of sale is the better matching of products and product availability to consumer desires and needs. Examples abound, particularly but not solely in the fashion trade, of how technology is being used to ensure the retailer is stocking in the store what is selling rather than what the retailer hopes will sell. Retail buying and merchandising retain elements of retail knowledge and risk-taking, but increasingly consumer behaviour patterns are used to channel that knowledge and help decision making. Merchandising and buying are becoming increasingly dependent on information technology assistance and this also then impacts on distribution flows. W. H. Smith for example is able to merchandise newspapers and magazines at local stores through the use of geodemographics to 'spot' likely bestsellers. Local stores become tailored to the local market, with distribution practices taking account of local variations.

Changing consumer tastes and habits have conditioned such developments, but have also included other extensions to product ranges with which retail operations have to cope. In food for example, there have been extensions into frozen and chilled products, whilst in many trades the concepts of own-label or private-label have affected retail operations. The more mobile and affluent consumers of the 1980s are also much less tolerant over shortcomings in retailer offerings. Distribution becomes all the more important. Retailing has seen the rise of larger and more powerful companies across many retail sectors. These companies are crucial buying points for suppliers. Modern multiple retail companies have centralised authority and control and are setting high operational standards for their business. These standards are set in response to increasing consumer demands for services and facilities in retailing. Retailers and wholesalers now place a premium on having the right products in the right place at the right time and are very careful to ensure that the distribution systems that service stores are as efficient and effective as possible.

The changes in business organisation have a number of implications for physical distribution. In particular the implications of retail concentration are twofold. First, the stores themselves are changing, and in many cases getting larger. This changes the distribution requirements, and on a local scale involves new locations with, for example, edge-of-town stores replacing the high street outlets. The physical distribution demands of a large food superstore are vastly different to the requirements of the shops it replaces. The centralised control of small units in chains ensures that their distribution requirements also are different. Modern shopping centres, pedestrianisation schemes and other traffic management measures also change the distribution requirements. Second, the size of these retail companies and their dominance of the market mean that much of the retail distribution process is an exchange between a very limited number of manufacturers on the one hand and a small number of retailers on the other. It has to be remembered that the retailing distribution changes described in this chapter have counterparts in distribution changes by manufacturers at their end of the distribution channel. At a different retail level opportunities may also exist, however, in providing better distribution services to the small-shop independent retailers. It must not be forgotten that independent businesses make up the bulk of retail outlets in the UK and can provide a large market for good and appropriate distribution.

The changes in retail operations also have a number of implications. The development of own-labels for example has two main implications. First, own-labels are within the control of retailers for longer than manufacturers' brands and a close control can therefore be maintained throughout the distribution channel. This is well demonstrated by the detailed involvement for example that Marks & Spencer and Benetton have with their suppliers. Second, if a retailer has an own-label strategy then manufacturer brands often have to fight to obtain shelf space. One element of this fight is the adherence to delivery schedules and standards set by retailers. Accurate and effective physical distribution becomes a competitive tool for the manufacturers. The other changes in retail operations are similarly affecting physical distribution by placing higher standards on distribution operations. If retail outlets are improving handling, merchandising, availability and selling standards to the customer, then the implication is that the physical distribution system from the manufacturer and to the store has to perform to equally improved and exacting standards.

This brief introductory review has attempted to demonstrate that the changes that are occurring in retailing are causing major changes to be made in distribution systems. It is clear that the distribution operations of major retailers have now to be placed under close consideration if they are to serve the retail business properly. Distribution is, as Hornby comments, a critical success factor in a modern retail business and must be managed accordingly.[6] The remainder of this chapter considers how this should be undertaken.

7.3 Physical Distribution Management

Distribution is concerned with product availability and is often summed up in the adage of getting the right product to the right place at the right time. This implies that retailers must be concerned with the flows of product and information into their companies in order to make products available to consumers. In particular the concern is with the structure and management of marketing and physical distribution channels. Physical distribution is concerned with making products physically available for possession by consumers. The management task in physical distribution can therefore be summarised as:

> the planning, co-ordinating and controlling of the physical movement of products to provide a level of timely and spatial physical availability for customers, appropriate to the needs of the market place and the resources of the company.[7]

If we disaggregate this definition then it can be suggested that the management task in physical distribution is concerned with a number of elements. These elements can be described as the distribution mix and comprise:

— decisions about the number, type and location of the storage facilities;
— decisions about the levels of stockholding in terms of both quality and quantity;
— decisions about the transport to be used in moving products;
— decisions about packaging and unit sizes and how these are handled;
— decisions about communications both within the distribution elements and externally in the distribution channel.

These elements of the distribution mix (storage facilities, inventory management, transportation, unitisation, communications) have to work together. These core elements of distribution also provide the structure of the recent textbooks in the area.[8] The ways in which these elements interact can best be viewed by considering a simple retail example.

A retailer has to be aware of consumer demand, or to be able to forecast demand for a product. This demand knowledge or forecast has to be translated both into product orders to suppliers (manufacturers and/or wholesalers) and to re-supply shelves at the retail outlet. These communications trigger the setting of inventory levels at various storage points. Within these storage facilities the inventory will be handled in various sizes and ways. The communications trigger also forces product movement through transportation. All the elements interact in providing distribution and in setting service levels and costs incurred.

The distribution function has to manage these elements of the distribution mix to provide the correct balance for the market and the company between the lowest possible distribution costs on the one hand and the highest possible customer satisfaction on the other. Distribution is explicitly concerned with costs and customer service and the elements of decision-making that influence these. Customers are the life-blood of any retailer, and yet retailers cannot forecast precisely what demand is going to be. A balance has therefore to be struck. To a considerable extent it is the better awareness of the costs incurred in making this balance and the potential service gains that are available that are causing the emergence of the new professionalism in physical distribution. These relationships are shown diagrammatically in Figure 7.1.

FIGURE 7.1
The Elements of the Distribution Mix

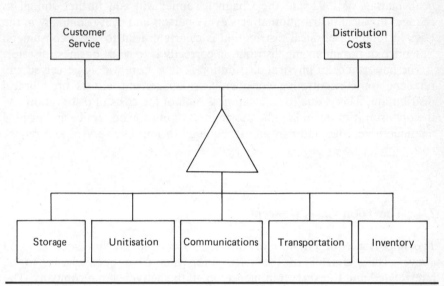

It is becoming increasingly common to see the term 'physical distribution management' replaced by the term 'logistics management'. In many cases the terms are used interchangeably although there are differences. Christopher defines logistics management as:

> the process of strategically managing the movement and storage of materials, parts and finished inventory from suppliers, through the firm and on to customers . . .[logistics] is thus concerned with the management of the physical flow which begins with sources of supply and ends at the point of consumption.[9]

Physical distribution is thus somewhat narrower than logistics management, being concerned with finished products rather than the combination of materials management of components and raw materials as well as finished products as implied by the definition of logistics. For retailers it would seem that whilst companies are extending their influence back into logistics management and concepts such as integrated distribution and just-in-time distribution are becoming increasingly important, the narrower concept of physical distribution management is more applicable. This is the term used here, but the importance of backward integration and co-operation by retailers should be emphasised.

At the national level, physical distribution is a vital component of the national economy of any country.[10] There is an enormous investment in infrastructure, facilities and the workforce, all of which are changing rapidly. Some of the companies involved in distribution or specialising in distribution management are among the largest companies in the UK. The open European market of 1992 and the Channel Tunnel will add further stimuli to change. Physical distribution affects every person and every company in the UK. In retailing physical distribution is clearly crucial to serve consumers. The price of not managing distribution correctly is to court business disaster.

The importance of physical distribution is now more widely perceived and retailers are concentrating considerable management efforts on physical distribution. This is due to an awareness both of the costs of distribution and the opportunities, including the possibilities of improving service and gaining a competitive edge and of using technology to improve service and reduce costs.

7.4   The Total Costs Concept

The importance of physical distribution to a company has been stressed above. The elements of the distribution mix have been shown to be interrelated and to exert an influence on all the activities of a company. The problem this raises is that it is often difficult to identify where the true costs of physical distribution lie. What is becoming increasingly obvious to retailers is that it is only by putting together the entire costs of physical distribution wherever they are encountered that the extent of the management issues for physical distribution can be ascertained. Analysis of the true costs of distribution can often lead to the identification of more efficient ways of operating. Detailed costing of distribution can lead to improved performance through the better matching of supply to consumer demand and to better targeting of a company's distribution offering. It is the identification of all these costs that lies behind the total cost approach to physical distribution.

The identification of the total costs in distribution allows a better understanding of the costs of undertaking distribution and the likely effects of changing the distribution operation. The identification of costs allows the search for 'trade-offs' between one area of costs and other areas. A 'trade-off' occurs when costs are consciously incurred in one activity centre in order to achieve increased benefits from another activity centre, or from the aggregated effects of other activity centres. In all cases, the objective is to achieve a net gain in service or cost terms. For example, a decision by a retailer to centralise distribution would not only change the cost structure compared to previous systems but also change the service provision to stores and thus consumers. Costs in warehousing may vary, but so too will costs in stockholding and transportation as well as communications. In some cases it will be possible to externalise some costs onto manufacturers. Retailers have to examine their distribution system to see if alternative methods of provision can provide the necessary costs and service balance. Such a total cost approach is not easy, but it is argued the benefits can be considerable.

7.5 Customer Service in Distribution

The discussion above on total costs has been couched in terms of the need to find a cost and service balance. This service element is of enormous importance in retail distribution. The precise composition of 'customer service' is not easy to specify. Customer service varies by product, location and company and comprises a host of tangible and measurable elements such as the number of stock-outs as well as less tangible and unquantifiable elements such as telephone manners or store design. It is also important to recognise that a true customer service orientation by a retailer involves service by everyone in all their activities. For a retailer customer service is important in terms of relations with consumers and suppliers, but it is also important within the organisation where for example the retail outlets are the distribution centre's customers and have to be serviced accordingly.

Customer service has become a key element of many retail offerings and is seen as an integral element of retail strategy.[11] In distribution terms this can be seen as being because of the pressure on costs and thus the cost/service balance, the intensification of competition, the opportunity to provide a competitive edge, the increasing integration of systems and the striving for supply chain management and just-in-time distribution.

The standard way of examining customer service provision is by disaggregation into elements of pre-transaction, transaction and post-transaction service. Pre-transaction service tends to be policy related and arises prior to the transaction taking place. It could include, for example, the provision of a customer service statement to the customers. Such a statement might outline policy on specific occurrences, e.g. Marks & Spencer returns policy. Design or technical information or help can be considered as pre-transaction service. Transaction elements of service are the more direct and quantifiable elements of service. They include for example stockout levels, order cycle time, order accuracy, product substitution as well as elements such as provision of order information and expedited shipments. These elements are the operational aspect of customer service in retail distribution. Post-transaction elements are those that arise once the transaction has been completed. Service in such cases not only includes warranty and installation for example, but also covers tracing products or owners and audit-trials etc. Whilst it is easy to consider such elements in terms of customers of a retail outlet, it is also instructive to consider such elements at other levels in the distribution channel. For example, the supplier/retailer interface can contain many of these pre-transaction, transaction and post-transaction elements. Similarly the relationship between a distribution centre and the retail outlets it serves contains the same basic elements, all of which need to be in balance for top quality distribution to occur. The danger is that only some of these elements are considered important in providing service, whereas in fact all aspects are crucial (Figure 7.2).

Retail distribution clearly has a major concern in the transaction elements of customer service. For example, most retailers assess their suppliers on a regular basis in terms of their delivery reliability into distribution centres, the number of errors in which can be measured easily. Retail outlet managers are often instructed to inform retail head office if delivery to the store, from the company's own distribution centre, is missed, late or in any way inaccurate. Systems can be put into place to monitor such service provision and to remedy recurrent problems. Sainsbury, for example, produces each morning an operational distribution report summarising performance in distribution for the past 24 hours. Problems have to be identified and actions indicated. Two hours later a retail division report is produced about the service received from distribution. Daily, Sainsbury can monitor and improve on its distribution performance.[12]

Such operations and quantifiable reports are important in the performance of any business. Retailers are now, however, turning their attention to the other elements of customer service. Attention is being focused on the ease of placing an order, on the way in which complaints or changes are handled, on vehicle and driver appearance and knowledge of the job, the company and the systems in place. From a concentration on meeting quantifiable targets the service issue has moved to being one of total quality in customer service. For retailers this means a first class service feeding the retail outlets, allowing customers to be served. Such a service involves suppliers and distribution specialist companies as well as the retail company itself.

This emphasis on service and a total quality service approach, together with the general rise in importance of distribution management in retailing, are reflected in changes to the elements that make up the distribution mix. These can be examined in turn.

FIGURE 7.2
Customer Service in Physical Distribution

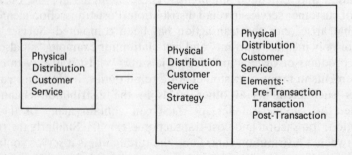

7.6   Inventory, Packaging/Unitisation and Warehousing

Inventory

Inventory performs a number of different functions within a retail company, but they are all related to the basic retail fact that it is not often possible to be totally sure about the demand for products or the sales or supplies of a company. The main role that inventory plays therefore is that of 'buffering' or linking the elements within a retail company or within a distribution channel. This linking process is also required because there is generally a temporal and spatial separation between production and consumption. Only rarely are goods produced and consumed almost instantaneously and at the same place. Inventory takes account of these separations.

Retailers generally consider inventory as being of three types: in-transit, cycle or safety inventory. *In-transit inventory* is that which at any time is moving from one part of the distribution channel to another. *Cycle inventory* is the inventory required because of time lags or other inconsistencies in the system. Retailers may, for example, have to hold inventory because of the need of production runs or because of seasonal fluctuations. *Safety inventory* is the inventory required as it is not possible to be totally accurate in most business forecasts and it is important to have an 'emergency' supply on which to draw. Clearly the size of this safety inventory is a careful management decision involving a trade-off between costs and service. This safety inventory is a mixture of a measure of belief in forecasts and a willingness to incur costs through holding inventory in order to provide service to the consumer.

The danger in classifying inventory in this way and encouraging retail outlets and retail buyers to develop stockholding patterns around inventory types is that there is a tendency to over-rely on inventory and incur excess costs. There is a danger of wanting inventory 'where it can be seen' or having inventory 'just-in-case'. Inventory is built up and not properly managed and customers are being provided with (although not realising or using it) 'excess' service at enormous costs. It is against this tendency that retailers are turning to the concept of 'just-in-time'. The concept of just-in-time distribution aims to eliminate waste, which includes in its purest form, *all* inventory. The idea is to provide the right number of products in the right place at just the right time, i.e. immediately before they are needed (or sold). Thus a retail outlet would hold the bare minimum of product to cover anticipated sales, relying instead on frequent replenishment from a distribution centre which in turn is frequently replenished from manufacturers. Logically manufacturers would also be producing product just ahead of demand, so reducing the temporal fluctuations in physical distribution and allowing efficient information and product flows to overcome spatial separations. The volume of stock in the entire system is reduced, releasing valuable capital but hopefully maintaining or improving service levels. The keys to approaching this ideal position are the better forecasting and reporting techniques now available, the use of data (particularly point-of-sale data) throughout the distribution channel, the sharing or integration of information, management control of business service levels, and the better location of inventory

Packaging/Unitisation

Even in a just-in-time situation, and most retailers are some way off this, products have to be held and transported throughout the distribution channel and within a retail company. There is need therefore to consider packaging requirements and the sizes in which products are best transported and handled.

Packaging has many roles to play, and at times these roles are in conflict. For example, the best packaging for protecting a product may make it too bulky or heavy to handle. The best packaging for promotional purposes may not allow electronic identification of a product. The most 'consumer-friendly' shape for a new product may simply be impossible to package into convenient shapes or sizes for handling

The effect of these conflicts is to encourage the idea of regularity in packaging and product handling. Regular sizes and shapes are used as a compromise between the varying conflicting roles. These regular sizes and shapes may themselves be packaged together in some way so as to provide a regular or unit size for handling. Unitisation may be a standard size carton, box or tray, or a roll cage, or a pallet load etc. If a standard or unit size can be agreed then costs of handling can be reduced dramatically by maintaining this size throughout the distribution channel if possible. For example, retailers may specify the maximum dimensions of a shrink-wrapped pallet load. These dimensions would then be used in distribution centre and shop storage space construction, in vehice design and purchase, in handling or conveyor systems etc. The savings can be considerable in terms of efficiency and effectiveness.

At the same time there are gains to be made from the more careful and thoughtful design of individual products and how these fit together to form unit loads and how they occupy space on shop shelves, vehicles and in distribution centres. The current tool in vogue in retail management is that of DPP. As part of its calculation DPP involves examining occupancy and handling costs at various stages of the distribution channel. Products that are poorly packaged or have awkward shapes and sizes tend to perform poorly in DPP calculations and there is then pressure to regularise shapes and sizes and thus gain from handling and occupancy savings.

Warehousing

It has already been suggested that retailers are more concerned now with just-in-time concepts in distribution rather than the old emphasis on the management of inventory. Taken to an extreme, it can be seen that just-in-time distribution obviates the need for warehouses or distribution centres. It is difficult, however, for many reasons, to envisage retail systems being able to function reliably and efficiently without any warehousing function. Warehousing is necessary to retailers for a number of reasons:

— to achieve transportation economies
— to obtain quantity discounts
— to maintain a source of supply
— to meet changing market conditions
— to achieve operational efficiencies
— to achieve handling benefits
— to accomplish supply chain management.

Retailers are not likely to have a static distribution system in terms of warehouses, as efficiencies can be gained by closely examining operations. For most retailers the need for warehousing is proven. The questions then become ones of:

— what type?
— how many?
— where?

These questions are clearly interlinked and retailers have to develop an overall strategy for warehousing as for other elements of their operations. In retailing such questions take on an added importance as many distribution facilities have been present in the company for a long time or may have been 'gained' during a takeover or merger. The warehousing system may therefore be an inefficient collection of relict features rather than an efficient and effective modern system.

The basic question of the type of warehouse is merely at a general level a question of public or private warehousing. The distinction is between private warehousing which is for the use of only one client on a permanent basis, and public warehousing which involves renting space in a warehouse shared by other users. For large retailers this is not a major problem as private warehousing is the preferred option. Major retailers are likely to use public or common user warehousing only in exceptional circumstances. At a specific level, the fitting out of warehouses changes their 'type' considerably and retailers will want to customise warehouses to their own operations. The specific requirements of mail order, for example, lead to very particular warehouse operations.

The number of warehouses in a distribution system will vary by retailer and will be dependent on several factors including costs and service. The basic decision that retailers face is whether to go for a centralised or a decentralised warehouse system. The trend in most retail sectors has been to centralise the warehousing as far as possible. In some companies the centralisation process can be taken as far as having only one national distribution centre. For other retailers, however, the service level required and the product characteristics favour the development of a small number of regional distribution centres.

Whilst this may appear not to be a centralised solution, it has to be remembered that the situation it supersedes is stockholding at all retail outlets, supported by an extensive warehouse network. The new solution is therefore clearly one of centralisation.

The centralisation process is occurring across many retail sectors. In foods, Asda and Tesco for example are embarked upon a major development programme for centralised distribution centres; Boots, Storehouse and Burton are doing the same in non-foods; whilst mail-order companies such as GUS and Grattan are also investing heavily in centralised facilities. The benefits that are claimed in such circumstances include:

— greater speed, efficiency and flexibility in the flow of inventory to the store
— the spreading of overheads and a reduction in costs through the use of new systems and reduced inventory
— improved business control and service levels.

In addition to making decisions about the number of distribution centres in any retail distribution system, retailers have also to decide on the location of these facilities. Much effort has been expended on finding operational research models that aid in this process, but in many cases the assumptions inherent in such models bear little applicability to real life. What is clear from studies of the distribution centre locations of major retailers is that certain broad locations are favoured.[13] These as might be expected bear considerable relationships to the population centres, and thus the store locations, and also the infrastructure and transport networks. Provided a site has the necessary proximity and access to the road system, then the detailed location is almost irrelevant within broad areas. The location decision then becomes more concerned with the facilities available or proposed on site and the commercial deal that can be struck in occupying the site.

For example the present pattern of such centres shows that the motorway corridors of the M1, M4 and M6 are particularly common locations, and that the general areas in particular around Greater Manchester, West Midlands, West Yorkshire, Bristol, Central Scotland and London (West and North) are favoured locations. For non-food multiple retailers, and especially those with a single national distribution centre, locations tend to be within the area bounded by Birmingham, London, Leicester and Swindon.[14] The concentration of these centres at a relatively restricted number of locations suggests that common forces are at work in the selection of broad areas for retailer's depot location. It can also be seen for the location of manufacturer depots as well. What does have to be remembered, however, is that the pattern of depot location is a changing one as infrastructure etc. change across time. The development and extension of the motorway network for example has played a major role in the development of retailing in the UK and in particular in the distribution activities of retailers.[15]

Having devised a warehouse distribution system and chosen the locations, retailers have then to be concerned about the operations that occur in and around the distribution centre. At the outset such concern might focus on the building requirements and design specifications. This is both to reduce wastage and to improve efficiency. Other operational concerns continue on a more or less permanent basis. These include the control procedures of running a distribution centre, the handling system and locations for stock in the centre, and the degree of computerisation and automation.

The basic requirements of a distribution centre are to check goods in, check goods out and to be able to identify where goods are stored whilst they are in the distribution centre. Whilst these three basic tasks can be easily stated, their operation in practice can be highly complex and can incur enormous costs if not managed correctly. It is also clear that the more automation, mechanical handling or computer control of the procedures that can be introduced, the more efficient the processes are likely to be. This introduction of technology has, however, to be balanced against the costs in investment. Whether a system is automated or computer controlled or not, the important aspects of materials handling that have to be considered include the use of unit loads, the full use of the cubic capacity of the centre, the minimisation of movement and the control of flows. The exact specification of these aspects of warehouse operations will vary by company, and are dependent on such issues as product characteristics, throughput and other measures of service.

For some retailers there is a clear advantage to be gained from a high level of automation. For example mail-order companies such as GUS or Grattan can gain considerable benefits in cost reduction and service improvement through the use of automation in warehouses. Other retailers in which products can be standardised or handled in a regular fashion may benefit in the same way. Iceland Frozen Foods for example has invested heavily in a new automated distribution centre. Even retailers in the food trade, where much produce is fast-moving and may not be handled automatically, are benefiting from the introduction of advanced computer control systems and better operational procedures. Warehouses and distribution centres are now the focus of considerable management attention and investment whether in automated handling equipment or in computer systems such as World Wide Chain Stores or Dallas Systems.

This management attention and investment can be seen for example in Woolworth.[16] The problems that Woolworth had in its distribution function included very high stock costs, poor distribution centre productivity, unidentifiable service levels and a lack of control. Management attention with the aim improving the total cost position and service levels focused on the areas of centralisation, delivery scheduling, productivity, supplier liaison and stock management. All these areas can be seen to make up the warehouse issue for retailers.

The way to improve its position and achieve changes was for Woolworth to introduce supply chain control systems and in this particular case World Wide

Chain Stores was chosen. This system is supported by a family of systems including purchasing, marketing and supplier support, warehouse management, customer store ordering processing, labour management and forward buying. The important point to note is that whilst warehouse management plays a key role in cost reduction and service improvement it is but one component of supply chain management. The illustration of Woolworth suggests both how poor and inefficient some retailer distribution systems can become and also the possibilities for improvement if management attention and investment are directed towards solving the distribution problems in a coherent and integrated manner.

It is also apparent from this examination of the inventory and warehouse function in retail physical distribution that it can be a very complicated, expensive and time consuming management task. For these reasons, warehousing has been one of the areas of distribution that retailers have looked to sub-contract to distribution specialist companies. In such cases, however, the retailer has to be certain that the distribution activity is being carried out to the retailer's standards, service levels and specifications. Sub-contracting is discussed in more detail later.

7.7   Transportation

Physical distribution for retail companies involves moving considerable amounts of product over considerable distances. These physical links involve all elements of the distribution channel but fundamentally are concerned with the process of transporting goods into the retail outlets. For retail companies this process is focused on road transport. Whilst other forms of transport are used in stages of product movement and particularly the sourcing process, the main mode of transport used by retailers in moving goods in the UK is that of road. The reasons behind this are clear. For retailers, road transport offers the degree of flexibility, availability and speed they require in terms of vehicles to carry products and of access to sites and retail outlets. This flexibility can occur through varying sizes and capabilities of vehicles, including temperature controlled transport, as well as the handling characteristics that can be added to road vehicles, such as access for fork-lift trucks, tail-lifts, hanging garment rails, etc. In addition, road transport is able to offer through movement to retailers without the need to double-handle product. These advantages are not available in other modes of transport. The result is an overwhelming dominance in the use of road transport for retail physical distribution.[17]

The very prevalence and ease of use of road transport, however, bring its own problems. In particular two sets of problems can cause difficulties to retailers. These are restrictions on movement and fleet management issues. The restrictions on movement come in a variety of restrictive measures at both the national and local government levels. National government for example limits the weight of vehicles allowed on the road and also the length of time a driver is permitted to drive. Both these measures affect retailers' ability to carry out distribution as they would wish. At the local level the restrictions are generally in terms of the times of delivery to shops or of access to delivery areas. Local pedestrianisation schemes in town centres for example often involve limiting the times at which a retail outlet can be serviced. In such cases either alternative delivery routes need to be found, e.g. via a back-door to the outlet or from underneath in a planned shopping centre, or the less convenient times of delivery have to be accepted with consequent implications for stock-holding and replenishment.

An associated problem arising from the very success and nature of the road transport option is that of congestion. Vehicle congestion in major cities, whilst not due solely to deliveries to retail outlets, does cause problems in the frequency and reliability of deliveries to the stores. Sainsbury for example claim they lose £3m a year due to congestion in central London alone. The congestion of sections of the motorway network also causes excess costs in distribution. At micro-scale levels the problems of delivering to retail outlets in high streets is also well-known and causes congestion. Such problems have been tackled in a variety of ways, including the provision of more modern off-street access. There can be little doubting, however, the very real problem that vehicle congestion is causing, and seems likely to continue to cause, to retailers.

The fleet management issues in road transport are also considerable. Fleet management requires a great degree of attention if it is to be carried out effectively and efficiently. Because road transport is so prevalent, and also because of its flexibility, there are dangers for retail firms in its management. It is all too easy to mismanage a road vehicle fleet because it is so large or it is a complex task. The problems arise in operating and managing the fleet on a day-to-day basis rather than considering the wider issues in the fleet operation process, although these wider issues are the starting point in looking at fleet management.

These wider issues begin with the composition of the vehicle fleet. There is a tremendous variety of vehicles that are available for use in road distribution. The composition of the vehicle fleet needs therefore to consider issues such as the product, handling aids and the running use of the vehicles as these all affect costs. Certain products require specialised vehicles for transportation. Fragile products are one example, but the whole of the chilled and frozen food chains depend on specialist vehicles. Modern superstores demand products at a variety of temperatures. Frozen products require to be kept below certain temperature levels whilst other temperature levels are required for chilled products. Correct distribution therefore demands the proper mix of vehicles to carry these products. One response has been the development of multi-temperature vehicles which can improve vehicle flexibility, but at a cost. Similar complexities exist in terms of handling products on and off vehicles, the use of the vehicle space and the operational use to which vehicles are put. As with most aspects of distribution, the better matching of requirements with operations brings considerable savings.

Once the composition of the vehicle fleet has been determined, decisions have to be taken over how to finance the vehicle fleet acquisition. Broadly, there are three ways of acquiring a vehicle fleet. These are outright purchase, leasing and contract hire. The decision between these categories and the many variants within them will depend on the circumstances of individual retailers. Some retailers will wish to maintain the vehicle fleet within the company and will look for purchase or leasing arrangements. Other retailers will instead sub-contract the transportation to distribution specialists either as transportation alone or as part of a larger sub-contracting package.

Once the vehicle fleet has been established, it has to be operated efficiently. It is in this area of operating costs and the control and measurement of these that many of the problems occur for retailers. Close control and monitoring of vehicle and driver performance, as well as meeting legislative requirements on, for example, vehicle operation and maintenance, are crucial to the performance of any delivery operation. In retailing, with the recurrent need to re-supply the retail outlets, such issues take on a considerable importance. Vehicles and drivers in retail distribution are profitable only when in transit, and with so many journeys to be made there is a large multiplier effect of any under-performance. Here too, inefficient operation can incur considerable excess costs.

Because of the importance attached to the correct operation of the vehicle fleet many retailers have become increasingly interested in applying computer software. Such software has particular applications in the vehicle scheduling and routeing areas and many retailers have made investments here. The belief is that using technology in this way enables retailers better to match their investment in vehicles to requirements and to make full use of those vehicles they have available. A number of examples of this exist, but probably the best documented is that of Argyll's use of Paragon.

Christensen and Eastburn analyse the introduction of a computer system for delivery planning – Paragon – into the distribution system of Argyll Stores.[18] It is important to realise that physical distribution in Argyll has changed considerably, and was in a process of change at the time of this introduction. Argyll itself as a retailer has changed since its acquisition of Safeway, and the computer package has been updated and improved. It should also be noted that this introduction was but one aspect of technology introduction at this time into Argyll and its distribution system.[19]

The system as introduced by Argyll into their Felling distribution centre contained three main parts. First was a master data file about the stores and their delivery constraints. This was linked to the computerised road network in the computer. Second, was the automatic routeing section which generated routes and loads. Third, was an interactive facility which allowed manual over-riding of the computerised schedules. Christensen and Eastburn claim the benefits of introduction of such a system to include:

— greater vehicle utilisation
— improved service levels to stores
— reduction in transport costs and capital investment in vehicles
— the use of the system as a simulation tool.[20]

Computerised scheduling programs of this type can be used to solve the day-to-day problems of scheduling and also to plan routes for periods ahead where volumes are relatively fixed. This is the basic use normally envisaged of such programs and the main initial use at Argyll. In addition, however, increasing use is being made of such programs to allow strategic and tactical scheduling solutions to be tried or simulated on the computer before being made operational within the company. The use for simulation avoids the introduction of expensive changes and trials of unacceptable or less efficient schedules. Such simulation uses are likely to become more prevalent.

As with other functional areas of distribution, there are clear possibilities in transportation for sub-contracting some or all of the operations of the vehicle fleet to distribution specialists. With the growing complexity of fleet management it is likely that the main response by retailers to these problems in the future will be to sub-contract the operations to specialist distributors. This option will be examined in more detail below.

7.8   Information Systems and Communications

The sections of this chapter above have placed great emphasis on the physical flows of product through the distribution system. This has been the traditional focus of the analysis of distribution systems. It is increasingly being recognised, however, that for every physical flow there is a corresponding flow of information. Retailers are therefore beginning to place as much emphasis on the information flows as on the physical flows. By improving the use and the sharing of information, enabled by the new technology, it is hoped to rationalise the physical flows to those most necessary for the operations of the business, and to provide the correct costs and service balance. This rationalisation might in fact see an increase in the number of physical movements as the relative balance between the advantages of moving information as opposed to moving product change. This again is another manifestation of the search for a better matching of demand and supply in distribution.

The basic requirement of an information system is to provide accurate and timely information to allow physical distribution functions to operate in an efficient, effective and co-ordinated way. In particular the information system links the company to relevant systems external to it, co-ordinates the distribution functions within the company, monitors and controls physical distribution performance and also activates or acts as a trigger for the physical side of physical distribution. An example of these functions is provided below for a hypothetical retailer.

The head office of a retailer receives notification from branches (customers) for replenishment. This notification could be either details of sales or of stock required. This information may have been computer-generated or may have been collected by manual observation or data capture on portable units. The information is received by head office either electronically by computer, by other means, e.g. Fax, or in some cases by telephone or post. Head office processes this information. This processing will involve for example:

— checking the information for consistency, reliability etc.
— passing orders to distribution centres
— updating record files on branches, products, inventory etc.

At the distribution centres products will be picked, documented and transport scheduled for delivery. Reports from distribution centres will be sent back to head office or the order processing centre. Again links could be computer based or use telephones, Fax etc. The withdrawal of stock from distribution centres will allow replenishment at this level. Contracts and orders have therefore to have been placed with suppliers and records updated. These records will include performance monitoring of:

— suppliers
— branches
— distribution centres.

Throughout this procedure other relevant information such as invoices, etc. will also have to be distributed and recorded.

It is worthwhile considering in more detail the applications of information technology in physical distribution. It is not possible or useful to provide a list of the technology that has been applied by retailers in physical distribution. Instead, it is rather more useful to consider the functional areas that form the structure of this chapter and to consider the scope for technology in these. The following technology applications have already been mentioned in the context of these functional areas:

— handling systems for warehouse operations
— computer systems for warehouse management
— fleet management systems
— depot location programs
— vehicle routeing and scheduling programs.

To these can be added the 'support' functions of information systems in pursuit of total cost comparisons and customer service. Such systems require to be able to provide operational, tactical and strategic information to the relevant levels of management. What is clear is that for modern retailers the key to effective physical distribution management lies not only in applying technology to the functional areas and to management information systems, but also in ensuring that the links between these areas and between levels of management are improved. The earlier illustration of Woolworth has suggested the need for specific technology introduction and also the necessity of using technology to link together areas of a business to ensure supply chain management. These developments require considerable investment particularly in communications.

For a retailer, the value of internal communications within the company should be quite clear. If communications can be improved between the level of the retail outlets and the other levels of the company then the physical distribution aspects of the retail business can be improved. For example, communications can inform the head office of sales at the store level almost as soon as they take place. This allows the possibility of moving towards a just-in-time distribution system in retailing. It is also clear that of similar importance to a retailer are the external communications and in particular Electronic Data Interchange (EDI).

EDI aims to replace paper transactions amongst companies by electronic communications using a computer network. For this to occur there are two main prerequisites. First, standards are required to constrain and direct the communications. Second, there needs to be a network that enables different retailers and their computers to communicate with each other. For retailing, the standards used are mainly those enshrined in TRADACOMS, whilst the main network is that of TRADANET. TRADANET is run by International Network Services and allows the exchange of documents in TRADACOMS standards between companies. Thus, for example, orders and invoices can be sent and received electronically between retailers and manufacturers. With modifications to the standards, this and competitive services will be available on an international basis. In addition to its use by retailers and manufacturers, the concept of paperless trading is attracting the attention of other intermediaries in the distribution channel, such as specialist distribution companies. There is now a crucial necessity for electronic communications in distribution:

> the high cost of inventory, combined with the need for faster response times operationally, have tightened the service lead times and the need for speed and accuracy, whilst maintaining cost effectiveness, demands two-way electronic links rather than the movement of paper.[21]

What in effect is happening is that the advances in information technology and associated developments in uses of information systems and communications have combined to allow new developments in physical distribution. In particular, the operationalisation of the concepts of just-in-time distribution, integrated supply chain management and indeed, logistics management, would not have been possible without the developments in technology. 'Push' replenishment systems have been translated into 'pull' systems.

The distribution channel consists basically of four groups: retailers, manufacturers, consumers, and distributors/wholesalers. In three of these groups the unit size is getting larger, with the other group (consumers) – the target market – becoming more fragmented. The implication is that to meet these narrower markets the information systems and flows between the three trading groups – retailers, distributors/wholesalers and manufacturers – have to be much more effective and efficient (Figure 7.3). A 'pull' distribution system for example requires more efficient communication of sales data and thus order data from the retailers to the manufacturers, perhaps via a distribution specialist or a wholesaler. One method of ensuring both speed and accuracy is through an integrated information system or via electronic communications such as VANS/EDI. Such links and such networks are becoming increasingly important in physical distribution. The importance of electronic communications and networks will be seen not just within retailers and by retailers, but within manufacturers and by manufacturers. Electronic communications on an international level are going to have a fundamental effect on physical distribution.

FIGURE 7.3
The 'New' Physical Distribution

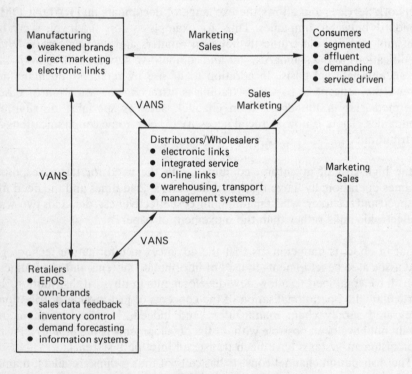

Note: VANS – Value Added Network Services (including Data Services).

7.9 Sub-contracting Distribution

The earlier sections of this chapter have already noted the potential that exists for the sub-contracting of elements, or indeed all, of the retail distribution function to distribution specialists. For example distribution specialists have been considered in terms of warehousing, vehicle fleet operations and computer systems and links. It is a relatively short step to sub-contracting all of these activities and the remainder of the distribution function to specialists. For many large retailers this route of sub-contracting is indeed one that has been pursued, and dedicated distribution systems set up and run by specialists on behalf of retailers are now relatively common.[22]

One effect of this process has been the emergence of large operators in the specialist distribution field. In the same way as in the manufacturing and retailing sectors earlier, the process of concentration is changing the market characteristics of the specialist distribution contractor. Companies such as the National Freight Consortium and the Transport Development Group are major operators. What is clear from the services offered by these companies is that the concern is no longer with *running* elements of the distribution function, but with *managing* the distribution chain as an entirety based on sound planning at operational, tactical and strategic levels. As retailer distribution has become more complicated and sophisticated, so a market opportunity has emerged for companies able to take on this aspect of the distribution channel.

Contract distribution has expanded over recent years not only for retailers but also for manufacturers. The distribution channel is increasingly one comprising large players at all levels. Specialist distribution companies have been successful because they have met the market needs. This success has been founded on a number of reasons. These include:

— the centralisation of retail distribution
— the growing complication of distribution requirements
— the increasing requirement of retailers to control distribution and to manage the distribution channel
— the need to reserve retail management and resources for the key retail tasks
— the awareness of manufacturers that physical distribution is a vital area of their operations.

As has been seen earlier, retailers have begun to look closely at their policy of stockholding and their use of expensive high street and other retail space. At the same time the problems of delivering to a multiplicity of stockholding (as opposed to sales) locations whilst maintaining customer service have developed into a major management issue. The solution of consolidation or centralisation eases many of these problems. Centralisation also has the effect of more clearly defining a distribution activity rather than a retailing one, and so the logical step is to utilise specialists to provide the regional distribution centres and the associated operations, including transportation.

Retail distribution has also become more complicated in terms of the products that have to be handled. In food retailing, for example, there is a requirement for many of the leading retailers to take in products at a variety of temperatures. The developments of the cool chain, chilled chain and frozen chain each complicate the distribution requirements and necessitate the development of specialist handling systems. The continued increase in quality and freshness required of many products also changes the distribution requirements. Retailers have chosen in a number of cases to deal with increasing complexity by sub-contracting complete channels, e.g. frozen goods handling, to specialists.

In non-food retailing the requirement has been to become more responsive to the market, to develop new products and offerings and to improve quality and presentation. These trends too lead to an increase in complexity, and again specialist distributors have seen a market in, for example, fashion goods handling or the handling of fragile products.

Retail distribution and distribution channels have also been the scene of a power battle between manufacturers and retailers. The past position of manufacturers controlling distribution and pushing goods through the distribution channel to retailers has been upset by the changing structure and relationship of retailers and manufacturers. The new distribution sees retailers pulling goods through the distribution channel from manufacturers. Retail control of information and the changed power relationship allow *retailers to exert control and management authority* over the distribution channel. This concentration of control and management authority allows retailers to specify performance levels and standards and employ distribution specialists to carry out many of the distribution tasks. Control and authority is with the retailers, the responsibility is with the specialists.

As retailers have become more powerful so they have exerted their power by taking control of the distribution channel. The main reason for taking control of distribution is cost: it is a much more effective operation when controlled by one retailer rather than myriads of suppliers. There are other reasons, however, and Quarmby cites three.[23] First, control by the retailer allows an improvement in the quality of the distribution service. Second, management control at the store level is aided by retailer control of the distribution level. Third, retailer control allows a flexibility of response that is lacking in the less-ordered manufacturer controlled systems. The net effect of the changing balance of power in distribution terms is that management attention is focused on cost-effectiveness and the quality of the distribution service. Good service at acceptable cost by the retailer is a prime competitive edge. Realising that edge has increasingly become possible through the use of distribution specialists enabled by technological developments. Quarmby notes that the growth of contact distribution is a reflection of the development of power of information technology and communications. In Sainsbury for example it allows 'control by information' rather than 'control by doing it yourself'.

Retailing is a highly competitive industry and retailing management has consequently to be continuously aware of changes in the market. This has two main implications for physical distribution. First, it places *greater emphasis* on physical distribution by seeing distribution as a potential generator of a competitive edge. If distribution specialists are available, then tight control of these will yield an efficient distribution system. The alternative is to do it all within the company, buying in the key management. Second, it places *operational priorities* away from in-house physical distribution by stressing the key management tasks at the store level and the investment priorities of retail not physical distribution. Distribution specialist companies are contracted in to provide the management and reduce the financial involvement. Individual retailers will see the justification for using distribution specialists in different ways.

In the same way that retailers have questioned the key aspects of their business and used specialist distributors to carry out selected tasks, so many *manufacturers* have begun to question whether they need a great involvement in distribution. This questioning has focused particularly on whether the sub-contracting of operations to specialists can provide financial benefits, concentrate management resources and activities, and provide the required service levels. Where retailers have used specialist contractors, it makes sense in some cases for manufacturers to use the same specialists to feed their goods into the retail system. In some cases retailers will instruct their specialist distributors to collect product from the manufacturer, thus improving vehicle efficiency and use and gaining cost savings from being able to take partial loads and purchasing on an ex-works basis.[24]

From both ends of the distribution channel therefore pressure has been applied to introduce distribution specialists to carry out distribution operations on behalf of both retailers and manufacturers. By applying specialists to the distribution task, a service can be offered that appeals to markets in both retailing and manufacturing. The new distribution system increasingly combines large companies at all levels of the distribution channel including distribution specialists.

Given these reasons for the growth of distribution services it would seem that retailers perceive certain advantages of sub-contracting distribution. These advantages include financial benefits, better management of change processes in distribution, the purchase of specialist expertise, a concentration of activities and improved business relationships. Against these advantages, however, are often claimed to be certain disadvantages of contract distribution, or alternatively advantages of retaining distribution in-house within retailers. It is suggested for example that contracting out distribution loses management control, acts against operational integration, provides lower customer service and makes little sense when in-house distribution systems are efficient and providing the required service.

Sub-contracting physical distribution to distribution specialists has been an increasingly used option in recent years. This is undoubtedly because distribution specialists have been able to offer a product or service which fitted requirements in both the retail and the manufacturer market places. This is not to say that sub-contracting is the right procedure for all retail companies in every circumstance – it is not. It is also not to say that sub-contracting is a soft option. There can be no such thing as 'out-of-sight, out-of-mind' in retailing and physical distribution. If sub-contracting is pursued then the advantages and disadvantages have to be carefully weighed and the disadvantages minimised by tight control and monitoring of distribution performance.

7.10　Physical Distribution Strategy

Strategy in retailing is often seen as being solely concerned with the positioning of the retail company in the market place. This is to ignore the necessary physical distribution flows that underpin a company's performance. It also ignores the vital questions about physical distribution or supply strategy. In many cases it can be argued that developing a strategy to supply a retail outlet structure consistently and regularly is at least as important as developing a market strategy.

The strategies in physical distribution for retailing at a general level follow certain distinct paths. McKinnon distinguished three basic strategies for getting goods from the manufacturer to the retailer's outlets.[25] These were direct delivery from the supplier, centralised stockholding and load consolidation, and collection of supplies. Beyond these three possibilities there are only limited options for retailers. Strategy for retail distribution management is in fact encompassed by limited possibilities. Once the broad strategy is decided, the operational mechanics of the distribution system can and will vary amongst retailers. For example, some will sub-contract whilst others will not.

The real message about physical distribution strategy is that it is all about managing the supply chain and ensuring maximum influence and control over the product and information flows in the distribution system. For many retailers this act of taking control has seen the development of centralised systems enabled by technological and communication advances. By such a strategy retailers maximise control, improve the level of customer service and gain competitively. Whilst very apparent in the food retailing sector, such developments are increasingly found in other retail sectors as well. This can be illustrated by examining briefly Boots and Tesco, although similar points are made about distribution strategy in the examples used by McKinnon[26] and Walters.[27]

The need for strategic planning by retailers concerned about their physical distribution systems is not confined to the food sector although many of the example are drawn from there. Murrell has shown how Boots the Chemist have applied many concepts and operational aspects covered in this chapter to a redesign of their distribution system. The main problems for the company were the complexity of distributing a very wide range of products to over one thousand stores of tremendous size variation and the reliance on an old replenishment system. The triggers for change in the company were the general factors of the need to be more effective and to improve competitive position, and the more specific factors for Boots of the realisation of the *ad-hoc* nature of much current distribution operations, the opportunities presented by investment in technology particularly at the point-of-sale, and the scope offered by the new professionalism in physical distribution.[28]

Murrell argues that the response required was a new strategic approach and that this comprised four major strands. First, was a move to vertically integrated supply chain management which basically meant all levels of the distribution chain anticipating the requirements on them from final consumer demand. The prerequisite for this was better item level recording and data dissemination. Second, consolidation of delivery was introduced which involved the use of a nominated carrier and collection of products on an ex-works basis, and the reduction of direct to store deliveries. Third, was a reduction in stockholding by the search for just-in-time supply. This involved better use of data as indicated above, more frequent ordering and replenishment, and more thorough control of the location and amount of stockholding. Finally, a more rigorous definition of service prioritisation for products and customers was introduced. All these elements worked together to produce the desired outcome of the new physical distribution strategy and demonstrate both the interlinked nature of the entire distribution channel and also the potential for improving existing retailer distribution systems.

A further example of changing strategy of retail physical distribution is afforded by Tesco stores. This is a particularly well-documented and analysed case, which shows clearly the development of a strategy over a period of some years.[29] The strategy is currently being refined further to improve the efficiency and effectiveness of the company's distribution activities.[30]

The Tesco distribution system in the late 1970s in the wake of Operation Checkout almost came to a halt. The volume of goods being moved by Tesco proved too large to handle in the timescales required. The decision was then taken to move away from direct delivery to stores to centralisation. Tesco adopted a centrally controlled distribution service delivering the vast majority of stores' needs, utilising common handling systems, with deliveries within a lead time of a maximum of 48 hours. Seven key areas of this strategy can be identified. First, there has been an extension and change to the fixed distribution facilities, including the building of new distribution centres. The location of these facilities is aimed at more closely matching distribution needs to the store location profile. Second, lead times have improved. Improvements in technology have allowed faster stockturn, allied to which is the scheduling of vehicles at all points in the channel. Third, common handling systems are in use at the distribution centre and the stores to handle stock replenishment more easily. Fourth, the demands of modern retailing have required multi-shift working. Fifth, computer software throughout the system can model company decisions allowing the best use of all facilities. Sixth, contract carriage has been used to meet high levels of performance. The standards required are set by Tesco and monitored by them. The contractors have to meet these specifications. Finally, new technology is used to maintain a strict inventory control.

The effect of this strategy for Tesco has been to produce a more rationalised network of distribution centres, computer-linked to the stores via head office. The proliferation of stockholding points has been reduced. These new centres are the hubs of the network, being larger, handling more stock, more vehicles and requiring more efficient organisation. Control of the system ensures the stores obtain the goods they require. The technology has enabled this control, which in turn reflects the strategy. The implications of these changes are to alter the spatial locations of the physical distribution structure and alter the transport patterns.

The major change to the strategy as presented above is that the company is now concentrating its distribution further by focusing on the development of composite distribution. Composite distribution uses specially designed vehicles with temperature controlled compartments to deliver any combination of frozen, chilled, fresh or grocery products. The composite distribution process will be focused on eight distribution centres. Seven of these are new purpose-built composite distribution centres with the other an extension at Livingston in Scotland. Centralising distribution of these products in this way reduces costs and improves sales and productivity. These eight centres will replace 26 centres in the previous system and will allow daily delivery to stores of products in good condition.

The eight distribution centres will each service a region of the country. The sites are all close to key motorway intersections or junctions allowing rapid access. Of the eight composite distribution centres only one will be run by Tesco. The remainder are to be operated by specialist distribution companies with Glass Glover running three, the National Freight Consortium two, and Hunter Distribution and Hays Distribution one each. Cross-comparisons of performance of these centres and the sub-contractors will be produced to enable 'league tables' to be drawn up of performance. Changes to sub-contractors are possible if performance warrants.

The composite centres will be computer linked to head office to allow the passing of data and the imposition of monitoring and control. For all products handled by the composite centres, forecasts of demand will be produced and transmitted to suppliers. The aim of the system is to allow suppliers to have a basis for preparing products. This is particularly important for short life products where the aim is to operate a just-in-time system from the factory through the composite centre to the store. To meet such targets on delivery etc. each supplier needs information on predicted replenishment schedules.

Composite distribution is more complex than can be described here. By introducing the system Tesco aims to improve its business performance still further. This is to be done by developing an efficient and effective distribution system around the expertise of the distribution specialists, the standards set by Tesco, the sharing of data with suppliers and the speed of data transmission by communications. At the same time operational aspects of the system are also being improved to provide enhanced service to the stores and thus the consumer. This new strategy will in turn be refined as enhancements become possible. Distribution in Tesco has developed a long way from the problems brought on by Operation Checkout.

7.11   Conclusions

The changes in retailing described and analysed elsewhere in this text comprise a revolution. Changes are also occurring on the manufacturing side. The challenge for physical distribution in retailing is to perform the distribution task to the standards set in the distribution channel and thus to support retailers and manufacturers in their desires to improve the product offering in the widest sense. With the power of retailers it is now incumbent on those in retailer distribution to respond to their challenges. This involves developing a reliable, consistent distribution performance that operates at the required efficiency within acceptable costs. The challenges are relatively easy to state, but their resolution requires major changes in attitude and performance, and investment of both time and money.

One area of investment that is clearly required and one that is increasingly prominent is in technology and systems. Retailer investment in technology and systems for distribution has been discussed, and the distribution channel is increasingly using advanced technology. Computer links are now being used to connect head offices, distribution centres and customers. Such systems handle stock replenishment to and from distribution centres, increasing the level of management control, reducing purchasing costs, decreasing the level of paperwork and providing timely stock information. Electronic data interchange is now integrated into a number of companies, including specialist distribution companies. The use of communications in this way is aimed at better control – thus producing stronger links, reducing stockholding and enabling retailers and manufacturers to operate a more effective physical distribution system. Some wholesalers similarly are using technology to link the retailers they serve, again to improve their competitive position.

Within and associated with the distribution centres themselves, further investment is being directed at technology and systems in a number of ways. First, control of stockholding and movement in distribution centres is increasingly monitored and organised by computer. These systems control the stock from the receipt of the pallet load through to the issue of goods to the store. Typical systems will perform the whole series of stock control functions, eliminating inefficiencies in stock handling and movement. Second, there is also a much higher level of use of sophisticated hardware in distribution centres to minimise stock handling, involving AS/RS systems, conveyors, carousels, pallet stations and laser scanning stations for control. Complicated flow and sortation systems based on carousels or conveyors are in operation in many centres. Finally, investment is alo being directed at the movement issues associated with deliveries to and from the distribution centres and retail outlets. Increasingly, computers control the timing of goods into the warehouse from suppliers and the scheduling and routeing of vehicles and goods from the distribution centres to the stores.

Throughout this chapter stress has been laid on the control of operations and the way in which this has become an important issue. Retailers will therefore have to become more aware of the time and effort needed in setting appropriate standards for operations and in the monitoring of performance against these standards. Control can be aided by technology, but an integral part of providing service to set standards and improving service is the role of people. Companies will be forced to improve the training for their employees to ensure that the personnel in distribution are of the right calibre and motivation to carry out their jobs to the prescribed standards. There is a need for a more professional approach to the personnel in retail distribution; a need that is being recognised by good companies who, as *Retail Week* noted, are employing a 'new breed of professionals'.[31]

Distribution is about connecting elements of a channel and providing links. The approach that has to be taken therefore is a total logistics one emphasising these links and the broad concept of logistics management. This involves other areas of companies as well as distribution and requires a rethink about the management and integration of distribution activities within retail companies.

One further aspect of this chapter deserves emphasis above all others as it underpins the challenges that distribution faces. The concept of customer service has been stressed here and must be stressed in retailing. There is a danger, however, that customer service in retailing is becoming associated solely with customer service at the retail outlet. It is imperative to realise that the distribution function to the retail outlets equally has an important role in customer service. A customer service orientation is crucial to modern distribution's ability to deliver the goods. Customer needs must be clearly identified, agreed and then satisfied on a regular and reliable basis.

Retailing is undergoing major changes. The effects of these changes at the retail level are fundamentally altering distribution requirements. Changes such as concentration and product range extension are being reflected in the centralisation of distribution facilities, which are increasingly run by distribution specialists. With the increasing use of technology enabling further changes, retailers are examining their distribution chains. The effect is to shorten the chains, provide greater control for the retailers and to minimise the linkages. There is a reduction in stockholding and a changing location of the stock that is held. As stock control becomes more crucial, and retailers and manufacturers try to approach a just-in-time retail distribution system, so the location and efficiency is increasingly produced through the movement of information rather than the movement of products. Accurate and timely information flows enable accurate and timely product movement.

In the same way that the retailer revolution has more years to run, so the physical distribution effects and implications will continue to reverberate for a number of years, challenging distribution practices and businesses. The challenge will be met by forward-looking, customer-service oriented companies who are willing to invest in appropriate technology, personnel and logistics management. These companies will emerge over the coming years to dominate the distribution business, providing the service for the 1990s and beyond. A final caveat, however, is necessary. Companies must not assume that the distribution challenges can be met easily. In the same way that the retail revolution has caused major casualties, recent evidence suggests that some companies are treating too lightly the complexity of modern physical distribution systems. The new distribution is not easy; it requires considerable time, effort and skill to get it right.

References

1. L. Sparks, 'The Retail Sector', in P. Jones (ed.), *Management in Service Industries* (London: Pitman, 1989).
2. J. A. Dawson and L. Sparks, *Issues in Retailing* (Edinburgh: Scottish Development Department, 1985).
3. D. W. Walters, *Strategic Retailing Management* (Hemel Hempstead: Prentice-Hall, 1988).
4. Ibid.
5. F. Belussi, 'Benetton: information technology in production and distribution', *SPRU Occasional Papers* (University of Sussex) No. 25, 1987.
6. S. Hornby, 'The Place of Distribution in a Modern Business', *Focus on Physical Distribution Management*, Vol. 5, No. 1, 1986, pp. 4–8.
7. M. Christopher et al., *Effective Distribution Management* (London: Pan, 1983) p. 19.
8. J. Cooper (ed.), *Logistics and Distribution Planning* (London: Kogan Page, 1988); and A. Rushton and J. Oxley, *Handbook of Logistics and Distribution Management* (London: Kogan Page, 1989).
9. M. Christopher, *The Strategy of Distribution Management* (London: Heinemann, 1986) p. 1.
10. Cooper, *Logistics and Distribution Planning*.
11. J. W. Hummel and R. Savitt, 'Integrated Customer Service and Retail Strategy', *International Journal of Retailing*, Vol. 3, No. 2, 1988, pp. 5–21.
12. D. A. Quarmby, 'The Importance of Quality in Retailing', *Focus on Physical Distribution and Logistics Management*, Vol. 7, No. 7, 1988, pp. 15–19.
13. A. C. McKinnon, *Physical Distribution Systems* (London: Routledge, 1989).
14. Ibid.
15. L. Sparks, 'Spatial-Structural Relationships in the Development of Retail Companies: a case study of Kwik Save Group PLC', *Service Industries Journal*, Vol. 10, No. 1, 1990, pp. 25–84.
16. C. Wiggett and B. Grange, 'Woolworths: Achieving Supply Chain Control', *Logistics Today*, Vol. 7, No. 2, 1988, pp. 31–5.

17. Cooper, *Logistics and Distribution Planning*.
18. L. R. Christensen and M. P. Eastburn, 'Introduction of a Computer System for Delivery Planning: Argyll Stores – Case Study', *Focus on Physical Distribution Management*, Vol. 4, No. 6, 1985, pp. 21–7.
19. Walters, *Strategic Retailing Management*.
20. Christensen and Eastburn, 'Introduction of a Computer System for Delivery Planning'.
21. *ANA News*, May 1988, p. 1.
22. J. Fernie, 'Contract Distribution in Multiple Retailing', *International Journal of Physical Distribution and Materials Management*, Vol. 19, No. 7, 1989, pp. 1–35.
23. D. A. Quarmby, 'Developments in the Retail Market and their Effects on Freight Distribution', *Journal of Transport Economics and Policy*, Vol. 23, No. 1, 1989, pp. 75–87.
24. G. Murrell, 'Management of the Retail Supply Chain', *Logistics Today*, Vol. 7, No. 2, 1988, pp. 5–9.
25. A. C. McKinnon, 'The Physical Distribution Strategies of Multiple Retailers', *International Journal of Retailing*, Vol. 1, No. 2, 1986, pp. 49–63.
26. A. C. McKinnon, 'The Distribution Systems of Supermarket Chains', *Service Industries Journal*, Vol. 5, No. 2, 1985, pp. 226–38.
27. Walters, *Strategic Retailing Management*.
28. Murrell, 'Management of the Retail Supply Chain'.
29. L. Sparks, 'The Changing Structure of Distribution in Retailing Companies: an example from the grocery trade', *Transactions of the Institute of British Geographers*, Vol. 11, No. 2, 1986, pp. 147–54; and the same author's 'Technological Change and Spatial Change in U.K. Retail Distribution', in R. S. Tolley (ed.), *Transport Technology and Spatial Change* (Institute of British Geographers: North Staffordshire Polytechnic, 1988) pp. 123–48.
30. Tesco Stores, *Composite Distribution* (Cheshunt: Tesco PLC, 1988).
31. 'A New Breed of Professionals', *Retail Week*, 14 April 1989, pp. 16–17.

Retailing Organisation Structure and Personnel Management **8**

8.1 Introduction

The management of people in any retail organisation creates inevitable opportunities, costs and stress for all those who are employed, supplied by, or served. The dynamics of human relationships and the reaction of people responding to changing needs, priorities, perceptions, and expectations provide the essential ingredients affecting the authority and role of a personnel manager. The body of knowledge and expertise encompassed by the term personnel management undoubtedly has the capacity to contribute significantly to the success of any retail enterprise, even though the profession has its critics both within and external to retailing. Such criticism does not usually assert that the problems of resourcing, motivating and administering a skilled labour force now and in the future are relatively trivial. Rather, the ability, expertise and influence of individual personnel managers is not always commensurate with the task. Time and effort may be largely spent solving crises, reacting to events, becoming aware of situations when it is too late to offer effective help, not learning from admitted past mistakes and generally being incapable and removed from any position of influence in the company. Regrettably personnel managers may not be seen as motivating forces developing a company philosophy, affecting decision-making and establishing achievable standards of performance for all staff. Personnel managers, especially in retailing, need to help design the organisation structure, making it efficient as well as cost effective, to develop and communicate a culture which embraces not just a legal, but an ethical code of behaviour. In this way all employees can believe in themselves and others, and will encourage everyone to share a common purpose within a changing environment.

Introduction
  The problems of providing personnel services in retailing.
  The importance of establishing a coherent strategy.

Retail employment
  The size, structure and composition of the labour force.
  Implications for Personnel Management in retailing.

Personnel Credibility in Retailing
  Challenges faced by personnel managers.
  A strategy for acceptance and influence.

Creating the right climate
  Standards set by 'excellent' companies.
  The role of Personnel Management in retailing.

Changing management types and practices in retailing
  The effect of charismatic leadership.
  Mechanistic bureaucracy in retail.
  Sensitivity to changing consumer and employee expectations.

Retail skills and qualities
  Employee skills and performance in retailing.
  Environmental and trading demands.

Personnel expertise in retailing
  — Employee relations
  — Recruitment and selection
  — Training
  — Performance appraisal
  — Staff counselling
  — Employee redundancy and dismissal
  — Employee services

Conclusions.

Personnel specialists more than other managers not only have to co-operate with others, but also have to influence, persuade, and yes, sell ideas to other line managers and technical staff. To be credible within an organisation personnel managers have to be thoroughly acquainted with the business of retailing, the merchandise, the trading pattern of the stores and to be visible and responsive when and where personnel services and advice are sought. The term human resources management better describes this pro-active strategy of social and technical engineering especially in retailing, where appropriate attitudes and interpersonal skills of management and staff need to be communicated to each other for the ultimate purpose of providing a sensitive, effective and realistic consumer offer.

The plan of this chapter is to identify the particular features of employment in retailing which will help to explain the distinctive demands that are made on those with responsibilities for personnel and human resource management. Because personnel management as a profession has evolved in a mainly non-retailing context, its services are not universally recognised as useful, let alone vital to the needs of retail businesses. Personnel managers have not always helped their own cause. Can lessons be learned from those companies generally acknowledged as being successful? Are there service-based, consumer-led organisations which fully recognise the importance of the personnel/human resources specialist and entrust to them commercial decisions that affect the job and lives of everyone in the company? The answer to be given is a considered yes, although there is not one universally accepted formula for success.

Retail companies are themselves experiencing both evolutionary and sometimes revolutionary change, and the opportunities are always present for human resources practitioners to manage those initiatives which are appropriate to the ways that businesses are developing and adapting to the needs and expectations of the market.

The management of human resources in retailing can be assessed according to the ability to achieve results in relation to the cost involved. As the direct wage and salary costs of employing people in retailing are usually second only to that of the merchandise, there is the clear need to monitor such expenditure and to seek means of measuring and promoting labour productivity. Other employment costs can also be sizeable, arising out of low staff retention, high absenteeism, skill shortages, low shopping basket volume and value, and shrinkage – not always given as separate items in the profit and loss account. One national chain of electrical retailers estimates that labour costs from all sources comprise more than 30 per cent of the operational budget.

The chapter then considers those personnel functions that are demonstrably relevant to retailing and where, arguably, personnel managers are providing acceptable standards of service, in the areas of staff planning, recruitment and selection, training and employment services. In other respects, notably in management systems affecting industrial relations, wage and salary administration, performance appraisal and the overall climate of employee relations, further investment in time, money and expertise will create additional strengths in the personnel armoury.

8.2 Retail Employment

Retailing activity is characterised by its great diversity in the merchandise and services offered, the dynamic and often volatile nature of the business transactions taking place, and the variety of management systems that operate in a competitive culture. In comparison with many other industries, retailing is big, broad and busy. Sales in excess of £100 billion were recorded in 1989 in those 350 000 separate establishments employing over $2\frac{1}{3}$ million people. Some of these retail establishments in excess of 200 000 square feet are comparable to medium-sized factories as they employ several hundred staff on a day and night basis, including legal and illegal trading over seven days. They each catered for over 1 million shopping trips and earned several million pounds in revenue in the month before Christmas 1989. Retail employment has expanded in the period 1980 to 1989. The *Employment Gazette* statistics of the Central Statistical Office show there has been an increase of 9.2 per cent in retail and wholesale employment. Areas of significant increase have been in food retailing, up by 12.5 per cent and wholesale distribution, 11.8 per cent. Large store developments have been a major feature of the 1980s. In the food retailing sector alone there were over 1000 stores each in excess of 25 000 square feet trading in 1989. There has been some transfer of business. Companies especially in the confectionery, tobacconist and newsagents' sector have declined, with a net employee loss of 8.1 per cent in the same period.

Retailing is also broadly based. A definition of retailing by the author 'as any type of business whose marketing efforts are directed towards selling merchandise and services to the final consumer', embraces food and fashion, toys and travel, money (banks) and mail order, dresses and DIY, books and breweries, leisure and lingerie, household products and horticulture, pets and perfume – to name but a few. Retailing is characteristically busy, but the pace of retailing activity can vary considerably – that in itself being a source of employee stress requiring appropriate staff deployment and counselling. Productivity in retailing has increased considerably in recent years. J. Sainsbury has acknowledged a 12 per cent increase in labour productivity every year since 1980. Marks & Spencer reported a 22 per cent increase in store productivity during 1989. At the Marble Arch store sales of some £$\frac{1}{4}$ million were achieved by each full-time equivalent member of staff during 1989. IKEA, the Swedish furniture chain, traded over 2 million visitors (customers) at its two UK stores during the four weeks before Christmas 1989.

The increase in the size of the retail labour force in the 1980s is, however, more apparent than real. Of the 600 000 new jobs that were created from 1984 to 1989, only 12 per cent were for full-time employees. It is estimated by the University of Warwick that 28 per cent of all retail jobs by 1995 will be for part-time workers. Together with the growth of part-time employment in retailing there has been an increase in the number of women employees, so that by the end of 1989 they comprised over 62 per cent of the labour force. In certain areas such as department stores, multiples, food and CTNs, women account for over 72 per cent of those employed. Only 12 per cent of males employed in retailing work on a part-time basis, whereas for females the figure is 55 per cent. The number of women in managerial positions is, however, relatively small and to be found mainly in personnel, training, merchandising, retail operations, consumer services and office administration.

The wholesale sector has a different pattern of employment. There, part-time work is not characteristic as it comprises only 16 per cent of those employed and involves mostly women. Over 62 per cent of the jobs in this sector are performed by men.

Trade union membership in retailing is relatively low and at best patchy. Overall, less than 30 per cent of retail employees are estimated to belong to a trade union. Of these most would belong to the Union of Shop, Distributive and Allied Workers (membership 390 000), the General Municipal and Boilermakers Trade Union (total membership 500 000) and the Transport and General Workers' Union (total membership 1.1 million). Retail companies such as J. Sainsbury, Tesco, Asda, CWS and CRS have recognition agreements with certain trade unions and enter into collective bargaining arrangements with them.

What accounts for the relatively high number of part-time women employees in retailing and the tendency for retail companies to employ non-union labour? Retail companies anxious to control labour costs prefer to schedule their staff according to the trading pattern of their stores. For some, over 60 per cent of an average week's business may occur either during lunch times or after 4.00 pm on Thursdays, Fridays and all day Saturday and Sunday. During the year, for some retailers 40 per cent of the annual revenue is concentrated in the six weeks prior to Christmas. Companies require staff who are flexible about their working hours and live near their place of work. One major food retailer operates a staffing rota with some 148 different permutations of half hours, days and locations, where its employees may be asked to work. In response to the employer's needs, it may not be too surprising to note that women with domestic responsibilities and family commitments can often readily work a varied and flexible number of hours during the day or in the evenings and weekends.

They may regard the income as a useful, if not an essential supplement to family earnings, especially if they find the work convenient, flexible and convivial. Staff turnover tends to increase when retail companies request their staff to adjust their hours and earnings with little regard to their personal circumstances and job security. Some retail companies were experiencing staff turnover in excess of 150 per cent in 1989 for stores in London and Home Counties. USDAW estimates average staff turnover in retailing for the same year to be 62 per cent, a level which requires 100 000 newcomers to join the union each year to avoid a net decrease in membership.

Retailing is essentially a young person's industry as over 25 per cent of young people who left school in 1989 at the age of 16–19 entered employment or training that was retail related. It is quite usual for store management appointments to be made at the age of 21, and there are many key executives who have been recruited to appointments in buying, marketing and IT systems and distribution before reaching the age of 28, commanding salaries in excess of £30 000 plus company benefits.

The character and composition of the retail labour force poses its own blend of problems and opportunities for personnel managers. As retailing is an industry dominated by women and managed by men, considerable scope exists to break down attitude barriers affecting career development and equal opportunities. Considerable differences in salary levels exist within retailing. That in itself creates tensions. Low pay characterises many jobs. One major food retail company estimated that over 70 per cent of its full-time staff employed in stores were in receipt of state family income support. Little opposition, challenge or even support to management authority seems to be forthcoming from the trade union sector. This places even more responsibility on management to safeguard the interests of those it employs and to ensure that adequate consultation and communication is taking place. High staff turnover inevitably creates an unstable, untrained, demotivated labour force which is expensive to maintain. In such circumstances resources that should be used to train and develop staff are instead diverted to recruitment and line supervision. Demographic changes are already causing many retail companies to rethink their recruitment policies. The decline in the number of 16–19 year olds, by some 23 per cent over the period 1988–95, is leading to a certain reduction in recruitment standards of education, presentation and experience. Recruitment drives aimed at people over 50 years of age and women with dependent children are intended to substitute for the reduction in young people. Retailing as a whole will need to compete for the employment of tomorrow's youth, and schemes designed to foster links with schools and further and higher education will demand increasing attention by retail companies. Above all, an emphasis on in-house training and the opportunity to obtain vocational qualifications will serve to address the problem of fewer high calibre young people entering the labour market and seeking employment with retailers.

8.3 Personnel Credibility in Retailing

How far is it possible for those with a retail personnel responsibility to respond effectively to the challenges they face? Retailing is inevitably affected by the spontaneous actions of human behaviour as it attempts to respond to those complex and continuous changes previously indicated.

Personnel managers employed at various levels of retailing organisations are not always regarded as being able adequately to meet the demands placed upon them, and can be considered by some as 'a repository for odds and ends of managerial work not having a logical place elsewhere'.[1] Whether personnel management as a function has credibility in a retail context or not must depend on judgements made by different companies. Part of the problem may be explained by the evolution of personnel management within extractive, manufacturing and processing environments, and its association with the power conflict between capital and labour interests during the best part of the last 150 years. Retailing, as it employs over 11 per cent of the working population of the UK and is characterised by large, complex, national and multinational organisations, is a comparatively recent phenomenon, and still it is argued needs to establish its identity as a profession in its own right and not to be regarded merely as an employer of professionals. Personnel management may consider retailing to be a further application of its traditional professional practice and expertise, but the legacy of its upbringing brings both advantages and drawbacks affecting its acceptance and integration into retailing.[2] Perhaps it is apparent insecurity that causes certain personnel and training managers in retailing to become hypersensitive and defensive about their role in the companies. As one managing director in one of the top five UK food retailers said, 'Personnel management is a burden on our profitability, but is occasionally useful'.

Until relatively recently, personnel departments in many retail companies have been given only lip-service by other managers. But for the day-to-day operation of the business certain personnel specialists occupy a low-profile role – strategic business decisions often being taken in functional areas with little or no consideration given to the consequences affecting personnel related issues. Where personnel departments exist in UK retail companies, and some successful organisations such as Kwik-Save do not have them, they tend to be allocated problems affecting staff welfare, wages records, counselling and staff recruitment for hourly paid sales assistants. Personnel issues, however, should incorporate everything that an organisation does or is to be concerned about doing, and become more of a vision-leading activity, involved in creative people building. Personnel departments in the traditional isolationist sense need only exist where the culture of the company considers it unnatural for everyone to assume responsibility for people.[3] This view cannot be reconciled readily with the definition of personnel management propounded by the Institute of Personnel Management[4] as 'that part of management concerned with people at work and relationships within an enterprise that . . . aims to bring together and develop into an effective organisation men and women . . . having . . . regard for the well being of the individual and working groups . . . to secure . . . the best contribution to success'. At least there is a professional body, the IPM, which seeks to promote the interests of personnel practitioners by providing specialist training, disseminating knowledge and expertise, and promoting a code of ethics. It must be admitted, however, that the high academic and business reputation of personnel management is not yet universally recognised by other managerial groups in business and industry.

Perhaps it is the difficulty to get hardened 'self-made' autocrats wth an obsessive 'live-to-work' syndrome to admit they can be poor managers of people, dangerous drivers and bad lovers. How can personnel managers not merely justify their existence, but enable other managers to allow themselves and others to be more effective? Not by a naive detachment from commercial reality of costs, timescales, competition and pressure; neither by blindly transposing into a retail environment, techniques, practices and attitudes which have been accepted elsewhere; but rather by modifying, applying and developing those personnel functions which have evolved over many decades.

8.4 Creating the Right Climate

Accepting the premise that successful personnel practice needs to permeate throughout the veins of a company, what examples exist in large multinational organisations with some retail and marketing interests? Peters and Waterman[5] refer to such 'excellent' companies as IBM, Bloomingdales, Caterpillar, McDonald's, Hewlett Packard, Mars, Delta Airlines, General Electric, Proctor & Gamble and Disney Productions. Their survival, it is argued, has come about because these organisations have been highly adaptive in responding to the changing requirements of their staff, products, services and customers. Even though many of these companies are either American and/or non-retail organisations, it is considered valid to refer to them as examples to the retail sector for a number of reasons.

The ability successfully to manage change in a corporation is a business skill which can be translated to other sectors of the economy. It matters little if you sell products in bulk to wholesalers or provide services to individual customers. It is broadly recognised in global terms that America and Japan have led the world of the 1980s in personnel techniques, and have created large, dynamic and powerful multinational organisations. What UK based retailers are significant on a global basis or even in Europe for that matter? Even Marks & Spencer needs additional time and opportunity to acquire the status of a truly international retailer.

It is therefore difficult to illustrate what certain 'excellent' UK companies are doing to manage change which distinguishes them from those that are relatively less efficient. Highly successful companies (e.g. Marks & Spencer, J. Sainsbury, Whitbread, IKEA, Harrods) are acknowledged as highly competent at competitive analysis, sourcing, reducing tasks to quantifiable objectives, monitoring performance and implementing consistent practice throughout their organisations. Personnel issues are not usually regarded as a major influence accounting for their success. But for long-term stability, vitality and survival it is essential that the organisation consists of people who are equipped and motivated to secure the company's future. Career development and management succession planning is not a sleight-of-hand gimmick intended to massage staff turnover statistics in the short term.

The requirement for organisations to develop chameleon skills of adaptation has become increasingly important as the information revolution gives managers more opportunity to respond much more quickly and make decisions on the basis of a larger volume of relevant data. No company would admit its willingness to allow competitors an advantage.

Competition is a potent force, and those organisations and managers that were nurtured and developed in more traditional operating environments than those of the present and future will have systems, strategies, policies, procedures and attitudes that will inhibit and blunt the contribution of computer-based business and technical innovation. Financial investment in computer harware and software is not enough even for those who can afford it. The philosophies, cultures and systems that enable all employees, and not just managers, to make best use of the information is the more demanding challenge for an organisation to respond.

A highly adaptive organisation has a need to centre its future strategies around five key concepts: creating total customer responsiveness, pursuing fast-paced innovation, achieving flexibility by empowering people, learning to love and thrive on change, and building systems for a 'world turned upside down'. If organisations design systems around 'Thriving on Chaos',[6] and not the 'ideal situation' which never exists anyway (what apparently successful retailer is ever satisfied), then the organisation is at least increasing the odds in its favour to succeed when others are not.

The special feature of these 'excellent' companies is that they fight against the latent inertia that big organisations inevitably create. It can be very difficult for anything big to get anything done. The anti-bureaucracy drive by Lord Rayner in Marks & Spencer in 1983 may have helped to stem the tide. 'Excellent' companies acknowledge the dumbness that size creates by concentrating on communicating simple unambiguous messages to customers, suppliers and employees. Thus IBM means 'Service'; McDonald, 'Quality, Service, Cleanliness and Value'; Caterpillar, 'Twentyfour hours service anywhere in the world, or they're free of charge'; Next Directory, 'Delivery within 48 hours'; Marks & Spencer 'We give peace of mind'.

Such companies, although big, are close to their customers. Their organisations are not obsessed with exotic systems that require an arrogant expectation that everyone will want to conform and subserve. Neither are they driven by high technology that can throw up its own culture standards and conventions. The world's top car salesman for most of the mid-1970s and 1980s, Joe Guard showed he cared for his customers. The 13 000 birthday, New Year, Christmas and Easter cards he sent out every month proclaimed the message.

Smiles may not cost money, but can be a powerful part of a salesperson's behaviour and contribute significantly to the value-added service a company can give. How many customers are there who consciously or unconsciously decide they will visit a store because the staff there are helpful and treat them as a friend?

At IBM customer care is extended to full job liability. If an account collapsed, a sales representative could have the full value of commission earned to date deducted from his salary. As the president for marketing says,

'It's one of our little ways of trying to get people to pay attention to today's customers'. Such companies place appropriate emphasis on the quality and effectiveness of training and communications programme. It also ensures full acceptance, interest and support by everyone in the organisation. The value-added product and service which results ensures economic viability. Differentiation between competitive products depends entirely on the way the company chooses to run its business. Why else then can Marks & Spencer achieve a mark-up of up to 100 per cent on brown eggs? Biologically and nutritionally there is nothing to distinguish the St Michael product from eggs sold on a market stall.

'Excellent' companies have another pointer to their success. They stimulate autonomy and entrepreneurship. There is a chance for tens of thousands of people to use their initiative. This approach is based on the hypothesis of Jewkes[7] that nothing works out right the first time it is tried. A process of error reduction and a willingness to accept and learn from constructive criticism forms an essential climate to cultivate flair and innovation. Jewkes considered 58 major innovations, some 46 of them came from the wrong place, at the wrong time, by the wrong person, in the wrong industry and with the wrong end user. Quinn[8] studied the formal innovation processes of some major American companies – Bell Labs, Polaroid, Xerox, IBM and General Electric – over 25 years and concluded that 'not a single major product has come from a formal planning process'. One of the major degree initiatives of the 1980s, Manchester Polytechnic's BA(Hons) Retail Marketing degree, was not created by setting up a formal development committee. Informal discussions (often over a pie and a pint and a game of snooker) led to a concentrated brain-storming residential week-end where the structure and pattern for future development was conceived. Often worthwhile results are achieved because entrenched opposition said 'it couldn't be done'; so jet aircraft, television, laser technology all had difficult, if unnecessarily difficult, births.

A belief in a 'mission impossible' often drives key groups of employees to superhuman efforts. An organisation needs to allow such esoteric behaviour, especially at senior levels. As Drucker[9] points out, 'Whenever anything is being accomplished, it is being done, I have learned, by a monomaniac with a mission'. A crisis, a challenge, a fear of competition, a burning ambition to achieve a notable result, a self actualisation need,[10] can all produce exceptional responses. The presence of irrational, erratic, monomaniacal eccentrics can be seen in industry, business, science, education and the arts. Descriptions given to Nobel Prize-winners include the terms, peasant toughness, resilience, streak of lactality, killer instinct and a strong finisher – not necessarily the most intelligent, physically fit people, but almost invariably the most persistent. Henry Ford was regarded by many to be a real pain in the neck with his obsessional attention to detail, but he did more than anyone else to create the automotive age for the mass public. Organisations need to be designed so as to allow such people to thrive. There is little that can succeed without the energy of such persistent, highly motivated, often emotional and irritable idea engines.

'Excellent' companies are experts in achieving productivity and efficiency through people. Every organisation in the UK, if not in the world, will publicly declare it is people orientated. The human resource management policies of Hewlett Packard, IBM, Johnson & Johnson are especially noteworthy. They are different especially to the extent that they treat people with respect and dignity, expect to receive contributions and ideas from them, and listen and respond to what is expressed. Certain UK retail companies reflect this management style, albeit in a patchy and confusing manner. There can be a tendency, according to the flavour of the month, to insist on staff expressing their opinion, then to bang the table and impose an arbitrary solution. One notable example of where the policy of openness is consistently followed by management is IKEA, where co-workers are allowed and even encouraged to enjoy a considerable level of autonomy in its stores.

Contact with people reinforces their commitment and motivation. The practice of United Biscuits to start the day with an executive breakfast encouraged managers to make contact with colleagues and technical specialists they would not normally meet in the course of the day. Periodic changes in the seating arrangements in the staff restaurant can also redefine social patterns of interaction and discourage people from sitting together in small groups for years on end. It is amazing what people find they have in common once they take the courageous move of making new contacts. The open door policy may be old hat but it pays dividends. At IBM there is the fundamental acceptance that managers exist to support their people and not vice versa. At MFI the design of the head office purposely ensured there was no executive floor and that each director is located in his own department in order to be accessible to his people. The layout and positioning of work stations affects the frequency of contact considerably. If staff are separated by distance, floor level or noise, they will create communication barriers as well. Digital and Hewlett Packard deliberately encourage their people to travel throughout the USA and Europe so as to see each other. The new headquarters of Intel in Silicon Valley is lavishly equipped with boards and flipcharts to increase the opportunity of having informal brain-storming sessions with people from different specialisms and professions.

Studies by Rothlisberger and Dickson[11] have indicated that people who have more control over their lives will be more productive, even though they may not always be willing or want to exercise their right to use that control. Research showed that in an experimental group which had the authority to turn off unwelcome background noise by pushing a button, levels of productivity were up to five times higher than for the control group which had no such right. There is a clear benefit for companies to give people more control, or perceived control over their work. Certain retail companies such as Marks & Spencer, Makro, J. Sainsbury and Next are giving more autonomy and discretion to department managers. As Paul Smith, personnel executive of Marks & Spencer stated in 1986 'our function is to take the stress and anxiety out of people's jobs'.

'Excellent' companies are positively minded in their assessment of people's performance. IBM sets goals for its employees which are achievable. The top 80 per cent of its salesmen qualify for entry to the one-hundred per cent club. The top 3 per cent qualify for gold circle status. The best results come when the middle 70 per cent performers are helped to achieve more, not by alienating 90 per cent of the people by rewarding just the 10 per cent. Dixons and MFI deliberately incentify their management teams with promotions, targets and competitions. The winners are normally judged on increasing their own performance, rather than first past the post. Keeping in touch is more than arranging frequent meetings and encounters. Companies can successfully manage change if they value a management style that is very much hands on and by having a clear vision and set of values; there being only one way to inculcate the message – in the field by visible demonstration, not by means of policy statement. The Hewlett Packard company refers to this approach as MBWA (management by wandering about). Retail branch managers should spend very little time in the office. Rather they should be out in the store and with their people and customers, and sense what is taking place before the computer printout tells them. At McDonalds members of the public can be served by area and regional managers, but because they dress and act the same as the rest of the crew, no one would know it. This company is very clear about its business objectives and can respond quickly and sensitively to customer needs. Immediately after Eddie Carlson took over United Airlines he and the top management team spent 60 per cent of their time on the road for eighteen months, taking the message and commitment to the field. The creation of student work placement experiences for seven cohorts of BA (Hons) Retail Marketing studies (over 600 since 1984) at Manchester Polytechnic was not brought about by writing letters to faceless personnel and training managers, but rather by visiting the stores, taking part in their own recruitment activities, experiencing the practical realities of retailing at first hand, serving customers, drinking tea and generally sharing a common interest in retailing activity as it was taking place.

Hands-on management certainly enables the company to keept its finger on the pulse of commercial reality. Even though the market research department is important, real live visible evidence has no substitute. Had General Motors or Ford moved to the West coast of the USA in the early 1970s they would have seen the smaller Japanese cars on the freeways. However, at the same time around Detroit where company cars are the norm, all around are seen in large numbers the large American limos. Ivory towers are just as dangerous as rose-tinted spectacles. Distance between head office and stores can be potentially disastrous. MFI's head office at Colindale is built on top of a store. This permits the merchandisers, buyers and personnel staff to go to the ground floor and try out ideas where the takings are .

These 'excellent' companies invariably have an organisation which is simple in structure and a lean cost-conscious staff. Lines of communication are simple and more direct. The matrix structure has shown itself to be a recipe for confusion and demarcation. What can an individual achieve with half a dozen bosses and a tenth of the responsibility for a task? Efficient companies can respond to the demands of a multi-dimensional complex society without creating a formal, ineffective and cumbersome organisation that is inflexible and not responsive to change. Are there lessons here for those more traditional high street department store retailers?

Mars, which has a $7bn turnover, sixty divisions and 60 per cent of sales outside the USA, is managed from a small building which houses twenty officers and twenty secretaries. This is in contrast to the 10 per cent of Marks & Spencer labour force employed in administrative head office functions and Ford's seventeen layers of management. Toyota by contrast can manage its multinational operation with five. Johnson & Johnson and General Motors give their operating divisions considerable independence. The board of directors in each division can actually create the advantages of healthy rivalry and competition rather than the potential damage that product duplication can bring.

Large, successful enterprises create an overall identity of purpose and product differentiation. For example, 3M's more than 100 000 products all have the common link arising from bonding or coating technology – e.g. Scotch tape, video and audio cassettes, post-it-notes and office copier products. There is the dichotomy of having an apparently loose structure, yet ensuring rigid control and almost fanatical attention to quality performance. The development of 'own label' products and exclusive brands by retailers can do much not only to foster customer loyalty and repeat purchases; it can stimulate employee pride in the job. People working in such cultures become obsessive about their work – as one food hall manager said 'there's real beauty in a can of beans'.

8.5 Changing Management Types and Practices in Retailing

'Excellent' companies are a product of their own creation, where different methods worked best. First generation excellence revolved around charismatic leaders who were a legend in their time. Simon Marks's endeavours with a market stall in Leeds, Robert Owen and his concern with the well-being of all his workers, Tom Watson of IBM who established 'respect for the individual' and 'service to customers' were men of their time. Paternalism was their slogan, profit-making their aim. There is a tendency, however, when such people are no longer active in the business, and when no obvious successor survives, for there to be a perpetuation of past practice by those who have not the ability to manage well. When commercial or technical difficulties arise there is a tendency to make excuses, blame others, become defensive and uncritical of themselves.

Second generation 'excellent' companies perfected the mechanistic bureaucracy which attempted to predict problems and prescribed solutions before they occurred. This was the antithesis to original thought and innovation. Weber[12] advocated the virtue of formal structure and rigid lines of communication – fine, where there are stable environmental conditions and a static technical infrastructure with unquestioning obedience from staff. However, success depends ultimately on senior management delivering the right answers for most if not all of the time as they not only have the power but also all the information and expertise. Many retail companies have and are experiencing such a mechanistic culture – particularly some in the food retailing sectors.

Whatever criticisms are levelled at these bureaucratic organisations, invariably they are cost-conscious enterprises seeking to minimise the dangers of risk and uncertainty. The credibility and strength of these second generation companies lies in their stability. Value is placed on position, title, status, promotion and salary, rather than on doing things differently. Such companies were anxious to grow, but only on the basis of providing more of the same. Why change a winning formula? The institution's needs come before those of individuals; this is the culture of the organisation man.[13] The necessary ingredients for success in the information age – flexibility, innovation and creativity – are lacking as each level of the hierarchy in the organisation acts as a filter inhibiting change. Every level has the authority to say 'no' and be negative; rarely would they have the right to say 'yes' if the organisation has not yet thought of the approved method to respond.

The third generation of companies have the undoubted ability to transform their products and organisation in response to social, legal and economic changes, and consumer buying habits and preferences. Who in food retailing would be rash enough not now to provide health conscious environmentally friendly products and services? A lot has happened in the last five years: customers and retail staff are better informed, better educated, more discriminating and can transfer their shopping and employment loyalties to those companies that are perceived as better able to supply their social, moral as well as their material needs. The development and extension of own-label products has created new challenges for some companies that had never previously thought about producing merchandise for sale themselves. As in the case of Woolworth's Focus Strategy of 1986, one by-product has been the improvement in the confidence of the sales staff who become better informed about what they are selling and identify themselves more with the company and its own merchandise.

Third generation 'excellent' companies do not need to provide and operate formal staff morale-building programmes. The working environment and shared values of the company provide in an informal manner what is expected from each person. It is the excitement and zest the companies generate that stimulates people to do their very best. In this new cultural environment quality without compromise is applied not just to the product but to the way everyone in each department does his job, from finance to reception to sales. The setting of attainable objectives ensures that most people succeed most of the time.

However, the transition between first, second and third generation companies is not automatic. There are fundamental differences in culture, attitude, behaviour and work styles. Those who are comfortable and successful in one environment would be uneasy and feel threatened in another. The purpose of a personnel and training department is to see that adequate preparation, monitoring and feedback characterise an individual support programme or a personal assistance plan (PAP) – for example, as provided by Whitbread.

Not many of the companies that have been cited as 'excellent' in global terms so far have extensive retailing interests. That does not mean that this is a permanent state of affairs, but rather that many retailers have not yet achieved universal recognition as excellent managers of people, customers and resources. The maxim 'pile it high, sell it cheap' dies hard. Training is still seen to depend on last week's takings. Mergers, acquisitions, takeovers and buyouts may be justified in financial terms and as part of a strategy to increase market share, but as to the effects on the people who work there – well personnel are there to 'pick up the pieces and get rid of those who are surplus to requirements'. Even some personnel specialists take a cynical view of their contribution to success. To quote one personnel director of a DIY retail company, 'The trouble with training is that it is not a separate item on the Balance Sheet. You start off the year with training at the top of the priorities needing urgent attention and it gets downgraded to the bottom of the heap after a month or two'.

8.6 Retail Skills and Qualities

Yet retailing by its very nature is a people-centred activity. All those problems and demands that companies experience in a traditional manufacturing and industrial environment are there, and more besides. For personnel managers to contribute effectively to the needs of the retail business, the impact that retailing activity has on the working lives of the staff has to be appreciated and recognised. Retail employment is a high-profile experience. Staff have visually to conform to accepted standards of dress and appearance. For some people, it is often better to be warned off before tackling the very real demands that retailing imposes, and thus avoid all the bitterness, tears, loss of time, money, opportunity and confidence that could be experienced. Four major skills and attributes a person needs to possess (arguably given varying emphasis by retailers) are numeracy, critical awareness, social sensitivity and stamina. Expertise in solving quadratic equations, calculus and logarithms is not usually a sought-after technique in retail. Rather, a knowledge of percentages, ratios, measurement and the statistical presentation of data, and an ability quickly and accurately to assimilate large amounts of numerical data with confidence and certainty to achieve deadlines are essential requirements. Over and above these technical skills must be an accurate perception of relative amounts of money, time, space and distance. A figure wth an extra nought in it must be instantly recognised as not conforming with reality. A 2 per cent increase in the sales turnover of a store must, by association, mean something in terms of the company's profit margin break-even point and operating budget. There is also the need to be aware of the competitor's position in the market. If they are reporting a 10 per cent increase in turnover you are in all probability losing your share of consumer expenditure and need to ascertain reasons for this state of affairs, and whether it is likely to be a temporary or long-term trend. Figures, like words, will only provide a clear understanding of what is actually happening if the correct questions are posed in the first place. It may then be possible to judge, interpret and deduce trends correctly from the available data.

Successful retailers almost invariably have a keen eye for detail. A moment's visual inspection of a fruit and vegetable display can reveal possible problems with the range, colour, freshness, correct pricing and labelling. Observing a rack of ladies' dresses can indicate if there is anything wrong with the seams, cut, colour or range, and whether its position in the store is appropriate and is attracting attention. It can be most useful to note whether customers stop and talk while examining the garments or totally ignore them and rush by. Do customers shop in small groups, or are they always on their own? What types of customers make a purchase, and have they been before? These and other features of shopping patterns do not escape the notice of the keen observer.

Social sensitivity may be developed through training and experience, but there must be a predisposition to be interested and concerned for others in the first place. Involving others in what you are doing, which may on occasions cause a sacrifice of your own time and effort, are the hallmarks of a person who is socially committed. Sometimes the intention to help those who apparently need it is misinterpreted, as when a young man gave up his seat on a bus and smiled to an apparently frail old lady. He was sharply rebuked with the acid comment, 'What do you think you're doing? I'm not that decrepit'. At the very least, some acknowledgement and an attempt to remember a face, a name and a person's interests and activities shows some effort to relate to others.

Social skills do not merely mean being 'nice to people'. Comments from a wide range of store managers, personnel and training officers and retail trainees themselves emphasise the crucial importance of 'people skills'. One must be sincerely interested in a wide range of social activities, creating events and situations through and with others, demonstrating a task or merely listening and showing attention can all be valuable social skills. Listening and not just hearing is a major positive social attribute in retail, especially in a department store when a number of bored, lonely or insecure customers may eventually buy goods or services from attentive staff who have taken the trouble to listen to their problems and have shown patience and persistence. Social skills is that convenient generic term which is used to include what is being said as well as the way it is being said within the context of the totality of the visual and non-verbal behaviour which is taking place. Thus nodding one's head at the correct time, smiling, gestures and looking towards, but not necessarily at, the other person are some of the more usual positive requirements. Noticing and recognising these aspects of customer and employee behaviour can be of enormous help. One's own approach and demeanour can be adjusted if necessary. A lack of eye contact can denote disinterest, and a stance with feet apart and arms folded may be interpreted as an intimidating or defensive posture. It can often be the case that an individual, no matter how gifted or talented, may display boredom, uncertainty, insularity, dominance or impatience.

To some the whole idea of selling or offering a service may imply servility, and if the hostile warning signs are detected in an applicant then every effort should be made to dissuade that person from retailing.[14] Such is the importance that is being attached to social and interpersonal skills that an in-depth study of this whole area is considered by a number of retailing organisations to be an essential part of an individual's management training and development. It is certainly possible through a programme of social awareness to raise and extend an individual's verbal and auditory threshold so as to notice far more about what actually is taking place.

For many of the jobs in the retail stores, and especially in the stockroom and warehouse, evidence of stamina and endurance must rank as an essential qualification. It is not just the heavy or bulky boxes and merchandise that has to be moved, but the sheer distance that many people have to cover. One sales supervisor who worked on three floors of a department store was recorded as covering 21 miles in a nine hour day. For those who are fairly static there may be little chance to sit down, although there ought to be some facility nearby. Standing for long periods on tiled or mosaic floors in many a food hall can be extremely stressful. Some staff working in a ladies' fashions department where shag pile carpets were newly laid complained about trudging through the thick pile which made their ankles ache. Being actively involved with the shopping public, as the majority of retail staff are, brings them directly into contact with all the viruses, germs and bacteria associated with the whole range of human ailments. It is a practice for some companies to arrange for their staff to receive inoculations, and some checkouts are fitted with perspex shields, which are not only security devices, but can also offer some protection against infection from others. Where staff are required to work variable hours or shifts, an individual's health can be affected through changes in personal eating and sleeping habits. The pattern of human metabolism can become upset and normal resistance to various forms of illness is reduced in individual cases. Then there are those occasions when staff are working on loading bays receiving goods, or in cold rooms when there can be exposure to frequent changes of temperature and humidity. Some people may be more susceptible to these conditions than others and can suffer more from chills, colds, influenza and bronchitis.

8.7 Personnel Expertise in Retailing

Personnel practitioners in retailing have developed expertise in a number of key personnel functions, notably in staff planning and development, recruitment and selection, training, performance appraisal, staff counselling and employee services.

Employment Relations

Staff planning and development can be based on sophisticated models which identify factors that affect the number, location, skills and competences of staff required now and in the future, based on projections of business activity, productivity performance and wage costs. It is possibly in the major food retail companies such as J. Sainsbury, and in mail-order firms such as Littlewoods and pub retailers Greenall Whitley where personnel managers devise, amend and operate computer programs that facilitate data analysis and employment modelling for use in staff projections. Further development could identify future staffing sourcing and recommend the most cost effective means of capitalising an opportunity in times of labour scarcity. Sophisticated management information systems identify those areas where particular expertise is needed. EPOS data from the point of sale is an indispensable part of personnel scheduling in stores for J. Sainsbury; but readily to respond to problems of shortages and delays identified by IT and caused by inadequate staffing elsewhere in the business, is still a challenge that many personnel managers in retailing need to address. The sophistication of IT can enable personnel managers to monitor changes in sales revenue in relation to those labour costs that are more easily controllable by line managers in the short term. Computer based modelling can identify not only potential areas of cost saving, but also the likely beneficial effects on employee performance resulting from redeployment, retraining or changes in the pattern of working hours that are worked. IT is already providing stores and head office with much more relevant, immediate and detailed data from which to make better decisions and to assess, if not always to reduce, the level of risk arising from management actions.

Data used to compile labour budgets do not only include projections of future sales. They also reflect costs which are necessarily incurred from company restructuring or new developments where additional skills and experience need to be acquired by staff. Training costs can also be influenced by the current and projected level of staff turnover.

Labour budgets in retailing can be calculated on the basis of sales per employee per hour during a standard working week and related to a figure which meets financial objectives. Alternatively it can be calculated as a percentage of projected sales turnover. Whatever method is used, the labour budget should be sub-divided into areas, stores and categories of staff with an amount included for training and staff development. For those companies able to measure and reward employee productivity, the labour budget must be flexible and responsive to short-term changes in sales revenue. Staff development and succession planning necessitates a more stable and assured financial budget covering a time period of several years so that a full opportunity is given to a personnel manager to bring about reconstruction of the labour force.

Recruitment and Selection

Some personnel managers in retailing companies, especially in department stores before Christmas, spend more than two thirds of their time on staff recruitment and selection. Consequently many feel this is the area where they have most to offer their company. But do they? Is it more a case of recruiting in haste and regretting at leisure?

The key to successful recruitment and selection lies in preparation. A thorough job analysis which identifies the scope of the job, its key duties and responsibilities, its position and authority in an organisation, is a prerequisite. Information about the job can be gathered from the current post-holder, if there is one. He or she will tell you what they think they are doing. The post-holder's super-ordinate will explain what ought to be taking place. If there is a difference in their perception, then independent observation may provide additional insight. From the data so obtained a job description is drawn up which identifies the duties and responsibilities considered necessary for effective performance in the job. A job specification can provide in more detail the standards that apply to the tasks to be undertaken, as well as giving a clear indication of the skills, qualities and experience of the 'ideal' candidate. Once reliable criteria for assessing an applicant's suitability are agreed, including positive and negative indicators of success, a personnel or line manager is much more likely to succeed in the attempt to appoint a person who is competent and has potential for further development. Appointees are far more likely to remain in the company and progress their career if systematic matching exercise is thoroughly conducted in the first place.

Retailers proliferate the variety of recruitment and selection techniques that are used. Tesco and increasingly J. Sainsbury are advocates of psychological tests such as NP6, WP3, CP3/7, VI, NC 2, 16PF, OPQ, AH4, AH6, Wasson Glaser, FI0/B and SCII, as well as structured interviewing, group discussions, observation and practical exercises. One sometime wonders why certain tests are used to assess candiates' abilities and skills, and whether the results obtained are significant and realistic. There is also the problem of accurately and objectively assessing behaviour especially in group situations. What to one observer is clear evidence of a stubborn, brash demeanour, another may not have thought of as significant; and yet another may regard what was heard, rather than seen, as tough, forthright and decisive. However, clearly this is the one opportunity the personnel manager has to influence the size and composition of the workforce and at the same time ensure the full involvement of line management in the process, the results of which they must be able to live with,[15] meet the interests of the company and provide fulfilling opportunities for applicants best suited for the work.

Training

Training, it is said,[16] compensates for the inadequacies of the selection process. The reputation of training in selling techniques, display and merchandising by such companies as Littlewoods, Debenhams and Harrods is legendary; that for product knowledge, operational systems is thoroughly covered by J. Sainsbury and Waitrose; Marks & Spencer provides a breadth of operational training and facilitates leadership development.

Current interest in training includes attention being paid to self-instructional packages, computerised training systems and an emphasis on a broader educational development for middle and senior management leading to externally recognised qualifications such as MBA. Future development in retail training at all levels will be very much influenced by the need to create greater standardisation and uniformity of practice.[17] The introduction of competence based levels of attainment by the National Retail Training Council will facilitate transferability of skills and a recognition of work-related experience qualification in its own right. Many retail companies are likely to seek external accreditation and validation of their in-house management training from institutions in the higher education sector, possibly leading to the award of their own diplomas or degrees. Who says that training and staff development is cheap? Expenditure on training initiatives is likely to attract an annual budget of 2 per cent of total staff costs in the coming decade.[18] This level of investment is still, however, only modest when compared with leading retail companies in Germany and Japan.

Performance Appraisal

Performance appraisal is the one area which personnel managers in retailing often regard as a minefield.[19] Companies such as Debenhams, Marks & Spencer, and J. Sainsbury have used criteria-based referencing as the basis for management assessment. Difficulties may arise if a manager is appraised on aspects of his work that do not fully reflect the range of responsibilities and expectations placed on him at the time. The comment 'I'd have seen to that more carefully had I thought it mattered so much' shows that performance review needs to be clearly related to the agreed realities and demands of the developing situation that exists. Personnel managers need therefore to devise and implement a strategy for performance appraisal that stimulates managerial growth and innovation, yet which enables each person to be aware of the broader objectives of the company and to create achievable targets that are mutually agreed. To this end, the revised appraisal and performance review procedure of Marks & Spencer in recent years, and that of Thomas Cook, invite more active participation on the part of the appraisee, who reviews his or her own experience, and what they would like to achieve in the future with the support of the organisation. The mechanism for operating staff appraisal and performance development is a systematic training programme to enhance the interviewing and observation and listening skills of line management, and to monitor and evaluate judgements which are made so that reasonable consistency is assured. Job and performance profiling is seen as another innovation by larger retailers such as Tesco, J. Sainsbury and the Peter Dominic Group. Critical incident assessments CIA and the use of the 'Repertory Grid' RG record current experience of managers deemed to successful performers. CIA identifies and prioritises those aspects of the job considered to be significant. R.G. provides a profile of those skills and qualities which help to distinguish particular jobs in an organisation. Follow up of these procedures is vital, otherwise yet another bureaucratic process is created which gives arid results. Deficiencies in current performance may be rectified either through training or the temporary or permanent removal of the individual concerned from the specific job or area in the company. Recognition and incentive packages appropriate to the specific situation need to be delivered. Yet again a personnel manager with an interest in developing human resources in the company should influence the decision and action that affects the future career development of individual staff.

Staff Counselling

Staff counselling may be likened to the casualty department of a hospital. No one knows when they may need the service; yet when they do there is the expectation that expert help is available, and that following the crisis the patient can be returned to an active life. Personal assistance programmes (PAP) as operated by a number of companies – a notable example of which is Whitbread – do in fact cater for a range of stress-related problems, which may often be of a temporary nature. Difficulties arising from alcohol abuse, and problems in forming satisfactory personal relationships characterise the cases that are referred to specialist help. Such a service needs to be regarded as something more than another example of a caring organisation. As well as being part of a broader social and community obligation, help and support given by PAP, especially by those who are in the best position to provide it, makes sound commercial sense. It shows commitment by the company to an employee at times when such action matters most. Personnel managers therefore take to themselves the role of providing an effective rescue and recycling programme.

Employee Redundancy and Dismissal

The volatile nature of retailing, with its inevitable changes and opportunities, makes long-term planning difficult. This, together with those flaws and imperfections found in people working in a tempting environment, can cause companies actively to seek selective or total termination of employment. Personnel managers need to advise managers about the complexity of employment law which determines whether a particular case is one of redundancy, resignation, wrongful, fair or constructive dismissal. Indeed, the actions or lack of action on the part of the company or any member of staff can materially affect the legal judgement made in individual cases brought before an industrial tribunal. (See Chapter 7 for more detailed reference to this.)

The mergers, takeovers, amalgamations, rationalisations, buy-outs and other euphemisms of organisational change have affected many sectors of retailing in recent years. Many staff, especially those on part-time contracts, or having less than two years service, have no legal right to redundancy compensation. In practice many examples exist where retail companies take a compassionate attitude, either giving an *ex-gratia* payment and assisting their staff to find alternative employment. Membership of employers' or trading associations such as the Retail Consortium provides retailers with an additional source of advice and practical assistance in such cases. Where disputes and grievances have arisen over the offer and termination of employment, matters are not always helped if the original contract of employment is vague, ambiguous or patently fails to meet the requirements of current employment law. The multiplicity of job titles, grading structures and entrenched practices affecting salaries, job responsibilities and fringe benefits provides a fertile ground for disputes and grievances that can affect the industrial relations climate. Every retail organisation needs to have a clearly worded, understood and accepted statement of employment policy which stipulates not only employee rights, but their obligations to conform to acceptable standards of behaviour. What precisely constitutes gross or serious misconduct requires explicit explanation. Because termination of employment, redundancy and dismissal can inevitably occur in an emotional atmosphere charged with mistrust and recrimination, formal practices ought to be devised and objectively administered. In addition the personnel manager should become accepted as counsellor, conciliator and mediator and provide the necessary overview as conscience to the company.

Employee Services

It is in the area of employee services that retail companies excel. Based on a social, moral and often religious concern for the welfare and safety of all those who work in the store, paternalist retailers have historically provided what they considered the full range of welfare facilities: living-in accommodation, company outings, library, education, medical treatment and pensions. In fact, what it took to provide a fit, well turned out, obedient, loyal and industrious workforce who were accessible and obligated to the company for their generous treatment.[20] Times have changed. The self-conscious retailer is anxious to be regarded as a 'caring' employer providing for the material and psychological wellbeing of its staff. A chiropody service, cervical-screening, subsidised meals, staff discounts are some of the usual benefits that are provided. Even so, disputes and grievances may arise when there are more occasions and examples for individuals to feel disadvantaged if not discriminated against if other staff are perceived as receiving better or undeserved treatment. Indeed personnel management may often have to pay attention to the means and methods of delivering the staff welfare package rather than concentrating on the often thankless task of deciding 'what new benefit can we provide now?' For welfare provision to be seen to be benefiting the business as a whole rather than a few favoured people must always be the concern of the personnel specialist.[21]

8.8 Conclusions

Are there areas of employment where the latent as well as actual demands of retailing activity find personnel managers lacking either in experience or determination? There are, notably in the field of industrial rather than employee or human relations. How many retail companies are satisfied that they are able realistically to measure and assess the productivity performance of their staff and relate it to the wage and salary cost to the business? IT resources are certainly able to generate the means to do this. Is there an adequate response to the challenge of European labour law and practice which will affect UK retailers after 1992? There is a different approach towards employee access to information and consultation at the place of work on the Continent, as provided for in the Delors social contract. Perhaps the more entrenched autocratic leadership styles of senior retail managers in the UK need to be replaced by a more open, accountable and consistent approach. Is there adequate consideration being given to the impact of a skill shortage in the UK labour force in the 1990s especially brought about by a dearth of young people?[22] In these and related issues no retail organisation is an island sheltered from the same circumstances that affect employment as in other companies. The reduction and prevention of unnecessary stress factors is such an issue. Work done by FIET[23] (Federation Internationale des Employés Techniques) examines the benefits of ergonomic design at the checkouts, of monitoring the effects on operators engaged in the concentrated observation of computer data on printout or on screen, the physical dangers of theft and violence, and the need to harmonise work and non-work interests and priorities for employees. Retailers are beginning to respond.

Marks & Spencer is considering career break programmes for its staff; Tesco and Asda are designing checkouts that will reduce operator fatigue; security screens are being fitted and staff are trained in first aid. Retailer support is continuing to grow for the arts, education, minority interests and social rehabilitation programmes in the community.

However, it is the strategic issues such as wage and salary performance, the creation of a coherent wage and salary structure, and the delivery of a democratic culture that encourages participation as a right rather than as an expedient, which will enhance the credibility, authority and influence of personnel management in the 1990s. In these and other issues retail companies are well placed to extend environmentally friendly, commercially sound and socially beneficial policies to the staff they employ, not only in the UK but in a truly international setting.

Personnel management has come a long way to convince retail companies of its value and service. However, like a school report, the assessment 'Is doing quite well, but needs to achieve consistent results in the future' seems a fair summary comment.

References

1. D. Torrington and J. Chapman, *Personnel Management* (London: Prentice-Hall, 1983).
2. D. G. Couch, 'Personnel Management in Retailing – A problem of credibility?', *Institute of Grocery Distribution Bulletin*, May 1988.
3. W. F. Whyte, *Organisation Man* (Harmondsworth: Pelican, 1963).
4. IPM Definition. *Institute of Personnel Management Handbook 1979*.
5. T. Peters and R. Waterman, *In Search of Excellence* (London: Harper & Row, 1982).
6. T. Peters, *Thriving on Chaos* (London: Macmillan, 1988).
7. J. Jewkes, *The Sources of Innovation* (New York: W. W. Norton, 1970).
8. J. Quinn, '*The Mythology of Innovation*', in *Readings in Management, Innovation* Ed. Trashman, Michael and Moore (New York: Pitman, 1982).
9. P. Drucker, *Innovation and Entrepreneurship* (London: Pan, 1986).
10. R. Maslow, *Motivation Behavior* (New York: McGraw-Hill, 1947).
11. F. J. Rothlisberger and W. J. Dickson, *Management and the Worker* (Cambridge, Mass.: Harvard University Press, 1939).
12. M. Weber, *The Protestant Ethic and the Spirit of Capitalism* (London: Allen & Unwin, 1930).
13. W. H. Whyte, *Organisation Man* (Harmondsworth: Pelican, 1963).
14. D. G. Couch, 'Students on Industrial Release – Pleasure or Pain?' *IGD Bulletin*, May 1987.
15. A. Roger, *Interviewing for Selection* (National Institute of Industrial Psychology, 1964).
16. S. Tyson and A. Fell, *Evaluating the Personnel Function* (London: Hutchinson, 1986).
17. K. T. Abella, *Building Successful Training Programmes – a step by step guide* (Wokingham: Addison-Wesley, 1986) p. 156.

18. R. Chapman, 'Personnel Management in the 1990s, *Personnel Management*, January 1990, p. 30.
19. T. Peters and N. Austin, *A Passion for Excellence* (London: Collins, 1985).
20. P. C. Hoffman, *They Also Serve* (London: Porcupine Press, 1953).
21. J. Morgan, *Managing Change in Personnel* (London: Macmillan, 1986).
22. N. Alexander, 'The Internal Market of 1992, Attitudes of Leading Retailers', *Retail & Distribution Management*, January 1989, pp. 13–15.
23. D. G. Couch, *Retailing: a Self Starter* (Harmondsworth: Penguin, 1989).

Government Control in Retailing 9

9.1 Introduction

Although government intervention has long been accepted as a feature in the provision of such social welfare services as education, health services, income security, housing etc., it is not recognised as a characteristic in the provision of retail services where, traditionally, market forces have been thought to predominate and it has been believed that the profit motive would ensure the best use and provision of resources. Even so, most Western style, capitalist economies and all communist countries possess a considerable body of legislation relating to retailing. In many cases this has emanated from a concern for the protection of public interest, and it would seem that certain governments have extended to the retail sector the view that the 'principle of free competition, which is applicable to the production of things for private demand, is not applicable to the production of things where public interest is involved'.[1]

Rather unfortunately, 'the retailing-public sector interface has not been studied in anywhere near the degree that is needed'.[2] Apart from the pioneer work of Boddewyn and Hollander,[3] which is now somewhat dated, there have been few detailed studies and no major attempts at evaluation of the achievements of the various policies. There are several reasons for this and, excluding the lack of finance, Feldman has suggested there are essentially three.[4] First, the large-scale emergence of public policy issues in marketing is a relatively recent phenomenon and inevitably there has been a 'research lag'. Second, there is the fact that for scholars of marketing such issues have some political significance and, as such, differ markedly from those with which they are accustomed to dealing. Third, Feldman suggests, is the fact that such issues are in many ways intractable, whereas research in marketing, traditionally, has confined itself to subjects which are relatively easy to define (i.e. market sizes, product prices, etc.).

For these, and doubtless several other equally important reasons, the relationship between government and retailing remains relatively unexplored and under-researched. The purpose of this study, therefore, is to go some way towards rectifying this situation, by providing an overview of the whole field of public policy and retailing but, at the same time, concentrating on those policies relating to the planning of retail systems.

9.2 The Nature of Policies

Although recognition of the importance of government intervention has been only recent, there exists in most countries of the Western world a considerable body of legislation which affects the retail trades, either directly or indirectly. Even in the United States of America, where the philosophy of *laissez-faire* has prevailed perhaps more than in any other country, there is 'an enormous volume of retailing-related legislation'.[5] Much of this legislation reflects the political activity of small traders, particularly in periods of economic recession, and many countries do possess policies specifically intended to protect small unit retailing. However, in reviewing government policies towards retailing, perhaps the first point that ought to be made is that the retail trades are affected not solely by direct marketing-oriented legislation but by indirect legislation aimed at other economic or social objectives. As Hollander has observed:

> Overall economic policies that contribute to prosperity or depression affect not only the volume of goods purchased through the retail system, but also the supply of retail workers and would-be entrepreneurs. Postwar American policies that have encouraged highway construction and the development or suburban one-family housing have probably done as much as any other phase of action in shaping contemporary retailing.[6]

Clearly such an observation is not confined to America and is not exhaustive of the range of policies that affect retailing in this way. For instance, government taxation policies can have very considerable ramifications for the structure of retailing, as was the case with Selective Employment Tax in Britain,[7] while policies relating to urban renewal can also affect retail organisation and structure,[8] as can energy conservation policies.[9]

Apart from these very broad-ranging policies which have indirect (sometimes unintended) implications for retailing, there is a large number of policies which relate directly to retailing, and it is on these that attention will be focused. In this context, the second point which has to be made is that these policies are themselves extremely difficult to classify satisfactorily. The main reasons for this are that, in the first place, the policies have been derived, often, in a very piecemeal fashion in response to particular problems or pressures from particular sectors of society. As a consequence, few countries possess a national plan towards retailing or a set of coherent policies aimed at achieving a specific objective with respect to retailing. Equally, however, classification is difficult because differences sometimes exist, as will be shown later, between the actual and ostensible purpose of the legislation. Hollander cites a number of examples where this is the case and concludes that 'in view of all the ambiguities in public policies and the differences between policies in different countries, few universally valid generalisations can be offered'.[10] However, several classifications do exist,[11] but none is fully comprehensive or mutually exclusive, so that certain policies can be placed in more than one category. Perhaps one of the most valuable attempts at classification is that by Dawson which distinguishes between policies aimed at improving the efficiency of retailing and those concerned with providing equity solutions.[12] While this provides a very useful framework for discussing retail planning policies, particularly given the greater social awareness of marketing in recent years, it does suffer from the fact that policies which may appear to be promoting retail efficiency may also be interpreted in a social responsibility/equity context and vice versa.

This is certainly true of land-use planning policies, which are concerned not only with the spatial efficiency of retailing but also with the needs and requirements of minority groups, most notably the underprivileged and the deprived sectors of society. As Hollander points out 'efficiency in retailing may be valued as a means toward the improvement of consumer welfare . . . as a means of removing marketing obstacles facing other sectors'.[13]

Conscious of the problems involved in classification, three main categories of public policy have been recognised here: those which regulate competition, those which safeguard consumer interests, and those which regulate trading conditions. Each embraces a wide set of legislation and it is under each of these broad headings that the subject of government control will be examined.

9.3 Policies to Regulate Competition

These constitute one of the most important but controversial sectors of government intervention in retailing. Essentially, governments can regulate competition by controlling the spatial pattern of retailing (through land-use planning controls) and by manipulating the structure of retailing (through either the control of restrictive marketing practices or the promotion/restriction of innovation in retailing). Most Western societies have developed a relatively comprehensive set of legislation relating to both sets of policy, but it is relatively rare for both to be employed equally in any one region. Perhaps the two extreme examples are the United States of America and the United Kingdom, the former relying very heavily upon the control of restrictive marketing practices to regulate competition, while the latter has depended, to a very large extent, upon policies relating to development control. This does not mean that neither country has developed alternative legislation. Increasingly, American planning is placing greater emphasis on zoning ordinances, and there is evidence that land-use controls have been used to shelter established firms, for instance, from the emergence of new types of competition.[14] Equally, Britain has developed, largely since the late 1940s, a very complex and intricate set of competitition laws, though unlike the American legislation, the British laws do not include general prohibition on price discrimination.[15] At this point, perhaps it is important to recognise the distinction between what might be termed 'free competition' and 'fair competition'.

Competition in retailing takes three forms:

(a) horizontal competition – the conflict among competitors of the same type, such as the competition between two independent grocers,
(b) intertype competition – the conflict among different methods of distribution as, for instance, the conflict between independent and multiple retailers,
(c) vertical competition – the conflict between different stages in the same line of distribution, such as the conflict between retailers and suppliers over prices and margins.

The legislation relating to competition in retailing relates to all three types and, in general, has been based upon the premise that 'free competition is the situation most beneficial to the community at large'.[16] In other words, the legislation has tended to encourage, rather than discourage, competition. In certain instances, however, one trader or one type of trader may possess an unfair advantage over the other and, in these circumstances, the competition may be regarded as being unequal. Probably this is most frequently experienced (or at least most readily recognised) in the context of intertype competition where, frequently, independent small traders have asserted that the selling prices of the major retailing organisations are lower because of their unfair use of bargaining power in negotiations with suppliers. That is, the intertype competition between small and large traders is unequal because of the inability of small traders to compete as effectively as the large traders in terms of vertical competition. In several countries, but most notably the United States, the result has been the introduction of measures to prevent such competition through the regulation of prices.[17] However, the whole issue is shrouded in controversy since, almost inevitably, the promotion of 'fair competition' involves a measure of control over 'free competition'. As a consequence, while many Western-style capitalist societies have introduced legislation to stimulate free competition, legislation to promote fair competition is, as in Britain, somewhat less common.

Policies to Promote Free Competition

Markets can be regarded as lying on a continuum ranging from completely monopolistic to perfectly competitive. While complete monopoly is relatively rare in Western society, perfect competition (in the strict economic sense) is equally unusual. In general, most markets can be regarded as being imperfectly competitive – i.e. offering a blend of monopoly and competition – but the situation is somewhat complicated by the fact that the concept of monopoly is extremely complex, involving consideration not only of the number of suppliers, but also of the products being marketed, the geographical area of the market and the time factor (i.e. a supplier may have a temporary monopoly). As a consequence, the commercial policies of most Western style governments are characterised by legislation to control the development of monopoly situations.

The control of monopoly power is one of the oldest problems of competition policy, and in most countries the laws relating to monopolies and mergers are extremely complex.[18]

It should be appreciated that the laws relating to monopolies and mergers rarely condemn *per se* the concentration of economic power. Rather, it is widely accepted that there are sound economic reasons for enterprises wishing to expand their size and share of the market, and the laws tend to concentrate, therefore, on the abuse of that power: on those situations where market dominating enterprises 'violate public interest', 'interfere with the normal operation of the market', 'secure unreasonable prices' or 'create unfair business conditions' etc.

To this end, two distinct types of legislation have been developed. The first attempts to prevent or to dissolve the formation of unreasonable or undue market power, being based on the view that the adverse effects of market power cannot be controlled as long as the position of power continues to exist. The second approach takes the opposite viewpoint and is based on the belief that interference with such structural changes could prevent the achievement of improved efficiency. Under the second approach, therefore, the formation and existence of market power is left unaffected but the business practices of powerful enterprises are subjected to government control. While these are the two main approaches, they are not mutually exclusive and, in several countries, are applied concurrently. Even so, it is possible to recognise two sets of competition laws: those which control the formation of market power and those which control the conduct of market dominating activities. The former relate to mergers and monopolisation (the formation of monopolies) and as in Canada, France, Japan and the USA, take either an administrative or a criminal form. The laws controlling the conduct of market dominating enterprises take two different forms. They may:

(a) prohibit the abuse of power and subject the offenders to criminal, quasi-criminal or administrative sanctions. This is the situation in Spain, France, Germany and Switzerland.
(b) provide for administrative powers to intervene. The legislation belonging to this group does not prohibit abusive practices automatically, and essentially it can either be designed specifically to deal with these

practices (as in Belgium, Holland, Germany and the United Kingdom) or it may be applicable against anti-competitive practices in general (as in Denmark, Norway and Switzerland).

While retailing is subject, in many countries, to these general laws governing the restraint of economic concentration, it is also subjet to laws which are designed to control restrictive trade practices or restraints on trade. Such laws are directed at trade agreements intended to stifle competition, and these range in form from legally binding contractual agreements (cartels) to situations where firms merely 'act in a similar fashion and it is virtually hopeless to ascertain whether they are doing so in pursuit of an arrangement to act in concert, or whether they are merely manifesting an individual but identical response to the prevailing market conditions'.[19] Essentially, there are two types of agreement: horizontal agreements between parties at the same level of business activity (e.g. agreements between retailers) and vertical agreements between parties at different levels (e.g. agreements between retailers and suppliers). However, the range of subjects included in such agreements is extremely wide and the corresponding legislation is exceedingly complex, particularly as it is not uniformly developed throughout Western society. Perhaps the most extensive body of restrictive practices (anti-trust) legislation is that developed in America where the 'anti-trust system is possessed not only of a comparatively lengthy history, but also of a fervour that has won for it worldwide fame'.[20]

Irrespective of the precise nature of the legislation, such laws relating to restrictive trade practices have very considerable influences on the relationship not only between retailers within any given retail system but also between retailers and their suppliers. Equally, there can be little doubt that they have done much to preserve an element of competition in the distribution systems in which they are found, and this is reflected in the spatial, structural and organisational patterns of the respective retail systems.

Policies to Promote Fair Competition

As mentioned earlier, situations exist in which the promotion of free competition is, in reality, the promotion of unfair competition. In such situations, the question arises as to 'whether laws should exist not only to protect the public by promoting free competition but also to protect the trader by promoting fair competition'.[21] The whole subject is one of controversy. Some argue that laws to promote fair competition are unnecessary, while others suggest that since unfair competition drives competitors from the market it reduces competition and laws are required, therefore, to protect the interests of both the trader and the public. Whatever the case, laws do exist which attempt to promote fair competition. Usually these laws relate to the regulation of prices and focus on resale price maintenance (r.p.m.) agreements and price discrimination practices.

Resale price maintenance is the procedure by which the producer controls the price of goods. Essentially it takes two forms: vertical price agreements (between, for instance, manufacturer and wholesaler or wholesaler and retailer) or horizontal agreements (between a number of manufacturers or a number of wholesalers). Invariably it results in the elimination of price competition and tends to be outlawed in those countries with laws promoting free competition. In many countries, however, this has not always been the case, and most countries which now outlaw such practices once possessed laws which promoted price maintenance agreements. While this pattern of acceptance and rejection is repeated in many countries,[22] not every country has abolished resale price maintenance, or did so as early as America and Britain. In Germany, for instance, abolition occurred in 1974 only, while in Italy resale price maintenance agreements are permitted, and in France a supplier may recommend that his customer resells a product at a given price so long as there is no implication of a minimum price.

The exact impact of these various regulations relating to resale price maintenance is difficult to determine. As Kjolby has observed in his review of the situation in Denmark, 'a widespread use of resale price maintenance is said to preserve too many small retail shops operating at a low rate of efficiency',[23] and there is little doubt that major structural changes have occurred in many countries once retail price maintenance has been removed. However, the evidence from America does not appear to 'support the contention that the enactment of fair trade laws lessens the number of retail failures or bankruptcies or increases the number of retail stores'.[24] Whatever the precise effects of the resale price maintenance legislation on the structure of retailing, the subject is so shrouded in controversy that 'there may one day be brought about a statute which completely reverses the present situation'.[25]

Laws prohibiting price discrimination are probably encountered less frequently, though particularly interesting examples are to be found in the commercial legislation of America, Canada and Australia.[26] Price discrimination consists, basically, of charging customers different prices for products of 'like grade and quality' in an attempt to lessen competition. Essentially it takes two forms:

(a) A national or regional company may differentiate in the prices it charges in different areas. In many cases this will be necessary to cover variations in, for instance, distribution and operating costs. In others, however, the major objective may be the elimination of competition. The company may slash prices in one area to such an extent that competitors are forced out of business. Often this involves selling at cost or below, the retailer using profits generated in other stores to offset losses thus incurred. Once competition has been eliminated, prices are usually permitted to rise to the level of those charged in other areas, and in the process of eliminating competition the retailer has discriminated in the prices charged to customers in different areas.

(b) A large retailer may use his position to negotiate favourable (lower) prices with a supplier, causing the supplier to discriminate (out of fear of losing custom) between large and small retailers. Clearly there are considerable cost savings involved in handling large volumes and it is not unreasonable for the large retailer to be given a share of these savings. Frequently, therefore, suppliers provide a 'cost-justified' discount based upon the costs involved in handling orders of various sizes. In certain circumstances, however, very powerful retailers are able to negotiate discounts additional to those reflecting the cost savings to the supplier (i.e non-cost-justified discounts). Since the smaller, less powerful retailers are unable to negotiate such favourable terms, the end result is the eventual elimination of the smaller competitor.

Reactions to price discrimination are extremely varied. Some regard it as a most valuable exercise in free competition since it helps reduce prices (in the short term at least) and eliminate inefficiency, while for others the 'elimination of competitors is the elimination of competition'.[27] Accordingly, policies relating to price discrimination range from general acceptance (as in the United Kingdom) to the prohibition of loss-leader selling (as in Belgium and France) and the very elaborate legislation relating to price discrimination developed in America and copied to a certain extent in Canada and Australia.

While the precise impact of such legislation is difficult to determine, it is regarded by some as having 'economic justification in attacking the monopsonistic power of large buyers,[28] but by others as being 'anti-competitive and inconsistent with the objectives of a competitive economy'.[29] Indeed, it has been argued that such legislation discriminates against the large buyer, thereby 'weakening the position of just those retailers who have proved most likely to innovate and engage in price competition'.[30]

The Promotion or Restriction of Innovation

In their conclusion to *Public Policy Towards Retailing*, Boddewyn and Hollander make the point that 'the major retailing development conducive to the growth of public policy has certainly been the continuous appearance of new, aggressive forms of retailing and concomitant growth of inter-type competition'.[31] In certain situations, however, public policy has emerged as a result of the very lack of competition and innovation to which Boddewyn and Hollander refer. Communist countries have been particularly active in this respect in their search for greater efficiency, but within Western capitalist society perhaps France provides one of the most recent and interesting examples. Throughout the 1960s, the French government evolved a retail trade policy intended to facilitate the re-organisation and modernisation of retailing. The numerous procedures and measures which constituted this policy have been described elsewhere,[32] and although it is impossible here to review them in any detail, it should be noted that they included measures to regulate prices, promote competition, stimulate investment and improve management. As a result of these measures, retailing in France has been completely transformed and it can be argued that 'the spirit of initiative in fact developed only because the actions of the State tended to favour innovation in trade'.[33]

Not all government policies towards retailing are as positive as the French policies of the 1960s, however. As Hollander and Boddewyn have observed, government officials 'are often anxious to preserve existing institutions and shopping districts and consequently may use their planning powers and other means to discourage new and marginal entrants'.[34] Perhaps the most effective method of dampening innovation is the procedure known as development control. This is the procedure which, as its name implies, controls the form, location and size of proposed developments, be they commercial, industrial or domestic. It can be backed, as in France in recent years, by specific state legislation or can exist as a less formal, but equally effective planning doctrine or philosophy, as in Britain. The French legislation is contained in the Loi d'Orientation du Commerce et de l'Artisanat of 1973 (better known, perhaps, as the Loi Royer). The aim of the provisions has been to curb the excessive growth of large stores and shopping centres; but while the number of large store openings has declined since 1973, it is difficult to determine precisely the effect of the legislation. Rather strangely, perhaps, the Ministry of Trade has argued that the reduction in the number of large, new stores is due not to the new law, but to the recession in the French economy, the increase in construction costs, the increased costs in financing new development and the increased scarcity of sites suitable for development. However, if the law 'had really been as ineffective as the Minister of Trade claims . . . there would be no point in retaining it'.[35] Indeed, there can be little doubt about the general effectiveness of the law in 'slowing down the building of hypermarkets' in France, if nothing else, through the delays caused by the procedure itself.[36] Indeed, a similar situation occurs in Japan where the Large Scale Retail Store Law of 1974 (amended in 1979) has successfully reduced the rate of large store growth in Japan.[37]

The British approach is, perhaps, less formalised but equally effective. Although the British planning system requires that all new buildings (or substantial alteration or extension to an existing building) receive 'planning permission' before development, Britain possesses no formal policy legislation relating specifically to out-of-town shopping centres or large new stores, other than a largely advisory note (Development Policy Control No 13) issued by the Department of the Environment in 1972 and again (in revised form) in 1977. The latter document requires that the Secretary of State is notified of all applications for stores in excess of 9290m^2 (4645m^2 in the original document) outside existing town or district centres. This is to determine whether 'planning issues of more than local importance are involved' and whether the applications should be called in for a decision by the Department of Environment. Initially the DOE took the view that such operations were harmful to the retail structure of Britiain's towns and cities – a view held not solely by planners at the national level, but often by their local government colleagues. In 1972, in fact, it was probably fair to suggest that British 'planners almost to a man have set their hearts against these forms of development'.[38] Throughout the 1970s this became less extreme, and by the end of the decade Britain possessed approximately 220 superstores and hypermarkets but only one planned out-of-town regional shopping centre (at Brent Cross in North London) and this only after some thirteen years of planning objections and revisions.[39] When compared with developments elsewhere in Europe, however, it was probably true to suggest, that 'there is no other country in Western Europe which has sought to contain the process of decentralisation to the same degree as in Britain'.[40] So, it would appear that without the support of either formal legislation or the formulation of a specific national retail policy, British planning had attempted to restrict innovation with the aim of preserving the traditional pattern of retailing, both structural and spatial. In effect, therefore, British planning has been regulating competition, as in France, through its policy relating to development control and the granting of planning permission. Subsequently a less restrictive planning approach has been adopted in Britain. Although the 1980s witnessed a general decrease in governmental intervention in the British economy, possibly the turning point for retailing occurred in July 1985, when in response to a Parliamentary Question, the Secretary of State asserted that 'since commercial competition as such is not a land-use planning consideration, the possible effects of a proposed major retail development on existing retailers is not in this sense a relevant factor in deciding planning applications and appeals'. As a consequence of this statement, the controls on new developments were removed and by 1989, Britain had over 600 superstores and hypermarkets either trading or with planning permission.

Ensure Spatial Competition

Despite this British government ruling, considerable concern has been expressed, when considering the implications of modern trends in retailing, about the possible creation of monopoly situations through the elimination of local competition. In his book *The Politics of Distribution* Palamountain makes the point that 'despite the idyllically competitive picture assumed by those who decry supposed modern trends towards monopoly, in the "good old days" retail markets were often monopolistic'.[41] In this context he points to the local monopolies that existed (and still exist) in many small settlements and argues that the most effective monopoly was, and often is, that held by the small local trader.

   Clearly the spatial component is important in the consideration of monopoly power. Rarely does it feature as a primary consideration in competition policy, however, being more characteristic of policies relating to urban and regional planning. When considering the question of spatial competition, the planner has to take account of the various levels at which competition occurs. Accordingly, planning policies towards retailing relate generally to three different levels of provision: the regional or inter-urban, the settlement or inter-centre, and the centre or inter-shop. At the regional level concern is focused on the interrelationships amongst settlements, while at the level of the settlement, attention is paid to the interrelationships amongst different retail centres within one settlement. These are the two levels to which, traditionally, planners have paid most attention. The third, the level of the centre, concerns the interrelationships amongst the shops within any one centre. This is a comparatively neglected area from the planning viewpoint and relatively few planning authorities have evolved policies towards the retail mix of individual centres. Rather, planning has tended to concentrate on policies relating to the overall provision of retail floorspace, leaving the more detailed question of retail mix either to the free play of the property market or the policies evolved by the shopping centre developers. Obviously, the situation varies from country to country, and it is noticeable that in Holland the planning system requires that local authorities make detailed forecasts of retail floorspace requirements within centres. However, even in countries such as Holland where such detailed planning does exist, it is normally related to the particular needs of the local community, and overall policies towards retail planning at the local level (with regard to actual shop provision) act more as guidelines rather than firm statements of policy.

Often policies at the regional and settlement level are more formalised and clearly defined. For many, the basis has been central place theory. First developed in Southern Germany in the 1930s the theory puts forward the concept of a hierarchy of central places, each with their own hinterland in which the lower order (smaller) centres provide only highly dispersed services and are, themselves, within the hinterlands of higher order (or larger) centres fulfilling more specialised, less dispersed functions (Table 9.1).[42] The literature on central place theory and its application to planning is extensive,[43] and it is necessary here merely to point out that over the years the initial formulation of the theory has been considerably modified (most notably by Losch)[44] and extended (by Berry and Garrison)[45] to include consideration of the provision of services within urban areas. Equally, it should be recognised that the theory has been the subject of considerable criticism, and doubt has been expressed over whether the strucural regularities of the hierarchy proposed by Christaller actually occur in reality.[46] On balance, the weight of empirical evidence seems to assert the validity of the hierarchical concept and the consensus of opinion seems to be that a five-tier system exists at both the regional and the settle level (Table 9.2) though often not all levels of the hierarchy are represented.

No universal agreement appears to have been reached, however, about thresholds (i.e. the minimum levels of demand necessary to support the various types of business activity) and ranges (i.e. the distances consumers are prepared to travel to obtain the various goods and services offered). Even

Table 9.1
Christaller's Central Place System

Centre	Theoretical no. of centres	Theoretical no. of trade areas	No. of types of goods offered	Typical population of centres	Typical population of trade areas
Landstadt	1	1	2 000	500 000	3 500
Provinzstadt	2	3	1 000	100 000	1 000
Gaustadt	6	9	600	30 000	350
Bezirkstadt	18	27	330	10 000	100
Kreisstadt	54	81	180	4 000	35
Amstort	162	243	90	2 000	11
Marktort	486	729	40	1 000	3.5

SOURCE: W. Christaller, *Die zentralen Orte in Suddeutschland* (Verlag, 1933).

so, central place theory has been widely adopted by the planning profession in countries like Britain 'where it represents the main organisational principle not only for the retail provisions but also for educational, medical and other welfare services',[47] and in Holland, where it forms the basis for the settlement network servicing the population of the reclaimed polders[48] and where there has developed 'a rather inflexible and straightforward hierarchical system of shopping centres'.[49]

Since the late 1960s, central place theory has lost much of its popularity, and it functions more as 'a guide and reference system than an automatic solution within which planning decisions are to be taken'.[50] Certainly this has been the case in Britain where, for much of the subsequent period, emphasis has been placed on determining retail floorspace requirements through the application of retail allocation models.[51]

Probably the group most frequently applied are those known as the spatial interaction models. Basically these are refinements of Reilly's Law of Retail

Table 9.2
Typical Five-Tier Hierarchies

Level	Regional	Settlement
1st order	Metropolis	Central Business District
2nd order	City	Regional Shopping Centre
3rd order	Town	Community Shopping Centre
4th order	Village	Neighbourhood Shopping Centre
5th order	Hamlet	Isolated Corner Stores

Gravitation.[52] This states that 'two cities attract trade from an intermediate town in the vicinity of the breaking point approximately in direct proportion to the population of the two cities and in inverse proportion to the squares of the distances from these two cities to the intermediate town'. Such break-points can be found for several pairs of places within a region, and a set of trade area boundaries constructed. However, trade area delimitations of this type are meaningful only for settlements broadly similar in size. For this and several other reasons the original formula has been extensively revised, most notably by Huff and Lakshmanan and Hansen.[53]

The model derived by Lakshmanan and Hansen has become the most common reference model used in British planning research into shopping systems. Basically it is a model designed to estimate the impact of new planned shopping centres on existing retail systems. Developed to evaluate strategies for locating satellite shopping centres in Metropolitan Baltimore, it was first used in Britain in the early 1960s to assess the likely impact of the proposed out-of-town regional shopping centre at Haydock Park.[54] Since then 'there has been a tremendous advance in technical capability associated with this kind of model' as Wilson[55] has observed, but because of the relative difficulty involved in implementation, usage is far from universal.

9.4 Policies to Safeguard Consumer Interests

In many countries, as the previous section has demonstrated, the preservation of free competition is regarded as an important contribution to the protection of the consumer. However, although many of the measures introduced by governments to preserve competition can be regarded as protecting consumer interest, most governments now possess a set of policies specifically orientated towards the consumer. Many of these policies have been reviewed by the OECD Committee on Consumer Policy,[56] and detailed accounts are available for individual countries.[57] As a consequence, it is necessary here merely to emphasise the main policy approaches, particularly since the implications of much of the legislation are greater for production than they are for retailing.

As was pointed out earlier, much consumer policy has stemmed from the pressure exerted by consumer organisations and the general dissatisfaction of the consumer with the goods and services offered. This dissatisfaction, as Renoux has observed, is expressed in three ways:

1. Shopping system dissatisfaction involving the availability of products and retail outlets.
2. Buying system dissatisfaction concerning the process of selecting and receiving products from stores patronised.
3. Consumer system dissatisfaction resulting from problems in using and consuming goods and services.[58]

With each of these various aspects of consumer discontent, different interest groups are involved, different levels of government intervention are encountered and retailing is affected to a greater or lesser extent (Figure 9.1). Clearly, much of the competition policy referred to earlier is intended to reduce or eliminate shopping system dissatisfaction, and obviously this affects very considerably the structure of the retail trades.

Traditionally, government intervention has not been a characteristic feature of either the buying or the consuming system where the resolution of consumer dissatisfaction has been the responsibility of the companies concerned – their success in eliminating dissatisfaction being measured in terms of company profit levels. Increasingly, however, governments have become involved in the problems of the buying and consuming systems, and a large body of public policy has been evolved to eliminate consumer dissatisfaction at both levels. Essentially three areas of consumer policy can be identified:

(a) *Consumer protection policies*. These take two forms: those intended to protect the consumer in a physical sense and those intended to protect the consumer's economic interests. The former are very extensive and long-established, being part of the notion of public health, and are of two

---

FIGURE 9.1
The Consumer Policy Formulation Process. (Adapted from Renoux, 'Consumer Dissatisfaction and Public Policy' in F. D. Allvine (ed.), *Public Policy and Marketing Practices* (Chicago: American Marketing Association, 1973).

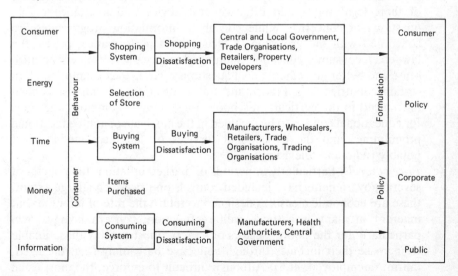

---

types: 'those designed to protect consumers against products that are unsafe and endanger health and those intended to secure greater and more enduring product safety.[59] They range from banning dangerous products to attempts to eliminate or reduce the quantity of dangerous substances in them and, where this is not possible, to the labelling of products warning consumers of the hazards involved in their use. Clearly the implications of these policies are greatest for producers. Retailing is more affected by the policies produced to protect the consumer's economic interests, the main objective of these regulations being 'to protect the consumer against fraud and deception'.[60] It is impossible in the space available to review the full range of legislative procedures which have been adopted, but generally governments have introduced legislation to prevent fraud, to control aggressive sales methods, to outlaw deceptive or misleading sales techniques and inaccurate or misleading advertising and to limit consumer credit. Coupled with this, most countries have tended to strengthen the consumer's contractual position by imposing clear, inescapable obligations on the trader.

(b) *Consumer information and education*. The effectiveness of consumer protection, however, depends upon action taken by the individual consumer, and most governments have recognised the need to inform and educate consumers. In many countries, governments have done much to stimulate consumer information and education. Usually consumer information programmes are organised by both public and private concerns and involve comparative tests (to inform the consumer of the specific characteristics and performance of goods and services), labelling (to help the consumer make rational choices and protect against inaccurate statements or descriptions), and advisory services (to inform consumers of their legal rights and offer general advice and assistance on all questions of concern). While consumer information programmes are concerned with the provision of facts (about performance, prices, the law, etc.), consumer education is intended to give the consumer 'a critical sense and better judgement on all questions relating to consumption'.[61] In certain countries (e.g. France and Italy) consumer education has been introduced to the curricula in schools, but the most common practice is for educational courses to be included in the curricula of adult educational programmes and the educational services of the mass media, most notably radio and television.

(c) *Price controls*. Particularly in periods of marked inflation, the policies of several governments have included controls on prices. To a large extent, these are economic measures designed to retard the rate of inflation; but inherent in many is a social welfare function, concern being shown particularly for the poorer sectors of society, most notably those unable to increase their incomes through collective bargaining (e.g. the aged, infirm, unemployed, etc.). Although difficult to enforce, the most usual practice is for there to be a general freeze on prices, often coupled with a similar, possibly voluntary, freeze on wages. Additional procedures, adopted in countries like Portugal, include the setting of maximum prices for staple goods or, as in Austria, the introduction of legislation to control excess profits. Of particular interest are government food subsidies and/or tax compensation payments. Both systems are employed in Norway, for instance, where compensation for value added tax is paid by the government on about twenty food items.[62]

By definition, the measures to aid the consumer are not retail policies. However, they do have, in many cases, implications for retailing and the structure of the retail system is affected in a number of ways. First, certain types of retailing, such as pyramid selling in France, are regarded as being harmful to the consumer and are banned by law, thereby modifying the structure of the retail system by preventing the development of one (or more) retail form. Second, the general extension of bureaucracy through the development of policies to protect the consumer can, and frequently does, discourage entry or stimulate closure. Often this affects most considerably the marginal sector of the retail system but, as in Britain,[63] the effects of closures can have a considerable impact on the structure of the retail system. Third, the consumer is becoming better informed and more discriminating, and the implications of these developments are quite considerable, particularly for retail management.

For some time, for instance, there have been signs that the modern consumer is becoming dissatisfied with the 'pile it high, sell it cheap' philosophy, traditionally associated with the supermarket trading. It could be, therefore, that the supermarket is reaching the end of its life-cycle in its present form – a development which could have a very considerable effect on the retail systems of most advanced economies.

9.5 Regulation of Trading Conditions

In most countries the growth in consumer awareness has not been matched by improvements in the quality and technical ability of sales staff. Indeed, in many countries the opposite is the case as the situation in Canada demonstrates. Here it was discovered that the 'manpower employed in the distribution service was less experienced in 1967 than in 1947'.[64] Since then the Canadian government has made positive efforts to improve the level of skilled manpower in retailing. This is a development which is repeated elsewhere in the Western world and it has become one of the more important areas of government involvement in terms of business regulation.

Vocational Training

One procedure for improving the level of expertise in retailing is to prevent unqualified persons from establishing new businesses. Usually this involves the issuing of a licence to trade only to those persons who have completed successfully a course in retail management. This is the situation in Holland, for instance, where special retail trade schools have been established 'to prepare young people for entrepreneurship in retailing'.[65] Being orientated to business managers and owners, the benefits of the procedure are somewhat limited, and rather than raising the general level of skill in the retail trades, perhaps such an approach is more appropriate for restricting the number of new entrants to the retail system. Certainly it is not a policy which is widely pursued in Western society, except in certain particular circumstances (e.g. the operation of retail pharmacies). Policies relating to the training of employees are more widespread and range from essentially voluntary schemes (as in Britain) where firms are encouraged to train their employees to compulsory training programmes and apprenticeships (as in Germany).

Business Hours

A second area where government policies are important in the regulation of trading conditions is the area of opening times. In most countries, business hours are regulated by law and, in so doing, the legislators are attempting to strike a balance between the interests of the shopkeepers, the employees and the consumers. Many countries prohibit Sunday trading (on religious grounds) and restrict the length of the working day but regulations vary considerably. In France, for instance, the regulations are extremely liberal and are based on labour regulations. All businesses employing staff must allow a weekly period of rest (usually on a Sunday) and although the maximum weekly working period is 46 hours in the food trades and 42 hours in non-foods, it is possible for large establishments to keep open at night by employing overlapping or succeeding shifts. Since the regulations apply only to paid employees, businesses not employing staff are free to choose their own hours. More stringent regulations, possibly the most restrictive in the world, occur in Germany where the Store Closing Law of 1956 was introduced. Ostensibly this was to protect employees, but it was strongly supported by the small traders who wanted to avoid the situation whereby large enterprises could stagger employee working hours and thereby stay open for longer periods. Essentially, the law limits the hours of business to between 09.00 hours and 14.00 hours on Saturday, and 07.00 hours and 18.30 hours Monday to Friday. Certain exceptions are provided for in the law, as, for instance, the extension of opening hours to 18.00 hours on the first Saturday in the month and the last four Saturdays before Christmas. Originally these regulations were opposed by the large firms since they were seen as favouring the small trader. Over the years, however, the town centre department stores and supermarkets have become major supporters of the regulations as they have realised that since store opening hours and office working hours are very similar, many working consumers have little time to shop around and prefer large stores that carry a wide selection under one roof to the small conventional store, or prefer to shop downtown because the stores near their homes are ready to close by the time they return from work.

The Store Closing Law has had, therefore, a very profound and possibly unintended effect upon the structure of retailing in Germany by maintaining the importance of both the town centre and the department store in the retail system. As Soldner[66] has observed, still further implications have arisen as a result of the law. Although Germany possesses numerous modern suburban shopping facilities, one of the efforts of the law has been to regulate the rate at which superstores and hypermarkets have been developed and to retard the rate at which decentralisation has occurred. As a consequence, the town centre department stores have tended not to be represented in the newly-developed regional shopping centres, there has been a remarkable growth of wholesale cash and carry warehouses which, as wholesale operations, are not subject to the Store Closing Law, and mail-order trading has become an established feature of the retail system.

In Japan, the legislation relating to business hours reflects quite clearly the desire to protect the small trader since it relates solely to large department stores, not permitting them to open before 10.00 hours or after 18.00 hours. However, the motive underlying this policy is consumer protection – the law must be seen in the context of Japan's overall policy 'to protect the consumer's interest by assuring the owners of small-to-medium-size enterprises the opportunity to compete'.[67]

In Britain, there has been considerable debate over the issue of trading hours which are regulated by the now somewhat outdated and idiosyncratic Shops Act 1950. Over the past thirty years there have been numerous attempts to change the hours of retail trading. All have encountered strong opposition (particularly from trade unions and religious groups) and all have failed to gain the necessary majority in parliament. The most recent, in April 1986, reflected defeat for a government with a parliamentary majority of 140-plus. Even so, the legislation does require modification to ensure that the hours of retail trading, in the words of the prime minister, do 'correspond to modern patterns of living'. As the National Consumer Council has demonstrated, there is strong public support for a revision of the law on Sunday trading,[68] but there is little doubt that the complete liberalisation of the hours of retail trading would have a very profound effect on the structure of the retail system[69] and the conditions of employment in retailing.[70]

9.6 Conclusions

In this review of public policies and retailing, an attempt has been made to demonstrate that in most countries the workings of the system are not left to the free play of the market but are regulated and manipulated by government action. Clearly it has not been possible to consider every aspect in detail or to cover every piece of legislation. For instance, most countries possess legislation relating to hygiene in shops which places restrictions on the ways shops operate, and there is a whole series of indirect policies which have very important and significant influences on the structure of the retail system. This latter group of policies has been mentioned very briefly already, but given the space available, it has not been possible to consider them in any detail here. Rather, attention has been focused on the major policies which relate specifically to the working of the retail system.

While most countries possess policies which relate to retailing few possess an overall policy towards retailing. In most Western capitalist countries, however, the overall objective appears to be the protection of consumer interest through, in the most part, the promotion of competition. Legislation has been evolved, therefore, to restrict restraints on trade, to make competition fair and to enable consumers to shop more discriminatingly. Not infrequently, however, these individual objectives are in conflict, with the result that one set of legislation appears to be working against another. This situation is made worse by the fact that the effects of the legislation often develop in a way unforeseen by the policy formulators and/or the real purpose of the legislation is not made clear at the outset. Still further problems arise from the fact that policy formulation inevitably lags behind changes in objectives, and inevitably a discrepancy exists between the policy needs and the capabilities of the existing body of legislation. As a result of all these factors and influences 'government policies toward retailing are usually fragmentary, unconnected and even inconsistent'.[71] To counteract this situation, perhaps there is a need for governments to have 'a clearer definition of what the goals and objectives of retail and commercial planning should be, with the goals conceived as a national set of aspirations and the objectives the instruments by which policies are formulated at the local level.[72]

References

1. M. Dobb, *Welfare Economics and the Economics of Socialism* (Cambridge: CUP, 1970) p. 10.
2. J. J. Boddewyn and S. C. Hollander, *Public Policy Toward Retailing: An International Symposium* (London: Lexington Books, 1972) p. 1.
3. Ibid.
4. L. P. Feldman, 'A Framework for Research on Public Policy Issues in Marketing', in F. D. Allvine (ed.), *Public Policy and Marketing Practices* (Chicago: American Marketing Association, 1973).
5. S. C. Hollander, 'Retailing and Public Policy: Retrospect and Prospect', in Allvine (ed.), *Public Policy and Marketing Practices*, p. 342.
6. Ibid., p. 341.
7. W. B. Reddaway, *Effects of the Selective Employment Tax: First Report on the Distributive Trades* (London: HMSO, 1970).
8. B. J. L. Berry *et al.*, *The Impact of Urban Renewal on Small Business: The Hyde-Park Kenwood Case* (University of Chicago Centre for Urban Studies, 1968); and R. L. Davies and D. J. Bennison, *The Eldon Square Regional Shopping Centre: The First Eighteen Months* (Retail Planning Associates, 1978).
9. J. A. Dawson, *The Marketing Environment* (London: Croom Helm, 1979).
10. Hollander, 'Retailing and Public Policy', p. 58.

11. Boddewyn and Hollander, *Public Policy Toward Retailing*; Hollander, 'Retailing and Public Policy'; and OECD, *The Distribution Sector: Evolution and Government Policies* (Paris: OECD, 1973).
12. Dawson, *The Marketing Environment*.
13. Hollander, 'Retailing and Public Policy', pp. 59 and 60.
14. L. F. Bartlet, 'Shopping Centers and Land Controls', *Notre Dame Lawyer*, Vol. 35, 1960, pp. 184–209; and G. H. Steadman, 'Shopping Centers and Local Government – Collision or Co-operation', *Journal of Retailing*, Summer 1955, pp. 80–1.
15. A. R. Everton, *Trade Winds: An Introduction to the U.K.'s Law of Competition* (Alan Osborne and Associates, 1978); Monopolies and Mergers Commission, *Discounts to Retailers* (London: HMSO, 1981, HC 311); and Office of Fair Trading, *Competition and Retailing* (London: OFT, 1985).
16. Everton, *Trade Winds*, p. 7.
17. J. C. Palamountain, *The Politics of Distribution* (New York: Greenwood Press, 1968).
18. OECD, *Market Power and the Law* (Paris: OECD, 1970).
19. Everton, *Trade Winds*, p. 9.
20. Ibid., p. 38.
21. Ibid., p. 55.
22. B. S. Yamey, *Resale Price Maintenance* (London: Weidenfeld & Nicolson, 1966).
23. H. Kjolby, 'Denmark', in B. S. Yamey (ed.), *Resale Price Maintenance*, p. 176.
24. S. M. Lee, 'The Impact of Fair Trade Laws on Retailing', *Journal of Retailing*, Spring 1965, Vol. 41, pp. 1–6.
25. Everton, *Trade Winds*, p. 58.
26. A. R. Everton, *Price Discrimination: A Comparative Study in Legal Control* (Bradford: M.C.B. Monographs, 1976).
27. Ibid., p. 2.
28. L. E. Weiss, *Economics and American Industry* (New York: John Wiley, 1961) p. 437.
29. R. F. Gwinner *et al.*, *Marketing: An Environmental Perspective* (London: West, 1977) p. 359.
30. Weiss, *Economics and American Industry*, p. 437.
31. Boddewyn and Hollander, *Public Policy Toward Retailing*, p. 431.
32. P. Cortesse, 'France', in Boddewyn and Hollander, ibid.
33. J. Freis, 'Government Intervention in France: How Has it Affected Development?', *Retail and Distribution Management*, 1978, Vol. 6, No. 2, pp. 41–5.
34. S. C. Hollander and J. J. Boddewyn, 'Retailing and Public Policy – An International Overview', *Journal of Retailing*, 1974, Vol. 50, No. 1, p. 56.
35. J. A. Dawson, 'Control Over Large Units in France: The Loi Royer and Its Effects', *Retail and Distribution Management*, 1977, Vol. 4, No. 6, p. 15.
36. Freis, 'Government Intervention in France', p. 45.
37. D. A. Kirby, 'Government Policies Towards the Small Retail Business in Japan', *International Small Business Journal*, 1984, Vol. 2, No. 4, pp. 44–58.
38. Pragma, 'Planners Versus Shopping Centres', *Journal of the Royal Town Planning Institute*, 1972, vol. 58, p. 244.
39. UPRI, 1978.
40. R. L. Davies, *Marketing Geography* (London: Methuen, 1977) p. 177.
41. Palamountain, *The Politics of Distribution*, p. 40.
42. W. Christaller, *Die zentralen Orte in Suddeutschland* (Verlag, 1933), translated by C. Baskin as *Central Places in Southern Germany* (New York: Prentice-Hall, 1966).
43. B. J. L. Berry and A. Pred, *Central Place Studies: A Bibliography of Theory and Applications* (Regional Science Research Institute, Philadelphia, 1965).

44. A. Losch, *Die Raumliche Ordjung Der Wirtschaft* (Berlin: Verlag, 1944), translated by W. H. Woglom and W. F. Solper as *The Economics of Location* (Yale: Yale University Press, 1954).

45. B. J. L. Berry and W. L. Garrison, 'Report Developments of Central Place Theory', *Papers and Proceedings of the Regional Science Association*, 1958, Vol. 4, pp. 107–120.

46. R. Vining, 'A Description of Certain Spatial Aspects of an Economic System', *Economic Development and Cultural Change*, 1955, Vol. 3, pp. 147–95.

47. Davies, *Marketing Geography*, p. 29.

48. J. P. Thysse, 'Second Thoughts About a Rural Pattern for the Future in the Netherlands', *Paper of the Regional Science Association*, 1968, Vol. 20, pp. 69–75.

49. J. G. Borchert, 'Retail Planning and Retail Planning Research of the Netherlands', in R. L. Davies (ed.), *Retail Planning in the European Community* (London: Saxon House, 1979) p. 84.

50. K. Robinson, *Central Place Theory II: Its Role in Planning with Particular Reference to Retailing* (London: Centre for Environmental Studies, 1968) Working Paper No. 9.

51. R. L. Davies and D. S. Rogers, *Store Location and Store Assessment Research* (London: John Wiley, 1984); and A. Ghosh and S. L. McLafferty, *Location Strategies for Retail and Service Firms* (London: Lexington, 1987).

52. W. J. Reilly, *The Law of Retail Gravitation* (Knickerbocker Press, 1931).

53. D. L. Huff, 'A Probability Analysis of Shopping Centre Trade Areas', *Land Economics*, February 1963, Vol. 53, pp. 81–9; and T. R. Lakshmanan and W. G. Hansen, 'A Retail Market Potential Model', *Journal of the American Institute of Planners*, May 1965, Vol. 31, pp. 134–43.

54. *Regional Shopping Centres in North West England (Part II)* (Manchester University Department of Town Planning, 1966).

55. A. G. Wilson, 'Store and Shopping-Centre Location and Size; a review of British research and practice' in N. Wrigley, *Store Choice, Store Location and Market Analysis*. (London: Routledge, 1988).

56. OECD, *Consumer Policy in O.E.C.D. Member Countries* (Paris: OECD, 1972).

57. G. Borrie and A. L. Diamond, *The Consumer, Society and the Law* (Harmondsworth: Penguin, 1968).

58. Y. Renoux, 'Consumer Dissatisfaction and Public Policy', in Allvine (ed.), *Public Policy and Marketing Practices*.

59. OECD, *Consumer Policy in O.E.C.D. Member Countries* (1972), p. 6.

60. Ibid., p. 7.

61. Ibid., p. 13.

62. C. Blythe, 'Norwegian Nutrition and Food Policy: Consumer Information and Price Policy Aspects', *Food Policy*, 1978, Vol. 3, No. 3, pp. 163–79.

63. J. A. Dawson and D. A. Kirby, *Small Scale Retailing in the U.K.* (London: Saxon House, 1979).

64. OECD., *The Distribution Sector: Evolution and Government Policies* (Paris: OECD, 1973) p. 54.

65. J. F. Haccou and P. J. M. Lubers, 'The Netherlands', in Boddewyn and Hollander, *Public Policy Toward Retailing* p. 262.

66. H. Soldner, 'West Germany', in Boddewyn and Hollander, *Public Policy Toward Retailing*.

67. M. Yoshino, 'Japan: Rationalising the Retail Structure', in Boddewyn and Hollander, *Public Policy Toward Retailing*, p. 215.

68. National Consumer Council, 1983.

69. D. A. Kirby, 'Shops Act 1950: Restrictions Out-trading', *Area*, 1984, Vol. 16, No. 3, pp. 233–43.

70. J. A. Kay *et al.*, *The Regulation of Retail Trading Hours* (London: Institute of Fiscal Studies, 1984).
71. Hollander and Boddewyn, 'Retailing and Public Policy', p. 55.
72. R. L. Davies, *Retail and Commercial Planning* (London: Croom Helm, 1984).

Legal Issues in Retailing 10

10.1 Introduction

In all business organisations, the law exerts a considerable influence on management. It is essential, therefore, that retail managers have a clear understanding of their rights and duties under the civil and criminal law – and appreciate the penalties that may be incurred by them or their employer if they fail to remain within the law in exercising their managerial functions. Some reference has already been made in a number of earlier chapters to the role of the law in retailing. In this chapter legal issues are explored in more detail. The main areas to be considered are the legal relationships between retailers and their suppliers, customers and employees. Planning and competition issues have already been dealt with in the previous chapter.

10.2 Legal Background

Before dealing with specific legal issues it may be helpful to make some preliminary observations on the sources of law and the main legal categories. There are two major sources of law in the United Kingdom legislation and case law. In Scotland the 'Institutional' writings of certain authors of legal treatises are also regarded as sources of law. Legislation is now by far the most important source of law. It consists not only of Acts of Parliament such as the Sale of Goods Act 1979 and the Wages Act 1986 but of what is called delegated or subordinate legislation. It is not possible for parliament to deal directly with the detail involved in drawing up legal rules in many cases, so authority is given to someone else, often a government minister, to draft further rules. A good example is to be found in the law of consumer credit. The Consumer Credit Act 1974 is a lengthy statute regulating the credit industry. Long as it is, it cannot deal with the very detailed regulation thought necessary. The Act therefore gives authority to others, mainly the Secretary of State for Trade and Industry, to make detailed rules fleshing out the principles set out in the 1974 Act itself.

Case law or judge made law is also important as a source of law. This derives from the decisions of the judges in cases before them. The principle behind a decision in one case will govern the decision of a lower court in a similar case. While not as important quantitatively nowadays as legislation, it is a major source of law and we shall see that many important areas of law relevant to retailers, such as contract law, have their origins in judge made law.

In addition to these domestic sources of law, our membership of the European Community has added another dimension. Community law prevails over domestic law and must be enforced by UK courts which are also bound by the rulings of the European Court. European Community law is to be found in the treaties setting up the Community and in the decisions of the European Court; but in addition the Community has its own methods of legislating. For present purposes the directives and regulations of the Community are of importance. Directives are statements of objectives to be achieved by member states in order to harmonise their laws. For example, the law on manufacturers' liability for defective products was the subject of a directive. In the UK this required parliament to pass the Consumer Protection Act 1987 in order to comply. Regulations on the other hand are legal rules promulgated by the Community which become legally effective without any further action by member states.

There are a number of ways in which the law can be classified. For present purposes it will be enough to note that there is a major division between criminal law and civil law. Both are important in the regulation of business activity, but it is important to distinguish between them. The criminal law is concerned with forbidding certain kinds of conduct and punishing those who engage in the prohibited acts by means of fines and imprisonment. In a retail context the Trade Descriptions Act 1968 provides a good example. It makes it a criminal offence to make misleading statements about goods and services. Civil law deals with the rights and obligations which arise between individuals (including companies), or between individuals and the state. Important areas of civil law are the law of contract, property law, and the law of tort which seeks to compensate victims of certain forms of harmful conduct. Enforcement of the civil law is the responsibility of the individual, whereas the criminal law is enforced by the state. It is important to note that the same act may give rise to both civil and criminal sanctions. For example, misleading statements about goods by a retailer might be a breach of the Trade Descriptions Act 1968 rendering him liable to a criminal prosecution. In addition, a customer who was deceived by the statement might be able to claim compensation in a civil action for breach of contract.

10.3 Supply of Goods

Retailers are in business to supply their customers with goods and they must acquire their stocks from manufacturers or wholesalers. These everyday processes have legal implications. Central to the relationship of retailer and customer and retailer and supplier is a contract of sale. As the contractual relationship is basically the same in both cases it is possible to deal with the two situations at the same time, for the most part, leaving some matters relating to consumer protection to be dealt with separately.

Sale is defined by the Sale of Goods Act 1979 as 'A contract by which the seller transfers or agrees to transfer the property in goods to the buyer for a money consideration called the price'. Sale is to be contrasted with various forms of supply on credit which are referred to below. A less usual legal form is barter. In its classic form of the exchange of one product for another this is rarely found in modern retailing; but what is known colloquially as 'trading-in' is very common. It is not altogether clear how trading-in should be classified. Depending on the circumstances, it may be regarded as a sale or as a separate contract. In England and Wales the question of classifying trading-in is not now of great moment following the enactment of the Supply of Goods and Services Act 1982 which for most purposes has resulted in barter having the same legal consequences as sale. That Act does not apply in Scotland where there is less certainty about the correct legal classification of trading-in.

Formation

If there is no credit element in the contract for supply of goods then there are no special formalities. A contract for the sale of goods no matter what its value does not need to be in writing. However, where goods are sold on credit or are hired it is necessary to observe certain formalities, and these are described below.

An individual does not have full legal capacity until the age of eighteen. In practice this does not cause problems for retailers because the contracts of those under eighteen are still enforceable if they are for what the law calls 'necessaries'. Most purchases by teenagers will fall into this category which would include such things as food, clothes and personal belongings.

In a retail sale a contract is concluded when the retailer accepts the purchaser's offer to buy. The significance of this is that the mere display of goods is not an offer and thus the retailer is not obliged to sell what he displays or advertises. This will avoid some of the difficulties if demand for goods advertised exceeds supply or an article has been incorrectly priced.[1]

The Contract of Sale

Not only is it not necessary for contracts of sale to be in writing, it is not even necessary for the parties to consider the precise terms on which they wish to do business. The retailer and the customer or the supplier will have to agree on the item that is to be the subject of the sale but they may not expressly agree on anything else. Not even the price may have been agreed and in this case the Sale of Goods Act says that the buyer 'must pay a reasonable price'.[2] More commonly, they may not give any thought to their rights should the product be in some way defective, or what is to happen should the goods be damaged before being delivered. The Sale of Goods Act has rules which apply in the absence of the express agreement of the parties and, especially in relation to quality, will imply terms into the contract. Such terms have been implied by statute since the enactment of the Sale of Goods Act 1893 and are now to be found in the Sale of Goods Act 1979. They have sometimes been described as a consumers' charter which, since legislation starting in the 1970s was passed, is now a reasonable description. Prior to the enactment of the Supply of Goods (Implied Terms) Act 1973 it was possible for the retailer to exclude these rights. In the case of consumer sales this is no longer possible. In commercial transactions it is possible to exclude these implied terms, though this will only be effective if it can be shown that such exclusion was fair and reasonable.[3]

10.4 Transfer of Property in the Goods

The essence of a contract of sale is the transfer of ownership, or what lawyers call the property in the goods, from seller to buyer. Exactly when this occurs it is important to know because it may determine who bears the loss should the goods be accidentally damaged or destroyed; and will be important if one of the parties has become insolvent before payment has been made. It is therefore necessary to summarise the rules in the Sale of Goods Act relating to the transfer of ownership.

The Sale of Goods Act makes a distinction between 'specific goods' and 'unascertained goods'. Specific goods are those identified and agreed on at the time a contract of sale is made; unascertained goods are those which are not identified and agreed on when the contract is made. For example, an order from a retailer to a potato wholesaler for 100 tons of potatoes would be for unascertained goods because it would not be possible to say precisely which potatoes from the wholesaler's stock were intended. The potatoes could become specific goods if they were set aside and earmarked for a particular customer.

The Sale of Goods Act states that the property in specific goods passes when the parties intend it to pass, and to ascertain the intentions of the parties 'regard shall be had to the terms of the contract, the conduct of the parties and the circumstances of the case'.[4] Even in commercial contracts, let alone consumer contracts, the parties do not always consider this issue so the Act provides rules for ascertaining their intention.[5] Thus if the contract is unconditional and the goods are in a deliverable state the property passes when the contract is made.[6] Note that this may be before the buyer takes delivery. However, if the seller has to do something to the goods to put them into a deliverable state, or they have to be quantified in order to work out the price, the property does not pass until that has been done and the buyer informed.[7] If goods are sold on a sale or return basis property passes when the buyer indicates his acceptance or the time for return of the goods expires.[8]

In the case of unascertained goods property cannot pass until the goods have been ascertained.[9] If the parties have not applied their minds to this issue the Act says that they become so when 'appropriated to the contract'.[10] This will happen when goods are earmarked for a particular buyer.

If we now recall that the risk normally passes with the ownership, it will be seen how important it is to take account of these rather technical rules. It is quite possible for the goods to be at the buyer's risk before they come into his possession. Such a risk can easily be covered by insurance provided the buyer is aware of his liability.

Another problem connected with the transfer of ownership concerns obtaining payment. It is not uncommon for goods to be supplied on extended credit terms. If the buyer becomes insolvent before payment has been made but after he has become the owner of goods the seller is an unsecured creditor for the price. In an attempt to protect themselves sellers have often resorted to retention of title clauses which state that ownership is not to pass until payment is made. This works well enough where the goods are still in the possession of the buyer, but becomes more complicated where he has re-sold them or mixed them with other goods in a manufacturing process.[11]

The Implied Terms

As stated above, the Sale of Goods Act 1979 implies certain terms into contracts of sale, and in the case of consumer sales it is not now possible to exclude these terms. These terms relating to title, description and quality are discussed below.

Title

There is an implied term on the part of the seller that he has a right to sell the goods, and in the case of an agreement to sell, that he will have that right when he has to pass the property in the goods to the buyer,[12] a good example is provided by the case of *Rowland* v. *Dival* (1982).[13] Mr Rowland bought a car from Mr Divall for £334 and used it for four months. He then discovered that Divall had bought it from someone who had stolen it. Divall, therefore, although unaware that the car had been stolen could not become the legal owner and could not pass ownership to anyone else. The car had to be returned to the true owner. Mr Rowland sued Mr Divall and recovered the purchase price as Mr Divall was in breach of s.12 of the Sale of Goods Act.

Having considered the implied term about title it is appropriate to look at some other aspects of transferring title. As a general principle the law takes the view that one cannot pass on a better title than one has oneself, a principle summed up in the latin maxim *nemo dat quod non habet*. This can be inconvenient and, indeed, can work injustice, with the result that the principle has not been rigidly followed for reasons which were well explained in a judgement of Lord Denning MR:

> In the development of our law two principles have striven for mastery. The first is for the protection of property; no one can give a better title than he himself possesses. The second is for the protection of commercial transactions; the person who takes in good faith and for value without notice should get a good title.[14]

There have thus grown up a number of exceptions to the *nemo dat* rule, though these have been described as 'arbitrary and capricious'.[15] It should be emphasised that these exceptions will be of no relevance to the customer in those cases where he is dealing with a solvent retailer. The customer will simply rely on his right to be provided with goods which the retailer is entitled to sell and will obtain compensation if this is not the case. However, should this not be possible the customer may be forced to seek refuge in one of the exceptions.

The exceptions are now set out in the Sale of Goods Act 1979. Where, for example, what is called 'a mercantile agent',[16] of which a retailer would be an example, has possession of goods with the consent of the owner a sale by him would confer a good title on the buyer. Sales in 'market overt' confer good title on the purchaser.[17] Market overt means shops in the City of London and markets established by charter or custom in England though not in any other part of the United Kingdom. The sale must have taken place during daylight.

A retailer may have obtained his supplies from someone who has what lawyers call a voidable title. This most commonly arises where the true owner has been induced to part with goods by a trick. However, section 23 of the Sale of Goods Act states that the purchaser obtains a good title if he buys before the true owner has done something to assert his right of ownership.[18]

It is not unusual for the seller to remain in possession after he has received payment for a consumer durable because he cannot deliver for a few days or it is not convenient for the customer to accept immediate delivery. Should the retailer deliberately or accidentally purport to resell the goods to someone else that other person will obtain a good title. Similarly, it may happen that the buyer may obtain possession of the goods before legal title is transferred to him. If he should sell, section 25 provides that the purchaser from him obtains a good title even though the original buyer never actually obtains good title from the original seller.

Description

Where there is a sale by description there is an implied term that the goods will correspond with the description.[19] A sale is by description not only where the buyer does not see the goods before he buys them, as where they are selected from a mail-order catalogue, but also in many other circumstances. Even where the buyer has seen the goods and, perhaps, selected them himself, it may still be a sale by description, provided he has relied to some extent on a description. The case of *Beale* v. *Taylor* (1967)[20] provides an example. Mr Taylor advertised his car for sale in the classified columns of a newspaper as a 1961 Triumph Herald. Mr Beale came to look at it before buying it. He later discovered that the car was an amalgam of the rear half of a 1961 Herald and the front half of an older model. The English Court of Appeal decided that although he had inspected the car he was entitled to damages because he had relied to some extent on the description in the advertisement.

The courts have tended to take a tough line with any departure from the seller's specification of his goods. For example, a company agreed to supply 3000 tins of Australian canned fruit packed in cases containing thirty tins each. When the goods were delivered, it was discovered that about half the consignment was packed in cases containing twenty-four tins. The buyers decided to reject the whole consignment because of this departure from the contract and the courts upheld their right to do so.[21]

Quality and Suitability

Section 14 of the Sale of Goods Act 1979 deals with the quality of goods by implying terms about merchantability and fitness for purpose.[22] Two preliminary points need to be made about these implied terms. It is clearly established that liability for quality under s.14 does not depend on fault. As it was put in one case:

> If there was a defect in fact, even though that defect was one which no reasonable skill or care could discover, the person supplying the article should nevertheless be responsible, the policy of the law being that in a case in which neither were to blame, he, and not the person to whom they were supplied, should be liable for the defect.[23]

A good example is *Frost* v. *Aylesbury Dairy Co* (1905).[24] The dairy had supplied Mr Frost and his family with milk which turned out to have been infected with typhoid germs. As a result his wife died. It was proved that the dairy's production methods were extremely careful and that the typhoid germs could only be detected by prolonged investigation. It was decided that there was an implied term that the milk would be reasonably fit for consumption and it was irrelevant that the defect could not be discovered at the time of the sale.

It is the seller who is liable under the Sale of Goods Act not the manufacturer. In the consumer context this almost always means that it is the retailer who is the person to whom the consumer must look for redress if the goods do not prove to be satisfactory.

The goods to which the terms about quality apply are not just the article specified in the contract but include the 'goods supplied under a contract of sale'. So, if a container in which goods were supplied were defective the quality term might be breached. There have been cases where the goods themselves have been of the appropriate quality but some foreign substance, such as a detonator in a bag of coal, has been present.[25] In these circumstances the goods have been regarded as not meeting the statutory standard. More recently it has been decided by the courts that the implied terms might not be complied with if the goods were supplied with inadequate instructions.[26]

(a) Merchantable quality

Before discussing what merchantable quality means it should be noted that it does not apply where defects have been specifically drawn to the buyer's attention, or where the buyer has examined the goods and the defect was of a kind which that examination ought to have revealed.

The term merchantable quality has exercised the courts on numerous occasions, and the one thing that can confidently be said about it today is that it is widely regarded as being unsatisfactory especially in relation to consumer transactions. As the recent Law Commission report, *Sale and Supply of Goods* (Cmnd 137) observes:

> If the word 'merchantable' has any real meaning today, it must strictly be a meaning which relates to 'merchants' and trade; the word must be inappropriate in the context of a consumer transaction. The expression 'merchantable quality' is, and always has been a commercial man's notion: this explains why the original Act [the Sale of Goods Act 1893] did not define it – commercial juries needed no direction on how to make the appropriate findings.

To try to alleviate the problem of what the term means a definition was introduced by the Supply of Goods (Implied Terms) Act 1973 and is now set out in s.14(6) of the Sale of Goods Act 1979. It reads as follows:

> Goods of any kind are of merchantable quality within the meaning of subsection (2) above if they are as fit for the purpose or purposes for which goods of that kind are commonly bought as it is reasonable to expect having

regard to any description applied to them, the price (if relevant) and all the other relevant circumstances.

It now seems clear, following the decision of the Court of Appeal in *Aswan Engineering Establishment Co* v. *Lupdine Ltd*,[27] that where goods have more than one normal purpose they pass the merchantability test if they are fit for one of those purposes.

Before exploring some of the grey areas of the definition it will be useful to consider situations where goods can confidently be said not to pass the statutory test. Much emphasis is placed in the statutory definition on the fitness of the goods for their purpose or purposes. So a car which will not go, a hi-fi system which does not reproduce sound, a kettle which does not boil water and a refrigerator which does not keep its contents cold are not of merchantable quality.

While there is no express reference to safety in the definition there is little doubt that an article which is unsafe is not of merchantable quality.[28]

One of the grey areas where the differing expectations of commercial and consumer buyers could be important is in relation to goods which work but have cosmetic or other minor defects. In consumer situations recent case law tends to suggest that there is a better appreciation amongst the judiciary of the problems of consumers. In a recent case involving a new Range Rover which had a number of minor defects it was decided that the vehicle was not merchantable. In deciding on merchantability it was said that:

> one would include in respect of any passenger vehicle not merely the buyer's purpose of driving the car from one place to another but of doing so with the appropriate degree of comfort, ease of handling and reliability and, one might add, of pride in the vehicle's outward and interior appearance. What is the appropriate degree and what relative weight is to be attached to one characteristic of the car rather than another will depend upon the market at which the car is aimed.[29]

The court went on to point out that the fact that the defects could be repaired was not relevant to deciding whether the vehicle was merchantable at the time of delivery; nor was the fact that the purchaser was entitled to have repairs carried out free of charge under the manufacturer's warranty.

While *Rogers* v. *Parish (Scarborough) Ltd* is a welcome decision for consumers there is still a good deal of doubt about whether minor defects in complex products like cars render them unmerchantable especially where these defects can easily be repaired. In considering this issue it is relevant to remember that the definition states that goods are to be as fit for their purpose 'as it is reasonable to expect having regard to any description applied to them, the price (if relevant) and all the other relevant circumstances'. In a Scottish case it seems to have been suggested that a relevant circumstance was the well-known fact that new cars have some minor defects on delivery.[30]

There is no express reference to durability in the statutory definition of merchantability and there is some confusion as to whether goods need prove to be durable. It has been stated in a number of cases that the implied terms as to quality fall to be satisfied at the time of delivery and not at some later date. However, the fact that a product broke down shortly after purchase may be evidence that at the time of purchase it was not of merchantable quality.[31]

Second-hand goods are required to comply with the merchantability standard just as new goods must. This does not mean that the buyer of second-hand goods is entitled to the same quality. The merchantability standard is a flexible one, and the fact that the article was second-hand would be one of the factors to be taken into account when applying the statutory definition. As Lord Denning MR put in *Bartlett* v. *Sidney Marcus* (1965) in relation to a car:

> on the sale of a second-hand car, it is merchantable if it is in usable condition, even if not perfect . . . A buyer should realise that when he buys a second-hand car defects may appear sooner or later and, in the absence of an express warranty, he has no redress.[32]

(b) Fitness for purpose

There is an implied term that the goods sold should be fit for their purpose where the buyer, expressly or by implication, makes known to the seller any particular purpose for which the goods are being bought. Where there is an obvious purpose it is not necessary to state it. This implied term will frequently overlap with that of merchantability, but there can be circumstances where goods are of merchantable quality but do meet the specific purpose which the buyer had in mind.

While discussing the quality of goods it is convenient at this point to refer to consumer safety legislation. The Consumer Protection Act 1987 Part II has various provisions designed to ensure that unsafe goods are not sold by retail. There is a general duty to provide goods which are safe and it is a criminal offence to breach this duty. In addition the Secretary of State for Trade and Industry is given power to make detailed rules about the design and packaging of goods in order to ensure that they are safe. Breach of the general duty or the rules is a criminal offence.

Sample

There is another implied term which also applies only to business sales, and that is that where goods are sold by sample the bulk must correspond with the sample; and the buyer must have a reasonable opportunity to compare the bulk with the sample.[33]

The Buyer's Remedies

Where the goods supplied do not conform to the standards required by law in that, for example, they are not of merchantable quality the buyer has two remedies: the goods may be rejected, i.e. they may be returned and the purchase price repaid; or damages may be claimed. Rejection is available for only a relatively short time. The buyer loses the right to reject when he informs the seller that he has accepted the goods; he does anything inconsistent with the seller's ownership, e.g. gives them to someone as a present, or a retailer sells them; or does not reject within a reasonable time.[34] What is a reasonable time is a question of fact.[35] It seems that time can run out before the buyer has had a reasonable opportunity to have discovered the defect. It was said in a recent case that this provision in the Sales of Goods Act was:

> directed solely to what is a reasonable practical interval in commercial terms between a buyer receiving the goods and his ability to send them back, taking into consideration from his point of view the nature of the goods and their function, and from the point of view of the seller the commercial desirability of being able to close his ledger reasonably soon after the transaction is complete. The complexity of the intended function of the goods is clearly of prime consideration here. What is a reasonable time in relation to a bicycle would hardly suffice for a nuclear submarine.[36]

Applying these principles the judge in that case, involving a consumer sale, decided that the right to reject a car was lost after three weeks during which the buyer had driven only 140 miles. The rejection period for less complex articles must be extremely short especially as the period in the *Bernstein* case seems to have been extended because of the illness of the buyer.

Although the right to reject may have been lost, or the buyer prefers not to exercise that right, he is still entitled to damages where the implied terms have not been complied with. Where the goods are defective the amount of damages will be assessed by asking what amount of money will put the buyer in the position he would have been if the contract had not been broken. This may well be the difference between the value of the goods as delivered and their value if they had been of the standard contracted for or the cost of a repair. It should not be forgotten that other types of damage may flow from a breach of a contract of sale. If the buyer is injured by defective goods the damages for repair of the goods may be trivial compared to the compensation for physical injury caused by them.[37] Damages for breach of contract do not normally include a sum for the inconvenience caused. However, if it is clear that breach of the contract will inevitably cause disappointment and distress damages on this basis may be obtained. This occurred in a case where a new car was bought from a garage who knew that it was going to be used for a foreign holiday which was ruined because the car frequently broke down.[38]

Retailer's Liability to Others

In English and Scottish law liability under a contract is normally limited to the parties to the contract. Thus, in the context of contracts of sale, only the purchaser can enforce the Sale of Goods Act rights just discussed. If some third party such as person to whom the purchaser has given the product is injured because it is defective they do not have a contractual remedy against the retailer. Such a person will normally have to prove that the retailer was in some way negligent and so caused the harm to them. This is often difficult or impossible to do in the case of the retailer especially where pre-packaged goods are involved, and in the past a negligence action would have been more likely to have been brought against the manufacturer. Recent legislation, the Consumer Protection Act 1987, has made such an action easier as it has removed the necessity to prove fault, thus introducing strict liability for manufacturers. The Act has also slightly extended the liability of retailers. They will be liable without proof of fault under the Consumer Protection Act 1987 to those, other than their customers, if they cannot say who supplied them with the defective goods. This provision emphasises the need for good record keeping on the part of the retailer.

Selling on Credit

Selling on credit is of immense importance in the retail economy. As Galbraith has pointed out 'The process of persuading people to incur debt and the arrangements for them to do so are as much a part of modern production as the making of the goods and the nurturing of the wants'.[39] There are a number of different ways in which credit can be provided, and these can be subdivided into two main groups. The first is lender credit, where a debtor is advanced a sum of money which is repaid over a period of time together with interest. In many examples of this such as bank overdrafts or personal loans there is a clear distinction between the provider of the credit and the supplier of the goods, and the lender will have little control over how the loan is to be used. In the case of vendor credit the supplier of the goods may also supply the credit, or will have a close arrangement with a credit provider.

Vendor credit can take a number of forms which have differing legal consequences. Hire-purchase is a contract where goods are first hired to the buyer who pays instalments and at the end of this period can, for a small sum, exercise an option to become the owner. It is only at this point that the customer becomes the owner. The significance of this is that until that point he is not in a position to sell the goods as he is not the owner; and from the lender's point of view he has some security for his loan.

Another form is conditional sale which is very like hire-purchase. The buyer obtains immediate possession of the goods in return for regular instalments. He does not become owner until some specified condition is fulfilled. The difference between this and hire-purchase is that under conditional sale the buyer is committed to buying from the outset. A third method is credit sale in which ownership of the goods passes to the buyer at the start of the agreement and the price is paid in instalments.

Although, strictly speaking, not a form of instalment credit it has become common for rental agreements to be used in effect as a form of credit arrangement. Long-term car leasing as an alternative to hire purchase to the consumer is not uncommon.

In addition to lender and vendor credit other types of credit, such a credit cards, have developed which do not easily fit into these categories. Another example was the development of personal loans provided by finance companies to the customers of retailers with whom they had existing arrangements. The attraction of this method prior to the Consumer Credit Act 1974 was that the lender had no legal responsibility for the quality of the goods.

Prior to the Consumer Credit Act 1974, which implemented many of the recommendations of the Crowther Committee, credit law had developed in a haphazard manner, and economically similar transactions had legally different consequences. The 1974 Act seeks to rationalise this situation and recasts consumer credit law. Although the Act was passed in 1974, such was its complexity that it did not come fully into effect until 1985. It will be appreciated that in the space available it is not possible to do more than outline its more important aspects as they affect retailing.

In summary the Consumer Credit Act 1974 seeks to control malpractice in the credit industry, redress bargaining inequality between consumers and traders, and regulate the remedies for default. The methods used to achieve these ends are various. One of the most important is the licensing system operated by the Director General of Fair Trading which applies to virtually anyone involved in the consumer credit industry including those offering consumer hire facilities. Not only those who grant credit but those involved in ancillary credit businesses such as credit broking or debt collection need licences. Retailers will require a licence, not only if they themselves provide credit, but also where they have an arrangement with a finance company under which hire purchase can be arranged, because this is a form of credit broking.

Licences will only be granted where the applicant can show that he is a fit person to hold such a licence and that the name under which he applies is not misleading or otherwise undesirable. Factors taken into account are whether the applicant, or persons associated with the applicant, have committed any offence involving fraud, dishonesty, violence or a breach of consumer law; practised discrimination on the grounds of sex, colour, race, or ethnic or national origin; or engaged in deceitful, oppressive, unfair or improper business practices. It is a criminal offence to engage in an activity requiring a licence without holding one;[40] and an agreement entered into as a result of the activities of an unlicensed trader is unenforceable without the approval of the Director General of Fair Trading. This means, for example, that where a retailer does not have a licence as a credit broker any credit agreement entered into by a finance company as a result of an introduction by him cannot be enforced by the finance company even though that company is properly licensed.[41]

It is not all credit agreements that are subject to the legislation which applies to what it calls 'regulated agreements'. These are defined in the Act[42] as personal credit agreements by which the creditor provides the debtor with credit not exceeding £15 000. The Act does not make a sharp distinction between consumers and others, and the debtor can be anyone other than a corporation, thus including partnerships or sole traders. Certain agreements are exempt, including those involving not more than four instalments; certain types of credit card transaction such as American Express where the amount outstanding must be paid off in full each month; and certain low cost credit arrangements.

Where a credit transaction is subject to the Act there are a number of ways in which it is controlled. The Act places considerable emphasis on the disclosure philosophy which is exemplified by the 'truth in lending' provisions designed to ensure that credit consumers know the true cost of credit and can make meaningful comparisons. There are also extensive rules on the ways in which credit can be advertised and restrictions on canvassing loans.[43] Parts V–IX of the Act regulate the form and content of individual credit or hire agreements, the rationale of these provisions being that the agreements should be easy to understand and comply with; and that information should be presented clearly. The credit agreement in the statutorily approved form must be signed by the debtor and he must be provided with a copy of the completed agreement.[44]

The credit consumer is further protected in other ways. In order to curb the activities of doorstep salesmen credit agreements not signed at trade premises are subject to a five day cooling-off period. As has been explained above, in some forms of credit transaction the actual supplier of the goods and the person regarded in law as the seller are different. In the typical hire-purchase transaction the retailer sells the goods to a finance company which then enters into a separate contract with the consumer to hire the goods to him. In theory the legal seller, e.g. the finance company, would have no liability for legal wrongs of the actual supplier, the retailer. Under the Consumer Credit Act the finance company is made liable for the wrongs of its agent the retailer. In other transactions involving a cash price of more than £100 where the lender under a pre-existing arrangement provides a loan to enable goods to be purchased there is joint liability on the part of the retailer and the credit provider for breaches of contract or misrepresentation by the seller.[45]

10.5   Termination

Most consumer credit and consumer hire agreements terminate when all the payments have been made as envisaged in the agreement and, in the case of credit agreements, the customer has become the owner of the goods. There are a number of provisions in the Consumer Credit Act which deal with situations where for one reason or another termination takes place in different circumstances. It may be that the customer finds that it is possible to pay off the debt faster than had been anticipated. Section 94 of the Act gives a non-excludable right to make early repayment and the possibility of obtaining a rebate of credit charges.[46]

Most of the rules in the legislation dealing with termination relate to less happy circumstances where the customer is in some financial difficulty. Section 99 of the Consumer Credit Act provides that a conditional sale or hire purchase agreement can be terminated and the goods returned at any time before final payment is due by giving notice to the person to whom payments are made. All outstanding liabilities must be discharged and the debtor must normally bring his total payments up to one half of the total price.

If the purchaser falls into arrears and is in default, to use the technical term, there are various ways in which his position is protected. Where goods are 'protected goods', i.e. the purchaser has paid more than one third of the total purchase price, the goods cannot be repossessed without a court order.[47] If the creditor intends to take other action under the agreement, notice of default must be served on the purchaser and seven days given to put right the default.[48]

One notable feature of the Consumer Credit Act is that it gives wide discretionary powers to the courts in relation to the control and enforcement of agreements. For example, time orders can be made varying the payments to be made by the purchaser. Another unusual power given to the courts is the power, in effect, to rewrite an agreement where its terms are considered extortionate.[49]

10.6   Advertising and Marketing

Advertising and marketing have central roles to play in retailing, and in this section the legal background to these activities is considered. The common law has taken a tolerant attitude to sellers' methods of promoting their products. The blatantly false advertisement would, almost certainly, involve criminal liability for fraud and might give rise to a civil action by the defrauded customer. This is not, however, the usual kind of case. The real issues are those of providing information which is complete and not misleading and which does not offend public taste. For detailed regulation of advertising it is to legislation and self-regulation that one must look.

In the past the statutory regulation of advertising has been piecemeal. However, with the implementation of the European Communities Directive on misleading advertising there has been a move towards a general prohibition on misleading advertising.[50] Most of the specific legislation is negative in character, though there are some examples of legislation requiring information to be supplied to consumers, of which the Passenger Car Fuel Consumption Order 1983 made under the Energy Act 1976 requiring the results of fuel consumption tests to be given is an example.[51]

More commonly advertisements are regulated by legislation which makes it a criminal offence to make false or misleading statements. Some of these relate to specific types of product such as food[52] and medicines;[53] or certain aspects of retailing such as the legislation on weights and measures.[54] Of general application is the Trade Descriptions Act 1968, a statute enforced by trading standards officials employed by local authorities. The Act makes it a criminal offence to make false or misleading statements about goods or services. In relation to statements about goods, an offence can be commited without having any criminal intention: it is enough that a statement which is false or misleading has been made. This apparently harsh approach is ameliorated by the provision of defences such as that the commission of the offence was the result of someone else's error, or incorrect information supplied by another person. The separate offence in relation to services does involve proof of some degree of guilty intention.[55]

The control of misleading indications about prices has proved a difficult and controversial matter. Previous attempts to do so under the Trade Descriptions Act 1968 and the Price Marking (Bargain Offer) Order 1979 proved unpopular both with business and enforcement staff. Part III of the Consumer Protection Act 1987 introduces a different approach. Instead of attempting to prohibit specific practices, as the earlier legislation did, it creates a wide general offence of giving to consumers a misleading indication as to the price of goods, services, accommodation or facilities.[56] To assist traders the Secretary of State for Trade and Industry has drawn up a code of practice[57] which has evidential value in a prosecution. Failure to comply with the codes does not by itself give rise to criminal liability, but it can be referred to in order to establish an offence, while compliance with the code may be relied on to show that no offence has been committed.

Discussion of advertising regulation would be incomplete without reference to self-regulation. In 1962 the advertising industry established the Advertising Standards Association as an independent body funded by the advertising industry to act as a watchdog over advertising. Its remit extends to advertising in print, cinema and poster media, and it oversees the British Code of Advertising Practice. This code contains rules which most of those involved in advertising in the United Kingdom have agreed to abide by. The basic principles behind the code are summed up in a slogan often used by the ASA that advertisements should be 'legal, decent, honest and truthful'. The code attempts to go beyond legal standards and influence matters of taste and good practice which may not easily be regulated by law. Radio and television advertising are subject to very similar codes though strictly speaking these are not voluntary as they are required by legislation.[58]

Certain marketing methods are subject to statutory regulation. The Trading Stamps Act 1964 regulates the way in which trading stamps can be used to promote goods and services. Pyramid selling schemes have been regulated since the scandals of the late 1960s by Part XI of the Fair Trading Act 1973. These apply to schemes where profits are made not so much by the sale of goods or services as by the recruitment by existing participants in the scheme of other participants. What is sometimes referred to as inertia selling, that is the sending of goods to people who have not ordered them in the hope that the recipient will pay for them, is now regulated by the Unsolicited Goods and Services Act 1971. This is done by providing that unsolicited goods become the property of the recipient without payment after they have been in his possession for certain periods. It is also a criminal offence to demand payment for unsolicited goods.

10.7   Enforcement of Consumer Protection Legislation

Responsibility for the enforcement of much of the legislation referred to above rests with local authorities. In England and Wales the non-metropolitan county, metropolitan district and the London borough councils all have consumer protection functions and enforce a wide range of legislation including the Weights and Measures Act, the Trade Descriptions Act 1968, the Food Act 1985 and the Consumer Credit Act 1974. In Scotland the regional councils carry out these tasks. Another important institution in relation to business regulation is the Office of Fair Trading. In the context of retail trading the powers of the Director General of Fair Trading to prevent what Part III of the Fair Trading Act calls 'persistent unfair conduct' towards consumers are worth noting. Under these provisions the Director General can discipline traders, the ultimate sanction being imprisonment or a fine for failure to abide by promises given to desist from unfair conduct.

10.8   The Retailer and his Employees

The law regulates the relationship between the employer and employee in great and ever increasing detail. A number of weighty tomes have been written upon the subject of employment law. Indeed, individual works have been penned upon most of the sub-topics considered below. It can be appreciated then, that the author has had to be very selective in his treatment of the issues in this area, with no issue being examined in depth. The reader must look elsewhere if he requires detail, and some assistance is provided for him in this respect. The relationship between retailer and employee is largely governed by the same principles as regulate the relationship of employer and employee generally, and the treatment of the subject will reflect this. In certain respects, nevertheless, retail employment is treated differently. For obvious reasons these are the only aspects of the subject to be treated in any detail.

In order to assist the reader in following this section of the chapter and making subsequent reference to it, a brief contents list is given below.

Recruitment
Discrimination generally
Employing part-timers
The Contract of Employment
The Written Statement of Terms and Conditions of Employment
Remuneration
    Form and manner of payment
    Amount of remuneration
    Making deductions from wages
    Sick pay
    Itemised pay statements
    Equal pay

Hours of work and holidays
    Breaks
    Half-days
    Sunday employment
    Employing those under sixteen

Health and safety at work
    Common law duties
    Vicarious liability
    General statutory duties
    Statutory duties applicable to retailers
    Duties of employees

Dismissal
    Giving notice
    Written statements of reasons for dismissal
    Redundancy payments and unfair dismissal

Transfer of undertakings

List of abbreviations used
EPA 1975   = Employment Protection Act 1975
SDA 1975   = Sex Discrimination Act 1975
RRA 1976   = Race Relations Act 1976
EP(C)A1978 = Employment Protection (Consolidation) Act 1978

Recruitment

This is the most obvious starting point for a consideration of the relationship. The law exerts an influence here by insisting that an employer may have to pay compensation[59] if he refuses to recruit an individual on sexual[60] or racial[61] grounds.[62] An employer, moreover, commits a criminal offence if he publishes or causes to be published any job advertisement which indicates an intention to discriminate.[63] It is also a criminal offence to instruct another person to commit a discriminatory act.[64] Thus an employer cannot evade responsibility by, for example, allowing an employment agency to recruit on his behalf, but making it clear that he expects them to recruit in a discriminatory manner.

The only circumstances relevant in the present context in which it would be lawful to practise discrimination in recruitment would be where being a member of a particular sex or racial group is a genuine occupational qualification[65] for the job in question. Few potential genuine occupational qualifications are relevant in a retail context. Still, being a member of a given racial group can be a genuine occupational qualification where food or drink is served to the public in a particular ethnic setting,[66] e.g. an Indian restaurant. Equally, a job might have to be held by a man[67] since it involves intimate physical contact with men or being in the presence of men who are in a state of undress.[69] This genuine occupational qualification has been raised in two cases concerning respectively, a woman seeking work in a men's tailoring establishment[70] and a man seeking work in a woman's clothing shop.[71] In each case the defence failed to be established since it was shown that the individuals could carry out the vast majority of their duties without outraging decency, while there would always be an employee of the appropriate sex on hand to deal with the more sensitive aspects of the job.

Reference has so far been confined to direct discrimination, i.e. treating an individual less favourably on racial or sexual grounds.[72] (It is also sexual discrimination to discriminate against married persons.)[73] Yet indirect discrimination is also unlawful. This occurs when one applies equally to all a requirement or condition the effect of which is that a considerably smaller proportion of members of a particular sex/racial group can comply with it. A member of that sex/racial group who is unable to comply with that requirement or condition may seek compensation for that discrimination, unless the employer can show the requirement/condition to be justified on grounds other than sex or race.[74] For example, refusing to contemplate recruiting anyone with a beard would be indirectly discriminatory against Sikhs, so that an employer, if challenged, would have to show that the condition served some purpose, e.g. hygiene in relation to foodstuffs.[75] In the context of sex discrimination it is indirect discrimination to refuse to employ a woman on the basis that she is responsible for looking after children.[76] Accordingly, employers should be careful not to display too great an interest in an individual's family background when conducting interviews, lest the impression be conveyed that such matters are important to their decision.

The last point leads on to an observation about the nature of indirect discrimination. As noted above, it revolves around the application of a requirement or condition. It has been held[77] that one does not apply a requirement or condition by taking a factor into account, if it is not conclusive to one's decision. Thus if an employer decides aginst employing an applicant on account of the latter's poor command of English he applies a requirement that applicants, to be employed, must be reasonably competent in English. This would discriminate indirectly against certain racial groups, obliging the employer to justify the condition if challenged. However, if the poor command of English is only a single factor dissuading an employer from recruiting an individual, and not decisive in itself, then no requirement or condition is imposed, and no discrimination occurs.

Discrimination Generally

Having explained the idea of discrimination in the context of recruitment, let us now consider how else it may affect the employer. Generally he may not discriminate on sexual or racial grounds as regards terms and conditions of employment, promotion, access to benefits etc. Naturally, disciplining or dismissing the employee on such grounds is also unlawful discrimination.[78] Racial segregation is automatically treated as discrimination.[79] Sexual or racial harassment also amount to discrimination.[80] An employer will be liable for all discriminatory acts perpetrated by his employees in the course of their employment,[81] whether against fellow employees or otherwise, unless he can show that he took all steps as were reasonably practicable to prevent such acts.[82] A policy on discrimination (especially harassment) might therefore be important, as might informing employees that engaging in such behaviour will be treated as a serious disciplinary offence. Yet, it seems that if no reasonable steps would have prevented the behaviour in question, an employer may satisfy the above test by doing nothing.[83]

Certain forms of sexual discrimination are lawful. Men cannot complain of special treatment afforded to women in connection with pregnancy and childbirth,[84] e.g. maternity leave. Also it is possible under British statutes to discriminate with regard to the range and level of benefits available on death or retirement, e.g. occupational pensions.[85] However, this area of valid discrimination will become narrower over the next few years.[86] Indeed it is already unlawful under EC law for British employers to operate sexually discriminatory pension schemes.[87] Finally, it is not discrimination at all to insist that female employees refrain from wearing trousers, if rules as to the proper attire for male employees are also maintained.[88]

Employing Part-timers

This subject is allied to those of recruitment and discrimination. With the vast majority of part-timers being female,[89] any differential treatment of part-timers must be indirectly discriminatory against women.[90] Accordingly, employers who deny part-timers the full range of benefits available to full-timers, or who provide part-timers with terms and conditions inferior to those enjoyed by full-timers, or who select part-timers for redundancy ahead of full-timers, should be able to justify their stance – presumably by demonstrating the economic or organisational advantages of full-timers. The cases are undecided as to whether an employer's insistence that the employee must work full-time can be a requirement or condition. This can be important where the employee for family or other reasons wishes to go part-time. It may be that certain jobs are in their nature full-time, e.g. managerial posts. Thus employers may not have to justify their refusal to let a female employee work part-time.[91]

Part-time and full-time are not terms with specific legal meaning. No statute seeks to define them. There is no minimum working week to justify the term full-timer. Everything depends on the context of the individual workplace. Any person who works significantly fewer hours than 'full-timers' in that place could be described as part-time. Yet, beyond the context of discrimination one finds situations where precise legal significance may be attached to an employee working only a certain number of hours per week. This is because to qualify for most employment rights an employee must have a certain minimum period of continuous employment.[92] Those whose contracts envisage them working fewer than eight hours a week never build up a period of continuous employment, while those whose contracts envisage them working at least eight but less than 16 hours a week are only regarded as having continuous employment after five years service.[93] In other words, such an employee after four years and 51 weeks service has no continuous employment; a week later he has five years continuous employment. It is only those employees whose contracts envisage them working at least 16 hours per week who will begin to build up a period of continuous employment from their first week in the job.[94] An employee who works one week on and one week off will never build up a period of continuous employment, no matter how long he works and how many hours he works in the week on.[95] Unfortunately, we have no room to say any more about this important subject, but readers should bear the preceding discussion in mind when they encounter references to periods of continuous employment hereafter.

The Contract of Employment

Outside of the many statutory rights and duties, the employment relationship is governed by a contract of employment. Every employee has one, whether there is anything in writing or not. The contract determines the range and nature of the employee's rights and obligations and specifies what he is forbidden to do.

The Written Statement of Terms and Conditions of Employment

In practice it can prove difficult to discover what, if anything, the contract says on a particular issue, especially if it is not in writing. Thus every employee with 13 weeks continuous employment is entitled to a written statement of terms and conditions of employment[96] (unless the relevant details are already covered by an actual written contract).[97] The aim of the written statement is to provide employees with details of the more important rights and duties.[98] It must tell the employee when the employment began, how much he is paid and how often, what hours he must work, what holidays and holiday pay he receives including his entitlement to accrued holiday pay on termination of employment, conditions relating to sickness and sick pay, pensions and pension schemes (if he is not entitled to holidays, holiday pay, sick pay or a pension the statement should say so),[99] what notice he must give or be given to terminate the contract, what his job title is. The statement must provide details of a grievance procedure. Finally, where when the employee's employment began the employer had at least 20 employees, the statement must detail any disciplinary rules applicable to the employee, and specify a person to whom the employee can apply if dissatisfied with any disciplinary decisions relating to him, together with any procedure to be followed.

Clearly, such a statement may be fairly lengthy. A permissible shortcut is to refer the employee for details of all or any of the above mentioned terms to a reasonably accessible document,[100] e.g. master contract, collective agreement. Equally, eventually some of the terms will become outdated. Employers must inform employees of any changes in the terms covered within one month of the change occurring.[101] Yet, if details of any term are contained in such a reasonably accessible document, and employees have been informed that changes in a given term will be recorded in the document, then it is enough that this is done.[102] Should an employer fail to notify a change, it does not necessarily signify that a change has not happened.[103] Nor will employees necessarily be taken to have agreed to a variation of any term merely by failing to challenge the intimation of a change – especially if the change in question has no immediate practical effect.[104] Courts, moreover, are reluctant to accept that an employee who signs for a statement thereby acknowledges the accuracy of its contents.[105]

Either party may challenge the accuracy of a statement and have it corrected by an industrial tribunal.[106] Furthermore, where no statement or an inadequate statement is provided, an employee is entitled to apply to an industrial tribunal to discover what the missing terms should be.[107] Often this will be obvious or may be easily worked out from what happens in practice. Where this is not so, the tribunal must work out what the parties would have agreed, if they had turned their minds to the term in question. Where even this approach fails, one case suggests that the tribunal should consider what would be just in the circumstances, bearing in mind that it is the employer's failure to meet his statutory obligations which has created the difficulty.[108] Accordingly, although no penalty is imposed for failure in any of the above obligations, employers would be wise to ensure that they provide adequate written statements, for fear that an industrial tribunal may find itself compelled to invent certain terms of the contract.

Although the matters discussed above *must* be dealt with in the written statement or contract, employers can cover a variety of other rights or duties therein – a fact to be borne in mind as we proceed.

Remuneration

Form and Manner of Payment

It is up to the parties to agree as to the form and manner of remuneration. Thus they may agree that it take the form, wholly or partly, of payments in kind, and it is indeed quite common for remuneration packages to include a variety of non-cash benefits. They can also decide whether the money wage is to be paid by cash, cheque, or directly into the employee's bank account. An employer who against his employee's will moves over to a system of cashless pay is unlikely to invite serious legal trouble, despite perhaps committing a technical breach of contract. Yet any attempt significantly to alter the balance between cash and non-cash benefits might raise the spectre of constructive unfair dismissal (see below) even if the value of the total remuneration package was undiminished.

Amount of Remuneration

Usually this depends on the terms of the contract. The written statement should provide clear information as to how remuneration is earned. However a number of wages councils are active in the retail industry.[109] (The government has mooted the possibility of abolishing wages councils, but no such steps have been taken so far.)[110] Wages councils issue wages orders. These orders set a minimum hourly rate, and sometimes a minimum hourly overtime rate, which comes into effect once a certain number of hours (specified by the order) have been worked in the week.[111] The rate set by a wages order applies to all workers aged 21 or more in the area of operation of that wage council, whatever their grade. Orders do *not* apply to workers below the age of 21.[112] Their rate of pay depends entirely on the contract. An employer may pay above the wages council rate, but commits an offence if he pays below that rate, even if the employee has agreed to do so.[113] Such employees, moreover, may claim the difference between what they should have been paid and what they were actually paid.[114]

Wage councils are obliged to send details of wages orders to each employer who appears to them to be affected thereby,[115] while employers on receiving such details are obliged to post them in a place where they can be seen by any

worker covered thereby.[116] The system is policed by the Wages Inspectorate[117] who are entitled to demand relevant information. It is an offence to
supply false information. Inspectors may enter premises and interview any
person. Once again it is an offence to obstruct an inspector or knowingly to
supply him with false information. Inspectors must be allowed access to wages
records, which must be retained for three years. Failure to do so is an offence
as is the falsification of records.[118] Despite these references to offences, it is
very rare for the Inspectorate to prosecute.[119]

Making Deductions from Wages

Complex rules govern the making of deductions from wages.[120] (In this
context the term deduction also covers a simple failure to pay the agreed
wages, unless this results from a genuine mistake.)[121] Deductions are lawful
only in certain circumstances. Obviously, they are lawful if authorised by
statute, e.g. PAYE, National Insurance.[122] If, however, the deduction is
authorised by the contract of employment, then assuming the relevant term to
be in writing, a deduction will be lawful if the employee receives a copy of
that term prior to the deduction being made.[123] If the term is not in writing,
then the employee must receive a written explanation of its existence and
effect prior to the deduction being made.[124] (Once such a copy/written
explanation has been provided, it validates all subsequent deductions under
that term.)

Should an employer find that the contract confers no power to make a
particular deduction, a deduction may still be valid if the employer can
persuade the employee either to agree to vary the contract to confer such a
power, or to give his written agreement to such a deduction being made.[125] In
such cases, none the less, the agreement/variation may *not* permit deductions
to be made in respect of events occurring prior to the agreement/variation.[126]
Suppose then, that the till of a check-out operator is consistently short, but
that the contract does not permit the employer to recover the shortfall from
the employee's wages. Should he persuade her to give her written agreement
to the making of deductions in such circumstances, then deductions could
only be validly be made in relation to shortfalls arising *after* that agreement.

The above principles apply to all employees. Yet extra restrictions apply to
the making of deductions from the wages of retail employees, where the
deductions are made because of cash shortages or stock deficiencies arising
out of retail transactions. Firstly, even if otherwise valid, no such deduction
can be made more than 12 months after either the date when the employer
discovered the shortage or deficiency, or if earlier, the date when he ought
reasonably to have discovered it, e.g. where a yearly stock-taking or daily till
check occurs.[127] The only exception to this rule is that where the first in a
series of deductions occurs within the 12 month period it is permissible for
others in that series to occur after the period has elapsed. Secondly where a
deduction is made from the wages of a retail worker on the above grounds,

then no more than 10 per cent of the *gross* wages can be taken at any one time.[128] The 10 per cent restriction is lifted, however, as regards the final payment of wages, i.e. that relating to the final period of work,[129] or, if paid later, any payment in lieu of notice. Even so, any element in the final payment which relates to an earlier period of employment, e.g. accrued holiday pay, continues to be subject to the 10 per cent limit.

An employee may complain to an industrial tribunal of an invalid deduction. If the amount has not been repaid by the date of the hearing, the tribunal shall order the repayment of the deduction or the invalid percentage thereof. The employer thereupon loses the right to recover that sum forever.[130]

Sick Pay

The terms of the contract determine whether the employee is entitled to be paid while off ill. Yet every employee (with a few exceptions) is entitled to Statutory Sick Pay. Since this is essentially a social security payment paid through the medium of the employer, we cannot deal with it here.[131]

Itemised Pay Statements[132]

Every employee each time wages are paid must receive an itemised pay statement detailing the gross and net amounts paid, plus the nature and amount of any deductions. Invariable deductions may alternatively be notified via a standing statement of fixed deductions. The standing statement details the nature and amount of each fixed deduction. Once the employee has received a standing statement, then his pay statement need only record the aggregate amount of fixed deductions (as well as specifying non-fixed deductions). If any fixed deduction changes, then the employee must receive an updated standing statement. Should the employer provide no or an inadequate itemised pay statement, the employee may complain to an industrial tribunal which, if it supports his complaint, *may* award compensation – subject to a maximum figure of the amount of unnotified deductions over the 13 weeks immediately preceding the tribunal application.

Equal Pay[133]

Although a woman normally claims equal pay with a man, a man can claim equal pay with a woman. Equal pay is something of a misnomer since the legislation permits one to claim equality in relation to most terms of the contract. It operates through a woman insisting either that a term in her contract should be upgraded to the level of a similar term in the contract of her male comparator, or that she should receive the benefit of a term in his contract which is not in hers. A woman can compare herself with men working for her employer or an associated employer in the establishment where she works, or in other establishments in Great Britain where common terms and conditions operate. In other words, if the employer has a number of branches, the employee can compare herself with a man at another branch unless he observes completely different terms and conditions at the two branches.

For a comparison to be successful the comparator must be employed on like work, work rated as equivalent or work of equal value. (It is up to the woman to choose her comparator. Neither the tribunal nor the employer can suggest that another would be more appropriate.)[134] Like work means that the jobs are broadly similar.[135] Work rated as equivalent means that the jobs have been rated as equal by a job evaluation study (or would have been had the study not been sexually discriminatory). Work of equal value means that the jobs have been assigned equal value in a special job evaluation study carried out by an independent expert appointed by an industrial tribunal. An equal pay claim can still be defeated even where the comparator is shown to be employed on like work/work related as equivalent if the employer can show that the man's superior terms are due to a genuine material difference other than sex, and even where the comparator is shown to be employed on work of equal value, if it can be shown that the superior terms are due to a genuine material factor other than sex. Examples of genuine material differences include, that the man is in a higher grade[136] (assuming the grading system is not discriminatory), or that he has been recruited at his former salary.[137] The concept of genuine material factor is wider than genuine material difference and might include the fact that the remuneration packages of the comparators are quite different[138] and perhaps even a market forces argument.

If an employee's equal pay claim succeeds then the terms of her contracts are automatically adjusted. She may be awarded compensation or arrears of pay covering the two years prior to her claim.

Hours of Work and Holidays

Generally, the law leaves it to the parties to agree what the hours of work and holidays (if any) should be. Yet retailing is an exception to this rule due to the provisions of the Shops Act 1950.[139] We shall consider these in some detail.

Breaks[140]

Where the hours of employment include the period from 11.30 a.m. to 2.30 p.m. then if lunch is not eaten in the shop or within the same building an hour must be allowed for lunch, otherwise 45 minutes must be allowed. Additionally, no person can be employed for more than six hours without a break of at least 20 minutes. Moreover, when the hours of employment embrace the period between 4 and 7 p.m. a meal interval of at least 30 minutes must be allowed.

There are exceptions to these rules. Shops where the only employees are members of the occupier's family who are part of his household are not covered. Also, where a weekly market day or the day of an annual fair occurs, then the lunch interval described above need not be permitted as long as the same length of interval is allowed, ending prior to 11.30 a.m. or commencing after 2.30 p.m. The same provision applies generally to those employed in the sale of refreshments or intoxicating liquors. Those who run pubs, cafés and restaurants may indeed choose not to apply any of the foregoing provisions, if they apply others instead.[141] These alternative provisions involve giving every employee not less than 45 minutes of meal break(s) on every half day and not less than 2 hours on every other day. Nor can any such employee be employed for more than 6 hours without an interval of at least 30 minutes. If an employer wishes to operate this system, he must conspicuously maintain a notice to that effect.

Half-days

Every employee must have at least one half-day during the week, i.e. work ceasing no later than 1.30 p.m. He may be refused a half-day during the week before a public holiday if he is not employed on that holiday and also has a half-day during that week. It is up to the employer to fix the half-day, and he may of course fix different half-days for different employees. Where employees are employed in premises for the sale of refreshments then, instead of the foregoing provisions, the employer may apply a different system provided he conspicuously posts a notice to that effect on the premises.[142] This system requires that (i) no employee be employed for more than 65 hours in a week, excluding meal times; (ii) every employee must have at least 32 weekdays off each year, at least 2 days per month, with at least 6 consecutive days holiday on full pay (Two half holidays a week are deemed equivalent to a whole weekday off); (iii) every employee must get at least 26 Sundays off each year and no employee may work three Sundays in a row.

Sunday Employment

In Scotland, apart from the fact that the business of hairdresser or barber may not be engaged in on a Sunday, there are no restrictions on Sunday trading.[143] In England and Wales on the other hand Sunday trading is generally prohibited, subject to a wide variety of exceptions,[144] and where shops are open on a Sunday certain requirements must be complied with.[145] Thus any person who is employed for more than 4 hours on a Sunday must get a whole day off during that week in addition to his half holiday, unless he has already had a day off during the preceding week for working that Sunday. Such a person may not be employed on more than two other Sundays in that month. A person who works for 4 hours or less on a Sunday must receive an extra half holiday during that week, unless he has had an extra half holiday during the preceding week for working that Sunday. The employer commits an offence if he fails to keep a record of those who work on a Sunday and of the holidays they receive as a result.

Employees engaged in certain activities are not subject to the above restrictions[146] – sale of intoxicating liquor, delivery of milk, post office, butcher, registered pharmacists where the employer is obliged to open on a Sunday.[147] Finally, the restrictions do not apply where in relation to those involved in the sale of refreshments, the special system described in the section on half-days has been adopted.

Employing Those Under School-leaving Age

Legislation[148] imposes considerable restrictions on the employment of those below school-leaving age. Thus no person can be employed (i) before age 13; (ii) before the close of school hours on any schoolday; (iii) before 7 a.m. or after 7 p.m. on any day; (iv) for more than 2 hours on any schoolday; (v) for more than 2 hours on Sunday.

Health and Safety at Work

Both statute and common law impose upon employers a variety of duties designed to ensure the health and safety of their employees. If an employee is injured as a result of breach of these obligations, then generally he may recover damages from the employer. Additionally, breach of many of the statutory obligations renders the employer liable to criminal prosecution, whether injury is caused or not. As will be seen there is often a substantial degree of overlap between common law and statutory duties.

Common Law Duties

The law in the main holds individuals responsible where their negligence results in harm to others, if such harm was a foreseeable consequence of negligence. This applies equally within an employment context,[149] but its application in this context is usually regarded as giving rise to three recognisable duties:

(1) The employer must provide a safe system of work,[150] i.e. he must ensure that the way in which the work is done is as safe as possible, avoiding all unnecessary risks, providing all feasible precautions against injuries, and ensuring that employees are not only aware of the risks and the importance of avoiding them, but trained to be able to do so.

(2) The employer should ensure that all equipment and premises are as safe as possible.[151] An employer is probably not in breach of this common law duty where equipment which has been provided by a reputable supplier and which is not obviously defective, turns out to be faulty, injuring an

employee.[152] Unfortunately statute[153] renders an employer liable for injuries suffered by any of his employees due to defective equipment where that defect is (wholly or partly) attributable to the fault of a third party (whether identifiable or not).

(3) The employer will be liable to employees for injuries caused by their colleagues if the latter are being asked to undertake work which is beyond their capabilities, or are known to be incompetent or irresponsible.[154]

Vicarious Liability

It may be noted in passing that employers are liable for wrongs committed by employees in the course of their employment – even where they are deliberately disobeying his instructions.[155]

General Statutory Duties

The Health and Safety at Work etc. Act 1974 imposes a number of duties on *all* employers – particularly an overarching duty to ensure, so far as is reasonably practicable, the health, safety and welfare at work of all his employees.[156] This is supplemented by a number of more particular duties:[157]

(1) To provide and maintain plant and systems of work that are, so far as is reasonably practicable, safe and without risk to health;

(2) To make arrangements for ensuring, so far as is reasonably practicable, safety and the absence of risks to health in connection with the use, handling, storage and transport of articles and substances;

(3) To provide such information, instruction, training and supervision as is necessary to ensure, so far as is reasonably practicable, the health and safety at work of all his employees;

(4) To ensure, so far as is reasonably practicable that any place of work under his control is maintained in a condition that is safe and without risk to health, and that means of access and egress are provided and maintained in a similar condition;

(5) To provide such information, instruction, training and supervision as is necessary to ensure, so far as is reasonably practicable, the health and safety at work of all his employees;

(6) To provide and maintain so far as is reasonably practicable, a working environment which is safe, without risk to health and affords adequate facilities for the welfare of employees at work.

On top of the above duties, any employer who has five or more employees must prepare, and revise as often as appropriate, a written statement of his policy regarding his employees' health and safety at work and the current organisation and arrangements for implementing that policy. He must also bring this statement and any revision thereof to the attention of all his employees.[158] Finally, the Health and Safety Executive has produced a poster

and a leaflet, both describing the major effects of health and safety legislation. An employer must give each of his employees a leaflet, or display the
poster where every employee can read it. The leaflet must be accompanied by
and the poster must contain the addresses of the local offices of the Health
and Safety Executive and the Employment Medical Advisory Service.[159]

A number of duties are imposed by other statutes:

(1) Employers must be insured against liability for bodily injury and disease
sustained by employees in the course of and arising out of their employment;[160]
(2) Employers must have a fire certificate for any premises unless 20 or fewer
people work there at any one time, or not more than 10 people work
other than on the ground floor at any time.[161] If premises do not require a
certificate then it should at least be ensured that (a) no doors through
which an employee might have to pass in order to escape are locked and
fastened so that he cannot easily and immediately open them (b) there
should be free passage to escape (c) appropriate means of fighting fire
should be readily available for use.[162]
(3) Employers must provide adequate and appropriate first-aid facilities and
ensure that there is an adequate number of individuals who are trained to
render first-aid to employees should this become necessary.[163]
(4) Employers must notify the local authority of any fatal accident, major
injury,[164] dangerous occurrence,[165] or notifiable disease,[166] and must also
maintain records thereof.[167]

Statutory Duties Particularly Applicable to the Retail Trade

A number of particular requirements to ensure the health, safety and welfare
of those employed in shops[168] is imposed by the Offices, Shops and Railway
Premises Act 1963. The Act does not apply, however, where the only
employees are close relatives of the employer.[169] The major requirements are
summarised below.

All premises furniture and fittings must be kept clean, with floors and stairs
being cleaned at least once a week.[170] Overcrowding is not permitted.[171] A
reasonable temperature must be maintained in every room where employees
work for other than a short period. Where the work does not involve physical
effort, a temperature of below 16°C after the first hour is not reasonable. Yet
this does not apply where the maintenance of such a temperature would not
be reasonably practicable, or would cause deterioration of goods. Nevertheless, where this is so, employees must have a reasonable opportunity to use a
convenient and easily accessible means of warming themselves.[172] Adequate
lighting and ventilation (artificial or otherwise) must be maintained.[173]

Suitable and sufficient sanitary conveniences must be provided. They must
be clean, well maintained and properly ventilated.[174] Similar duties are
imposed in relation to the provision of washing facilities, but here there must

also be supplied hot and cold/warm water plus soap and towels or some other means of cleaning and drying oneself. Such facilities and the place where they are located must be kept clean and tidy.[175] A supply of wholesome drinking water must be provided in a reasonably accessible place or places.[176] At suitable places there should be provision for persons to hang and dry clothing not used during working hours.[177] Where persons have in the course of their work a reasonable opportunity to sit down without detriment to their work, suitable and conveniently accessible seating facilities must be provided.[178] Where the work or a substantial part thereof can be done seated, any seats provided must be properly designed, e.g. with foot and back rests.[179]

All floors, passages, stairs etc. must be properly constructed and maintained, and so far as is reasonably practicable be kept free from obstruction and any substance likely to cause persons to slip. Every staircase must have a substantial handrail on the open side. If a staircase has two open sides, or is otherwise specially dangerous, then a handrail must be provided on both sides. All openings in the floor must be securely fenced, except insofar as the nature of the work renders fencing impracticable.[180] Every dangerous part of machinery must be securely fenced, unless it is as safe unfenced. If a fixed guard cannot be provided, there must be some other device which automatically prevents the operator coming into contact with the dangerous part.[181] No person under 18 shall clean any machinery if he is exposed to risk of injury by a moving part of this or adjacent machinery.[182] No person shall work on any prescribed machine[183] unless made aware of the dangers arising and precautions to be taken, has been properly trained, and is supervised by someone with experience on the machine.[184]

Every lift must be well constructed, adequately maintained, and inspected at least every 6 months. Every liftshaft must have gates which cannot be opened unless the lift is at a landing, while the lift should not be able to move unless the gates are closed. Each lift should be marked with the maximum load which should not be exceeded.[185] Finally no person can be asked to carry, move or lift a load so heavy as to be likely to cause injury to him.[186]

Duties of Employees

The Health and Safety at Work etc. Act 1974[187] imposes two duties on employees – to take reasonable care for the health and safety of himself and those who may be affected by his acts or omissions at work and to cooperate with his employer in so far as is necessary to enable the latter to comply with any legal requirement or perform any legal duty imposed by the relevant legislation. The employee is also subject to an implied common law duty to exercise proper care and skill in performing his work, and may be asked to indemnify his employer if he occasions the latter loss through a failure in this duty.[188]

Dismissal

It would appear logical to conclude this section by examining the various legal consequences of the termination of the employment relationship.

Giving Notice[189]

Every employee is entitled under statute to at least a week's notice (or a week's wages in lieu of notice) after 4 weeks' continuous employment. Once an employee has reached 2 years' continuous employment, he is entitled to a week's notice for each year of continuous employment up to a maximum of 12. The employee must also give at least a week's notice once he has 4 weeks' continuous employment, but the minimum period of notice he is obliged to give does not increase. The contract of employment may require either party to give longer periods of notice than these, but not shorter. Failure to give the proper notice of dismissal is a breach of contract, but an employee can recover as damages for breach of contract no more than the wages he would have earned during the period of notice to which he was entitled.[190] It is rarely worth suing an employee who walks out without giving notice.

An employee may be dismissed without notice when in serious breach of contract, e.g. dishonesty, violence, gross insubordination, breaking important work rules. He may resign without notice where the employer is in serious breach of contract. This is known as constructive dismissal since it counts as dismissal for statutory purposes,[191] e.g. unfair dismissal. Constructive dismissal may arise where, for example, the employer fails to observe any of the major terms of the contract, or where he treats the employee without proper respect.[192]

The Written Statement of Reasons for Dismissal[193]

If at the date of dismissal the employee has at least 2 years' continuous employment, he may demand a written statement of reasons for dismissal. The employer has 14 days to comply. The employee may complain to an industrial tribunal if the employer fails to comply or supplies an inaccurate or inadequate statement. If the employee proves his case, the tribunal may declare what it finds the reason for dismissal to be, and *must* award the employee a sum equivalent to 2 weeks' pay.

Redundancy Payments and Unfair Dismissal

Preliminary Conditions – Before an employee can claim either unfair dismissal or a redundancy payment he must have at least 2 years' continuous employment at the date of dismissal.[194] However, entitlement will be lost if at the date of dismissal he/she has reached the normal retiring age for the job.

Where there is no normal retiring age, or where it is 65 or above, or where there is a different normal retiring age for men and women, then an employee is disentitled if at the date of dismissal he/she has reached the age of 65.[195] (If the normal retiring age is above 65 the right to claim unfair dismissal is not lost until that age is reached.)

Redundancy – To qualify for a payment an employee must be dismissed for redundancy. Redundancy arises in either of two situations[196] – firstly, the employer closes the business down, either entirely or in the place where the employee works – but that may not be where the employee happens to work. It is any place where he can be asked to work under his contract. Thus if, for example, the contract allows the employer to require the employee to work anywhere in Britain, the fact that the employee has always worked in place X is immaterial. Should the employer close down in place X but offer the employee work elsewhere, the latter cannot claim that he is redundant.[197] The other situation contemplated by the concept of redundancy is where the employer needs fewer employees to do the work which the employee is employed to do. It is not necessary that the amount of work declines. If the employer decides that the same amount of work (or even more work) can be done by fewer employees, then those displaced are redundant.[198] The definition concentrates on the actual job to be done, rather than the conditions under which it is done.[199] Thus a shelf-filler is redundant if more cashiers but fewer shelf-fillers are needed, but a part-time shelf-filler is not redundant if the employer decides that he does not need part-time shelf-fillers, and asks him to go full-time. The terms of the contract are also important in this context. If it stipulates that the employee is employed primarily as a shelf-filler, but can be required to undertake any other non-managerial work, then a shelf-filler who is moved permanently to cashier's work is not redundant.[200]

If there is other work which is beyond the terms of the employee's contract, but which would be suitable for him to do, then should such work be offered to him (in writing) and he unreasonably turns it down, he loses his right to a redundancy payment. An employee has a four week period to try out any such new job. If he remains in the job for any longer, he cannot claim a redundancy payment should he thereafter leave the job, even were an industrial tribunal to agree that the job is unsuitable.[201]

Unfair dismissal – In order to show that a dismissal is fair,[202] the employer must prove that he dismissed the employee for one of the following reasons (i) redundancy, (ii) lack of capability and qualifications to do the job, (iii) misconduct, (iv) the fact that the employee's continued employment would contravene a statute, (v) some other substantial reason, and also show that it was reasonable for him to dismiss the employee for such a reason in the circumstances. We shall consider all such reasons except (iv) in more detail.

It is automatically unfair dismissal to select someone for redundancy on the basis of race, sex, or membership/non-membership of a trade union. It is similarly automatically unfair to select an employee in breach of a customary arrangement or agreed procedure for selection, unless there are special reasons justifying that breach.[203] Apart from this, it is accepted that it is up to the employer to determine the method of selection, as long as it is objective and rational.[204] From a procedural standpoint, employers should consult with both the union (if any) and affected employees before implementing redundancies, and should always examine the possibility of relocating redundant employees within the enterprise.[205]

There are two main forms of incapacity – illness and incompetence. In relation to illness the issue is whether it is reasonable to refuse to keep the job open any longer in light of the pressures on the business, the employee's length of service, the period the illness has lasted, and its likely future duration.[206] As regards incompetence, it will be unfair to dismiss an employee who has not been properly instructed, or made aware of what is expected. An employee should normally be warned if failing to achieve the required standard and afforded an opportunity to improve.[207]

Conduct justifying dismissal would embrace things like violence, dishonesty, insubordination, serious breach of company rules, lack of cooperation, persistent lateness, absenteeism, etc. It can cover conduct outside of work if this would attract unfavourable publicity to the employer, or reflects upon the fitness of the employee for the job,[208] e.g. someone caught shoplifting in another store. Misconduct need not actually be proved to have occurred if the employer believes that it has, has reasonable grounds for that belief, and has carried out reasonable investigation into the situation.[209] Clearly, it can be of great assistance to lay down rules governing misconduct, defining what kind of behaviour is unacceptable, what justifies instant dismissal or carries a lesser penalty, how penalties accumulate towards dismissal.

The category of 'some other substantial reason' is obviously intended to sweep up dismissals which are not caught by the other categories. It is often used, however, to justify the dismissal of employees who refuse to cooperate with a business reorganisation by permitting changes in their conditions of employment.[210]

Once an employer has established one of the potentially valid reasons, he must show he has acted reasonably in treating it as justifying dismissal. In other words, was dismissal within the range of reasonable responses open to a hypothetical reasonable employer? Germane to the question of reasonableness is the issue of procedure, i.e. proper investigation, hearing/consulting the employee, considering alternatives to dismissal. An otherwise fair dismissal can be rendered unfair by deficient procedure. It is only where it is obvious at the time of dismissal that observing a certain procedural step could not make any difference to the decision to dismiss that it will be reasonable to omit it.[211]

If an industrial tribunal finds an employee to be unfairly dismissed, it may order him to be reinstated or re-engaged or paid compensation.[212]

Transfer of Undertakings[213]

The legislation in this area applies where the right to run a business (or any part thereof which can function as a going concern) is transferred by sale or otherwise, e.g. assignation of a licence, or of the tenancy of a pub. The effect of the legislation is that any employee of the transferor who remains at the time of transfer is automatically transferred into the employment of the transferee. Indeed, this result follows even where an employee is dismissed prior to the transfer in order to prevent him being transferred.[214] If the transferee refuses to accept any of the transferred employees he is regarded as dismissing them. This can be serious since the transferred employees bring with them all the rights they had in relation to the transferor, including their periods of continuous employment. Moreover, the dismissal of an employee for a reason connected with the transfer is judged to be unfair unless it can be justified on 'economic, technical or organisational' grounds, i.e. some reason connected with the running of the business. Finally, employers should be wary of altering the terms of the contracts of transferred employees, since a *constructive* dismissal connected with a transfer is automatically unfair, unless the employee has in effect been given a new job.[215]

References

1. *Pharmaceutical Society of Great Britain v. Boots Cash Chemists (Southern) Ltd* [1953] 1 QB 401. Mispricing might have criminal consequences under the Consumer Protection Act 1987 see below.
2. s.8.
3. Unfair Contract Terms ss. 19 and 20.
4. s.17.
5. s.18.
6. s.16 Rule 1.
7. s.18 Rule 2.
8. s.18 Rule 4.
9. s.16.
10. s.18, Rule 5.
11. The retention of title clauses is often referred to as Romalpa clauses from the name of the case which first brought them to prominence, *Aluminium Industrie Vaassen BV v. Romalpa Aluminium Ltd* [1976] 1 WLR 676.
12. s.12.
13. [1923] 2 KB 500.
14. *Bishopsgate Motor Finance Corp. Ltd. v. Transport Brakes Ltd.* [1949] 1 K.B. 322 at 336.
15. *Report of the Crowther Committee on Consumer Credit* (1971), Cmnd 4596 p. 178.
16. s.24.
17. s.22.
18. In England the courts have said that asking the police and the Automobile Association to trace a car obtained by deception is enough. See *Car and Universal Finance v. Caldwell* [1964] 1 All ER 290. In Scotland this is not

considered sufficient and it seems that only informing the person who practised the deception will suffice. See *McLeod v. Kerr* 1965 SC 253.

19. s.13.
20. [1967] 1 WLR 1193.
21. *Re Moore and Co. Ltd. and Landauer and Co. Ltd.* [1921] 2 KB 519.
22. Unlike the implied term about description, these implied terms only apply where the sale is made in the course of a business so if someone buys an article privately it is not possible to complain under s. 14 that it is defective.
23. *Randall v. Newsom* (1876) 45 LJQB 364.
24. [1905] 1 KB 608.
25. See *Wilson v. Rickett, Cockerell & Co. Ltd.* [1954] 1 QB 598.
26. See *Wormell v. RHM Agriculture (East) Ltd* [1986] 1 WLR 336.
27. [1987] 1 WLR 1.
28. *Godley v. Perry* [1960] 1 WLR 9. In *Lee v. York Coach and Marine* [1977] RTR 35 the English Court of Appeal decided that a car which could not be driven lawfully and safely on the road was not of merchantable quality.
29. *Rogers v. Parish (Scarborough) Ltd* [1987] 2 WLR 353.
30. *Millars of Falkirk Ltd v. Turpile* 1976 SLT (Notes) 66 Court of Session.
31. *Crowther v. Shannon* (1975).
32. [1965] 1 WLR 101.
33. s.15.
34. Sale of Goods Act 1979 ss.34 and 35.
35. Sale of Goods Act 1979 s.59.
36. *Bernstein v. Pamson Motors (Golders Green) Ltd* [1987] 2 All ER 232.
37. As in *Godley v. Perry* [1969] 1 WLR 9 where a child lost an eye when a toy catapult broke.
38. *Jackson v. Chrysler Acceptances Ltd* [1978] 474.
39. J. K. Galbraith, *The Affluent Society* (1970) p. 167.
40. Consumer Credit Act 1974, s.39(1).
41. Ibid., s.40(1).
42. Ibid., s.189 and s.8.
43. Ibid., s.49.
44. Ibid., ss.60 and 61.
45. Ibid., s.75, see *United Dominions Trust v. Taylor* 1980 SLT 28.
46. Consumer Credit Act 1974, s.95 and Consumer Credit (Rebate on Early Settlement) Regulations 1983, S.I. 1983, no. 156; there are similar provisions in relation to consumer hire agreements.
47. Consumer Credit Act 1974, s.90. It is doubtful if under common law in Scotland it is ever lawful to repossess goods without a court order.
48. Consumer Credit Act 1974, s.87.
49. Ibid., ss.137–140.
50. Control of Misleading Advertisements Regulations 1968, S.I. No. 915.
51. SI 183, no. 1486.
52. The Food Act 1984 s.6 and the Food and Drugs (Scotland) Act 1956 s.6. 429.
53. The Medicines Act 1968 Parts V and VI.
54. See the Weights and Measures Act 1985.
55. Trade Descriptions Act 1968 s.14 see *Wings Ltd v. Ellis* [1985] AC 272.
56. s.20(1).
57. *Code of Practice for Traders on Price Indications*, DTI November 1968.
58. Broadcasting Act 1981 s.9.
59. Up to a maximum of £8925 at the time of writing, SDA 1975, S65(2) as amended; RRA 1976 s.56(2) as amended.
60. SDA 1975, s.6(1)(c).
61. RRA 1976, s.4(1)(c).

62. And religious grounds in Northern Ireland – Fair Employment Act 1976, Part III.
63. SDA 1975, s.38; RRA 1976, s.29; e.g. barman wanted; no coloureds need apply.
64. SDA 1975, s.39; RRA 1976, s.30.
65. SDA 1975, s.7; RRA 1976, s.5.
66. RRA 1976, s.5(2)(c).
67. Or a woman.
68. Or women.
69. SDA 1975, s.5(2)(c).
70. *Wylie v. Dee & Co (Menswear) Ltd* [1978] I.R.L.R. 103.
71. *Etam PLC v. Rowan* [1989] I.R.L.R. 150.
72. SDA 1975 s.1(1)(a) RRA 1976, s.1(1)(c); see also SDA 1975, s.2.
73. SDA 1975 s.3(1)(a); see *Coleman v. Skyrail Oceanic Ltd* [1981] I.C.R. 864.
74. SDA 1975, ss. 1(1)(b), 3(1)(b); RRA 1976, s.1(1)(b).
75. *Panesar v. Nestlé Co Ltd* [1980] I.R.L.R. 60.
76. *Hurley v. Mustoe* [1981] I.C.R. 490.
77. *Perera v. Civil Service Commission* [1983] I.C.R. 428.
78. SDA 1975, s.6; RRA 1976, s.4.
79. RRA 1976, s.1(2); but voluntary congregation need not be prevented – *P.E.L. Ltd v. Mogdill* [1980] I.R.L.R. 142.
80. *Porcelli v. Strathclyde Regional Council* [1986] I.R.L.R. 134; *De Souza v. Automobile Association* [1988] I.R.L.R. 87.
81. *Irving v. Post Office* [1987] I.R.L.R. 289.
82. SDA 1975, s.41; RRA 1976, s.32.
83. *Balgobin v. Tower Hamlets L.B.C.* [1987] I.R.L.R. 401.
84. SDA 1975, s.2(2).
85. Ibid., s.6(4).
86. See Social Security Act 1989 s.23 and Sch V.
87. *Barber v. Guardian Royal Exchange Assurance Group* [1990] I.R.L.R. 240.
88. *Schmidt v. Austick Bookshops Ltd* [1978] I.C.R. 85.
89. 79% – *Employment Gazette* 1989 185. Nearly half of all female employees work part-time ibid., 301.
90. *Clarke v. Eley (IMI) Kynoch Ltd* [1983] I.C.R. 165.
91. Compare *Home Office v. Holmes* [1984] I.R.L.R. 299; with *Clymo v. Wandsworth LBC* [1989] I.R.L.R. 241.
92. The main exceptions are protection against unlawful discrimination and dismissal for membership/non-membership of a trade union.
93. EP(C) A 1978 Sch. 13 para 6.
94. Ibid., para 4.
95. *Opie v. John Gubbins (Insurance Brokers) Ltd* [1978] I.R.L.R. 540.
96. EP(C)A 1978 s.1(1).
97. Ibid., s.4.
98. Ibid., s.1(2)–(6).
99. Ibid., s.2(1).
100. Ibid., s.2(3).
101. Ibid., s.4(1).
102. Ibid., s.4(2)–(3).
103. *Parkes Classic Confectionery v. Ashcroft* [1973] ITR 43.
104. *Jones v. Associated Tunnelling Ltd* [1981] I.R.L.R. 477.
105. *System Floors (U.K.) Ltd v. Daniel* [1981] I.R.L.R. 475.
106. EP(C)A 1978 s.11(2).
107. Ibid s.1(1).
108. *Mears v. Safecar Security* [1982] I.R.L.R. 185, but see *Eagland v. British Telecommunications PLC* [1990] I.R.L.R. 328, for a different approach.

109. The Retail Food and Allied Trades Wages Council, the Retail Trades (Non-Food) Wages Council, the Licensed Non-Residential Establishment Wages Council.
110. See H. C. Debs, 21st March 1989, vol. 149, No. 1479.
111. Wages Act 1986, s.14(1).
112. Ibid., s.12(3).
113. Ibid., s.16(2).
114. Ibid., s.16(1).
115. Ibid., Sch. 3, para 2; Wages Council (Notices) Regulations 1987 S.I. 1987/863, para 5.
116. 1987 Regulations, para 6.
117. On the powers of the Inspectorate see generally, Wages Act 1986, s.20.
118. Ibid., s.19.
119. See F. Davidson – A Guide to the Wages Act 1986, p. 44.
120. Ibid., ch. 2; The law also regulates in much the same way the exacting of payments from workers. Unfortunately the space does not exist to consider this subject in full.
121. Wages Act 1986, s.8(3).
122. Ibid., s.1(1)(a).
123. Ibid., s.1(3)(a).
124. Ibid., s.1(3)(b).
125. Ibid., s.1(1)(b).
126. Ibid., s.1(4)(a)–(b).
127. Ibid., s.2(3).
128. Ibid., s.2(1)–(2).
129. Ibid., s.4(1)–(2).
130. Ibid., s.5.
131. See *Employers' Statutory Sick Pay Manual*, N.I. 270 published by the DHSS.
132. See generally EP (C) A 1978, ss.8,9,11.
133. See generally Equal Pay Act 1970, ss.1,2,2A.
134. *Ainsworth v. Glass Tubes and Components Ltd* [1977] I.C.R. 347; A woman can compare herself with a man who used to do the job in question. *Macarthys Ltd v. Smith (No. 2)* [1980] I.R.L.R. 209.
135. Thus any alleged difference must not be illusory – *Dance v. Dorothy Perkins Ltd* [1978] I.C.R. 760.
136. *National Vulcan Engineering Insurance Group Ltd v. Wade* [1978] I.C.R. 800.
137. *Rainey v. Greater Glasgow Health Board* [1987] I.R.L.R. 26.
138. *Reed Packaging Ltd v. Boozer* [1988] I.C.R. 391.
139. Any premises where retail trade or business is carried on is a shop – restaurants, public houses, and hairdressers are included see s.74(1).
140. s.19(1) Sch. III, Part 2.
141. s.21; as to retailers' obligations in relation to opening hours and early closing Part I.
142. s.17.
143. ss.66,67; and see s.22(7).
144. See Part IV.
145. s.22.
146. See s.22(1)(b) (i)–(v).
147. The pharmacist must not be employed for more than two hours; must not have been employed on the previous Sunday and on one day (other than his half day) of either the previous week or the week beginning with the Sunday in question he must not be employed before 10.30 am or after 6.00 pm – s.22(1)(b)(v).
148. Children and Young Persons Act 1933, s.18.
149. See *Wilsons & Clyde Coal Co. v. English* [1938] A.C.57.

150. See *General Cleaning Contractors Ltd. v. Christmas* [1953] A.C.180.
151. See *Latimer v. A.E.C. Ltd.* [1953] A.C.643.
152. See *Davie v. New Merton Board Mills Ltd.* [1959] A.C. 604.
153. Employers' Liability (Defective Equipment) Act 1969.
154. See *Butler v. Fife Coal Co. Ltd.* [1913] A.C.149; *Hudson v. Ridge Manufacturing Co. Ltd.* [1957] 2 Q.B.348.
155. See *Brydon v. Stewart* (1855) 2 Macq 30.
156. s.2(1).
157. s.2(2)(a)–(e).
158. s.2(3).
159. Health and Safety Information for Employees Regulations 1989, s.2. 1989 1682.
160. Employers' Liability (Compulsory Insurance) Act 1969.
161. Fire Precautions Act 1971.
162. Fire Precautions (Non-Certificated Factory, Office, Shop and Railway Premises) Regulations 1976, s.1 1976/2010.
163. Health and Safety (First-Aid) Regulations 1981, S.I. 1981/917.
164. I.e. major fractures, amputation of foot, hand, finger or toe, loss of sight in eye, any other injury resulting in hospital stay of more than 24 hours unless purely for observation, etc. see Reporting of Injuries, Diseases and Dangerous Occurrences Regulations 1985. S.I. 1985/2023 para. 3(2).
165. See ibid., Sch. I.
166. Ibid., Sch. II.
167. Ibid., paras. 2–6, 7, 11.
168. s.1(3) – covers take aways, cafés, restaurants and pubs – but if the employee is exclusively engaged in making, assembling, repairing etc. any article in a particular part of the shop it may be regarded as a factory – see Factories Act 1961, s.175.
169. s.2(1).
170. s.4.
171. s.5.
172. s.6.
173. ss.7 and 8.
174. s.9; The conveniences need not be on the premises as long as they are reasonably accessible. Whether the level of provision is adequate will be determined by the Sanitary Conveniences Regulations 1964, S.I. 1964/966; Roughly, one w.c. may be provided if the number of persons working in the shop at any one time does not regularly exceed 5. Above that there must be separate provision for male and female employees, rising according to the number of each employed – see Sch. 2.
175. s.10; and see Washing Facilities Regulations 1964, S.I.1964/965.
176. s.11.
177. s.12.
178. s.13; If persons work in that part of the shop to which the public have access, the facilities will be regarded as unsuitable unless at least one seat is provided for every three employees, s.13(2).
179. s.14.
180. s.16.
181. s.17.
182. s.18.
183. Prescribed Dangerous Machine Order 1964, S.I. 1964/970 – mincing, mixing, chopping, slicing machines.
184. s.19.
185. See generally, Offices, Shops and Railways Premises (Hoists and Lifts) Regulations 1968, S.I.1968/849.

186. s.23(1), see also Children and Young Persons Act 1933, s.18(1)(f).
187. s.7.
188. *Lister v. Romford Ice and Cold Storage Co. Ltd.* [1957] A.C.555.
189. See EP(C)A 1978, Part IV.
190. *Gunton v. Richmond-upon-Thames LBC* [1980] I.C.R. 755.
191. See EP(C)A 1978 ss.55(2)(c), 83(2)(c); The coming to an end of a fixed term contract also counts as dismissal for redundancy and unfair dismissal purposes – ss.55(2)(b), 83(2)(b), but an employee under a fixed term contract of a year or more can contract out of his rights in relation to unfair dismissal, while an employee under a fixed term contract of two years or more can contract out of his right to a redundancy payment, provided in either case he so agrees in writing before the contract has expired – s.142.
192. See S. Anderman, *The Law of Unfair Dismissal* (2nd edn) pp. 63–88.
193. EP(C)A 1978 s.53.
194. Ibid., s.64(1)(a), 81(4).
195. Ibid., ss.64(1)(b), 82(1).
196. Ibid., s.81(2).
197. *Rank Xerox Ltd. v. Churchill* [1988] I.R.L.R. 280.
198. *Delanair Ltd. v. Mead* [1976] I.C.R. 522.
199. *Chapman v. Goonvean & Rostowrack China Clay Co. Ltd.* [1973] 1 W.L.R. 678.
200. *Haden Ltd. v. Cowen* [1983] I.C.R. 1.
201. EP(C)A 1978, s.84; The amount of a redundancy payment is worked out by a formula employing as variables (subject to upper limits) the employee's age, weekly earnings and period of continuous employment. The current maximum redundancy payment is £5520 EP(C)A 1978 Sch.IV; The parties can agree that the statutory rights should be enhanced under the contract.
202. Ibid., s.57; It is automatically unfair to dismiss someone for being/not being a member of a trade union – s.58.
203. Ibid., s.59.
204. *Buchanan v. Tilcon Ltd* [1983] I.R.L.R. 417.
205. *Freud v. Bentall Ltd.* [1982] I.R.L.R. 443; *Thomas & Betts Manufacturing Ltd. v. Harding* [1980] I.R.L.R. 255.
206. *Spencer v. Paragon Wallpapers Ltd.* [1976] I.R.L.R. 373.
207. *Mansfield Hosiery Mills Ltd. v. Bromley* [1977] I.R.L.R. 301.
208. *Moore v. C. & A. Modes* [1981] I.R.L.R. 71.
209. *British Home Stores Ltd. v. Burchell* [1978] I.R.L.R. 379.
210. *Martin v. Automobile Proprietary Ltd.* [1979] I.R.L.R. 64.
211. *Polkey v. E. A. Dayton Services Ltd.* [1988] I.C.R. 142.
212. EP(C)(A) 1978 ss.68–75 Compensation is currently subject to a maximum of £14 545 except where the dismissal is on grounds of membership/non-membership of a trade union or where the employer refuses to comply with an order of reinstatement or re-engagement.
213. See generally Transfer of Undertakings (Protection of Employment) Regulations 1981, S.I. 1981/1794.
214. *Litster v. Forth Dry Dock and Engineering Co. Ltd.* [1989] I.R.L.R. 161.
215. *Delabole Slate Ltd. v. Berriman* [1985] I.C.R. 546. Crawford v. Swinton Insurance Brokers Ltd [1990] I.R.L.R. 42.

Conclusions 11

'the changes in the structure of distribution
in the past 25 years have probably been both
faster and more far-reaching than in any similar
previous period, and the pace of changes shows no
signs of slackening.'

Monopolies and Mergers Commission, *Discounts to
Retailers* (London: HMSO, 1981, HC 311) para. 3.3.

11.1 Introduction

The purpose of this final chapter is to draw together the major themes of
retailing and retail management dealt with in the previous individual chapters
of the text. An opportunity is also taken to look at some particular
contemporary issues in retailing in the UK. Reflecting especially the concerns
of Part One of the text, the principal topics of this chapter are the continued
evolution of retailing, competitiveness and efficiency in retail distribution,
retailing corporate strategy, information technology, and international retailing.

11.2 The Continued Evolution of Retailing

In the case of many social and economic phenomena, the tendency for
contemporary observers is often to exaggerate the extent to which they are
living through a period of rapid, even 'revolutionary', change. At times the
pattern of retailing appears to have changed quite slowly. For all of the
developments in individual shops, multiple retailing and department stores in
the last decades of the nineteenth century, the picture painted by Jane Austen
in her last complete novel of 'the dash of other carriages, the heavy rumble of

carts and drays, the bawling of newsmen, muffin-men and milk-men, and the
ceaseless clink of pattens' on a wet afternoon in Bath in 1813 does not appear
to be much different from that of the 'conglomeration of narrow, cobbled
streets, terraced houses, cat-smelling tenements and gas-lit cabinet-making
workshops . . . [where] Jones' Dairy supplied milk direct from the cows they
housed in an adjoining stable' in the East End of London at the end of the
same century.[1] We noted, however, in Chapter 2 above that the past forty
years have witnessed very considerable changes in the pattern of retailing;
and it is impossible living in the 1990s to avoid feeling that retail distribution is
developing very rapidly. A number of 'models' have been developed which
try to build some system into the trend of development of retailing over time.
These models seek to provide an explanation for the direction of changes in
the pattern of retailing, and can be applied at different levels: from the retail
trade as a whole to individual stores.[2]

Three broad explanations of retailing change have been advanced. The first
of these focuses on changes in the general *environment* of retailing. Here it is
argued that changes in the social or economic environment – such as rising
standards of living, increased participation in the economy by women,
urbanisation of the population, or technological advances in transport,
refrigeration, economies of scale or information processing – result in adaptive responses by retail organisations. These institutions, individually or as a
whole, respond or adjust to their changing market environment: meeting the
needs of a better-informed, more affluent, or ageing or urbanised population,
and thereby change the pattern of retailing. In doing so retailers take
advantage of technological changes that enable them to transport and display
goods in different ways, organise individual stores differently, manage larger
shops or enterprises, and collect, store and process information more rapidly
or at lower cost. The results of these changes at one time or another have
been the development of multiple shop organisations and department stores,
mail-order shopping, discount stores, and edge/out-of-town shops. The
prevailing pattern of distribution will thus closely reflect the predominant
environmental features of the time; and retailing forms which fail to adapt
sufficiently (conventional department stores) or which are overtaken by
changes in consumer shopping habits or technology (traditional mail order)
will experience a reduction in their share of the retail market.

Adding to the environmental forces for change in the pattern of retailing is
competition among retailers. Successful competitors, it may be argued, are
those who are the first to recognise and capitalise upon environmental shifts.
Such change can often be attributed to entrepreneurial individuals: Gordon
Selfridge in the case of department stores, Sir Thomas Lipton in multiple-
shop grocery distribution, Michael Marks and the variety chain store, the
Fattorini family's Empire Stores and mail-order retailing, Sainsbury in the
case of self-service grocery stores, and more recent or present-day entrepreneurs such as George Davies with Next and Anita Roddick with the retail
franchise operation Body Shop. These individuals and their 'new' forms of

retailing took advantage of economic changes creating new classes of consumers, changes in transport and distribution and other technologies permitting new physical and organisational forms, evolutions in consumer taste, or the emergence of particular market segments. In doing so there has been a trend towards differentiating one total retail product from another, and a general tendency to trade up. Thus in terms, for example, of their merchandise, pricing policies and customer service etc. the early multiple stores, department stores, variety chains, specialist multiples, discount stores, modern superstores and the most recent specialist retailers such as Sock Shop have sought to differentiate themselves from predecessor competitors. In the process they have tended, as a reflection of increased economic standards of living, to move 'up market', emphasising choice and service etc. rather than price competition.[3]

A third, more sophisticated model, or class of models, of retailing evolution comprises a number of *'cyclical theories'*. Originators of these theories claim to recognise some form of cyclical pattern in the evolution of retailing: either in respect of the retail sector as a whole, a particular category of retailing, or individual retail organisations. These empirical observations are then built up inductively into a cyclical 'theory'. Thus the principle of the 'retail accordion' is based upon the fact that at a number of levels one can observe a 'general-specific-general' cycle of merchandise policy on the part of retailers over time. The better known 'wheel of retailing' theory posits that a tendency in retailing competition towards less emphasis upon price and more upon merchandise quality and product range is generally followed after a period by discount retailing or 'no frills' shopping, but that these organisations in turn mature into high cost/price retailers. Finally, it may be argued that particular retail forms such as the department store or discount organisation experience a product market life cycle. Under appropriate economic and other circumstances they are established and develop; but possibly as a result of environmental changes and competition from other retail forms they decline. Each of these three forms of cycle may be observed at the present time. Some retail sectors such as household furnishings or DIY are characterised by large 'generalist' organisations, while parts of the clothing sector are experiencing a rise of newer specialists. There is a general trend, after the popularity of electrical discount stores and cut-price grocery retailing of the late 1960s and early 1970s towards greater service and 'quality' competition in these areas;[4] and it would appear that the traditional variety chain store and department store formulae are coming to the end of their life cycles.

Given that the three basic models of retailing evolution – environmental, competitive and cyclical – almost certainly interact with each other, and that there may be different forms of cycle occurring simultaneously, how useful are these theories and how can they explain or predict retailing developments? These models highlight three corresponding features. First, given its place in the production–distribution channel, retailers have to be particularly alert to changes in the 'environment' as this term was used in the context of retailing strategy discussed in Chapter 4 above. This applies as much to changes in the general environment of the economy as whole, including social as well as economic factors, as to developments in the task environment of the individual retailer. Changes in demographics, economic wellbeing, spending patterns and styles of living affect retailers first and foremost. Thus the broad pattern of retailing must reflect the money that people have available to spend and the directions in which they choose to spend it. Second, within this 'macro' setting retailers will compete among each other for consumer spending, and thereby create the 'micro' environment determined by entrepreneurial decisions at the individual organisation level. The subject of retailing corporate strategy is the basis for such decisions. Third, it may be possible in all of these competitive responses to environmental change to discern cyclical patterns. Some of these, such as the product life cycle of retailing institutions, will be determined by corresponding developments in the environment dictating that certain broad retailing formats such as variety chain stores, department stores or mail order may be more or less appropriate to circumstances. The 'wheel of retailing' and the 'retail accordion' reflect cycles of competitive behaviour among retailers and the adoption of changing strategies.

11.3 Retail Competition

The theme of competition in retailing is important in three major respects. First, it is argued that it is through the forces of competition in retailing (including competition between different 'types' of retailer and the balance of competitive power between manufacturers and retailers) that consumers' best interests are served. Second, as was pointed out above in considering the evolution of the pattern of retailing, competition among retailers is a major determinant of the structure of this sector, and indeed of certain aspects of manufacturing industry structure. Third, an understanding of retailing competition is an important input into retailing strategy.

In the last analysis, so it is argued in a capitalistic society, it is upon competition among retailers as well as manufacturers that we rely to ensure that final consumers are satisfied in the most 'efficient' manner consistent with the standard of retail service that they wish. That further progress remains to be made in this area may be judged from some of the findings of the Office of Fair Trading report *Consumer Dissatisfaction*. A survey in 1985 revealed that 42 per cent of the adult population felt that they had some cause for dissatisfaction in consumer transactions over the previous twelve months. In the cases of furniture and floorcoverings, and household appliances 8.6 per cent and 9.4 per cent respectively of consumer expenditure gave rise to dissatisfaction.[5]

Competition among a range of retailers provides for a variety of retail services, and encourages the provision of this at the lowest cost. The consumer is thereby protected in an impersonal manner which obviates the cost (both to the general public and to individual litigants), delay and uncertainty involved in the use of the civil or criminal law in promoting the welfare of consumers. Thus despite the body of law relating to retailing and consumers, it is generally accepted that anomalies in the application of this law together with problems of enforcement deter the general public from adopting this avenue to ensure adequate service. The Office of Fair Trading itself recognised that 'It is well established that consumers are usually reluctant to pursue grievances by going to court, even when they have a good chance of success, largely because of the cost, uncertainty and delay involved';[6] while Smith and Swann, in their combined economic and legal analysis of the issue of consumer protection, concluded that 'we can understand the dismay with which a consumer views the prospect of a court appearance'.[7] There is a case, therefore, for both monitoring the effectiveness of consumer protection legislation, and also ensuring that the whole area of 'competition policy' is implemented to allow both structure and conduct in retail markets to operate for the benefit of consumers.

It was noted in Chapter 3 above how the way in which the various 'types' of competition (horizontal, vertical and intertype) have changed the structure of the retail sector and also the balance of trading relationships between retailers and manufacturers. Horizontal competition, between retailers of the same class of goods, offering the same type of service and having similar cost patterns, has a less obvious impact upon the structure of retail markets. This form of competition tends to take place either among traditional convenience goods stores such as conventional grocers or corner shops, each of which tends to enjoy something of a geographical monopoly, or among groups of shopping goods retailers such as jewellers or shoe retailers in more recognisable centres of retailing. Recently there has been a tendency for edge- or out-of-town shopping centres to develop where multiple superstores such as Queensway, B & Q, Texas, MFI or Great Mills can be found competing in their overlapping merchandise areas within quite a limited geographical area. Horizontal competition among shopping goods retailers is undoubtedly beneficial to consumers in terms of greater choice of merchandise and the ability to make price comparisons, and raises no particular issues regarding the restructuring of the retail sector.

By comparison, intertype competition between retailers offering different combinations of merchandise/service and having different cost structures, has given rise to concern regarding the 'fairness' of such competition, and the consequent impact upon vertical relationships between retailers and their suppliers. After a period, particularly during the 1950s and 1960s when there was a very significant shift in the balance of, for example, grocery trading between independent and multiple retailers, it is possible to look back on this as an inevitable development. As long as such intertype competition is 'fair', in that it does not involve deception of the consuming public in pricing, or blatant loss leader selling by large retail groups, then the resultant changes in the structure of retailing must be regarded as a reflection of advances in technology and shifts in consumer tastes. There is no doubt that consumers can benefit from the development of large, multiple shop retail organisations in terms of price levels; and there is evidence to suggest that even more than independent retail outlets, grocery multiples pass on their cost savings to consumers in the form of lower prices.[8] This does not, however, entirely dispose of the problem of the small, independent shop whose particular difficulties were considered separately in Chapter 5.

This brings us to the vexed issue of vertical competition between retailers and their suppliers, and in particular whether 'discrimination' by suppliers in affording trade discounts to large retailers which go beyond a reflection of cost or other economies involved in dealing with them are detrimental to public welfare. We noted in considering the role of the small, independent retailer that a case had been made for restricting the power of large distributors in this respect on the grounds that in the long term it was likely to be detrimental to the public interest insofar as it encouraged undue market concentration among retailers, drove smaller retail competitors from the market regardless of their efficiency, and 'undermines the health and viability of manufacturing industry'.[9] The Monopolies and Mergers Commission on the other hand took the laconic view that 'Concessions made by a manufacturer to strong buyers may be said to be commercially justifiable in the sense that, if they were not, the manufacturer would not have made them'.[10] A fair conclusion on this issue must be that unusual Scottish jury verdict of 'not proven', if only because of the horrendous econometric problem of testing whether, for example, manufacturers can and do effectively recoup 'excessive' trade discounts granted to larger retail buyers by general increases in price or a narrowing of trade discounts to smaller buyers.[11]

The hegemony of large-scale retailers has had ramifications beyond the terms of trade between suppliers and their distributors. Increased retailer concentration has certainly been an influence on the trend towards third-party physical distribution in retailing as large stores such as Tesco, Sainsbury and Asda have implemented systems of centralised supply from a limited number of large depots. This has led to the demise of manufacturer delivery fleets and the growth of outside distributors such as BRS, SPD (part of the National Freight Consortium) and TNT.[12]

Retailers have also had a more direct influence on manufacturers as, for example, they come to play an increased role in product innovation *vis-à-vis* processors of food products.[13] In the furniture trade it has been held that it was the emergence of large-scale retailers and their reluctance to accept the perceived poor quality of British goods or to deal with a 'cottage industry' of suppliers that led to a significant rise in imports in this sector and the consequent loss of market share (and jobs) on the part of British firms.[14] A more detailed study looked at this same issue across the range of consumer goods industries. It recognised in particular the role of distributors, and especially large-scale retailers, in determining what goods are offered to final consumers. It would certainly appear that concentration among UK retailers does make it easier for importers to penetrate consumer markets than would be the case in an economy with a fragmented retailing sector; and equally, large-scale retailers in the UK may be tempted to look abroad to more significant suppliers on the grounds that were suggested above in the particular case of furniture. The conclusion of this study of the period 1974–85 was, however, that the role of large-scale retailers in increasing import penetration had been greatly exaggerated.[15]

Competition, in retail markets no less than in others, is the focal point of strategic decision making; and the clearer an understanding that management has of the nature of competition in a sector the better the basis of its corporate strategy. The competitive 'five forces framework' which was used as a focus in Chapter 3 for analysing retail competition is taken from the literature on corporate strategy. The sources of competitive impact upon individual retailers, the strength of these and the manner in which they are operated by other sellers in the market, potential entrants, suppliers and customers, taken together influence retailer's generic strategies on growth, diversification and integration in the market as well as more detailed choices of market segmentation, merchandise, facilities and customer services.

Competition and competitiveness is therefore a vital setting within which retailing activities occur. A number of dimensions of this have been changed quite significantly over the past few years by advances in information technology. A separate section is therefore now devoted to this before we turn to conclusions regarding corporate strategy in retailing.

11.4 Retailing Information Technology

Information technology – the gathering, processing, storage, retrieval, display and communication of information or data, normally by means of microprocessor equipment – is an increasingly important aspect of retailing management at both the strategic and operational levels. Advances in science and engineering have greatly reduced the cost and increased the reliability of the equipment involved.[16] Recent surveys forecast an increase in information technology spending by retailers, with a rise in the number of EPOS terminals in Britain from 58 000 in 1986 to 410 000 in 1993; and it was estimated that 3000 UK grocery stores, representing 75 per cent of total food turnover, would be scanner-operational by 1990.[17] In broad terms information technology (IT) can be used to improve both the strategic and the operational dimensions of an organisation as shown in Table 11.1. More specifically with regard to retailing, IT can be adopted in the areas shown in Table 11.2.

The usefulness of IT is to add value to the operations of the organisation and to allow the firm to implement its chosen strategy and

Table 11.1
Strategic and Tactical Opportunities for Information Technology

---

Strategic opportunity
- Possibility to build barriers to entry
- Possibility to build-in switching costs
- Possibility to change the basis of competition
- Possibility to change balance of power in supplier relationships
- Possibility to generate new products
- Possibility to change organisational objectives

Tactical/Operational opportunities
- Cost reductions and efficiency increases
- Elimination/reduction of clerical effort
- More timely information
- Greater flexibility
- New opportunities for practice
- 'New integrated systems'
- Less idiosyncratic judgements
- Reduction of co-ordination problems

SOURCES: M. Wright and D. Rhodes, *Manage IT!* (London: Frances Pinter, 1985) p. 31

---

merchandise policy in the most efficient manner. Retailers who most rapidly and efficiently adopt IT will gain a significant competitive advantage over other firms.

Strategy

IT offers retailers opportunities both to provide new products or services to their customers and also to change the structure of the market to their advantage. 'Home shopping' – allowing customers to view a range of priced articles from a catalogue on a screen in their homes, to order these by computer or telephone communication from the retailer, and to receive delivery within a matter of days – is really a sophisticated version of mail-order buying. This use of IT does, however, offer consumers a much more convenient service and has the potential for adoption in a number of areas of retailing.[18]

Table 11.2
Information Technology in Retailing

Strategy	Offering new 'products' or services – home shopping, EFTPOS
	Increasing retailer power over suppliers
Planning	Modelling of store and consumer behaviour
	Making 'what if' decisions
Analysis	Processing of market research information forecasting
	Immediate feedback on sales through 'bar coded' information
	Supplier monitoring
	Direct product profitability
Service	Reducing checkout queues
	Reducing the incidence of 'out of stock'
Operations	Faster checkout throughput
	Linking of sales, inventory and purchase orders
	Reduced stockholding

EFTPOS (electronic funds transfer at point of sale) is close to implementation despite reported retailer reluctance to adopt this, as a means of allowing retail customers to have their checkout bill settled immediately by an electronic transfer of funds from their bank or building society account to that of the retailer.[19] The advantages of this are improved service for customers and (one supposes) increased security of funds transfer compared with stolen chequebooks or credit cards. The cost of any EFTPOS system will fall very largely upon retailers themselves; and their present reluctance to move beyond small-scale local experiments suggests that they are weighing up carefully the strategic advantages against the capital costs.

In addition to making a strategic contribution to retailing through adding value to services, IT can be taken advantage of to change the competitive structure of the market in favour of retailers. In this context IT can be used to change relationships with both suppliers and competitors. The retailer is able to exert the power of possession of information over suppliers in the market chain because he is adjacent (physically, in trading terms, and psychologically or sociologically) to the customer, because he has easier and less costly access to information on consumer behaviour, and because the activities of gathering, processing and analysing the relevant information have decreased in cost in real terms as a result of the applications of IT.[20] In particular, by taking advantage of EPOS data on suppliers, retailers can carry out much more immediate and accurate supplier evaluation in terms of speed of turnover of goods, sales margins realised, and comparative prices, delivery performance and trade credit among suppliers. Sophisticated analysis of this information, such as the direct product profitability (DPP) system adopted by Boots amongst others, allows retailers, for example, to find out whether a new product line is increasing total sales or simply taking custom away from existing products in the shop; and can also be used to calculate the *net* profitability of product lines after allowing for various forms of 'shrinkage', warehousing costs etc. As retailers keep ahead of their suppliers in this respect their bargaining power is correspondingly enhanced.

EPOS affects the competitive structure in the retailing sector by increasing the incidence of scale economies arising from IT investment, and also creating large initial capital and knowledge requirements for entry into the sector. Both of these phenomena are likely to operate to the disadvantage of the smaller retailer, and also increase the emphasis in retailing upon sales growth and absolute size against which to write off the investment and overhead costs of IT.

Retailers are not likely to be in a position to dominate their customers through the use of IT; although wholesalers can do so by tying, say, voluntary group retailer customers to the wholesaler's computer-based ordering system and thus increasing the 'switching' costs of the former.

Planning

Use of IT allows retailers to develop 'models' of their operation for planning purposes. These may relate to consumer behaviour or cash flows, and may be easily manipulated to ask 'What if?' questions in respect of changes in overall consumer spending patterns or interest rates in the economy.

W. H. Smith has spent £250 000 on a system combining EPOS and CAD (computer-aided design) which allows it to model on a computer screen the interior of any one of its 365 UK stores. This involves in part modelling consumer behaviour in a store (distinguishing, for example, between adults and children), and seeking to maximise the net profit per square foot by changing the store layout on the screen – 'What if . . . ?' – to arrive at the optimally designed store.[21]

Analysis

Much of planning depends, of course, upon access to relevant information. General and task environment information is broadly available in conventional form to all retailers. IT, however, allows individual retailers much more cheaply and quickly to process their own market research data, and through EPOS reading of bar-coded information to gather and analyse data on sales and profit performance. Such analysis allows retailers to know not only how much of a particular product line is bought over a period of time, but also how often it is bought, at what time of the day or week, in what size of pack, as part of how large a single transaction or 'till', along with what other items, and possibly, with the advent of EFTPOS, by whom or at least what type of customer. The danger here is almost that of information overload.

Direct Product Profitability or DPP was mentioned above as having a contribution to make in increasing retailer power over suppliers as a result of distributors having more detailed information on product profitability and suppliers' terms. DPP has benefited enormously from the adoption of IT. This technique now permits the retailer to attribute to each product or product category the direct warehouse, transport and in-store costs associated with it. Allowance can also be made for direct revenues such as special manufacturer deals, prompt payment discounts etc. The retailer can thus arrive at an accurate refined margin or direct product profit; and this should influence merchandise decisions as well as directing the search for increased efficiency of store operations.[22] It was reportedly on the basis of DPP analysis that Boots made its original decision to drop pet foods from its product range.[23]

In terms of differentiating the product range, IT, and EPOS data in particular, is allowing retailers to tailor individual store merchandise ranges to local markets. While a 'core' of merchandise may be dictated for each store within a group by head office, 'micro marketing' provides for particular additions to this by individual branches on the basis of local differences in socioeconomic and competitive variables.[24] Dixons – the largest UK electronic, photographic and domestic electrical appliances chain – is using IT to implement its 'Operation Reap', which is designed not only to increase operating efficiency by, for example, reducing stockholding levels but also to customise the merchandise and pricing policies of individual stores on the basis of local socioeconomic and competitive variables.[25]

Service

In some cases there may be only a small distinction between offering consumers additional service related to the existing product and offering a new product. The latter was considered above under the heading of Strategy; while here we consider how existing retailer services to consumers may be improved by the use of IT.

Check-out queues should certainly move faster with EPOS, and eventually EFTPOS, systems. Equally, more efficient monitoring of stock positions and reordering should allow retailers to reduce, and possibly eliminate, the incidence of 'out of stock'. With the increased knowledge of their customers which IT can provide, retailers can identify the needs of individual customers and increase the level of personal service. This can be applied to motor car and domestic electrical appliance sales as well as having ready access to the measurements of existing customers in the area of bespoke tailoring. Mail-order retailers are using their databases on existing agents and customers to target sales more specifically: sending outsize ladies' clothing catalogues only to those who previously ordered larger sizes, targeting home electrical offers to previous buyers of videos, and not sending gardening catalogues to those living in flats.[26] In each of these cases IT allows retailers to provide a 'differentiated' service to customers at lower cost as well as economising on marketing efforts.

Also included in the 'service' which almost all major retailers provide is the store credit card, whose provision again reflects advances in IT. These are generally held to increase store loyalty and sales as well as providing retailers with a great deal of useful marketing information; but the efficient operation of such schemes depends much upon IT.

Operations

It is in the area of operations that the most obvious advantages of IT appear to retailers. Retail distribution is, after all, an information intensive operation. The larger mixed retail businesses (former variety chain stores) have over 50 000 product lines to manage, W. H. Smith has 60 000 product lines, a modern Tesco unit has 18 000 lines, and Sainsbury customers buy well over 100m items each week.[27] Furthermore, although rationalisation by individual retailers has sometimes reduced these numbers – Woolworth moved from 50 000 lines bought from 8000 key suppliers in 1982 to 20 000 lines and 1000 key suppliers in 1988[28] – the trend in food retailing, as Fernie points out, is for product lines to have proliferated as superstores have increased in size. In 1987 an average superstore accommodated around 10 000 product lines in its 30 000 sq. ft., compared with 4000 product lines in an average 17 000 sq. ft. a decade earlier.[29] Retailers on this scale buy from a large number of suppliers (each of whom is being monitored by the retailer), and sell to millions of individual customers each year, each of whom expects products to be accurately priced on the shelves and passed quickly through the check-out, and to be provided with an accurate bill for the shopping basket of goods.

EPOS equipment allows retailers to establish a link between goods passing out of the store, an accurate count of stock on the shelves or in warehouses, and efficient ordering from suppliers based upon their delivery times, store turnover and economic-order-quantity calculations. Reduced stockholding levels and more efficient ordering and delivery follow from this. So far as labour cost savings are concerned, this type of IT equipment reduces the amount of staff time that has to be spent checking stock on shelves, increases throughput at the check-out, and also reduces the scope for human error at this stage through accidental mischarging or check-out operators passing goods out at lower prices to friends – known in the trade as 'sweethearting'.

One other application of IT to the information-intensive area of retailing is electronic shelf labelling. This involves electronic shelf-edge labelling through liquid crystal displays (LCD) instead of plastic labels. Individual units of merchandise are no longer priced (thus reducing store labour costs), and the content of the individual LCDs is controlled centrally in the store or even the group, with the facility to change prices rapidly and at very low cost in response, for example, to the pattern of sales. Electronic shelf labelling has yet to take off in the UK; but as costs fall and reliability increases, this too will become a standard part of retailing.

IT, therefore, has an important role to play in retailing management and retailer competitiveness at a number of levels: from contributing to strategic analysis through to improving operational efficiency. In addition to permitting the creation of new retail products or services, IT in particular allows for proactive retailing strategy through providing relevant decision-making information at increased speed and reduced cost. In order to benefit from this, however, retail management must build IT into the corporate strategy of the organisation.[30] Indeed, some writers would go so far as to suggest that one has to create a business-wide IT culture: one in which the business as a whole is thought of as a 'system', with individual functions such as purchasing, stockholding, sales, etc. being seen as sub-systems.[31]

Retailing management has also to confront certain organisational issues arising from the introduction of IT. The adoption of IT systems centralises decision making over which there was previously greater discretion further down the organisation.[32] Check-out operators and even store managers will experience a considerable erosion of responsibility and interest in their jobs as the tasks of the former become increasingly automated and the merchandise, pricing and display decisions of the latter are made centrally in the store organisation on the basis of computer-controlled information and models. In Walters's view 'Field and branch operations management have already become disillusioned (and possibly have been so for some time) as an increasing amount of responsibility (and job satisfaction) has been transferred into a centralised organisation structure.[33] These organisational and staff motivation issues will have to be overcome if retail management is to obtain the maximum advantage from the adoption of IT.

11.5   Retailing Corporate Strategy

Chapter 4 in this text, dealing with retailing corporate strategy, was perhaps inevitably the longest, being concerned with the fundamental, long-term managerial decision making in retail organisations. Decisions in this area must be based upon the economic and institutional environment of the trade, the nature of competition, and the legal and planning framework of retailing; and from these strategic decisions follow merchandising and marketing strategies, organisation structure and human resource management policies, together with physical distribution management decisions.

Strategy making in retailing, and the merchandising and marketing decisions that follow from it, assume particular importance in the context of three significant current characteristics of the retail trade. First, as was emphasised in Chapter 4 above, retailers operate at the end of the production–distribution chain adjacent to consumers, and therefore have to respond rapidly to changes in the pattern of consumption in the economy. At the present time the retail trade is faced with two significant features in this respect. Not only is the age structure of the population undergoing a great change, but retailing expenditure is increasingly fluid and unpredictable. The rapid decline in the birth rate in the UK, particularly since 1965, has produced a situation where, for example, by the end of this century there will be two million more middle-aged consumers and two million fewer in the 15–24 years age group, with consequent significant changes in total spending patterns.[34] This demographic change is superimposed upon a general trend to affluence and individuality in society which many observers consider will see the end of mass markets and of more stable – and thus relatively easily forecastable – patterns of retail expenditure. As the American investment bank Goldman Sachs put it in the context of the UK market,

> It should never be forgotten that as living standards rise, so the degree by which retail spending can be switched from one area to another is increased. Once you have enough clothes on your back, food to eat and chairs to sit on, it becomes quite discretionary as to where you choose to spend any extra income.[35]

Retailing, as Walters puts it, has been affected by an 'expressive revolution' where:

> Because of the demographic and socio-economic changes that have occurred, aspirations and expectations feature largely in consumers' buying motives. Large groups of consumers seek to use their purchasing behaviour to express their views of themselves. In an age of conspicuous consumption the marketing opportunities are often based more upon consumer attitudes than on anything else.[36]

In this situation retailers have to concentrate upon knowing and understanding their customers as much as the products which they sell. This has greatly increased the significance of strategic and marketing skills in retailing; and has led to widely varied and changing strategies, embracing the 'low-cost' approach of the expanding Kwik Save group in groceries and Ratner in the jewellery market, the customer and merchandise focus of 'lifstyle' retailers such as Next, Body Shop etc., the increased diversification of Marks & Spencer, W. H. Smith and Boots along with Kingfisher (Woolworth),[37] as well as the differentiation strategy of the remaining department stores and firms such as Sainsbury in the grocery sector.

This leads on to the second important characteristic of contemporary retailing organisations: one also highlighted in Chapter 4, and which again increases the importance of the corporate strategic dimensions of retailing management. The largest retailing organisations now comprise portfolios of businesses or strategic business units; and this trend is likely to continue despite examples in the mid and late 1980s of the break-up of some diversified firms such as Asda–MFI and the Harris Queensway group, and Gateway's disposal of its Linfood cash-and-carry subsidiary and its Spanish super-markets. Large, diversified retail organisations – most of the major retail groups have overseas subsidiaries, and in the case of Next and Marks & Spencer as well as Littlewoods they embrace mail-order operations in addition to shops – need to think and manage strategically. They require to plan in terms of corporate objectives, the analysis of their environment and resources, the identification of individual strategic business unit strategies, and organisation structures and other features designed to ensure efficient implementation of strategies. Unfortunately not all retail organisations appear to have lived up to these requirements. It may be, as one 'quality' newspaper put it, an excess of those dominant City emotions of fear and greed that drove the p/e ratios of Next, Storehouse, Harris Queensway and Dixons down from an average of 36.3 to 9.3 in 1988;[38] but it would seem that retailing requires strong injections of strategic thinking and sound manage-ment as well as flair if it is to be successful. Sir Phil Harris himself, while still chairman of Harris Queensway prior to its acquisition by James Gulliver's Lowndes Group in the middle of 1988, admitted that 'It became apparent that the rapid expansion of prior years had not been matched by our ability to manage and control the business';[39] and the *Financial Times* comment in the wake of George Davies's dismissal by the board of Next as its chairman and chief executive in December 1988 was particularly trenchant.

> Like an alarming number of retailing heroes before him, Mr. George Davies appears to have been an autocrat, who could not delegate and was not sufficiently watchful of the bottom line. In short, he may have been an asset at the head of a small fashion chain, but at the top of a major retailing company he appears to have become a liability.[40]

In addition to those examples, at the time of writing, the Gateway grocery supermarket group (the third largest in terms of market share) and Store-house (embracing BHS, Mothercare, Richards and Habitat) are now under close scrutiny by investment analysts and potential predators. In both cases the criticism is essentially that the incumbent management is not operating the stores' assets sufficiently well, particularly in the aftermath of merger and acquisition.[41]

The third characteristic of the medium term for the retail sector is an increased competitiveness of its general environment. The 1980s saw a significant decline in the proportion of total consumer expenditure going into retailing. This trend began in the 1970s when the diversion of consumer expenditure to foreign holidays, housing and leisure pursuits resulted in retailers' share of consumers' disposable income falling from 41.4 per cent in 1971 to 36.4 per cent in 1980.[42] Data relating to the 1980s are set out below in Table 11.3.

Table 11.3
Personal Disposable Income, Expenditure and Retail Sales 1980–89 (£m at current values)

	Total personal disposable income £m	Total consumer expenditure £m		Total retail sales £m	
1980	160 317	137 324	(85.7%) *	58 377	(42.5%) *
1981	176 260	153 423	(87.0%)	63 164	(41.2%)
1982	191 281	168 545	(88.1%)	68 359	(40.6%)
1983	206 132	184 619	(89.6%)	74 664	(40.4%)
1984	220 899	197 494	(89.4%)	80 677	(40.9%)
1985	238 804	215 535	(90.3%)	87 920	(40.8%)
1986	256 940	237 369	(92.4%)	95 657	(40.3%)
1987	275 684	259 326	(94.1%)	104 009	(40.1%)
1988	303 400	289 840	(95.5%)	114 648	(39.6%)
1989	352 097	328 453	(93.3%)	122 736	(37.4%)

* Percentage of previous column.

SOURCE: CSO, *Monthly Digest of Statistics* (London: HMSO).

In summary, these figures show that while in money terms Total Personal Disposable Income rose by 119.6 per cent over the period, Total Consumer Expenditure rose by 139.2 per cent, and Total Retail Sales by 110.2 per cent. In real terms the 1988 index of Total Personal Disposable Income (1980 = 100) was 118.6, and the corresponding index numbers for Total Consumer Expenditure and Total Retail Sales were 132.2 and 138.7 respectively.

However, although the volume of retail sales, as reflected in the increase in real expenditure, rose at more than twice the rate of consumer disposable income, the proportion of total consumer expenditure feeding through into retail spending fell fairly steadily from 42.5 per cent to 37.4 per cent over the period 1980–89. Total retail sales volume was only able to increase to the extent that it did over the period because of the significant rise – from 85.7 per cent to 93.3 per cent – in the ratio of total consumer expenditure to disposable income. The level of total retail expenditure in the economy is thus increasing only as personal disposable income rises (which in turn is dependent upon an expansion of national income or a reduction in personal taxation) and as a greater proportion of this is spent, or added to by an expansion of consumer credit. It is not likely that we can imagine significant annual increases in the national income (or further reductions in the levels of personal taxation), nor a further significant decline in the personal savings ratio (or corresponding rise in consumer credit).[43] The result is that as a marginally declining proportion of consumer expenditure goes into retailing, retailers face a less buoyant general economic environment in the foreseeable future.

Within this threatened general environment retail markets are character- ised by oligopolists pursuing expansionist strategies, leading to the likelihood of oversupply certainly of floorspace in the market. Hence the *Financial Times* comment on the stores sector being characterised by 'a profits performance grossly impaired by massive overcapacity and competition'.[44] For retailing as a whole, the top ten firms account for an estimated 27 per cent of total sales, and in the food trades the top four non-co-operative firms (Sainsbury, Tesco, Argyll and Asda) account for half of the total.[45] Invest- ment in the sector has been expanding dramatically: one estimate has put this at 15 per cent per annum in real terms since 1982, as retailers have expanded floorspace and invested in both design and information technology. More- over, although in the food trades an estimated three quarters of the growth among the top five firms has been 'bought' through acquisition, a number of retailers in this category are still expanding internally through store openings. Sainsbury, for example, opened sixteen new supermarkets in 1987 and a further eighteen in 1988, and presently plans to open an additional twenty stores in 1991.[46] The result of this is bound to be an intensification of competition among large-scale retailers in particular, and the expansion of some retailers has equally been matched by redundancies and the need for financial restructuring on the part of established firms such as the Burton Group, Rumbelows, MFI, and Lowndes Queensway.[47]

Clearly, the combination of a deteriorating and increasingly complex general environment, expansionist plans on the part of some retailers and a context of oligopolistic competition is going to demand increased strategic sophistication on the part of retailers in the 1990s.

11.6 International Retailing

One of the most significant current trends in retailing is the internationalisa- tion of the operations of many of the largest retail organisations. In the past the more important international dimension of retailing was the spread to various economies of new forms of retailing such as the department store or hypermarket retailing.[48] At the present time, however, there is now a significant number of retail organisations that may be described as multina- tional – i.e. having direct investment in a number of different economies; and although this phenomenon is not new – both F. W. Woolworth and Sears & Roebuck were operating multinationally by the early decades of this cen- tury – a number of factors are presently operating to increase the trend to multinational retailing.

Among the most obvious 'push' factors encouraging UK retailers to expand by investing overseas are the reduction in the rate of growth in retail spending in this country (arising from slower population growth and GDP expansion), the maturity of many retail markets themselves, severe oligopolistic competition in a number of sectors of retailing, and saturation of retail floorspace provision. Corresponding 'pull' factors are the existence of higher-growth or less developed retail markets in other economies, opportunities to export a successful retailing formula, the risk-spreading benefits of overseas diversification, and a managerial desire to build a global retail business or to respond to particular events such as the final creation of a single European market at the end of 1992.[49] To this latter list should perhaps be added the increasingly internationally homogeneous nature of some branches of retailing, at least in more developed economies, and advances in transport and information technology which have reduced the costs of the movement of physical goods and information across geographical distances.

It is generally accepted that the more influential pressures upon UK retailers to expand overseas have been push factors. None the less, niche retailers such as Laura Ashley and Body Shop, or those such as Marks & Spencer which claim that they have a unique and exportable retailing formula, may be responding more to pull factors. Retail consumers in the UK have correspondingly benefited from the incursions of the Belgian GB-Inno-BM's Homebase DIY warehouses, the Italian Benetton in the sports goods sector, Swedish IKEA furniture stores, and most recently the German firm Aldi in discount grocery retailing.

As one might expect, multinationalisation strategies vary among retailers. While those such as Sock Shop and Laura Ashley offering a particular retailing formula expanded organically, more or less duplicating their UK retailing format overseas, others have bought existing retail operations in other countries as a more secure means of entering such markets. Examples of the latter strategy in the United States include Sainsbury's Shaws Supermarkets Inc., Dee Corporation's Herman's Sporting Goods chain, and even Marks & Spencer's 1988 acquisitions of the Brooks Brothers up-market clothing chain and Kings Supermarkets.

Within a broad strategy of seeking to achieve corporate goals with an appropriate level of control over foreign operations and dealing with the risks likely to be incurred, a number of 'models' of retail multinationalisation have been developed.[50] These distinguish, for instance, between the extent of the financial risk involved, the geographical spread of investment, the degree of central control maintained over foreign operations, and the contrast between reproducing overseas a successful UK retailing formula and adopting an individual 'local' presence in each host economy. Salmon and Tordjman, for example, distinguish between an *investment* strategy which involves taking a purely financial stake in existing overseas retail operations, a *multinational* strategy of setting up autonomous affiliates in a number of overseas economies which respond very much to the social and economic characteristics of the individual countries, and a *global* strategy, described as 'the faithful replication of a (retailing) concept abroad'.[51] Treadgold adopts a geographic-strategic scale spanning the more tentative 'border hopping' of *concentrated internationalisation*, the greater diversity of *dispersed internationalisation*, the increased scale of overseas operations of the *multinational retailer*, and, as in the case of the previous model, the almost world-wide presence of the *global retailer*.[52] This author then combines these various degrees of international commitment with market entry and managerial control styles to characterise retailers with overseas operations along a spectrum from 'cautious internationalists' to 'world powers'.[53] Retailers thus clearly have considerable choices open to them in adopting and implementing international strategies, depending upon their corporate goals, attitudes to risk, resource base and preferred management style.

As indicated in Chapter 4 above in considering multinational operations as a strategic option, this form of retailer growth is not without its pitfalls. Operations may often take much longer than anticipated to build up due to unforeseen differences in shopper preferences between economies, or an underestimation of the power of established competitors. Despite the considerable success over a number of years in the UK of the Next retailing formula, the firm was not able to translate this into overseas operations on a 'global' basis and closed down its four German stores after only eighteen months.[54] John Menzies opened its first Early Learning Centre in the United States in 1986 but has yet to realise any profits from this;[55] and Boots disposed of its 170 Canadian stores in 1988 having similarly failed to achieve adequate returns.[56]

The build-up and present scale of overseas operations by UK retailers, combined with the difficulties and lack of success of some of these ventures, means that '1992' is unlikely to see a major unleashing of further foreign investment by British retailers. As one study of these prospects pointed out, shopping is still an essentially domestic activity, with strong national differences in spending patterns and consumer tastes.[57] None the less, higher rates of economic growth in many other countries, and the move towards a single European market of some 320m consumers, will continue to exert a combination of push and pull forces encouraging major UK retailers to think in terms of multinational strategies. This trend will add further to the complexity of retail management and also create a greater distinction between the management characteristics of larger and small retailers.

11.7   Conclusions

This text has been concerned with the major issues in retailing and retail management in the UK. It has shown that over a period of three or four hundred years, and particularly since the last decades of the nineteenth century, retailing has emerged as a distinct part of the economy. It now forms an important part of total economic activity in the UK; and contemporary retailing organisations are large and complex businesses. It follows from this situation both that the efficiency with which this sector of the economy operates is important for consumer welfare, and related to this, that retailing organisations require considerable sophistication in their management. Hence the emphasis in the text both upon an analysis of the retailing sector through a consideration of its history, the role of competition and of government control in retailing, and also upon the management of retailing businesses large and small, not only through a consideration of corporate strategy in retailing but also merchandising and marketing decisions, physical distribution management, personnel and organisation structure issues, and the role of the law in retailing management.

It is hoped that the coverage of the issues in this text has indicated how worthy of such study the retail sector of the UK is at the present time, and that it may be a contribution both to a greater understanding of this area of economic activity and the efficient management of its consistuent business organisations.

References

1. Jane Austen, *Persuasion* (London: John Murray, 1818) Ch. 14; Harry Blacker, *Just Like it Was – Memoirs of the Mittel East* quoted in D. Clutterbuck and M. Devine, *Clore – The Man and his Millions* (London: Weidenfeld & Nicolson, 1987) p. 5.
2. This section draws upon two reviews of the literature in this area by Stephen Brown: 'Institutional Change in Retailing: A Review and Synthesis', *European Journal of Marketing*, 1987, Vol. 21, No. 6, pp. 5–36; and 'The Wheel of the Wheel of Retailing', *International Journal of Retailing*, 1988, Vol. 3, No. 1, pp. 16–37.
3. See A. Goldman, 'The Role of Trading-up in the Development of the Retailing System', *Journal of Marketing*, January 1975, pp. 54–62.
4. On this see in particular the case study on Asda Stores in D. W. Walters, *Strategic Retailing Management* (London: Prentice-Hall, 1988) pp. 50–60. An interesting contemporary example of the continued retailing revolution in the grocery field as the UK economy slows down in the 1990s is the arrival in this country of the German discount retailer Aldi whose strategy runs counter to the trend until recently in this sector of retailing to trade up. The advent of this new strategy may reflect both macroeconomic factors in the general *environment* and also a *wheel* effect as Aldi joins Kwik Save in adopting a low priced/reduced service grocery retailing strategy in contrast to the major grocery chains which in *competition* with each other have moved up market. See *Financial Times*, 6 September 1990.
5. See Office of Fair Trading, *Consumer Dissatisfaction* (London: OFT, 1986) paras 2.3, 3.19 and Table 4. Similar evidence arises in the more recent OFT report *Fair Deal* (London: OFT, 1988).
6. Office of Fair Trading, *A General Duty to Trade Fairly* (London: OFT, 1986) para. 1.10.
7. P. Smith and D. Swann, *Protecting the Consumer* (Oxford: Martin Robertson, 1979) p. 245.

8. See the evidence in Monopolies and Mergers Commission, *Discounts to Retailers* (London: HMSO, 1981, HC 311) Appendix 6, para. 13.
9. A. R. Everton, *The Legal Control of Buying Power* (London: National Federation of Retail Newsagents *et al.*, 1986) p. 11.
10. *Discounts to Retailers* para. 6.18. Although the food/grocery trade is the example most frequently quoted in analysis of intertype and vertical power, the Monopolies Commission clearly recognised the existence of these forces in its consideration of the 1989 proposed acquisition by Kingfisher of Dixons Group. This acquisition would have produced a combined market share of 21–26 per cent in the retailing of electrical goods, and the Commission appeared to accept that this enhanced horizontal power would have an adverse intertype impact upon smaller multiple and independent electrical goods retailers, and that the improved trade terms available to the largest of such retailers through their enhanced vertical power over manufacturers would result in a reduction in the number of these, while lower trade prices would not necessarily be passed on to consumers. By a majority the Commission recommended that the proposed merger should not be permitted. See Monopolies and Mergers Commission, *Kingfisher plc and Dixons Group plc* (London: HMSO, 1990, Cmd. 1079) esp. Ch. 4.
11. Ibid., paras 6.18–6.19.
12. See J. Lamacraft, 'A Load off the Mind', *Management Today*, October 1988, pp. 111ff.
13. See J. Senker, *A Taste for Innovation: British Supermarkets' Influence on Food Manufacturers* (Bradford: Horton Publishing, 1988).
14. See *Financial Times*, 19 April 1988.
15. See A. D. Morgan, *British Imports of Consumer Goods: A Study of Import Penetration 1974–85* (Cambridge: CUP, 1988) pp. 109–10.
16. See M. Wright and D. Rhodes, *Manage IT!* (London: Frances Pinter, 1985) Ch. 1; and Arthur Andersen, *1987 Guide to Distribution Software* (London: ILDM, 1987) Ch. 1.
17. See, for example, *Financial Times* 26 May and 1 June 1988; and N. Piercy, 'Retailer Information Power – The Channel Marketing Information System', in J. Gattorna (ed.), *Insights in Strategic Retail Management* (Bradford: MCB University Press, 1985) p. 96.
18. For examples of some of the latest developments in this area see Walters, *Strategic Retailing Management*, Ch. 4.
19. See *Financial Times* survey 'Retailing Technology', 28 March 1988.
20. See Piercy, 'Retailer Information Power', pp. 92–5.
21. See *Financial Times*, 7 March 1988.
22. See A. K. Pinnock, *Direct Product Profitability: An Introduction for the Grocery Trade* (Watford: Institute of Grocery Distribution, 1986).
23. *Financial Times*, 9 November 1988.
24. See annual Retailing survey, *Financial Times*, 12 September 1989.
25. See N. Travers, 'Kalms at the eye of the storm', *Director*, September 1989, p. 76.
26. See the chapter on Grattan in R. Nelson and D. Clutterbuck (eds), *Turnaround* (London: W. H. Allen, 1988) p. 187.
27. See data in *Financial Times* survey 'Retailing Technology', 28 March 1988; W. H. Smith, *1988 Annual Report*, p. 11; Nelson and Clutterbuck, *Turnaround*, p. 147; and O. Thomas, 'Ensuring Quality of Service for Sainsbury's customers', in B. Moores (ed.), *Are They Being Served?* (Oxford: Philip Allan, 1986) p. 160.
28. Nelson and Clutterbuck, *Turnaround*, p. 170.
29. J. Fernie, *Contract Distribution in Multiple Retailing* (University of Bradford unpublished MBA thesis, 1988) p. 19.

30. See M. E. Porter and V. E. Millar, 'How information gives you competitive advantage', *Harvard Business Review*, July–August 1985, pp. 149–60.

31. See D. W. L. Wightman, 'Competitive Advantage through Information Technology', *Journal of General Management*, Summer 1987, pp. 36–45.

32. See N. Piercy, 'How to Manage IT', *Management Today*, March 1984, pp. 72ff.

33. Walters, *Strategic Retail Management*, p. 273.

34. See figures in 'When the baby boom turned 40', *Financial Times*, 24 December 1988.

35. Quoted in *Financial Times*, 24 December 1988.

36. Walters, *Strategic Retail Management*, p. 3.

37. Paradoxically, Woolworth's recovery strategy in the early 1980s was referred to as 'Operation Focus', reflecting a retrenchment from its earlier vast merchandise range. Its present strategy even within the traditional Woolworth stores embraces none the less a wide range of merchandise in the identified areas of DIY, clothing, leisure, convenience, daily provisions, and housewares. See *Financial Times*, 30 August 1984.

38. *Sunday Times*, 18 December 1988.

39. Quoted in *Financial Times*, 24 December 1988.

40. *Financial Times*, 10–11 December 1988.

41. See *Sunday Times*, 9 October 1988; and *Financial Times*, 6 February 1989. Gateway was in fact taken over by Isosceles in the summer of 1989 in a leveraged buyout which resulted in 62 of its largest supermarkets being sold to Asda. See *Financial Times*, 12 September 1989.

42. J. Duncan, 'Retailing Strategies', *The Economic Bulletin*, Summer 1987, p. 20.

43. The 1980s have seen a very significant increase in consumer credit. Excluding borrowing for house purchase, consumer credit in money terms rose threefold from the end of 1981 to mid-1988 when it reached 14 per cent of annual household disposable income. In real terms this represented a rise of about 3 per cent per quarter over the period. This consumer credit expansion has undoubtedly fuelled rising retail sales levels, although interestingly the proportion of consumer credit provided by retailers fell over the period 1981–7 from 12.2 per cent to 7.1 per cent. See CSO, *Social Trends 1989* (Vol. 19) (London: HMSO, 1989) pp. 109–11.

44. *Financial Times*, 5 September 1989.

45. Ibid., 30 March 1989, 19 September 1988, 30 January 1989 and 26 January 1991.

46. See *Sunday Times*, 3 February 1991.

47. See *Sunday Times*, 3 September 1989; and *Financial Times*, 5 August 1989, 16 August 1989, and 18 August 1989.

48. An example of such comparative studies is E. Kaynak (ed.), *Transnational Retailing* (Berlin: de Gruyter, 1988).

49. See, for example, A. D. Treadgold and R. L. Davies, *The Internationalisation of Retailing* (Harlow: Longman/Oxford Institute of Retail Management, 1988) p. 10.

50. See W. J. Salmon and A. Tordjman, 'The Internationalisation of Retailing', *International Journal of Retailing*, Vol. 4, No. 2, 1989, pp. 3–16; and A. Treadgold, 'Retailing Without Frontiers', *Retail & Distribution Management*, November–December 1988, pp. 8–12.

51. Salmon and Tordjman, 'The Internationalisation of Retailing', p. 4.

52. Treadgold, 'Retailing Without Frontiers', pp. 8–10.

53. Ibid., pp. 10–12.

54. See G. Davies, *What Next?* (London: Century Hutchinson, 1989) pp. 102–3.

55. See Treadgold and Davies, *The Internationalisation of Retailing*, pp. 29–30 and 37; and *Financial Times*, 11 July 1989, and 30 January 1990.

56. See The Boots Company PLC, *1989 Annual Report*, pp. 13 and 20. Canada

appears to be a particularly difficult market for UK retailers to operate in, with both Marks & Spencer and W. H. Smith as well as Boots either losing money or withdrawing from this area. See *Financial Times*, 7 October 1989.

57. The Corporate Intelligence Group, *Retailing and 1992: The Impact and Opportunities* (London: Corporate Intelligence Group, 1989) p. 4.

Index

ACORN 57
Acquisitions 92
Advertising 248–50
Allied Suppliers 11, 14
Ansoff, H. I. 71
Argyll Group 158, 172–3
Asda xv, 51, 65, 81–2, 93, 147, 168
Australia 218
Austria 227

Bankruptcy 218
Belgium 217, 219
Benetton 158–9
Body Shop 33, 34, 156
Bolton Committee 32, 105, 117
Booker McConnell 32
Boots the Chemist 15, 47, 81, 91, 147, 168, 180–3
British Shoe Corporation 96
Burton Group 92–3, 154, 156, 168
Buyer's remedies 244

Canada 216, 218, 219, 227
Census of Distribution 16–18, 106–9
Central place theory 222, 223
Chandler, A. D. 71
Classification 214
Competition
    elimination of 218
    fair 215, 217, 230
    free 212, 215, 217, 219, 224
    horizontal 47, 215
    intertype 47–9, 215
    local laws 215, 221
    perfect 45, 215
    promotion of 220, 230
    unfair 217
    vertical 49–50, 215

Conran, Sir T. 151
Co-operative movement 12, 26–8
Consumer
    dissatisfaction 224
    information and education 226
    policy 224
    protection 224, 225, 230
    welfare 214
Contract of sale
    definition 236
    description 240
    fitness for purpose 243
    implied terms 237–43
    merchantable quality 241–3
    sample 243
    title 238–9
Contracts for the supply of goods 236
Credit 6, 245–7
Customer service in distribution 163–4

Davis, D. 9
Dawson, J. A. 111, 120
Demographics 192
Denmark 217
Department stores 12, 24–6, 229
Development control 220–1
Discounts 219
Dissatisfaction 224
Distribution mix 160–1
Diversification 91
Dixons 284
Dollond & Aitchison 93
DPP 157, 166

EDI 157, 175–6
Efficiency 214, 216, 218, 219
Employees
    dismissal 208, 265–6, 266–8

Employees (*cont'd*)
  hours of 259–61
  recruitment xiv, 252–3
  wages 256–9
Employment
  contract 255–6
  part-time 253–4
Employment relations 204
Enforcement of trading law 250
EPOS xv, 36, 110, 280
Equity 214
European labour law 209
'Excellent' companies 194–8

Fernie, J. 285
Flaschner, A. B. 148–9
France 216, 218, 219, 220, 221, 227, 228
Franchising 33–5
Fraser, W. H. 11

Germany 217, 218, 228, 229
Grattan 168–9
GUS 168–9
Guy, C. M. 58

Harris Queensway 90, 99, 288
Health and safety 261–4
Holland 217, 222, 223, 228
Hypermarket 220, 221

Iceland 169
Independent (small) retailers 31, 105, 213, 218, 219, 221
Information systems 173–6
Information technology 280–6
Innovation
  in trade 220
  promotion of 219
  restriction of 214, 219, 220
Institute of Personnel
    Management 193
Inventory 165–6
Italy 218, 226

Japan 216, 220, 229
Jefferys, J. B. 9, 12, 13, 17

Kingfisher (Woolworth) 15, 155–6, 169, 200, 285, 287
Kirby, D. A. 111, 116–7, 120
Knee, D. 82
Knickerbox 156
Kwik Save 65, 287

Labels (own/private) 59–60, 134
Land-use controls 215
Landmark 32
Law
  categories 235
  sources of 234–5
Legislation
  anti-trust 217
  direct 213
  indirect 213
Lewis, John 15
Licence to trade 227
Linfood 32
Littlewoods 15, 83, 133
Location 55–8, 83
Loi Royer 220

Mail order 35–6
Manufacturers' liability 245
Market power 216
Marks & Spencer 15, 47, 81, 83, 84–5, 90, 94, 140, 142–3, 156, 159, 163, 190, 287
Menzies, J. 12
Merchantable quality 241–3
McClelland, W. G. 4
McColl, R. S. xv
Monopoly 215, 216, 221
Multiple shops 11, 29–31
MFI xv

Next 36, 133, 288
Nielsen, A. C. 48–9, 119
Norway 217, 227
Nurdin & Peacock 32
Nyström, H. 61

Opening hours 51, 59, 228

Packaging/unitisation 166
Palamountain, J. C. 47
Performance appraisal 206
Personal assistance plan 201
Peters, T. 195
Pinpoint 57
Planning
  commercial 230
  urban 221
  regional 221
  retail 222
Policies
  consumer protection 224
  energy conservation 213

ensure spatial competition 221
land-use planning 214, 221
nature of 213
planning 220
promote fair competition 217
promote free competition 215
promote innovation 219
regulate competition 214
regulate trading conditions 227
restrict innovation 219
retail planning 214
Porter, M. E. 45, 46, 87
Portugal 227
Price
agreements 218
competition 219
controls 226
discrimination 215, 217, 219
reduction of 219
regulation 215, 220
Pricing 22–3, 52–5, 83
Physical distribution
management 154–86
Physical distribution strategy 180–3

Ratner 133, 138, 155, 287
Resale price maintenance 22–3, 29, 48, 52, 218
Restrictive marketing practices 214
Restrictive trade practices 217
Retail allocation models 223
Retailing
change 155–9, 274–7
competition 44, 277–80
employment 189
environment 72, 76–9, 109–12
functions 3–6
international 92, 290–2
marketing 131, 136–44
objectives 72, 75–6
operations 144
origins 8
resources 73, 79–81, 112–3
scale xiv
strategy 71

Sainsbury, J. 164, 171, 178, 285, 287
Sears, J. 89, 96
Selling
loss leader 219
pyramid 227

Shopping centres
hierarchy of 223
out-of-town 220, 221
regional 221
satellite 224
Smith, H. 3, 16
Smith, W. H. xv, 12, 89, 99, 122, 158, 285, 287
Social skills 202
Sock Shop 156
Spain 216
Spar 31, 156
Spitz, A. E. 148–9
Stacey, N. A. H. 25
Staff counselling 207
Storehouse (BHS) xv, 15, 82, 154, 168
Sub-contracting 177–80
Sunday trading 228
Supermarkets 227, 228
Superstores 221
Switzerland 217

Taxation
Selective Employment Tax 213
value-added 227
Tesco 51, 65, 91–2, 168, 180–1, 285
Tie Rack 33, 156
Total cost concept 162–3
Toys 'Я' Us 155
Trade stamps 24
Trade unions 191
Training 206
Transportation 170–3

United Kingdom 214, 217, 219, 220, 224, 229
United States of America 213, 214, 215, 216, 218, 219

Vertical integration 87–90
VG 31

Walters, D. 82, 132, 136, 286, 287
Ward, T. S. 63
Warehousing 166–70
White, D. 132, 136
Wholesalers 118
Wilson (Committee) 25